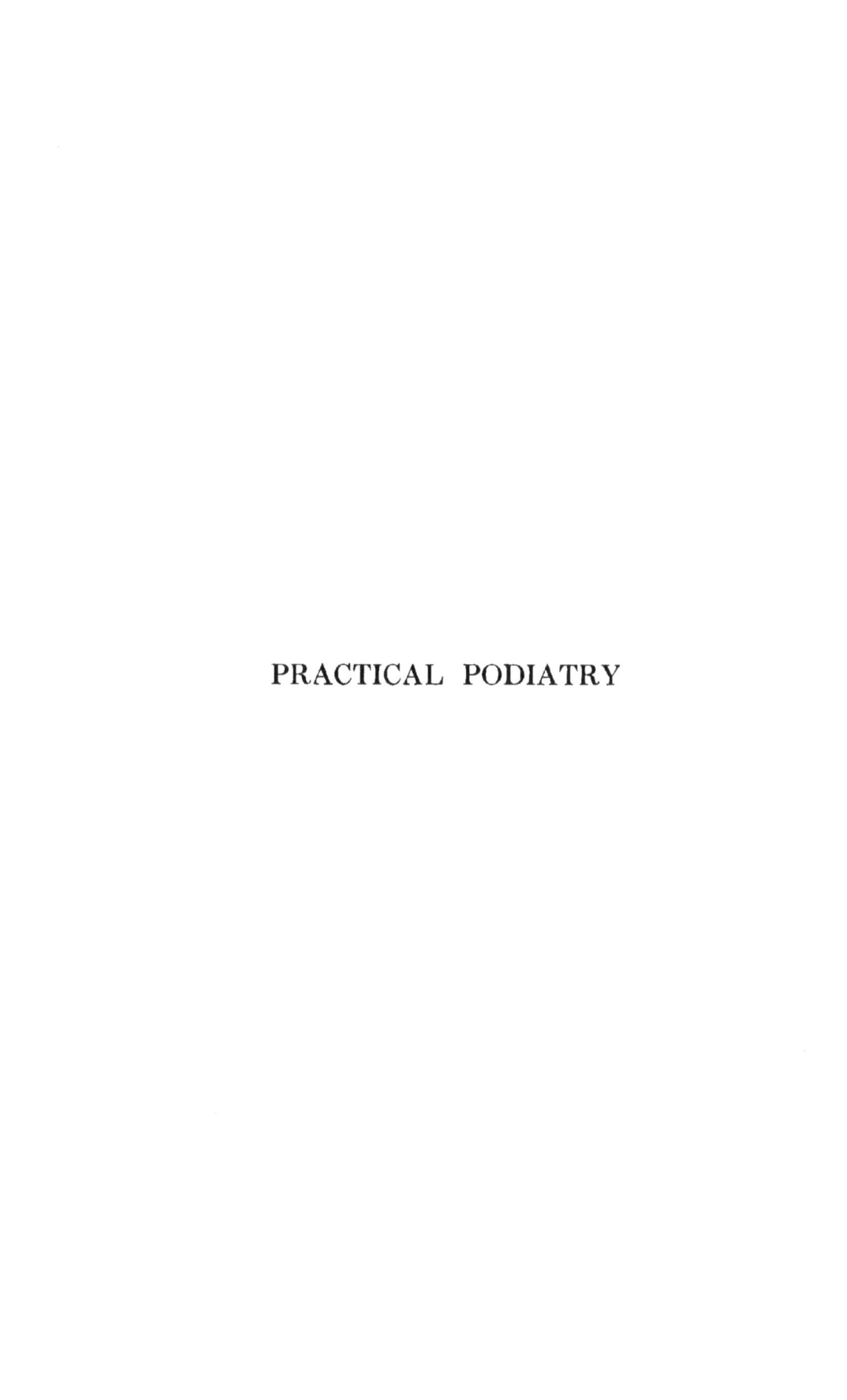

PRACTICAL PODIATRY

PRACTICAL PODIATRY

is the second volume of a series of books known as a complete System of Podiatry. The first volume

SURGERY
WITH
SPECIAL REFERENCE TO PODIATRY

has proven of worth and will be found in the libraries of all advanced podiatrists and of many progressive physicians.

PODIATRY ORTHOPEDICS

will be the next volume of the System to be published and will be followed by other books along special lines bearing upon a knowledge of foot lesions and their care.

PRACTICAL PODIATRY

BY

ALFRED JOSEPH

*Senior Professor of Podiatry, The First Institute of Podiatry, Ex-President,
Nat'l Ass'n Chiropodists, Editor, Pedic Items*

E. K. BURNETT

*Professor of Clinical Podiatry The First Institute of Podiatry, Vice-President,
Nat'l Ass'n Chiropodists Editor, The Podiatrist*

REUBEN H. GROSS

*Professor of Didactic Podiatry and Registrar, The First Institute of Podiatry,
Associate Editor, Pedic Items*

EDITED BY

MAURICE J LEWI, M.D.

*President, The First Institute of Podiatry Ex-Secretary, N Y. State Board of Medical Examiners,
formerly Professor of Medical Jurisprudence, Albany Law School, Ex-President, Albany
Co Medical Society, formerly Instructor, Albany Medical College; Member,
American Medical Association, Member, N Y State Medical Society, Member N Y Co Medical Society, etc*

PUBLISHED BY

THE FIRST INSTITUTE OF PODIATRY

213-215-217 WEST 125TH STREET

NEW YORK

COPYRIGHT, MAURICE J. LEWI, 1918

THE WILLIAM G. HEWITT PRESS
BROOKLYN, N. Y.

TO THE MEMORY OF

GEORGE ERFF
AND
ELLIOTT W. JOHNSON,

builders of the foundation upon which
the edifice of modern podiatry is
reared, this book is reverently and
appreciatively dedicated

THE beauties of contour of the human foot, coupled with its strength to perform the functions for which it was created, caused the ancient Greeks to glorify it in song and in art Medically and surgically it has always been a negligible factor in the world of science, notwithstanding the burdens which it is made to bear and in spite of the interference with locomotion and with general health which this non-care has occasioned for all centuries since creation Our propaganda recognizes the importance of this part of the anatomy and is causing the race to realize the need for footcare in health and for scientific foot treatment in disease

CONTENTS

CHAPTER		PAGE
	Foreword	ix
I	The Recent History of Podiatry	1
II	The Skin	11
III	Asepsis and Antisepsis	19
IV	Sterilization	39
V	The Care of the Foot	46
VI	Dressings and Bandaging	60
VII	Instruments	78
VIII	Shields and Shielding	96
IX	Local Anesthesia	143
X	Heloma	149
XI	Callositas	182
XII	Verruca	185
XIII	Calloused Nail Groove	205
XIV	Onychocryptosis	210
XV	Diseases of the Nails	237
XVI	Fissures, Blisters, Burns	248
XVII	Bursitis	263

CONTENTS

XVIII	CHIMATLON	283
XIX	DISEASES OF THE SWEAT GLANDS	297
XX	ULCERS	306
XXI	CUTANEOUS MANIFESTATIONS OF SUPER-ACIDITY	329
XXII	VOCATIONAL FOOT DISORDERS	339
XXIII	LOCOMOTION AS AN AID IN DIAGNOSIS	343
XXIV	MISCELLANEOUS FOOT LESIONS	357
	(Trench Foot, Ground Itch, Gas Infection, Syphilis, Focal Infection, Morton's Toe, Metatarsalgia)	
XXV	X-RAYS IN PODIATRY	385
XXVI	THE PODIATRIST'S OFFICE	405

FOREWORD

THIS volume has been compiled by men who started out in life as chiropodists. They have lived to see the genesis of podiatry from the trade which was theirs, and each of them has taken active part in the efforts which marked the transition from the old to the new order of things. The period of evolution has been extremely brief. Five short years have sufficed to transform the corn-cutters' trade to the podiatrists' profession.

One of the programmed features of the educational development of podiatry was the creation of a scientific literature bearing upon the practice of this branch of medicine. The earliest manifestation along the lines of this progress was the production of "The Text Book of Chiropody." This ponderous tome (1183 pages) contained matter pertaining to the teaching of medical and other scientific subjects that led up to the study of chiropody and to practical chiropody itself. The chapters on this latter topic were the first attempts of a scientific nature to collect material relating to podiatry practice. In consequence, the articles were few and their contents were meagre. Nevertheless this pioneer attempt to array chiropodical facts and methods of treating foot lesions proved efficacious in stimulating members of the chiropody profession to the higher educational needs, and all over the english-speaking globe this literature was hungrily masticated and digested by individual practitioners and by chiropody societies.

Bright and intelligent members of the profession utilized the material thus furnished them by practically applying suggested treatments and methods. Aspiring to augment their own knowledge and to add to this literature, they wrote up their experiences and, from time to time, their matured deductions were given publicity through the columns of "The Pedic Items" and "The Podiatrist." The instructors on the faculties of the various chiropody teaching institutions utilized these chapters in their pedagogic work, and medical practitioners turned to them to gain their first concrete knowledge of the subjects which they treated. These initial chapters thus filled an acute want and so proved their worth.

FOREWORD

In this volume, a more serious task has been undertaken. Each article will be found to have been prepared with a view to presenting the subject matter in its entirety, in scientific order and with accuracy. There has been no guessing as to cause and effect. Empiricism finds no place in these pages. The medical and surgical viewpoint is continuously in evidence and "Practical Podiatry" thus becomes the first medical work of its kind ever published, a sad commentary on the negligence of medical teachers and medical practitioners who have thus permitted non-medical graduates to compile the first facts relating to an important branch of medicine. The erstwhile tabooed "corn-cutter" thus becomes a leader in a collateral branch of medicine, and medical practitioners are compelled to glean their knowledge of this subject from laymen, who, without their material, moral or monied support—yes, often in spite of obstacles which medical practitioners have placed in their way—have succeeded in clearly and scientifically portraying features of essential medical practice which are to aid materially in creating a better species of the genus homo, and in relieving the woes of our race. Podiatrists may well feel a pride in this achievement and medical practitioners would do well to take home the lesson of indifference which this incident discloses.

Podiatry has not alone enriched the scholastic literature of medicine, but has also augmented the language of science. New terms have had to be coined to properly designate conditions, diseases and instruments. In order that these may be understood by the readers of this volume, their purport is given in the general glossary which will be found in the book. The etymologic construction of these new words is not explained because their origin will be readily apparent from their definitions.

"Surgery with special reference to Podiatry" was the first volume of this series to be published. In presenting "Practical Podiatry" to the profession and to the public, the second rung in the ladder of podiatry literature has been created and within two years it is hoped that the "System of Podiatry," of which both of the above volumes are a part, will have been completed.

Thus will be constituted a library for practitioners and students of podiatry which it is hoped will ever prove creditable to its sponsors, profitable to the profession and helpful to humankind.

M. J. L.

CHAPTER I

THE RECENT HISTORY OF PODIATRY

THE first steps in the movement for the enactment of a law governing the practice of chiropody in the United States were made in the state of New York, when, in 1895 C. S. Levy, H. Levy, L. B. Rosenberg, H. Mayer, E. Werther and M. M. Marks met at the residence of C. S. Levy to discuss this matter. As a result of this meeting, a bill drafted by Maurice Marks, a well-known New York lawyer, was subsequently presented to the New York State legislature. John B. Stanchfield, leader of the assembly, spoke at length on the question of "feet" and amid mirth and laughter (the question was considered somewhat of a joke), the bill was passed by the lower house. Shortly thereafter, the senate took similar action on the bill, whereupon Governor Morton promptly signed it.

In accordance with the provisions of the law, the Pedic Society of the State of New York was organized on the 3rd of June, 1895, and R. H. Westervelt was elected president, George Erff, treasurer and Louise Hartogensis, secretary. Wm. D. Gaige, Jonas M. Heimerdinger and L. B. Rosenberg were selected as the first board of examiners.

R. H. Westervelt served as president of the society for a period of two years, when he was succeeded by Elliot W. Johnson, who acted as chief executive officer for fifteen years. George Erff was the next president and he in turn was succeeded by Alfred Joseph, J. P. Solomon and Ernest Graff.

The affairs of the society improved with each succeeding

year, and much of the credit of its success should go to Maurice M. Marks, who acted as attorney for the society, and in addition, assisted wherever he could.

BIRTH OF "THE PEDIC ITEMS"

"The Pedic Items," which has done so much to advance the calling of podiatry, is the child of Alfred Joseph. In 1906 he outlined a plan to the members of the Pedic Society of the State of New York, whereby a journal could be created and conducted profitably. On January 1st, 1907, a leaflet called the "Pedic Society Items" was sent to the members. On April 1st, 1907, a four page paper was published, and after that Alfred Joseph was offered the position of editor. The "Items" appeared every four months for the first few years of its existence, and finally became a monthly paper which has grown to a sixty-four page book, and even this is inadequate to convey all that is new and of interest to the members of the profession. This book is now current podiatry literature in every english speaking country in the world. A number of chiropody publications have appeared from time to time, most of them, of no scientific value, and they died an early death. The newest paper, "The Podiatrist," is a thoroughly scientific journal, that has already found a place in the profession; it is edited and published by E. K. Burnett, one of the progressive members of the podiatry profession, and appears once each month.

FIRST SCHOOL OF CHIROPODY

At the March, 1911 meeting of the Pedic Society of the State of New York, Alfred Joseph, as chairman of a committee appointed to take the matter under advisement, read a report on the question of organizing a school, and asked that moneys be subscribed for the purposes of incorporating such an institution. In a short time, over $1,200.00 was subscribed and the corporation known as "The Chiropodists of

America" came into existence, with George Erff, president and Alfred Joseph, secretary.

This school was conducted along commercial lines, and although its purposes were good, it did not meet the standards which its promoters were hopeful of establishing for it and which it later secured through the action of the Regents of the University of the State of New York.

THE NATIONAL ASSOCIATION OF CHIROPODISTS

The October, 1911, issue of "The Pedic Items" contained the first announcement of a proposed plan to organize a national association of chiropodists. All chiropodists were invited to become members, and after a mail vote, Chicago was selected as the first convention city. On July 1st, 2nd, and 3rd, after the usual preliminaries, the organization was completed, and Alfred Joseph, who was the organizer of the association, was elected president. Ernest Graff was elected secretary-treasurer. This organization has grown from 225 members at its first meeting, to the present large society of over 1,000 members. The influence of the N. A. C is and has been decidedly salutory, and its organizers can well be proud of the work they have accomplished.

CHANGE IN THE CHIROPODY LAW OF NEW YORK

The members of the Pedic Society of the State of New York, after a brief experience, realized the shortcomings of the original law which governed the practice of chiropody. They sought to advance their calling and to provide so that those entering the profession should be properly equipped.

A committee of the Pedic Society of the State of New York composed of George Erff, Maurice Marks and Alfred Joseph, called upon Edward Milton Foote, M. D , a prominent surgeon, for advice as to procedure. Dr. Foote, in turn, advised that the secretary of the N. Y. State Board of Medical Examiners be consulted Thus it came to pass that these gentlemen met Maurice J Lewi, M D.

Dr. Lewi listened attentively to the request of the committee that he devise ways and means for improving the then inefficient chiropody law, fell in heartily with their objects and after outlining a plan of procedure, drafted a bill which, after receiving the sanction of the State education authorities, was introduced in the legislature. The bill was unanimously passed and became a law September 1st, 1912. Thereupon the State Education Department delegated Dr. Lewi to outline a standard for chiropody schools which they promply adopted. Much to the surprise of the officials of the New York School of Chiropody, these standards were so high that they feared it would be impossible for them to carry them into effect.

Conducting a school along the lines set by the State made it necessary to engage as its head one who was a medical practitioner, an educator, an executive and a man of character Where was such a man to be found? After much deliberation and numerous consultations, the committee of the Pedic Society decided that there was but one man known to them who combined all of these attributes and he was the very individual who had guided them in seeking to advance their profession, Dr Lewi. When the proposition was put to Dr. Lewi, he declined with thanks on the ground that his position as Secretary of the State Board of Medical Examiners was to his liking. The committee was insistent and pleaded with him to reconsider his determination For three months the committee and their friends labored with Dr. Lewi and finally, after making certain stipulations which placed the management of the school in his sole charge, he capitulated, and on January 1st, 1913, he assumed the presidency of the reorganized School of Chiropody of New York With meagre funds, but with earnest zeal he commenced his task and soon surrounded himself with a splendid faculty and with a modest but sufficient equipment. The school has flourished. It behooves every member of the profession of podiatry to remember that had it not been for the broad-mindedness and the foresight of Dr. Lewi, this calling which is gradually taking its place as a legitimate branch of medicine, would still be the trade it was, and the podiatrists of today would still be the "corn-cutters" of yesterday.

On September 27th, 1917, the Regents of the University of the State of New York granted a provisional charter to The First Institute of Podiatry and henceforth the School of Chiropody of New York will be known by that title

THE DEVELOPMENT OF OTHER SCHOOLS

After the organization of the new regime in podiatry education, the old system of conducting schools for gain only, was gradually eliminated and the need for schools to teach foot-ills in a scientific manner, became apparent. Since the organization of The First Institute of Podiatry, several other institutions have come into existence whose purpose is to equip their students to be true podiatrists The California College of Chiropody, situated in San Francisco, is the only institution west of Chicago, imparting knowledge of this character. In the middle west, the City of Chicago boasts of two schools, viz: the Illinois College of Chiropody and the Chicago School of Chiropody. The State of Ohio is well represented by the Ohio College of Chiropody in the City of Cleveland. Temple University of Philadelphia, Pa., has a Department of Chiropody and is educating specialists in conjunction with its medical course. The latest addition to chiropody teaching institutions is the University of Massachusetts in East Cambridge, Mass.

All of these institutions are endeavoring to educate their students along ethical and scientific lines, and it is but a question of time when they will have attained the status and educational influence of The First Institute of Podiatry.

ORGANIZATION OF PEDIC SOCIETIES

After the Pedic Society of the State of New York had been conducting its affairs for several years, podiatrists throughout the country, recognizing the advantages to be derived from a conjunction of individual interests into groups, created organizations in thirty-seven States of the Union. It is safe to predict that within the next five years, there will be a podiatry organization in each of the remaining States not now so organized.

Activities along these lines have not been limited to the United States alone. In England, the Incorporated Society of Chiropodists is a flourishing body, boasting a large membership. Ernest G. V. Runting is president of that organization and he and many others in the British Isles are helping to make podiatry a real profession. The other European countries are not progressive in podiatry work (possibly due to the war situation), but as the United States and Great Britain advance, so will the other nations follow. It is unfortunate that the people of many of these European countries do not fully appreciate the value of scientific foot treatment, but, as in other educational branches, it is only a question of time when every government in the civilized world will recognize the necessity for a full study of this important branch of medical science, and will also pass laws regulating podiatry practice.

In the United States, one of the first states to follow the example of New York, was California. In July, 1901, George Koenigstein called a meeting of the chiropodists in San Francisco, and an organization known as the San Francisco Chiropodists Association was formed. This society had for its prime purpose, the passing of a law governing the practice of chiropody in the State of California; the organization elected no regular set of officers but held desultory meetings once or twice a month at the office of Charles L. Scharff.

The bill that this society formulated was presented to

the legislature at Sacramento and Drs Scharff and Koenigstein were delegated to press it to passage. They worked like Trojans but to no avail. The bill was pigeon-holed and nothing more was heard of it. Subsequently the Society died a peaceful death.

In 1907, following the great fire in San Francisco, a few chiropodists again attempted to pass legislation in California, but this endeavor was also fruitless. In the latter part of 1911 and in the early part of 1912, stimulated by an article relating to the subject which appeared in "The Pedic Items," and fully realizing the benefits of chiropody organization, if properly conducted, several California practitioners were elected to membership in the National Association. Among these were Oscar L. Gruggel, S. Rutherford Levy, and Charles L. Scharff. These men became N. A. C. propagandists, and secured the applications of others in California for membership in the National Association. On January 12th, 1912, The Pedic Society of the State of California was permanently organized and chartered. Its first officers were, S. Rutherford Levy, President; William F. Leck, First Vice-President, Oscar L. Gruggel, Second Vice-President; H. H. Katz, Third Vice-President; Charles L. Scharff, Secretary-Treasurer, Z. L. Cornet, Sergeant-at-arms, and F. Schilling, Counsel for the Society.

This society attempted to pass a State law regulating the practice of chiropody (in 1913) and a bill drafted for the purpose by Mr. Schilling, was presented to the legislature. By almost superhuman effort on the part of every member of the society, the bill passed both houses of the legislature, but the Governor vetoed it on the ground that he was opposed to the creation of new State Commissions.

Dismayed, but not disheartened, the legislative committee immediately made arrangements to carry on the fight at the next session of the legislature. The new bill introduced, instead of creating a separate commission, placed the supervision of chiropody practice in the hands of the existing State Board of Medical Examiners. Changes agreeable to all concerned were made, and in the 1915 session of the legislature, the Benson Medical Act, 443, to regulate the practice of podiatry in California, was passed by both houses On June 8th, the bill was signed by the Governor and the law became effective August 8th, 1915.

In the State of Illinois, the first organization was effected in September, 1904. A charter was applied for and granted to Charles Kenison, Nicholas Von Schill, Frank Johnson and Ignace J. Reis. The officers elected were, Charles Kenison, President; Leonard Lower, Vice-President; C. G. Sims, Treasurer and Ignace J. Reis, Secretary.

On September 18th, 1912, the temporary organization of The Illinois Pedic Association was effected. The organization was made permanent on October 2nd, 1912, and the following were elected as the first officers:

President, Ignace J. Reis; Vice-President, Maximilian Pincus, M. D.; Secretary, Henry Schmidt; Treasurer, John Kenison; Trustees, Leonard A. Lower; Henry J. Riegelhaupt; Charles Kenison; Counsellors, Frank S. Lower, M.D , H. P. Kenison, M. Pincus, M.D.

In the year 1906, S. L. Lawton of Fall River, Mass., consulted with F. J. Coughlin of Boston as to the advisability of forming a state chiropody association. Harry P. Kenison of Boston was advised with and readily fell in with the plans. As a result, a meeting was called at the office of the latter and the Massachusetts Association was created. The first officers were J. P. Buntin, Boston, President; S. D. Lawton, Fall River, Vice-President; F. J. Coughlin, Boston, Secretary-Treasurer, and the following Directors: H. P. Kenison, F. E. Davis, C. R. Watkins, A. M. Brackett, W. E. Lee and G. M. Pettingill. This society has flourished and. due to the efforts of several of its members, including the present president of the N A. C., H. P. Kenison, the present law governing the practice of chiropody in Massachusetts was passed This was accomplished in spite of strenuous opposition on the part of medical practitioners and a few disgruntled chiropodists within and out of the organization.

In the West, there is gradually springing up a progressive spirit in all that pertains to podiatry. Much of this spirit has been created through the efforts of a few practitioners in the State of Colorado who have been extremely active in the past few years. In 1914, Bertha De Wolfe, having taken a course at the School of Chiropody of New York, located in the City of Denver. Realizing the necessity of organization, she immediately set to the task, and in December of that year, the Colorado Pedic Society held its first meeting. It was incorporated, January, 1915. Its first officers were, C. S Rees, President; A. M. Parker, first-Vice-President; Lucy Ballou, second Vice-President, and Bertha De Wolfe, Secretary-Treasurer.

The late Benjamin Oelsner of Bridgeport, Conn., was always an active member of the profession, and through his efforts, the Connecticut Pedic Society was organized, in the city of New Haven, March 23rd, 1910. This organization has grown rapidly, and because of its activities, Connecticut now has a chiropody law on its statute books.

The Rhode Island Chiropodists Society was organized November 8th, 1914, largely through the efforts of Alfred C. Moran, who represented the National Association of Chiropodists in that section of the country. This organization is gradually growing, and since the convention of the N. A. C. which was held in Providence, R. I., many practitioners who previously showed no interest in the union of podiatry forces, have become active workers in the interests of the profession. The officers of The Rhode Island Chiropodists Society are Charles T. Heilborn, President; Henry S. Batchelder, first Vice-President; F. S. Sargent, second Vice-President; Alfred C. Moran, Secretary-Treasurer.

LAWS GOVERNING PODIATRY PRACTICE

Since the first law governing the practice of podiatry passed in the State of New York, eighteen other states have taken similar action. The National Association of Chiropodists has been largely responsible for most of the success along these lines. The committee in charge of legislation has been a most active one, and its usefulness may be realized, when it is recorded that during the period from August, 1916, to July, 1917, six states in the union passed laws regulating the practice of podiatry. As the profession advances, and the academic requirements are increased, the laws are so changed as to create a greater scope of endeavor for our practitioners Thus in some states the law permits the podiatrist to perform operations of a major nature, while in others the practice is limited to structures involving the true skin only. It is safe to predict that in a few years, every state in the union will have enacted legislation regulating the practice of podiatry. The states now governed by such laws (New Jersey was the first) are Colorado, California, Connecticut, Illinois, Louisiana, Maryland, Massachusetts, Michigan, Minnesota, New Jersey, New York, Ohio, Pennsylvania, Rhode Island, Vermont, Virginia, Washington, West Virginia and Wisconsin *

Educators and the public generally throughout the entire country are beginning to realize the value of scientific foot care, and where the chiropodist was derided and scoffed at years ago, the podiatrist of today is gradually taking the place he so rightly deserves, at the side of the members of the other professions, honored and respected as a well trained, educated man who is proving a benefactor to the human race So it is, that the schools of chiropody are being developed, and in a few years when the academic requirements will have become the same as for the other professions, the courses of study at these schools will run on all fours with the schedules of study maintained at medical schools.

---
* The District of Columbia has now a similar law, passed since the above was written Ernest Stanaback former President of the N A C, and Harry P Kenison, the present President of the N A C, were potent factors in procuring most of the legislation in the above states

CHAPTER II

THE SKIN

Podiatry deals largely with ailments involving the skin or its appendages and it is deemed advisable to describe briefly the anatomy and physiology of that organ, so as to refresh the memories of those who study this work.

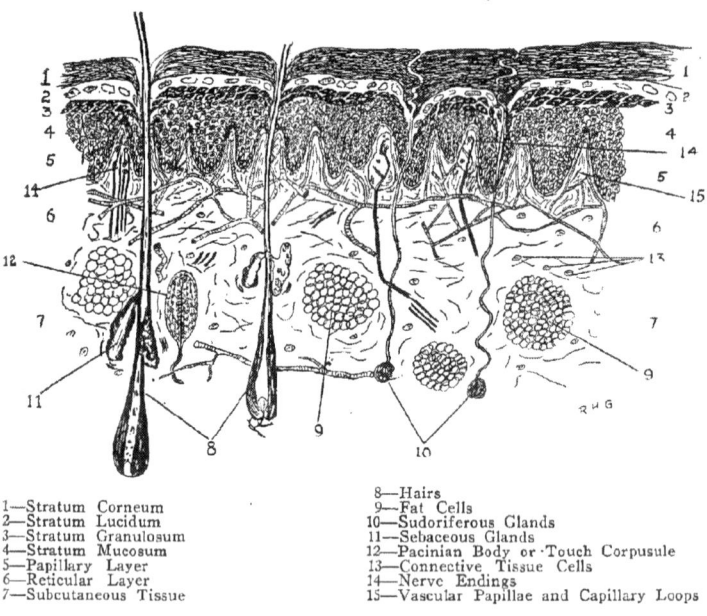

1—Stratum Corneum
2—Stratum Lucidum
3—Stratum Granulosum
4—Stratum Mucosum
5—Papillary Layer
6—Reticular Layer
7—Subcutaneous Tissue
8—Hairs
9—Fat Cells
10—Sudoriferous Glands
11—Sebaceous Glands
12—Pacinian Body or Touch Corpuscle
13—Connective Tissue Cells
14—Nerve Endings
15—Vascular Papillae and Capillary Loops

It is not the intention of the authors to enter deeply into this subject and the reader is referred to the works in this series which deal exclusively with anatomy and physiology, for a more intimate knowledge of the skin. It is an accepted fact that no one can intelligently comprehend pathology without knowing the normal structure and functions of the tissues of the body to be considered, and it is for that reason that the pages to follow have been written.

ANATOMY OF THE SKIN

The skin as a whole is composed of two distinct layers resting upon a third structure, the subcutaneous tissue. The outer portion is called the epidermis, cuticle or scarf skin, and is without blood and nerve supply, while the inner portion is called the corium, derma or cutis vera, and contains the capillary loops and nerve endings

THE EPIDERMIS

The Epidermis is divided into four layers, named from without inward, the stratum corneum, the stratum lucidum, the stratum granulosum and the stratum mucosum or rete Malpighii.

The Stratum Corneum, or horny layer of the skin, is composed of many layers of horny, non-nucleated scales which are being continuously displaced by exposure to weather, water, etc., and are being as continuously renewed by the deeper layers. This layer of the skin is involved in the simpler foot lesions such as heloma and callositas.

The Stratum Lucidum, or clear layer of the skin, is composed of a few rows of transparent cells, without distinct boundary, and, except on the palms and soles, is considered a part of the stratum corneum It is composed of from two to four layers of cells, which are like the cells of the horny layer except that they are brighter and more homogeneous. This layer is not often clearly defined and is of no importance

The Stratum Granulosum, or granular layer of the skin is composed of several rows of polygonal shaped cells which are well marked on the soles of the feet. The nuclei of the cells are not well defined and the cell itself refracts light.

The granules found in this layer are varied in shape and contain a fluid called eleidin and a peculiar solid substance called keratohyalin. This substance is derived from the cytoplasm of the cells and represents the first process in the cornification of the cells in the outer layers of the epidermis

The Stratum Mucosum, or mucous layer of the skin, usually called the rete, or rete Malpighii, is the deepest and most important layer of the epidermis. The basal layers of cells are separated from the corium by a basement membrane or membrana propria, and these layers, which are made up of columnar cells, contain the pigment of the skin. The next few layers show elongated, oval or rounded shaped cells, the form varying with the locality, the tendency being to a rounded shape, owing to the more even pressure on the cells from above and below. The cells are irregularly formed and are made up of a soft substance with large oval or rounded nuclei. In the intercellular spaces is found a fluid which is nutrient in character. In the stratum mucosum are found the prickle cells. These cells have hair-like processes on them which serve to hold the cells together.

THE DERMA

The Derma, or Corium, is divided into two layers, the outer, called the papillary layer, or pars papillaris, and the inner, called the reticular layer, or pars reticularis. It is composed of bundles of fibrous tissue, yellow elastic tissue and connective tissue cells, the reticular layer being more compact than the papillary layer. The derma contains blood vessels, nerves, lymphatics, touch corpuscles, hairs, sweat glands and sebaceous glands.

The Papillary Layer of the skin is composed of small conical elevations called papillae, which blend with the prolongations of the rete above. The best developed papillae are found on the under or flexor surfaces of the fingers and toes and attain their greatest length at this point. They are placed in double rows that underlie the cutaneous ridges on the fingers and toes. These cutaneous ridges remain unchanged throughout life and are so characteristic of each individual, that they are used as a means of detecting and identifying criminals and others. Papillae of two kinds are noticed, the one being very well supplied with blood vessels, and are called vascular, the others being only scantily supplied with blood, containing medullated nerves, and are called sensory papillae.

The Reticular Layer of the derma is composed of loosely arranged bundles of connective tissue which merge with the papillary layer without a distinct line of demarcation. In these bundles of connective tissue are found the sweat glands, the sebaceous glands, the hair follicles and the deeper lymphatics. This layer of the derma is made up of fasciculi of connective tissue which blend into each other obliquely and give it a plexiform appearance. As the bundles ascend towards the surface they divide into smaller and finer bundles, and when the papillary layer is reached, they have a close, felt-like appearance.

The Subcutaneous Areolar Tissue, or tela subcutanea, connects the skin with the deeper structures and should be considered a part of the true skin. It is made up of loosely arranged bundles of connective tissue which cross each other repeatedly and form well defined spaces. These spaces contain fat, and where there are large quantities of this fat, as on the soles of the feet, the tissue is designated as adipose. The subcutaneous areolar tissue also contains the deeper hair follicles and the deeper sweat glands.

Blood Supply. The layers of the epidermis are without vascular supply, but the derma and the subcutaneous tissue are well supplied with blood vessels. There are two plexuses, one superficial in the upper layer of the derma, and the other deep, in the subcutaneous tissue. The vessels of the upper layer arise from the deeper plexus and give off branches in all directions supplying the hair follicles, sweat and sebaceous glands. The papillary layer is richly supplied with delicate capillaries, which terminate in the papillae, and are called capillary loops.

Lymphatics. The lymphatics follow the vessels in a general way, there being two plexuses, viz: deep and superficial. Lymph spaces are found in the rete Malpighii, which connect with the channels of those in the derma. The papillae and the glands also have lymph channels.

Nerve Supply. The skin contains both medullated and non-medullated nerve fibres; these fibres are especially abundant in the soles of the feet and at the ends of the toes. They enter the skin with the more important ascending blood vessels. The non-medullated nerves terminate in the rete as fine filaments, and the medullated nerves end in the corium and subcutaneous tissue in special terminals called corpuscles. Examples of these are Pacinian corpuscles, tactile corpuscles and the end bulbs of Krause.

In addition to the sensory nerves, the skin also contains vasomotor nerves. These nerves are found on the smooth muscles of the skin and on all glands having such muscles, and have a direct action on these glands.

Muscles. Both striated and non-striated or smooth muscles are found in the skin. Those of the latter variety are most common, while the former are sparingly found. The smooth muscle fibres are found in connection with the hair follicles, the sebaceous and the sudoriferous glands, and they act upon these organisms.

Sudoriferous Glands. The sudoriferous glands, or sweat glands, are found in the reticular layer of the corium and in the subcutaneous tissue. They are simple tubular glands which are coiled into globular shape. The tubule of the gland empties into a gland duct which passes through the corium and the epidermis and opens on the surface of the skin in a funnel-shaped sweat pore. The sweat glands are very numerous, particularly on the soles of the feet It is estimated that there are 2,000,000 sweat glands in the adult human body.

Sebaceous Glands. The sebaceous glands, or oil glands,

are found in the reticular layer of the derma, usually associated with or in close proximity to a hair follicle. They may occur independent of the hairs however, as is the case in the lips. They vary in size from a simple pouch to a many pouched or multilobular gland. These pouches empty into a common duct, which in turn empties between the hair and the inner sheath. The ducts secrete sebum, which consists of fatty degenerated cells, in which is found epithelial waste matter. The sebum keeps the skin and the hair soft and oily.

NAILS

The Nails are a specialized form of epidermis, and are considered by many to correspond to the stratum lucidum of that structure. They are horny, elastic, transparent, quadrilateral plates, and are found at the distal ends of the fingers and toes, on their dorsal surfaces. The nails are convex on the outer surface and concave within. The nail itself is called the body and rests upon the nail bed. It has a free edge distally and two lateral and a proximal or short edge which latter lie in a groove called the nail or ungual fold. The ungual wall overlies the lateral and proximal portions. The nail is embedded into the derma at its proximal end by a root. This part of the nail is found beneath the ungual wall and is composed of cells which have not yet become horny.

The thin layer of skin, which extends forward from the nail groove at the beginning of the body of the nail, is called the eponychium or nail-skin. The lunula is the little whitish, crescentic spot, a portion of the nail-bed, which is found in front of the nail fold, and extends to the lateral edges of the nail.

The matrix of the nail is situated beneath the root of the nail, and is so-called because it is from this structure that the nail is produced. The matrix is thick, and raised in a series of longitudinal ridges, which are readily seen through the transparent nail tissue. It corresponds to the mucous layer of the epidermis, and is essentially of the same structure. The matrix is highly vascular, which accounts for the pink color seen through the nail, except at the lunula.

PHYSIOLOGY OF THE SKIN

The functions of the skin may be subdivided as follows:

>Touch Organ
>Protective Covering
>Excretory and Secretory Organ
>Temperature Regulator
>Organ of Respiration

The skin acts as a touch organ or as an organ of tactile sensibility, this power is supplied by special bodies found in the papillae. The degrees of consistency, of size, of form and of other qualities are recognized by this function. Other sensations are conveyed by these special nerve endings, such as heat and cold, burning, itching, tingling, etc. The sense of touch is well developed, particularly in the skin at the ends of the fingers, and this sense may be farther increased, as is the case with blind persons.

The skin acts as a protective organ to the body within, by excluding harmful agents such as bacteria, chemicals, heat, cold, etc. It is elastic and thick and is without sensation and thus protects the delicate structures beneath it from injury from various causes

The functions of excretion and of secretion are performed by the glands. The sudoriferous, or sweat glands, excrete the perspiration, and in this way also act as elimination organs, accessory to the kidneys. The body is continuously sweating. When there is no indication of this function, when the skin seems dry, the name "insensible perspiration" is applied; when the function is apparent, by the formation of drops of moisture on the surface, it is called "sensible perspiration."

The sebaceous glands are organs of secretion. They

give off an oily substance called sebum, which lubricates the hairs, and gives an oily, soft appearance to the skin. This tends to keep the outer layers elastic and pliable; where this function is absent, the skin becomes dry and is likely to form cracks or fissures.

The skin acts as a regulator of the body heat, by controlling the radiation of the heat as brought to the surface from within, and by regulating evaporation. The normal tension of the skin on the various parts of the body has an influence in the regulation of body temperature.

The function of respiration is, to some extent, duplicated by the skin, the process being analogous to the respiration that takes place in the lungs. The amount of oxygen absorbed is small, but water and carbon dioxide are freely given off.

CHAPTER III

ASEPSIS AND ANTISEPSIS

To understand thoroughly and rationally to practise asepsis and antisepsis, it is necessary for the operator to realize the difference between the two terms. There is a general belief among the laity—and, unfortunately, among some chiropodists—that these two words are synonymous, and that asepsis and antisepsis comprehend the same system of treatment. This is a fallacy.

Asepsis is a condition in which living pyogenic organisms are absent. Aseptic surgery comprehends the performance of an operation in a field free from pyogenic or septic germs, with sterilized hands, instruments, etc., preventing the introduction of germs from without.

Antisepsis is the process whereby germs causing disease, fermentation, or putrefaction are destroyed. Antiseptic treatment comprehends the use of certain drugs or a group of drugs which prevent the action of germs, which inhibit their growth, or which destroy them.

In the comparison of these two foregoing definitions the distinction between the two words is clearly brought out. We speak of a drug—mercuric chloride, for instance, as having an antiseptic action. We speak of a piece of sterile gauze—sterilized, we will say, by heat—as being aseptic. The mecuric chloride is an active substance which, applied to a septic area, will proceed energetically to its work of germ inhibition or destruction. The sterile gauze, placed over a similar area, has no power to prevent or even retard the action of the invading bacteria, let alone destroy them, but once having been rendered free from such germ life by an antiseptic, the aseptic gauze will keep the area in a germ free condition for a greater or lesser length of time

To sum up, then, the term "antiseptic" is applied to a drug or group of drugs from whose actions bacteria are rendered innocuous or are destroyed; and "aseptic" is applied to a condition in which no germ life exists, having previously been freed from such contamination by the use of an antiseptic agent.

Some years ago the term "germicide" was used in contradistinction to that of "antiseptic." This usage was brought about through the belief that some antiseptics would not destroy all forms of germ life Germicide, at that time, was used to distinguish a drug which would energetically attack and destroy all bacteria. Inasmuch as, on close survey, it was found that the antiseptics which would not destroy all germs were, in a great measure, weaker solutions, and that, if used in greater strength, they would be efficient as purifying agents, this distinction, today, has been done away with, and the terms germicide and antiseptic are used synonymously and will be similarly employed in this chapter.

ANTISEPSIS

Antiseptics to be actually efficient must be brought in direct contact with the septic area. There is an erroneous belief that all of the official germicidal agents and a majority of the proprietary preparations, the advertising matter of which latter claims for them great antiseptic proprieties, are efficient in deep seated septic processes by mere surface application This is wrong, and it is for this reason that in all septic inflammations, free drainage must be obtained and maintained, and the actual surface upon which the bacterial action is in evidence must be exposed before the beneficial action of antiseptic agents can be exerted or prove beneficial

The skin unquestionably does, at times, absorb a drug applied to its surfaces; but where an active infective process is present, the antiseptic action of a germicidal agent is practically nil unless the drug is brought into direct contact with the septic surface.

The present success of Dakin's solution, for instance, is not so much on account of the great efficacy of the solution itself—although it has potent germicidal properties—as it is due to the Carrel method of irrigation whereby this solution is carried to the most obscure recesses in which the infective process is present. Applied superficially, as must needs be done in chiropodial practice, we find that Dakin's solution is of no greater value than many other antiseptic agents, except perhaps that, on account of its being non-toxic, it can be used in cases where germicides with strong toxic properties are contra-indicated.

HISTORY OF ANTISEPTICS

The story of antiseptics is one of the most interesting in all the pages of medicine and surgery.

Antiseptics were employed as remedial agents long before the exact causes of putrefaction or fermentation were known. The Egyptians preserved the human body against the attacks of putrefactive organisms, without any knowledge of the character of the organisms causing decay. The wonderful state of preservation in which we, to-day, find the bodies of their kings, was brought about by means of balsams containing, probably, such antiseptics as benzoic and cinnamic acids.

In the sixteenth century the surgeons treated gunshot wounds with boiling oil. They knew that if these wounds were left untreated, putrefaction would ensue accompanied by great suffering, and the ultimate death of the patient. They also knew, empirically, to be sure, that boiling oil applied to the wound prevented the development of this putrefactive process, but they did not know why such was the case, nor did they realize that, by this use of superheated oil they were merely cauterizing the wound.

Ambrose Paré (1510-1590), who started life as an apprentice barber-surgeon in Paris, became a military surgeon in the army of Francis I, in Piedmont; and he, more from a humane feeling, as his writings tell us, than from any particular scientific knowledge, had the temerity to dispense with this oil boiling technic and to trust to a simple bandage saturated with a concoction of herbs. Pare, however, has no particular place in the development of antisepsis, his principal contribution to surgery being in the development of the use of the ligature for large arteries, which made amputation on a large scale possible for the first time.

Antiseptic surgery dates from the last few years of the nineteenth century, and among the names of its sponsors which will ever remain foremost, are Pasteur and Lister.

Lister's use of local antiseptics in surgery, however, should not, perhaps, be spoken of as a discovery. Without detracting in any way from the credit due him, it should be referred to, more correctly, as a practical application, in particular of the theories of Pasteur, and of several previous investigators.

Prior to Lister's use of phenol, the substance had already been described by Reichenbach in 1832, and by Runge in 1834, as one which would prevent putrefaction Long before these, tar and a number of similar products were advocated and used for foul ulcers, but the fact remains that Joseph Lister placed the use of antisepsis in connection with surgical procedures on a sound and practical basis.

Taking as a working basis the experimental researches of Louis Pasteur (Communications on the Theory of Fermentation 1853, 1858; The Germ Theory, read before the French Academy of Sciences on April 29th, 1878, and The Extension of the Germ Theory, which appeared in 1880), Joseph Lister, an English surgeon, developed his theory of antiseptic wound treatment. His first experiments were made public in 1860. At that time he stated that the evils observed in open wounds were due to the admission into them of organisms which "exist in the air, in water, on instruments, on sponges, and on the hands of the surgeon or the skin of the patient.'' Having accepted the germ theory of putrefaction, Lister applied himself to discover the best way of preventing harmful organisms from reaching the wound from the moment it was made until it was healed, or, if this could not be done, of using some agent to destroy the organism, either before it reached the wound or after it had lodged there.

Acting on the advice of Lemaire, who had already experimented with several substances which were known to be antagonistic to putrefaction, Lister chose carbolic acid, which he used first in the crude form.

His experiments extended over a number of years during which period he surmounted many obstacles, until in the early 80's he finally perfected his antiseptic treatment of wounds by means of carbolized sprays for the air of the room, carbolized solutions for irrigation, for instruments and for surgeons' hands, and carbolized dressings with mackintosh protection, as post operative procedures. To-day we smile at the idea of a dressing of phenol in any strength, covered with mackintosh protection; but in advocating this procedure, Lister had in mind, as nearly as possible, to cover the wound so that no external agencies might come in contact with it.

From this beginning, our present day antiseptic surgical technic has been gradually developed. Mercuric chloride gradually replaced phenol, and the use of the carbolic spray was discontinued on account of its chilling influences on exposed surfaces, which tended to lower their vitality.

Aseptic surgery owes its origin primarily to antiseptic surgery. Not long after Lister's rules for antiseptic procedure were generally observed, the realization came to many that the success of Listerian surgery did not depend so much upon the spray or the carbolized gauze, as it did upon cleanliness; the surgeon's hands, the instruments, the area to be operated upon, and the dressings must be clean—surgically clean.

To-day we have the rule of "the soap and nail brush," the sterilized instruments, the aseptic rubber gloves for the operator's hands, and the sterile dressing. The modern surgeon uses no antiseptics during operations; he uses instruments which are positively germless and the dressings of aseptic gauze are not impregnated with medications.

ANTISEPTICS

The important subject of antisepsis embraces such a variety of agents which may be employed in the numberless conditions arising, that it is usually divided into three groups. (1) general antiseptics; (2) local antiseptics; (3) internal antiseptics. For the purposes of the podiatrist, some knowledge of the first group is desirable, but his principal thought on this subject should be given to a thorough knowledge and understanding of the second group, those for local application. Inasmuch as the podiatrist is not allowed to prescribe internal medicines, no discussion of the third group, comprising internal antiseptics, will be included in this chapter.

General Antiseptics, or disinfectants, play so great a part to-day in preventive medicine that the podiatrist should at least inform himself on the general principles involved.

Under this group we find a number of agents which are employed for purposes of general disinfection. First on the list comes:

Sunlight. The bright, direct rays of the sun, coming into direct or immediate contact with germ life, are the best of all disinfectants. This does not mean their merely shining on one side of a carpet, or on small masses of blood, pus or sputum, but their penetrating each individual microorganism. When this can be accomplished, all germ life is destroyed in a few hours. But this cannot be accomplished in all conditions, and, unless the penetration of sunlight is thorough it is not dependable. For this reason we are forced to rely on other agents (thermal and chemical) to accomplish our purpose.

Heat. A direct flame will, of course, instantly destroy all forms of microscopic life; dry air heated to 160° C (320°F.) will destroy all disease germs—but not all spores —in one hour. Moist heat, water or air saturated with aqueous vapor, heated to 75°C. (167°F.) will destroy most germs.

Boiling water will even kill spores in ten minutes, if they are not in small masses. To break up such masses the addition of a small amount of baking soda will serve, not alone to dissolve these albuminous collections, but will also keep instruments from rusting (see Sterilization). Steam, or air which is supersaturated with steam, is fatal to pathogenic organisms, and at a much lower temperature than dry hot air.

Chemicals which may be included under this group of general disinfectants are formaldehyde, lime, sublimed sulphur and chlorinated lime.

Formaldehyde, formaline or formic aldehyde, is widely used as a general disinfectant. It is exceedingly powerful, one part of the gas rendering fifty thousand parts of air irrespirable. The action of formaldehyde is increased by moist heat, it does not actively corrode metallic instruments nor does it injure fabrics. The formaldehyde cabinet is used generally by podiatrists. (See Sterilization).

The official preparation of formaldehyde is a 37% solution known as liquor formaldehydi, U.S P For the disinfection of rooms, the solution may be applied directly by washing or spraying, or it may be used in vapor form. When the latter is employed, the windows and doors are tightly closed and all the crevices are plugged with paper.

Lime, calx, or calcium oxide, is extensively used but must be freshly prepared to be effective. Unslacked lime is a cheap, and an efficient means of destroying animal matter, but the milk of lime, freshly slaked, is by far the most desirable form.

Sublimed Sulphur, or flowers of sulphur, is not so generally used today as is formaldehyde. It should be used only in places where nothing can be injured by the corrosive action of the resulting sulphurous acid. As with formaldehyde disinfection, the vapor must come into actual contact with the microorganisms and the atmosphere should be moist.

Chlorinated Lime, improperly called chloride of lime, is a ready source of chlorine, and is a convenient and inexpensive agent for general disinfection purposes. It has a corrosive action, however, and therefore should not be used in places where this action will do damage.

There are a number of drugs which may be more or less successfully employed as general antiseptics and disinfectants. Phenol, cresol, potassium permanganate, mercuric chloride and copper sulphate are on this list, but as the podiatrist is principally concerned with the second group, local antiseptics, these drugs, which are included usually under that group, will now be discussed.

It is deemed wise before passing on to the subject of local antiseptics, to bring one important point to the attention of the student. Under no circumstances must the term deodorant be confused with disinfectant. A deodorant is an agent which merely destroys or conceals an offensive odor and has no power whatsoever to actually destroy or inhibit the growth or action of bacteria. Many disinfectants are also deodorants, but a deodorant may not always have germicidal properties.

Local Antiseptics are agents which are applied locally and externally for the purpose of arresting putrefaction. In podiatry there are a number of drugs belonging to this class which may be safely employed and whose beneficent action may be depended upon.

There has been a marked tendency in podiatry in the past toward the use of a number of proprietary drugs for germicidal purposes. Happily this practice is dying out, and a few years will find the therapeutics of podiatry established on a sound, rational basis.

The following local antiseptics can be safely employed in podiatry operations

Alcohol is used generally in practice to render fields of operation surgically clean. The pure grain alcohol is used for the immersion of instruments prior to operation, but a 60% solution is found more efficient for antiseptic action upon the body surfaces. A pledget of sterile cotton, saturated with alcohol and placed over a part, insures absolute asepsis in a short time. Alcohol alone cannot be practically used as a wet dressing. In this connection it is combined with boric acid, equal parts, and is efficient as an antiseptic

Liquor Alumini Acetatis, an 8% aqueous solution of acetate of aluminum, is used almost entirely as a wet dressing in infective inflammations. It is non-toxic and, while it is irritant to extensive denuded surfaces, it is usually employed for its astringent action.

Balsam of Peru is used chiefly in podiatry as a stimulating agent; its antiseptic properties, however, are well known and are probably due to the benzoic and cinnamic acid which it contains. It is used either alone, in ointment form, 3% to 10%, or in combination with collodion, 10%.

Boric Acid is employed principally as a wet dressing in cases of inflammations. It is quite free from toxicity and is but slowly absorbed. It is also used in powder form as an antiseptic.

Boroglycerine, U. S P., contains 30% of boric acid. It is found particularly effective in the treatment of indolent ulcers where a mild antiseptic lotion is desired.

Borate of Sodium (Sodii boras, U. S. P.), borax, has an alkaline reaction and for this reason is sometimes substituted for boric acid. It is soluble in 16 parts of water

Dakin's Solution is a solution of hypochlorite of soda, ½%. The preparation of the original solution is so difficult that large quantities of the drug are not easily obtainable. Chlorazene, an American product which is recommended by both Dakin and Carrel, is obtainable in tablet and in ointment form. One tablet dissolved in 8 ounces of water makes a solution, ½ of 1%. The solution is unstable, necessitating its being constantly made fresh, and for this reason the use of the drug is not practical in podiatry practice today. When used, the solution must be changed within twenty-four hours; if this is not done it becomes irritant, setting up an acute dermatitis. The drug is used as a wet dressing, but never with rubber or oiled silk covering.

Di-Chloramin-T, the newer form in which Dakin's solution is used, is a 5% or 10% hypochlorite of soda solution in oil of eucalyptus. This combination is found to be less irritating than the original solution. It is used as an antiseptic dressing.

Glycerinum, U. S. P., is not alone useful as a mild antiseptic but is also extensively used as a vehicle for many other substances in the treatment of skin lesions.

Hydrogen Dioxide, peroxide of hydrogen, is used principally in podiatry to decompose pus in which bacteria are protected from the action of other antiseptics. As the antiseptic action of hydrogen dioxide is dependent solely upon the liberation of its component oxygen, it is easily seen that once the ebulition occurring on its contact with albuminous surfaces ceases, it becomes inert. "Peroxide" is used as a pus germ destroying agent, and to loosen dressings which have become adherent from copious discharge.

Iodine, Tinct. Iodii, U.S.P., is 7% of iodine in alcohol, and presents the best agent known at the present time by which surface sterilization can be obtained. It is highly germicidal, but continued applications are decidedly corrosive and not alone inhibit the development of new granules, but also cause severe dermatitis, and at times symptoms of iodine poisoning. The one feature which prevents its use in some chiropodial procedures is the discoloration of the tissues produced by its application. It may be used full strength or diluted with water, as weak as a 1% solution

Iodoform, despite its unpleasant and suggestive odor, is an efficient antiseptic and is used in powder form. Its antiseptic action is principally derived by the slow liberation of its component iodine.

Several forms of mercury are used in podiatry.

Bichloride of Mercury, or mercuric chloride, is used, 1/2000, to prepare fields for operation, and from 1/5000 to 1/10000 as a wet dressing in infective inflammations. It is highly toxic and should never be used for any great length of time, or on a denuded surface of any size, as it is rapidly absorbed into the general system, and its corrosive action tends to inhibit the development of new granules. There are also systemic effects to be feared from its absorption.

Mercurous Chloride, calomel, can be used as an antiseptic dusting powder on many chiropodical lesions. It is combined generally with bismuth, equal parts, as an antiseptic and astringent application for blisters and burns.

Unguentum Hydrargyri, U. S. P, is a 50% ointment, used principally in chiropody in the treatment of parasitic diseases of the nails.

Unguentum Hydrargyri Ammoniatum, 10%, is an antiseptic ointment used safely in any case where such action is desired.

Phenol Liquefactum, U. S. P, carbolic acid, is used as an antiseptic in solution, 2½%. It is highly toxic and is never used as a wet dressing under any circumstances. Phenol, besides its toxic properties, has an anesthetic action on the peripheral nerves, and due to this action, many cases of carbolic gangrene have been reported.

Liquor Cresolis Compositas, U. S. P., also a coal tar product, can be advantageously used in a general spray for the foot, or for the special field of operation. It is antiseptic, and its saponaceous properties (it is a solution of cresol and soap) aid in softening the tissues as well as in cleansing them. It is used in 2% strength.

Lysol, an unofficial phenol derivative, is also used as a general spray, 2%, in water. Its odor is very strong and it is therefore objectionable to many persons.

Thymol is a phenol occurring in a volatile oil. It possesses strong antiseptic properties, but its comparative insolubility in water has prevented its more general use. The only official combination of thymol is

Thermolis Iodidum, U.S.P. Thymol iodide, or more correctly dithymoldiiodid, has been better known for years under its trade name "aristol." It is used as a dusting powder, is actively antiseptic by the liberation of iodine, and has become popular as an iodoform substitute.

Potassium Permanganate, U. S. P., has its greatest usefulness as a local antiseptic application where deodorant action is also desired. In the treatment of indolent, foul ulcerations it is very efficacious.

Sulphur is used principally in podiatry in the form of **Unguentum Sulphuris,** U. S. P. It is composed of 15% of washed sulphur, usually in a lanolin base, and has a mildly stimulating and antiseptic action.

There are any number of additional drugs, both official and unofficial, which can be and are used in podiatry practice, but it is deemed sufficient to name the foregoing which constitute a complete armamentarium for all antiseptic procedures.

THE FIELD OF OPERATION

For rendering the field of operation aseptic the following technic will be found efficient:

In addition to preparing the immediate field it is found advantageous to treat the surrounding areas to prevent the washing in of bacteria. To accomplish this the use of an antiseptic spray is to be advocated

Equipped as the podiatrist is with modern air compressing devices, this is a simple matter, the principal question being the selection of a proper spray.

An aqueous solution of alcohol is exceptionably suited for purposes of this kind and where a lesion is already present this drug should be used to the exclusion of all others.

Most cases the podiatrist is called upon to treat, however, present no lesion, yet asepsis must be procured in the event of a lesion being made during his operative procedures. In cases of this nature a spray of liq. cresolis compositus, U. S. P., 2½%, will be found to be an agreeable and efficient application. This solution has but a slightly disagreeable odor and has marked softening as well as antiseptic properties.

After the whole foot has been thoroughly sprayed and dried with a sterile towel, the immediate field of operation may be coated with tr. iodine, 3½%. This is one-half the strength of the official tincture and is advocated to obviate the deep stain occasioned by the use of the 7% tincture. In many cases, however, no stain whatsoever can be countenanced for fear of obliterating some diagnostic point, and it may be found advisable to dispense entirely with iodine, substituting alcohol, 60%, in its stead.

A pledget of sterile cotton saturated in this solution of alcohol and placed over the area under treatment, will produce asepsis in a short time. The penetrating qualities of alcohol are, however, found to be increased, if application is made by means of a cotton wound applicator, the mixture being rubbed vigorously into the parts.

The use of either of these two methods will procure a sterile field upon which any chiropodial operation may be commenced and completed in safety.

Should hemorrhage be caused during operation, it may be arrested in a number of ways: (1) Bichloride of mercury, 1/1000, may be applied on a pledget of sterile cotton. This will serve to check the blood flow by hastening coagulation, and at the same time will procure asepsis. (2) Tr.

iodine may be painted over the lesion and digital or tourniquet pressure applied until coagulation is complete. (3) Astringent and antiseptic dusting powders may be applied. (4) Styptics (Monsel's solution is efficient and the least irritating) may be used, but it must be remembered that these drugs combine no antiseptic qualities and therefore it is good surgery to apply tr. iodine before their use.

A hemorrhage arrested by any of the foregoing methods should be dressed antiseptically, as well. For this form of dressing, antiseptic ointments or dusting powders are found to be most effective.

ASEPSIS

The topic of asepsis will be found more thoroughly, discussed under the chapter "Sterilization."

Aseptic procedure comprehends the employment of all instruments and materials which have by some means been previously rendered free from germ life. Instruments are to be thoroughly sterilized by boiling in water for at least fifteen minutes, the hands of the operator are to be thoroughly cleansed, or are made as nearly germ free as is possible; the dressings used are to be surgically cleansed (usually by moist or dry heat) before application; and no antiseptic solutions are included in the treatment.

It is doubtful if aseptic procedures can be practised in podiatry to the exclusion of antisepsis. It must be remembered that after most chiropodical surgical procedures, the foot surfaces (again encased in a shoe) teem with septic matter which present the mediums best suited for the propagation of bacterial life,—heat, moisture and darkness.

An aseptic dressing having been employed, the length of time it will remain germ free is problematic; so it is found advisable in most instances where there is danger of infection, to resort to an antiseptic method of treatment rather than to rely solely upon the aseptic.

Dr. Edward Adams, Professor of Surgery at The First

Institute of Podiatry, lecturing to the students on "The Newer Antiseptics in the War," spoke as follows:

"The immense number and variety of wounds encountered in the present war, necessitating the care of many thousands of men at one time, and the entirely new situations created by modern warfare, have led to an amount of research heretofore unknown. True to its traditions, the medical profession has endeavored to discover the best methods in treatment and to render the best service in its power to bestow. Never has the surgeon had to face greater difficulties and never has he recorded more brilliant success.

"Where practically every wound is infected, antisepsis has necessarily received unusual attention, and the merits of different substances having antiseptic properties have been thoroughly discussed and have narrowed down to a very few. The fact is emphasized that those which are strong enough to be antiseptic must be used with great care, especially in cases where drainage is not free.

"After many trials and many discussions the tendency of men of the greatest experience, however, is to reduce the problem to very simple terms which may be expressed thus: (1) How to secure a clean wound. (2) How to give nature a chance with a minimum of interference, since, after all, she must do the healing.

"The early part of the war demonstrated the fact that both antisepsis and asepsis, as heretofore practised, have been vanquished by Mars. By some it was even considered that Lister's work went for naught. Now, however, antisepsis and asepsis, each in its proper place, have come into their own again and Lister is still the apostle of good tidings.

"The reasons are plain: first, at the beginning of the war we did not possess sufficiently effective antiseptics such as have now been given us; second, we were not masters of an efficient technic. We owe these innovations especially to two men, Dakin and Carrel, who have wrought a marvelous change. Lister taught us above all how to prevent infection; Dakin and Carrel, following his principles, have taught us how to conquer even the most virulent infections. For nearly half a century surgeons have been fighting strenuously against infection, but it required the stimulus of war to enable us to win a victory. Prevention and cure both are ours now.

"The newer antiseptics that have been discovered and used since the war are chiefly: Dakin's solution of hypochlorite of soda, di-chloramin-T, eusol and eupad, both preparations of hypochlorous acid, flavin, acriflavin, and proflavin, and a mercurial preparation known as mercurophen.

"These newer antiseptics, especially the flavin group, have pronounced bactericidal qualities, but it is too recent as yet for them to have been tested on a sufficiently large scale to permit of positive conclusions as to their value. Flavin is described in detail as to its process of manufacture and its action in an article by C. H. Browning and his colleagues in the Bland-Sutton Institute of Pathology of Middlesex, London (*British Medical Journal*, January 20, 1917, page 73). For technical reasons flavin as one of the acridin group is now called acriflavin, and a more potent preparation is called proflavin, which is described in the *British Medical Journal*, June 9, 1917. Dakin, in the same journal, June 23, 1917, endorses Browning's method of treatment with acriflavin. Its antiseptic action, instead of being diminished by blood serum, is increased thereby, even up to five times its potency. Moreover, as used by Browning, it is harmless to the tissues and does not interfere with the activity of the leukocytes nor with phagocytosis

"The most important paper yet published on these newer antiseptics is by Browning Culbranson and L. H D. Thornton in the *British Medical Journal*, July 21, 1917 The principal points brought out by their experiments with the use of acriflavin and proflavin are as follows: first, that the bactericidal power of acriflavin and proflavin, instead of being diminished and even destroyed by the contact of blood serum (as is the case with hypochlorite of soda, bichlorid of mercury, etc.), is greatly increased from 10 to 40 fold. Second, as a result, these two antiseptics, though acting at first merely by inhibiting bacterial growth, later become increasingly powerful and actively destroy the bacteria. After two hours' contact in the presence of serum, mercuric chlorid is practically equal to acriflavin in its lethal effect on the streptococcus and bacillus coli, but by this time the effective action of the mercury salt on the bacteria has come to an end, and a concentration which has then failed to kill the organisms, exerts little or no inhibiting effect on the proliferation of the survivors. On the other hand, concentrations of the flavins, which at this period have merely inhibited multiplication, later on prove bactericidal, so that finally the flavin compound is ten to twenty times more lethal than corrosive sublimate. Therefore, instead of renewing the solution every two hours, only one or two daily dressings are required. Moreover, they are apparently harmless to the tissues. Experiments show that such concentrations of flavin as will effectively control the bacteria do not interfere with phagocytosis

"Brilliant green, like the hypochlorites, in the presence of serum, soon loses its value as a bactericide; hence, if used it must be renewed at frequent intervals. On the other hand, it possesses the advantage of being an extremely potent bactericide, far exceeding the flavins in watery solutions, while at the same time it is comparatively harmless to phagocytosis, as well as to the tissues locally, and when applied to a wound it is devoid of general toxic action on the body. Its use by two hourly flushings after the Carrel method, has proved most encouraging.

"The Dakin Solution. The value of this antiseptic has been demonstrated by Drs. Carrel and Dakin. It is a carefully standardized solution of sodium hypochlorite and is usually prepared from chlorinated lime (bleaching powder), but may be prepared directly from chlorine gas. The formula has been varied from time to time. Some surgeons use an acid solution (anærobes do not live in an acid medium), others an alkaline solution, while Drs. Dakin and Carrel in their method, avoid an excess of either quality. In the solution now used by them which is made according to the formula of Dufresne, the chlorinated lime is combined accurately with both sodium carbonate and sodium bicarbonate, making a nearly neutral product which contains from 0.45 to 0.5 per cent. of sodium hypochlorite, because less is too weak and more is too strong. The advantages of this solution are as follows: (1) It is antiseptic and does not damage the tissues. (2) It is non-toxic and no danger is to be apprehended from its absorption. (3) It is hypertonic, that is, the concentration of the solution is greater than that of blood serum and tissue fluids, and therefore, it produces an outflow of lymph. (4) If used as an acid solution it is available against anærobic bacteria which require an alkaline medium.

"The fact that nearly all wounds of the present war are infected, in connection with the serious and often fatal nature of the infection, has stimulated an unusual amount of research with the hope that a reliable and safe disinfectant may be discovered—especially one that will not injure the tissues of the body, since these are more easily affected by the disinfectant than the bacteria themselves. This object has been realized in large part by the Dakin-Carrel solution, which, however, to be effective, must be frequently renewed according to the Carrel technique. It is also frequently very irritating to the skin, although this may be avoided by the use of petrolatum.

"According to the investigation of Dakin, a chemical action takes place between the hypochlorite in the solution and the proteins in the wound exudate with the formation of the new substances called chloramines. One of these chloramines has been prepared synthetically and introduced under the name of chlorazene, which is said to possess a germicidal power four times greater than the Carrel-Dakin solution itself and is unirritating to the skin but, like the latter, must be frequently renewed By dissolving one of these chloramines in an oily medium, however, it is possible to keep it in contact with the wound surfaces for a much longer time than can be done with a watery solution. The advantage of this is evident.

"The solution which is used at present has been named di-chloramin-T, the medium being chlorinated eucalyptus oil or paraffin oil. A ten per cent. solution of di-chloramin-T and eucalyptol may be kept in a colored bottle for at least one month with only slight change. It is applied to the wound surface in the form of a spray after the removal of infection foci and devitalized tissues. Deep cavities are filled with the liquid and drainage afterwards provided for. The high percentage of disinfectant contained in this preparation renders it active for a period of twenty-four hours because of the slow liberation of the germicide. It would appear that when applied with strict attention to detail it is not only less expensive than the Dakin-Carrel method, but will secure healing of a wound in a much shorter time. The gradual elaboration of the remedy makes it particularly applicable in cases that cannot be frequently dressed during transportation. Di-chloramin-T, hypochlorites and hypertonic salt solutions all have the power of dissolving dead tissue. A precaution to be remembered, however, is that if used near a blood-vessel hemorrhage may occur.

"For a detailed report of the use of di-chloramin-T in the treatment of infected wounds, read Dr H. T. Dakin's article in the *Journal of the American Medical Association*, July 7, 1917. For a still later description of the Dakin-Carrel treatment of wounds, see the report of the Surgical Commission to the Directors General of the British Army Medical Service reprinted from the *British Medical Journal*, November 3, 1917.

"To my mind the best preparations that can be easily used are   (1) Chlorazene (Abbott), in tablet form; (2) in form of a non-irritating surgical powder containing 1 per cent. chlorazene; (3) in form of a cream containing 1 per cent. of chlorazene in a sodium stearate base. These I can recommend''

CHAPTER IV

STERILIZATION

In the practice of medicine and its allied branches, it is recognized that no unsterilized object is clean; it is therefore necessary for every such object to be sterilized before being brought in contact with, or near to a wounded surface, or to a surface about to be wounded.

Previous to the time of Lister, who was the first one to practise and to advocate asepsis and antisepsis, it was considered normal for a wound to suppurate and the consequent appalling results were accepted as being in order Today, however, asepsis and antisepsis have been proven to be absolute essentials to intelligent treatment, and it is accordingly necessary that every practitioner treating the human body, should exercise the greatest care so as to prevent the invasion of hostile bacteria.

Sterilization may be defined as the act of rendering an object sterile (clean), by the destruction of microorganisms, preferably by means of heat To perform any operative work, so that there is perfect asepsis, or freedom from bacteria, depends entirely upon the care exercised in practising such asepsis. The instruments, the dressings, the field of operation and the hands of the operator are all media for contamination and the infection of wounds, and the sterilization of all these is necessary, as infection might come from lack of care in the preparation of any one of these details before an operation.

Instruments. The most efficient way of rendering instruments sterile, is by immersing them in boiling water for fifteen minutes. To each quart of water used in the sterilizer, is added one half an ounce of sodium carbonate (washing soda). This prevents rusting and also acts as a solvent for any fatty substance that may be on the instruments.

Superheated steam is used for sterilizing instruments, but this requires especially large and expensive apparatus which is not at the command of most practitioners. Dry heat will destroy bacteria, but it is not as effective as moist heat (steam). To procure absolute results requires a high temperature, which effects the temper of the steel in the instruments.

Instruments with sharp cutting edges, such as are used in the removal of helomata, are blunted by boiling. They are therefore best sterilized by immersing them in pure carbolic acid for a few minutes, followed by dipping in grain alcohol, the instruments being handled with a pair of forceps.

Dressings. Dressings such as gauze, bandages, absorbent cotton and other cloth materials are best sterilized by steam which is allowed to circulate through the material for fifteen minutes, and they may then be placed in dry heat for a short time, thus allowing the moisture to evaporate. If a steam sterilizer is not available, the dressings may be boiled, or they may be baked for ten minutes in a temperature not lower than that of the boiling point of water. Care should be taken that the heat is not great enough to scorch or burn the materials.

Sterilized dressings of all kinds may be purchased in convenient, hermetically sealed packages, and may be safely used without preparation. Once such a package has been opened and used, the contents do not remain sterile; the materials left over from an operation should not be used at another operation unless they have been again thoroughly sterilized.

Field of Operation. The skin of the foot is much thicker than that on the other parts of the body and in addition it usually does not receive the same hygienic care as does the rest of the skin surface. It is therefore highly essential that additional precautions be taken in preparing the foot for operation.

The entire foot should be scrubbed with soap and warm water so as to remove as much of the exfoliated skin and dirt as possible. It is then immersed in a solution of bichloride of mercury (1/2000) and wrapped in a sterile towel until ready for operation. The foot may also be prepared by first scrubbing with soap and water, washing with alcohol, 60%, and finally painting the part to be operated upon with tincture of iodine. Iodine has proven to be the best antiseptic in use today, but very often it interferes with chiropodical operations due to the stain it produces. This may be overcome to a certain extent by washing the part with alcohol after the iodine has been applied

Alcohol in a sixty per cent. solution is a very efficient antiseptic and wherever iodine cannot be used, it may be substituted. A piece of absorbent cotton, dipped into the alcohol, is placed in contact with the part to be treated and is allowed to remain for a few minutes. Like iodine, alcohol penetrates the layers of the epidermis and so destroys the bacteria that lurk between the outer layers.

Hands of the Operator. There are several ways of cleaning the operator's hands, but each such procedure is preceded by thoroughly scrubbing them with green soap and a nail brush for at least ten minutes, in warm water. Alcohol or ether should then be rubbed over the hands to dissolve fats, and they should then be dipped in a solution of bichloride of mercury (1/2000) for a few minutes A most efficient way of sterilizing the hands consists of the following: after scrubbing the hands as before described, take equal parts of chloride of lime and carbonate of soda (about one-half teaspoonful of each) and add enough water to make a paste. This is thoroughly rubbed into the hands and when the sensation of warmth has disappeared they are rinsed in sterile water.

The use of rubber gloves to protect the hands is of some advantage in that they may be thoroughly boiled before they are used; but unless the hands are sore or the skin is tender, they should not be employed, as they decrease the sense of touch so necessary in chiropodial procedures.

STERILIZING APPARATUS

There are many kinds of apparatus for each form of sterilization, and the podiatrist, in selecting a sterilizer, must be guided by the size of his purse as well as the amount of space he can afford for such an apparatus.

The steam sterilizer is unquestionably the best for general purposes, and the dual compartment arrangement is better than a single chamber outfit. Steam sterilizers for office purposes vary in size from the small single chamber, measuring four inches wide, eight inches long and four inches deep, to the larger double chamber which measures twelve inches wide, twenty-four inches long, the upper chamber twelve inches deep and the lower chamber six inches deep. The latter sterilizers are the best possible for the podiatrist's work, in that they allow for the sterilization of towels, dressings and instruments at the same time, and there is no direct contact between the instruments and the boiling water. The apparatus may be heated by gas or by electricity, gas being the most desirable as it is more easily controlled and regulated. The cost of the instrument equipped for gas heating is very much cheaper, and the operating expense is less than when electricity is similarly used.

As its name implies, the double compartment sterilizer is composed of two distinct sections which are easily separated, and when put together look as if they were one section. The lower compartment is more shallow than the upper and contains the water which is boiled for the manufacture of the steam to be utilized in the sterilization. The upper compartment has an inner jacket which is so arranged that the steam passing from below is collected in it, and is admitted into the compartment proper through a small opening at one end. This causes the steam to be forced in under a slight pressure, which increases the heat and adds to its power as a germ destroying agent. The opening is controlled by an inlet valve which may be adjusted so as to prevent the steam from entering the compartment. The steam then circulates around it in the jacket and in this way dry heat is generated in sufficient quantity to allow for dry heat sterilization. If space permits, it is advisable to have two such sterilizers, one for steam sterilization and the other for dry heat sterilization. The instruments, towels and dressings may thus be dried which prevents the rusting of the steel, and makes the linen more easy to handle. These sterilizers are, as well, an ornament to any office.

ELECTRIC STERILIZER

Where space is limited, the smaller electric sterilizers may be substituted for the larger outfits. There are many styles and shapes of this kind of instrument, but the principle is the same in all of them. There must be ample space for the reception of the instruments, and the cover must be closed when the water is boiling. The electric current is passed into a metallic disc, situated beneath the bottom of the water receptacle. As the current passes through this disc, it becomes hot, and the water in the compartment is gradually heated until the boiling point is reached. The current must never be left on when the machine is not in use, for when the water has evaporated, the heat will cause the solder holding the joints of the sterilizer to melt and cause a separation of the seams. This molten solder might even drip on something combustible and set it alight. There are some electric sterilizers which are equipped with safety devices which prevent this possible accident. The device provides so that when this heat is great enough, it melts a small piece of an alloy with a very low melting point. This metal is held in position by a clamp which is attached to the current flow and when this melts, the current is cut off and further heating is impossible. This is a very valuable attachment, particularly when one is inclined to be careless.

Another form of smaller electric sterilizer consists of a glass compartment into which is placed the heating apparatus. This latter is composed of coils enclosed in a metal protector. The protector is attached to a handle, through which pass the electric wires. This coil and handle is placed into the glass bowl and is held fixed by a small clamp. A cover is then placed over the bowl, which is so arranged as to allow the wires to pass through it.

FORMALDEHYDE STERILIZER

For sterilization with pure phenol and alcohol, it is necessary to have two wide mouth, glass stoppered, two-ounce bottles. When the instruments are being sterilized they may be left standing in either bottle until ready for use. A piece of felt, cut to fit the inside bottom of each of the bottles, should be placed in situ, so that when sharp edged instruments are placed in the bottles, their points will not be broken, by coming in contact with the hard glass.

Formaldehyde gas is an agent which has germicidal properties, and is used to a great extent where steam sterilizers are not available. Formalin, a concentrated solution of the formaldehyde gas, readily gives up its gaseous constituent so that when the liquid is placed on a flat tray, the gas will penetrate objects around it. Cabinets have been constructed which are so arranged that the lower shelf contains the solution, and the upper shelves may be used for instruments, dressings, towels, etc. When the cabinets, which vary greatly in size, are tightly closed, the gas will penetrate every object contained therein, thus destroying any microorganisms which might be present.

CHAPTER V

THE CARE OF THE FOOT

The Naked Foot. For many centuries the human foot was allowed to go naked, and our aboriginal ancestors never knew what foot clothing of any type meant. Much the same as with the rest of his body, unaided nature was allowed to minister to the needs of his pedal extremities. Research has shown that primitive man was very strong and able to withstand the abuses of the elements to a marked degree. The body adapted itself to nature and the elements, so that it could bear extreme heat or cold, wind or rain, or any condition of the weather, without giving way before these nature forces.

So it was with the foot of man during this period. The skin of the soles became thickened so that even the roughest surfaces caused no discomfort when borne upon by his bare feet. Even to this day, savage tribes that still go barefoot have skin on the soles of the feet that is tough and hardened. The author has seen natives of Central America, who are of this class, step on objects such as glass, lighted cigars, etc., without experiencing any appreciable discomfort.

In aboriginal man, muscular action of the entire foot was developed to its maximum. The muscles of the toes were under perfect control so that objects could be felt and lifted with them, much the same as with the fingers of man today. The leg muscles were well developed so that the position of the body in walking could be altered quickly and the body weight could be rapidly changed from one foot to another, so as to avoid contact with sharp pointed objects, such as burrs, sharp twigs, pointed stones, etc.

Nature was primative man's physician. Being continuously exposed to the air, skin exfoliation, evaporation of moisture and other normal functions were never interfered with. The objects with which the body came in contact in wading through small streams, or in walking through the wet grass and dewy underbrush, acted much the same as the bath brush of modern times. Further, man of that period, living on nature's foods, was never subject to the various conditions brought about by improper diet and which in turn manifest themselves in the feet as well as in other parts of the body.

Advent of Foot Clothing. As time went on and man became more and more civilized, clothing for the foot was gradually adopted, and from that time to the present the foot has undergone changes that make it necessary for the human race to resort to treatment for lesions that could not have developed if nature had had her way, and man had never adopted covering for the foot.

The first style of foot covering was the sandal. This caused no special trouble, but when man began to depend upon them for protection for the soles of the feet, nature consequently no longer required the tough, protecting, heavy skin, and gradually the integument of that region became thinner. The result has been, that today, slight trauma or irritation causes many disturbances on the soles, among which are the common helomata dura and verrucae.

An evolution of footgear followed the use of the sandal, and with civilization came vanity in foot dress and finally the modern shoe, completely at variance with nature's demands and causing so many disturbances that specialists in treating foot lesions became requisite to care for them.

Modern Footgear. The modern shoe, as compared to the normal foot, is worthy of special consideration. As a rule, the men who build shoes have from time immemorial been pure commercialists. Their purpose in engaging in the manufacture of footwear always has been and is to do business. They have attempted to create styles that would sell. They have produced wares that would be popular and therefore saleable. The question of the niceties of the anatomy and physiology of the foot and leg played no part in their calculations because they knew nothing about these features as factors in gaining results. The foot was treated as a whole, much as the hat manufacturer considers the human head when building a head covering. No consideration was given the natural beauties of the foot, so much appreciated by the ancient Greeks. The need for conserving the functions of the small bones of the foot so that their articulations would not be disturbed, caused them no pause. The necessity for allowing free play to all of the muscles which abduct, adduct, evert, invert, flex and extend the foot was and is a negligible quantity with the shoe-builder. There are few exceptions to this rule.

Suppose the dentist were to make sets of teeth to be fitted to the jaws of those who had become toothless, basing their manufacture of these dental adjuvants on the prevailing needs of groups of these tooth-defectives, and tooth-shops were to be instituted to fit these sufferers from wares in stock! The public would deride such an innovation. And still it is almost as ridiculous to suppose that our shoe-shops can properly clothe the feet of the public as they should be clothed from a stock of shoes which are made without careful relevancy to the anatomy and physiology of the foot. Let us take one feature of the modern shoe as a sample of this pandering to style: the high heel, so common on women's shoes, is a pure conceit. It is responsible for many of the foot lesions of to-day, and in addition causes systemic disturbances of a serious nature. When the body in standing is erect, the foot should be at right angles to the leg. When the heels are raised, however, it would be necessary to tilt the body forward to still maintain the right angular posture. It therefore becomes necessary in maintaining the erect position to allow for the mal-alignment of the body, due to the high heels, and this is accomplished in the knees, hips and spine. The knees are flexed, the hips rotated and the abdomen thrust forward. This latter interferes with the normal position of the abdominal organs, and thus arise many diseases common to women. The high heel is the etiologic factor. Locally, the calf muscles become contracted and an inward lateral displacement of some of the tarsal bones results. Gradually the other bones of the foot are displaced, and weak and flat foot result. Further, the high heel causes the foot to slip forward in the shoe and the toes are thus crowded. When the body weight is brought to bear upon the ball of the foot in walking, this crowding prevents the normal spreading of the metatarsal bones, and there is distortion of the bones, causing anterior displacement, or dropping of the anterior arch with resulting metatarsalgia.

Another illustration the function of the sudoriferous glands, namely, the elimination of liquid waste, in the form of sweat or perspiration, is going on continuously. As the fluids are brought to the surface by the gland ducts, evaporation takes place immediately, except under unusual circumstances, such as mental excitement, increased temperature, etc, in which instances the production may be very rapid or may be retarded. When the foot is encased in a shoe, or in a stocking that does not absorb moisture, such as silk or lisle, this evaporation is retarded to a greater or lesser degree, depending upon the leather of which the shoe is made. Such interference with normal functions is productive of many foot ills elsewhere noted in these pages. In this connection the podiatrist should be familiar with these facts: Vici kid is the most porous of all the leathers used in shoe manufacture, so that most if not all of the moisture excreted by the glands evaporates. Calf skin is not so efficient for foot covering, in that evaporation is limited; both of these leathers are far superior to either patent leather or colt skin, which latter are absolutely air and water tight, and should never be used as a foot covering The stocking should be of a material that will absorb moisture, and cotton or woolen hose are best for this purpose and will assist in keeping the feet dry and normal.

Again, the nails of the toes are often unfavorably affected by the modern shoe, especially the nails of the great toes. The toe box of the average shoe is made of stiff, unyielding material so that if the shoe is narrow or short, irritation or undue pressure is brought to bear upon the nail or the surrounding tissues, causing disease. It is especially necessary to obviate the possibility of pressure of the soft tissue of the nail groove against the hard nail substance, because if such a condition arises and is allowed to persist, calloused nail grooves, helomata and often ingrown toe nails result. In the same manner, pressure on the various parts of the nail may cause club nail, onychia or paronychia. Simple packing of the nail grooves with absorbent cotton, if properly done, is often the means of avoiding serious nail lesions, which, as a rule, are very painful.

In this connection it would be well to remember that it is most important that the nails be cut properly. The corners of the nails should never be removed, unless there is some trouble beneath the part. Removal of the corners of the nails changes the position of the surrounding soft tissues, which depend upon the hard nail substance for support, and thereby causes them to collapse. This is one of the primary etiologic factors of ingrown toe nail.

The bony structures of the foot have suffered extensively since the advent of modern footgear, and the treatment of the lesions in which the osseous tissue is involved is of importance to the podiatrist as well as to the surgeon or orthopedist. Many deformities of the foot are such that only the surgeon is qualified to successfully treat them, but the more common lesions properly come under the care of the podiatrist, and should be treated by him.

Pointed shoes cause displacement of the metatarsal bones, with subsequent nerve compression; hallux valgus is a common deformity due to misfitting shoes. These latter conditions are the result of improper footgear, as also of incorrect posture and of faulty locomotion.

The soft tissues of the foot have suffered to a great extent because of the modern shoe, especially the muscles that arise in the leg and are inserted in the foot. Upon these muscles principally depend the motions of the foot, especially those of flexion, extension, adduction and abduction. The calf muscles, as previously stated, become shortened, due to the high heels. Additionally the muscles on the outer side of the leg are shortened while those on the inner side are lengthened. The long extensors of the toe are also shortened.

When it is remembered that there are twenty muscles in addition to the twelve muscles of the leg inserted into the foot, the limited motion of this area, as compared to other parts of the body, is apparent. Take for instance, the movements of the toes in the average adult. The action of the great toe is markedly limited and that of the lesser toes is almost lost. This loss of action is brought about by a lack of use of the digits of the feet The hands and fingers being used continuously, the movements of these digits are active and numerous. The toes have a like muscular supply, but are far less efficient. The ability of the barefoot races to use their toes as accessory fingers, is proof that lack of development is due to lack of motion because of the toes being encased for most of the time in footgear.

Hygiene of the Foot. The many perverted functions of the foot that have been brought about by the use of modern footgear have made it essential that this part of the body be given special attention both by the specialist and by the individual himself. There are several essentials for proper foot care with which everybody should be familiar, and it is the duty of the podiatrist to instruct his patients in these essentials. The general hygiene of the foot is little understood by the average layman, and the fact that a patient takes a daily bath is no indication that the feet are being properly cleansed. To accomplish this the foot should be washed with soap and water, care being taken that any excrementitious matter which may have accumulated between the toes is thoroughly removed. It is best to use warm water for this purpose, and when the feet have been thoroughly cleansed they should be rinsed in cold water. This closes the glands which have become dilated by the heat; if allowed to remain open, they will over-functionate. The foot must be dried well, especially between the toes, and after this has been done, alcohol may be applied to assist in this purpose. Alcohol is both astringent and dehydrating. In cases of a normally dry skin, alcohol may be dispensed with; instead, a small quantity of an animal oil should be rubbed into the skin; lanolin is very efficient for this purpose.

Water, as a therapeutic agent, is used extensively and has many advantages that are lacking in other remedial measures. It is one of the most ancient of remedies, and its value has been recognized to such an extent that there are large institutes in this and other countries devoted exclusively to hydrotherapy.

No other agent is capable of producing so great a variety of physiologic effects as water; it is easily obtained and is also readily adaptable for the various conditions in which it is of benefit. Pastor Kneipp obtained excellent results with his water cure in Europe, and although his methods are not original creations, and their application was largely empiric, they attracted international attention. The entire system of treatment as practised by him was based upon some hygienic principle, and most of the results achieved were due to the application of common sense.

Water has three properties to which its value as a therapeutic agent are due; first, its power to absorb and communicate heat; second, its solvent properties, third, the ease with which it changes its physical state from the liquid to the solid or gaseous form. These three properties, either alone or combined, are to be considered when water is applied to the body as a therapeutic agent.

A given quantity of water by weight can absorb more heat than any other substance. The readiness with which this heat is absorbed makes it possible to apply either heat or cold to the body. Thus, ice applied to the body will melt, and in doing so will extract a large amount of heat from the tissues. It is valuable therefore in conditions such as local infections, in which the heat of the body is above normal.

Every substance is more or less soluble in water Water is therefore called the universal solvent. Water is the medium by which foods are dissolved and absorbed in digestion; water also dissolves and carries off the waste products to the various organs of elimination.

For therapeutic application, the temperature of water varies from 32 degrees, F. to 120 degrees, F., depending upon the condition in which it is used and also the purpose of its use. Foot baths are of special interest to the podiatrist, so that it is necessary to be familiar with the particular type of foot bath that is valuable in the treatment of foot lesions.

The *alternate foot bath* is used for stimulating the cutaneous circulation, and acts as a general tonic for the nerves and other tissues. The bath is given as follows· the feet are placed in hot water for two minutes and then plunged into cold water and kept there for 30 seconds. They are then returned to the hot water for two minutes and back into the cold water for 30 seconds. This is repeated a number of times, always starting with the hot water and finishing with immersion in cold water. This bath affords great relief to those suffering with tired feet after having worn shoes for a long period. As a general hygienic adjunct, the alternate foot bath is of great benefit, and should be employed at night before retiring.

Foot Care of Infants and Adolescents. About eighty per cent of the civilized, shoe wearing people, are foot afflicted to a greater or lesser degree, and most of this can be traced to neglect of the feet in infancy and youth. Many of the most common diseases found in adults might have been avoided if proper care had been taken and the causative factors removed in proper time.

The foot of an infant, which has never worn a shoe, is really a perfect foot, and it is the only stage in life in which the perfect foot is commonly found. The toes are spread and the forefoot is slightly adducted. When the first footgear is selected for the infant (it must be borne in mind that the foot grows rapidly at this age) the shoe should be of sufficient length and width to allow for this growth. The softest materials should be used for the first shoes of the infant, for as the feet are not used in walking at this age, the necessary support to locomotion received from the material in the shoe, is a negative factor.

When the child commences to walk, the shoes should be changed, and a sole should be provided. The upper should be of kid, and should extend slightly above the ankle. Laced shoes should be used, and continued throughout the entire period of infancy and youth. The normal adduction of the forefoot should be considered and the outer border should curve inward in a gradual line. The foot should be measured for shoes with the child bearing its weight on the foot. This allows for the spread of the foot in weight bearing, and measurements taken under these conditions give assurance of a proper fit.

As the infant grows, the muscular strength of the legs is increased, and eventually the limbs are strong enough to support and carry the body weight. It is at this time that the child will commence to walk by natural impulse or instinct. From the short, jerky, uncertain step, there is a gradual improvement and, with time, the infant gains confidence and strength and the step soon becomes firm and steady. The question is often asked of physicians and podiatrists by anxious mothers: "why is it that my baby does not walk?" It seems to be a source of worry to them, for as these mothers watch other children walking, they become envious and attempt to teach their children to walk. Walking is a natural function and it is foolhardy to insist upon infants attempting this foray until the bones to which the muscles are attached are sufficiently unyielding and the muscles involved can coördinate for that purpose. The use of artificial means of assistance for the child, viz., the various contrivances on the market that support the child under the arms and allow the feet to drag on the ground, should be discouraged.

Premature locomotion causes an unnatural strain upon the legs and feet and is often the cause of malformations which continue on in later life. Many foot and leg lesions can be attributed to an over-anxious mother who insisted upon her child walking before the time was ripe for it to do so. Therefore it behooves every mother to allow nature to have its way, and to wait until the legs are strong enough. In cases where walking is unsteady, it may be advisable to assist the strengthening of the muscles by massage and passive motion.

The use of appliances to assist a child which already walks should be guarded, and only when there is something pathologically wrong should they be employed. Weak-ankle shoes, or weak-ankle braces or supports, although they apparently help the child's gait, really retard the normal motions at the ankle joint, and there is little possibility of a compensatory increase in strength of the parts as a result of their use. When the ankle is continuously supported by some outside agent, the normal support, i.e., the muscles of the leg, become weaker. This is because they are not used, and atrophy is the result. When conditions are such that assistance must be sought, the part should be exercised by massage, exercises and passive motion. It is often a difficult matter to prescribe exercises for a child, but if given in a cheery way, so that the child thinks it is playing a new game or is having heaps of fun, the results are often remarkable. The First Institute of Podiatry is now planning an exercise room for children of the poor whose locomotion is impaired and the experiment will be watched with interest.

As the child grows into adolescence, the shoes should be changed often enough to allow for the normal growth of the foot. It is better to buy shoes oftener, than to attempt economy at the expense of health. The parents should acquaint themselves with an orthopedist or a podiatrist to advise and a competent shoe man, under the direction of the advisor, should fit the shoes of the growing child. Thus, caring for the same foot over a protracted period, such a specialist is better able to judge the size and shape best adapted for the individual. Walking and other forms of exercise should be encouraged, especially those exercises that develop the muscles of the foot and leg. It must be borne in mind that the flat foot and weak foot of later life are caused by deficient muscular action of certain groups of muscles.

Foot Care of Adults. After the foot has attained its full growth, and the bones have become calcified, correction of the lesions involving the bony tissue is difficult. Young persons who have been accustomed to wearing shoes with a straight inner line, and with broad toes, will pass into middle age without much, if any foot trouble. Slight friction or pressure may produce small helomata, but these are of little consequence and are easily relieved by intelligent care and treatment.

As previously stated, pointed and narrow shoes with high heels are responsible for many of the local foot lesions, and corrective treatment should be begun at as early a period as possible. When a person reaches middle age, the bones of the foot have become set. Attempts at correction, such as the prescribing of shoes with a straight inner line for such persons, cause the foot to be put into an entirely new position, and because the bones have become firmly set, such a new departure is frequently fraught with discomfort, and at times causes other bone and muscle troubles which are painful.

In younger adults, correction should be gradual. It is inadvisable to adopt radical measures for those who have been wearing incorrect shoes, or who have been walking and standing incorrectly for a long period of time. A woman who has been wearing high heeled shoes for a few years, has a shortening of the calf muscles which should be corrected, but to change from a two inch heel to one a half-inch high, without gradually reducing the height, will cause extreme discomfort. Appropriate exercises should be advised and the style of the footgear should be gradually and not abruptly changed as the foot responds to treatment.

Walking is one form of exercise in which every able-bodied person can indulge, and is a means of maintaining body health as well as of keeping the muscles of the foot and legs strong. Like every other form of exercise, it should be practised with caution. The individual who walks long distances is placing an undue strain upon the muscles of the lower extremity, and instead of being benefited, he is being harmed. The position of the foot is important in walking. The foot should point forward, and the forefoot should swing slightly inward with each step. In this way all of the muscles of the leg receive their proper share of work. The pace should be brisk and steady, yet not fast enough to cause the person to suffer in breathing. Slow, leisurely strolls are useless as a medium for muscular improvement, and are simply a waste of time.

The Care of the Soldier's Foot. The foot of the soldier is subjected to unusual strain, both on the march and while in the trenches, and special care is necessary if the maximum of efficiency is to be maintained. Hygiene should be practised to a greater extent than under ordinary circumstances, and immediate attention should be given to minor troubles that might pass unnoticed in civil life.

The feet should be washed daily, and if long marches are contemplated, they should receive this attention both before and after the march. The feet should be thoroughly dried after each washing, and dusted with some foot powder that will absorb moisture. Lycopodium is the best base to use in foot powders. Socks should be examined and if found torn or badly mended, should be discarded because the pressure of the spots that have been darned may result in painful troubles. Shoes should be large enough to accommodate the spreading of the anterior arch in walking, yet should be snug in the heel to prevent the foot from sliding and creating friction. When soldiers are to serve in the trenches their feet should be given special attention, to prevent the possibilities of trench foot and other foot lesions that are the result of trench life. It has been proven by those who have gone thoroughly into the matter that the water and mud which is found in the trenches is responsible for these lesions, therefore it is necessary to guard against it reaching the feet of the men. In addition to wearing rubber boots, the feet should be thoroughly rubbed with some greasy substance immediately before entering the trenches Mineral oils are best, and although the process of rubbing the feet and legs with oil is repulsive to the men, it should be compulsory, as it is the means of preventing loss of limbs. Cloths dipped in melted paraffin and then wrapped around the feet will suffice to keep the water from the skin.

Immediately after a siege in the trenches, the feet should be thoroughly washed with soap and warm water, carefully dried, and dusted with an antiseptic foot powder. One containing boracic acid and talcum will answer ordinary purposes If abnormal lesions develop, these should be treated in keeping with the requirements.

The men should receive instructions at regular intervals, and lectures on the care of the foot should be given by the officer in charge of that particular branch of the medical department. Foot inspections should be made at prescribed times, and during these inspections, the podiatrist can easily determine whether or not the men are in need of foot attention beyond that which comes with self-care. The feet should also be examined before a march of ten miles or more, and should be re-examined immediately after the march. This procedure will save the men from developing any serious trouble, as the beginning of any such trouble is thus detected, and proper preventive treatment can be applied, sufficiently timely.

One or two podiatrists should be attached to each ambulance train while the troops are on the march, so that they are available at short notice. The immediate application of a shield or pad over some part of the foot that is being irritated will often save the individual from foot infection that may be serious. Too much care cannot be given the feet of the soldiery as their efficiency is based upon their powers of locomotion. It was the opinion of the first Napoleon that an army moved upon its stomach. By that he meant that plenty of proper food was essential to every fighting force. In these times, it is conceded that the foot-whole alone can be counted as competent soldiers, important as may be the food question. It behooves us, therefore, to give to the men who are willing to offer up their lives for their country's weal, the very best possible care, and although the foot of the soldier has received no special attention in the past, the time is now ripe for the recognition of the podiatrist as an integral part of every officered unit in the Medical Corps of the Army and of the Navy. From a national economic standpoint alone, this recognition should be accorded because it must be clear that unless proper precautions are taken to note the condition of the soldier's feet before he goes overseas, thousands will be found unavailable for first line work and will thus constitute themselves an incubus rather than an aid to the fighting force of our country

CHAPTER VI

DRESSINGS AND BANDAGING

DRESSINGS.

Definition. A dressing is the material applied to a wound for the purpose of excluding the air, stimulating repair and protecting the affected areas from irritation and from other untoward conditions.

Four classes of dressings are used in podiatry, viz.: the moist dressing, the dry dressing, the ointment dressing and the occlusive dressing.

The Moist Dressing. The moist dressing is generally composed of several thicknesses of gauze applied to a part and moistened with some germicidal, antiseptic, astringent, antiphlogistic or sedative solution.

There are two forms of moist dressing: the evaporating and the non-evaporating.

The Evaporating Moist Dressing, generally known as the wet dressing, is an application of several thicknesses of gauze saturated with a solution and allowed to remain uncovered so that evaporation of the solution takes place. The gauze is remoistened from time to time so that it is kept continually wet. The action of this form of dressing, independent of the specific action of the solution employed, is heat reducing and causes localized anemia. It may be employed wherever infection or inflammation is present.

The Non-Evaporating Moist Dressing is composed of several thicknesses of gauze saturated in a solution and covered with some impervious covering such as gutta percha tissue, oiled silk or fishskin. This form of dressing, independent of the action of the solution employed, is heat producing and locally hyperemic. It is contra-indicated in the presence of pus, as the warmth and moisture produced by its use is congenial to the growth of bacteria. It should only be used when the skin is unbroken, in such cases as sprains and bruises, or where the action of a poultice is not contra-indicated.

The Dry Dressing. The dry dressing is composed of several thicknesses of sterile gauze applied to a part and allowed to remain dry. There are two forms of dry dressing, (1) that in which the gauze itself is alone applied, and, (2) one composed of dry sterile gauze or cotton used for the purpose of applying a dusting powder, having either antiseptic, astringent or stimulative qualities or in some instances, all three. The plain gauze dressing is used where asepsis and drainage alone are desired in a wound, all symptoms demanding the treatment by means of drugs having been eliminated. The gauze is used either as a "wick" and packed into a cavity as a drain, or in a series of thicknesses covering the whole affected area.

The dusting powder dressing consists in applying a powder to the affected surfaces and covering the same with several thicknesses of sterile gauze, or with a pledget of sterile cotton. The dusting powder is used when astringency is desired, as from bismuth subgallate (dermatol); or where stimulative and antiseptic action is desired, as from thymol iodide (aristol).

The Ointment Dressing. The ointment dressing is one in which an ointment, held in place either by lint, gauze or cotton, plays a conspicuous part in the repair of the lesion. The ointment is either spread upon the fabric used, or is applied directly to the affected areas by means of a spatula. This form of dressing can be used in the treatment of superficial inflammations, blisters, pernio, etc., but is contra-indicated in the presence of a discharge, as the fatty or oily base of the ointment interferes with the absorption of such a discharge and so prevents proper drainage of the part.

The Occlusive Dressing. The occlusive dressing is one

employed for the purpose of excluding the air and of completely sealing the parts. In podiatry this occlusion is obtained by the use of collodion, either plain or medicated, by a combination of collodion and cotton, or by the application of compound tincture of benzoin.

FABRICS.

There are a number of fabrics which may be used for dressing materials in podiatry. The three most important are gauze, cotton and lint.

Gauze is a thin meshed, loosely woven cloth employed in the manufacture of bandages and used for wound dressings; such gauze should be sterilized or impregnated with antiseptics.

The varieties of gauze which are of practical use in the practice of chiropody are:

(1) *Plain aseptic gauze,* either dry or moist; a gauze sterilized either by dry heat, so that the fabric remains dry, or subjected to moist heat (steam) sterilization from which the gauze retains a certain amount of moisture. The dry gauze is put up commercially in pasteboard boxes, and can be thus obtained in quantities of one square yard and upwards. The moist aseptic gauze is obtainable in as small a quantity as the former, but comes in sealed glass jars which may be kept upon the operating stand or cabinet.

(2) *Corrosive sublimate gauze* is put up in glass jars in quantities of one square yard and upwards. The gauze is saturated in a solution of mercury bichloride and may be obtained in strengths from 1/2000 to 1/10000.

(3) *Iodoform gauze* is put up for surgical use in the same manner and quantity as No. 2. The medication impregnates the whole fabric and constitutes an excellent method of applying the drug. On account of the suggestive odor of iodoform, however, this gauze has lost favor with the podiatrist.

(4) *Borated gauze,* or gauze impregnated with boric acid in 10% strength, is used in podiatry where a mild antiseptic dressing is desired. It comes in glass jars in quantities similar to the two foregoing varieties.

The forms in which gauze are used in podiatry practice are numerous. The following are the most important:

(1) *Bandage.* Gauze, in varying widths, makes a highly practical bandaging material. Cotton bandages are used, but cannot compare with even the poorer grades of linten gauze for durability. The reader is referred to the subheading, "Bandaging," at the end of this article.

(2) *Large gauze squares.* It is a common practice among podiatrists to cut large quantities of gauze into pieces about three inches square. These have two uses: (a), to dry off instruments dripping with alcohol or whatever germicidal solution has been used, before operation, and (b), as a dressing applied over the affected area. In the latter instance this size square is practical where the whole distal end of the toe is to be covered, as in applying a moist dressing in the treatment of ingrown nail, or where there

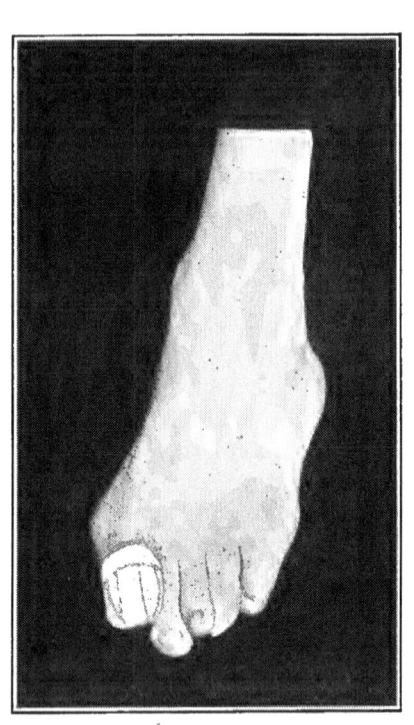

LARGE GAUZE SQUARE FOR DRESSING INGROWN NAIL

is a large area to be covered on the dorsum, plantar or lateral sides of the foot or upon the lower leg. As a "wipe" for instruments, one thickness, and as a dressing, three or four thicknesses are used.

(3) *Small gauze squares.* These are about an inch and a half square and have their principal use as a dressing to cover one side of a toe nail, or to cover a small area of the integument, or as a "wick" in the drainage of a large sinus or deep ulcerative condition. Both the large and small squares, cut to size, are sterilized by heat and are then placed in a formaldehyde sterilizer until used; this assures their absolute asepsis.

(4) *Nail Groove and Sinus Pledgets.* For the more confined areas of the nail groove or for a small sinus, gauze is cut into small pieces measuring about one-half inch long and one-eighth inch wide. Several thicknesses of the fabric are cut together so that even from a small amount of gauze many small pledgets or "wicks" are obtainable. These small gauze pieces are very practical for packing a nail groove, and, as the fibre is looser and the pledgets do not harden, they make a much softer and more yielding pad for the nail than does cotton.

In the drainage of a small sinus, these small pieces of gauze offer a very practical material for use as a "wick." Three or four strands of the fabric may be inserted at the mouth of the sinus to prevent surface granulation, while the repair in the deeper tissue is still incomplete.

Cotton. Cotton is the white, fluffy, fibrous covering of the seeds of the cotton plant which, when ginned and refined to a uniform smoothness, furnishes a medium which is used extensively in surgical dressings.

Aseptic absorbent cotton is manufactured by a number of firms and, except in the cheaper grades, no irregularities or foreign matter are found in the fabric.

Cotton is used in podiatry practice by winding it on the end of a wooden or metal applicator. The fabric, thus fashioned about the applicator, is used either dry or dipped in some medication for applying solutions to the foot. It is also used to dry parts or to wipe instruments; as a dressing, it is used principally in combination with collodion to make the cocoon dressing. This name is derived from its resemblance to the cocoon of the silkworm or the butterfly.

A cocoon dressing is a pledget of cotton, the fibre of which is smoothed and is placed in one direction, while the edges of the pledget are thinned out or "feathered." The cotton is applied over the part and collodion (preferably flexible collodion) is painted over it by means of a brush or a glass rod in such a manner as to bind the edges of the cotton firmly to the skin. The collodion when applied is semi-liquid, and as its constituents, ether and alcohol, evaporate upon contact with the air, the pyroxylin remaining becomes an integral part of the cotton, joining intimately with its fibres and with the surface of the skin. After the edges are bound down in place, the collodion may be painted once along the length and once across the fibre at the centre of the dressing, so as to bind the dressing into one cohesive whole; it is not wise, generally, to saturate the whole pledget with collodion, as when dried, the dressing will be hard and unyielding. In the procedure first described the dressing is semi-occlusive; in the latter, occlusive. The cocoon dressing is used principally as a covering for a part when an ointment has been applied and, as in these cases the parts beneath are tender, it is wise to have the dressing as soft and pliable as possible.

This form of dressing may be used alone or it may be applied as a covering and protection over the aperture of a shield after an ointment has been applied to the part. It is found very practical when applied over a nail fold and groove in which an ointment has been used. The dressing will confine the unguent to the proper areas and prevent it from running over that side of the digit. In dressing a blister or other irritated area, due to ill-fitting shoes or mended hosiery, the cocoon is also very practical. The cotton not alone serves to hold the medication in place, but acts as a padding so that the part may not be subjected to further irritation.

Cotton is also used in the form of a small pledget for packing a nail groove. The pledget or roll should be small and thin and is used to hold a medication in place; at the same time it constitutes a soft pad upon which the edge of the nail rests.

Lint. Lint is a flocculent material procured by ravelling or scraping linen.

Surgeon's absorbent lint as a dressing and shielding material, is continuously coming more into vogue. Otto Sjogren of New York is a great believer in its efficacy and in his demonstrations at The First Institute of Podiatry strongly advocates its use The late W. A. Kennedy of Philadelphia was also strong in his advocacy of lint as a dressing and is on record as follows: "The essentially favorable feature in utilizing lint for shielding purposes is that, when properly adjusted, there is no pressure on the parts which it serves to protect. Most, if not all, of the material of which shields are ordinarily made, is of an unyielding character, and, in consequence, the capillary circulation of the compressed part is disturbed If such a condition exists, absorption is prevented and the treatment is in most instances harmful rather than helpful. Because lint is a loosely woven cotton fibre, it does not pack in a hard mass, but always remains soft and yielding; nor is it necessary to apply it excepting in thin layers.

"The method of use should be as follows:

"Select a perfect sheet of lint and cut off a square or oblong piece slightly larger than the lesion and round off the corners so that they will not bulge when plaster strips or bandages are applied. Then cut a round opening in the lint, slightly larger than the lesion. Spread such medicament as is desired on the part requiring it, and then place the fluffy side of the lint next the skin, in situ, with the edges of the opening surrounding the part under treatment. Over this dressing, place a piece of lint so as to cover the existing dressing in its entirety and apply ordinary adhesive plaster to retain the whole in place. The thickness of the dressing represented in layers of lint will depend upon the necessities of each individual case, but in the experience of the writer, the most satisfactory results are obtainable where the dressing is least bulky. At times, when several layers of the lint are requisite to the patient's comfort, it will be found advisable to cut out the sides of one of the under layers for the purpose of making a half-moon dressing; then apply the top covering.

"In the accompanying illustrations most of the required dressings shown are of two thicknesses only, the under layer having the round opening and the upper layer acting as a protective as well as an absorbing medium. This method will be found useful, in that drainage may take place properly where there is a suppurating surface, and even though the patient does not return for treatment at the time suggested, there will be no danger of septic infection because of a damming in the flow of exudate, a menace which is so common in some forms of dressing. Patients will rarely complain that the plaster 'draws' offensively if the above dressing is properly applied.

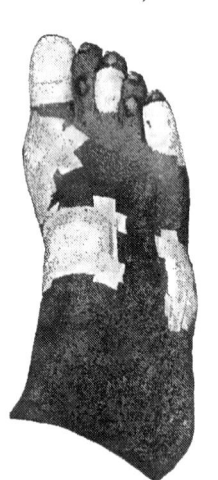

DORSAL LINT DRESSING

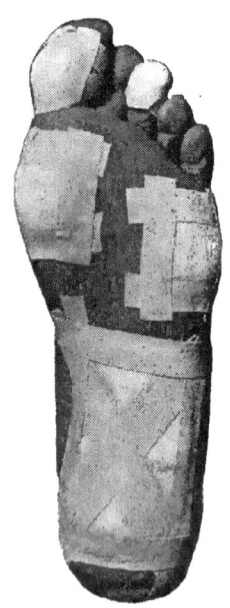

PLANTAR LINT DRESSING

"The plantar aspect of the foot exhibits four full dressings and half of another.

"The dressing covering the great toe may be utilized for any lesion from a callous to a perforating ulcer; the one on the distal end of the middle toe, for heloma or for any other condition usually met with in this region.

"The dressing covering the fifth metatarsophalangeal articulation can be applied for perforating ulcer, for callous or for vascular heloma and can be placed anywhere after treating this lesion The dressing covering the os calcis region is of a single thickness and can be used in varying sizes for any lesion found on the plantar surface.

"The partial dressing, covering the first metatarsophalangeal articulation is used from one to any required number of layers for covering bunions, enlarged joints, etc.; the other section of this dressing is shown on the dorsal aspect of the foot in the other illustration.

"The dressing covering the dorsal aspect of the great toe is used after any ingrown nail treatment and the dressings on the third and fifth toes are applied after the removal of helomata.

"The dressing covering the fifth tarsometatarsal articulation is very useful in combating the calloused and ofttimes inflamed area produced by the side seam of shoes, especially of the low-cut type.

"Lastly, the dressing covering the tarsal aspect is a comfortable arrangement to apply after removing the minute helomata produced by the eyelets of a shoe or for any other lesion found on the dorsal surface.

"In case of extensive ulceration or of profuse discharge from a lesion, it is advisable to use several layers of sterile or medicated gauze before applying the absorbent lint to the surface."

Collodion. Plain flexible collodion is used extensively in podiatry as an agent to bind cotton into place upon a part or as a vehicle of application for a number of drugs, or whenever an occlusive dressing is applied. Flexible collodion is ordinary collodion to which is added castor oil and turpentine. These drugs serve to reduce the contraction of the film during evaporation. Plain collodion, as evaporation takes place, contracts in area and when applied is liable to draw or "pucker" the skin about the part. Flexible collodion has practically no contractile tendencies during evaporation.

Flexible collodion, unmedicated, is used as an application over chilblains or in other conditions where occlusion is desired.

Medicated Collodions. Flexible collodion, medicated with various drugs, is also used extensively in podiatry. The four named and described below are the most important, and are most generally used.

Iodized Collodion (C. Iodatum, N. F.). Iodized collodion is a five per cent. solution of iodine in flexible collodion.

It is used in podiatry as a covering for the exposed tender tissues after removal of a callositas or an heloma. The film formed by the collodion serves as a protection against friction to the part and the iodine contained in the mixture acts as an antiseptic and counter-irritant This combination may also be used where any counter-irritant action is desired and wherever the tincture may be used.

Ichthyolated Collodion, 5 to 15% of ichthyol in collodion, is used for the same purposes as the iodized collodion in the protection of a previously pared callous, and as an antiphlogistic and stimulant in erythematous chilblain, this form of medication is used extensively and with good results. It forms an occlusive film over the chilled parts, and by the action of its constituent, ichthyol, serves to stimulate the deranged functions and to promote absorption in the congested parts.

Benzoated Collodion, 5 to 10% of tinctura benzoini composita in flexible collodion, may be applied in post-operative procedures in heloma, etc, as described in preceding paragraphs, and is also efficient as a stimulant in the treat ment of pernio and as a covering for blisters and other superficial lesions where no discharge is present.

Salicylated Collodion is a medicated collodion with the following formula:

>Salicylic acid, 30 parts;
>Ext. of cannabis Indica, 5 parts;
>Collodion, 240 parts.

It is extensively used in the medical treatment of heloma or callositas. This combination is disintegrative in its action and should not be applied on sound or normal integument.

Collodion, either plain or medicated, is contra-indicated in the presence of a discharging surface. By sealing the lesion, no drainage is possible, and the waste materials thrown off are kept confined to the detriment of the healing process.

Paraffin Preparations. Barth de Sanfort, a French naval surgeon, in experimenting for drugs to treat the cases of burns developing from the liquid fire and burning oil attacks of the Great War, discovered and perfected a substance known as "ambrine." The exact composition of this paraffin is a secret, and for this reason it has been received coldly in this country, but a number of similar paraffin preparations have been developed and are in general use today. The four most popular of these are known commercially as paraffin No. 7, paraffin No. 7-11, parresine and redintol.

Paraffin No. 7 (Dr. Hull) consists of paraffin (hard), 67%; paraffin (soft), 25%; olive oil, 5%; oil of eucalyptol, 2%, and resorcin, 1%. To prepare paraffin 7, first melt the hard paraffin, then add in the order named the soft paraffin, olive oil, oil of eucalyptol and resorcin.

Paraffin No 7-11 (Dr. Adams) consists of paraffin (hard), 69%; paraffin (soft), 25%; olive oil, 3%, and thymol iodide, 3%. The preparation of paraffin 7-11 is similar to that described for the preceding combination.

Parresine (officially adopted by the United States Army and Navy) is a wax-like substance, containing about 95% of paraffin, this is treated by the addition of a vegetable wax and mineral and vegetable resins so as to modify its physical character, especially as regards plasticity, ductility, pliability and adhesiveness. It also contains eucalyptol, a valuable antiseptic, which is added to cover the characteristically disagreeable odor developing from burned surfaces and other large abrasions during the process of healing.

Redintol is a mixture of paraffin and resins, having similar melting points. The firm manufacturing it have prepared a special form of sheet cotton for use in connection with the application of this product.

Technic. The technic of the application of these paraffin preparations is similar and is described in detail in the chapter on "Burns." The advantages of the wax treatment are numerous

(1) It is an inexpensive dressing (a pound of wax and a pint of liquid petrolatum, together costing about sixty cents, will dress many burns).

(2) It is a comfortable dressing because it is smooth, and the granulating surface does not grow through it as with the gauze. The paraffin is hard enough to make the dressing somewhat rigid and to act as a splint.

(3) It is a cleaner dressing, because the wound discharge is not permitted to soak through the impermeable wax covering, soiling all the linens that come in contact with the patient

(4) Superficial burns heal more readily under this treatment than with any other previously used method.

(5) It is a most comfortable dressing, for the reason that the granulations do not grow through it, and the dressing is lifted off painlessly

(6) The resulting scars are not as pronounced.

(7) It is a stimulant of granulations.

Disadvantages. The disadvantages of the wax treatment are·

(1) Some patients refuse to be treated with the wax (it is applied hot directly to the injured area) because of the pain.

(2) So many extravagant claims have been made for it, that the one who uses it for the first time will probably be disappointed.

(3) An infected wound is covered with a sealed dressing

(4) We have no way of controlling the temperature of the wax. Taken from the boiling water at 212 degrees Fahr., it is too hot. Cooling at 114 degrees Fahr., it is too cold. The degree of pain caused the patient is the only means one has of knowing if it is too hot, unless one tries it first on the back of the hand.

(5) Around the skin edges it is painful

IMPERVIOUS COVERINGS.

In connection with moist dressings, several varieties of impervious covering may be used.

Oiled Silk is a rubberized material of great strength, usually yellow in color and soft and smooth to the touch. The use of this material is quite general in podiatry for all moist, non-evaporating dressings. The technic of application consists in cutting a square of the fabric of sufficient size to cover the whole of the gauze dressing, also all sides of the toe (if this be the location of use) and a considerable amount of the surrounding healthy tissue. It is held in place either by a roller bandage, or by means of adhesive strips fastening down its edges to the adjacent surfaces. Dressings covered by oiled silk are apt to be bulky and for this reason, when the shoe is to be worn, it is not generally used.

Gutta Percha Tissue is a thin perishable material placed on the market by several firms. It is not to be compared with oiled silk for durability, but the dressing covered by gutta percha is not nearly so bulky, and for this reason it is popular and practical for use in podiatry. It is generally applied over the gauze by vulcanizing its edges to the surrounding integument. This is accomplished by means of heat, and, when completed, presents a neat dressing which is absolutely occlusive, and from which none of the solution used on the gauze underneath can escape. A square of the rubber tissue of sufficient size to more than cover the dressing is cut and held in place with the hand. A match is then applied to the edges of the square and while they are still melted they are lightly adhered to the surrounding skin. The tissue will adhere to the skin and will remain intact for a considerable period of time. The gutta percha is then covered by several turns of a roller bandage to protect the thin tissue from the rubbing of the shoe. Gutta percha tissue may also be held in place by means of adhesive strips as with oiled silk, but the vulcanizing process is by far the most popular and, insofar as confining the solution is concerned, it is also far more practical

Fish Skin is a manufactured material of tissue paper thinness and has proven very popular for use as an impervious covering. The technic of application is similar to that described for oiled silk and it is held in place by the same means. It does not make a bulky dressing and for this reason its popularity has probably exceeded that of oiled silk.

BANDAGING.

A bandage is a strip of gauze, muslin, flannel or other material of varying widths and lengths, used in the various branches of medicine for retaining dressings, applications and splints and to produce compression. Occasionally they are applied to retain heat. Bandages also help keep a wound clean by preventing the ingress of foreign matter.

Bandages are made of different materials, chief among which is gauze. This is made of lint, woven into a soft material, which is easily applied to all parts of the body.

Muslin is a heavier cotton material and is made of cotton or silk or of a mixture of both (lisle) with rubber. Flannel is wool woven into a soft, firm, semi-elastic material. Rubber bandages are used to induce excretion and for compression.

Bandages vary in width and length, depending on the size of the parts for which they are intended. For convenience, bandages are usually manufactured in widths varying from one-half inch to six inches, and in length from one to ten yards or more. Those which are used in podiatry vary in width from one-half inch to three inches. The standard length of bandages is five yards and ten yards. These may be cut and the unused piece preserved. A table of the widths of the various materials used in podiatry practice, showing the parts for which they are best adapted, follows:

	LESSER TOES	GREAT TOE FINGERS	ANKLE WRIST	ANKLE LEG	WRIST FOREARM	LEG FOREARM	LEG
Gauze	½"	1"	1½"	2"		2½"	3"
Muslin		1"	1½"	2"		2½"	3"
Flannel				2"		2½"	3"
Elastic				2"		2½"	3"
Rubber				2"		2½"	3"

A roller bandage consists of one piece of material rolled in the shape of a cylinder, having a core and a free end, and is the kind used in podiatry.

A double roller bandage consists of one piece of material, rolled from both ends, so that when it is completed there are two cylinders and no free end.

A plaster of Paris bandage is composed of a piece of gauze or crinoline into which is rubbed powdered plaster of Paris. This bandage is placed in water and then applied to a part, after a few moments the entire bandage becomes hard and solid. This form of bandage prevents mobility and is used for fractures and dislocations. In podiatry it is used for taking impressions of the foot for fitting mechanical appliances. Bandages are classified as follows:

Circular—being circular turns around a part.

Figure of eight—the turns crossing each other like the strokes of the figure 8.

Oblique—covering the part by oblique turns.

Recurrent—the turns returning to the point from which they originated.

Spica—the turns crossing and recrossing, resembling in arrangement the husks of an ear of corn.

Spiral—the turns ascending or descending, each turn covering about two-thirds to three-fourths of the preceding turn.

Spiral reverse—when the bandage is turned in reverse position so that the inner side becomes the outer and the outer side rests against the skin, in order to better adapt itself to the part.

Bandages are designated by various names, according to the shape they assume when completed, and they are sometimes named after the men who first used them; for example, "Barton's bandage" of the head.

The bandages used in podiatry are designated by the shape they assume. The names of the various bandages of the foot follow in the order of their importance

        Spiral bandage of the toes.
        Spica bandage of the foot.
        Figure of eight bandage of the ankle.
        Spiral reverse bandage of the leg.

The Spiral Bandage of the Toes. This bandage is applied to the great toe more often than to the lesser toes. Gauze, one inch wide for the great toe and one-half inch wide for the lesser toes, is used.

This bandage may be started by a few circular turns around the ankle, then diagonally across the dorsum of the foot to the base of the great toe; but this may be simplified by making a simple circular turn around the proximal end of the toe, with the free end towards the heel, which will firmly lock the bandage If the distal end of the toes is to be covered, the bandage is now applied from the proximal end of the toe on its plantar surface, over the distal end to the proximal end on the dorsal surface. This is repeated back and forth as often as necessary to cover the parts by what are known as recurrent turns. The spiral turns are now started and as the bandage moves toward the distal end of the toe, each turn must cover about two-thirds or three-fourths of the preceding one When the toe is covered, the spirals are continued back to its base, where the bandage is tied off. Many toes are not cylindrical but taper to a point; so that when the spirals reach the distal end of the toe, the bandage bulges on the inner side. This bulging may be avoided by making a reverse turn over the part instead of a simple spiral.

The Spica Bandage of the Foot. Bandage 1½ to 2 inches wide is used, depending on the size of the foot. The free end of the bandage is placed on the dorsum of the foot at the ankle joint, and is locked by several circular turns around the ankle. The bandage is passed diagonally forward across the dorsum of the foot to a point opposite the head of the metatarsal bone, then across the plantar surface of the foot to the opposite metatarsal bone, and diagonally backward across the dorsum of the foot, crossing the first half of the turn, producing an X. The turn is finished by passing the roller back over the tendo Achillis This is repeated, the second turn covering about two-thirds of the first and so on backward until the desired area is covered. The bandage is finished by a few circular turns around the ankle and is tied off in the usual manner

Figure of Eight Bandage of the Ankle. This bandage resembles the spica bandage of the foot in every way except that the first turn extends to the base of the metatarsal bone instead of to the head and, instead of tying it off at the ankle, a few spiral reverse turns are made up the leg. It is tied off as are the other bandages

The Spiral Reverse Bandage of the Leg. This bandage

is considered by many to be the most difficult of all the bandages of the extremities to apply A few figure of eight turns are made around the ankle and then the spiral turn is made; the bandage is reversed so that the inner side becomes the outer and the outer side rests against the skin. Each turn should cover about three-quarters of the preceding one, and care should be taken that at the point of reversing the bandage, no wrinkles or uneven folds are produced. The reverse turns should not be made over a wound or a part that may be irritated by additional pressure.

CHAPTER VII

INSTRUMENTS

TYPES, VARIETIES, USES, THEIR SELECTION AND CARE

No comprehensive monograph has yet been written discussing at any length the instruments of the podiatrist, and in compiling the following data there must necessarily be omissions. Up to the present moment no great amount of standardization has been accomplished along this line, either in the general use of a given instrument or in its name. It is the object of the author of this chapter to at least build a foundation upon which a complete and standardized line of instruments may be developed.

Many special instruments developed by practitioners who have refrained, for reasons best known to themselves, from giving their ideas and discoveries to the profession at large, must necessarily be omitted, and it is to be greatly desired that the next few years will be rich in the development and standardization of our instruments and appliances.

The instruments in general use to-day and manufactured by several companies, are all made practically of the same material and in the same manner, the differences between them, being due principally, to the finish. All such instruments as chisels, scalpels, spatulas, curettes, etc., are made from Sheffield steel, and are hand forged. The handles of these instruments are made of a silver or aluminum composite. Scissors, nail clips, thumb forceps, etc., are made also of Sheffield steel, but are drop forged.

Most instrument makers to-day have discarded the older method of finishing, known generally as the "crocus" polish.

This has come about principally for the reason that the application of the crocus polish or finish demands that the instrument be subjected to extreme heat. In accomplishing this, many instruments are rendered useless owing to the fact that the temper of the blade is ruined by the added heat

What is commonly known as a "satin" finish, accomplished by buffing, is now generally employed and does not tend in any way to injure the already highly tempered steel.

HISTORY OF INSTRUMENTS

With the exception of possibly two or three, it is doubtful, if chiropody has developed any really individual instruments. Our scalpels are similar to or are modifications of those of the surgeon; the nail chisels and excavators in general use have been borrowed from the realms of the dentist, as has the rotary drill, the nail clips, of course, are instruments which are purely for the purposes coming within the jurisdiction of the podiatrist; so, also are the various forms of the nail file.

The chisel used by a great number of practitioners for the surgical removal of helomata, is one of the oldest of chiropody instruments and is one which was unquestionably developed by the chiropodist for his own needs. There is no instrument in use by the surgeon which bears any resemblance to the chisel, and for this reason we can safely say that it is a true chiropody instrument and may therefore safely be called the helotomon—the podiatry surgical instrument. This also, in a measure, can be said of the soft corn spoon. This is, to be sure, nothing but a very shallow curette, but nevertheless no instrument in use in general surgery can be rated as being similar to it; it is therefore properly styled the podiatrist's curette.

Prior to 1909, the chiropodist found it necessary to select his own manufacturer and have his instruments made according to his own ideas, or to select them from the catalog of the surgical supply house This condition of affairs resulted in a wide diversity of styles. No two practitioners had similar instruments, and it seemed to furnish keen delight to one chiropodist to outdo his neighbor as to the size, finish and appearance of his instruments. Pearl handled scalpels were much in evidence and, when so, served to prove, without question, that the owner did no sterilization by boiling. Gold-plated blades and inlaid handles were frequently to be seen, proving nothing, unhappily, but the eccentricities of their owners.

In the year 1909, however, the manufacture of instruments as individual appliances for the chiropodist was started at the instigation of the late George Erff, by an instrument maker in Jersey City, N. J. His wares found such instant approval and the sales of his product so increased that it was not long before several other firms embarked in the business of manufacturing instruments solely for chiropodical work.

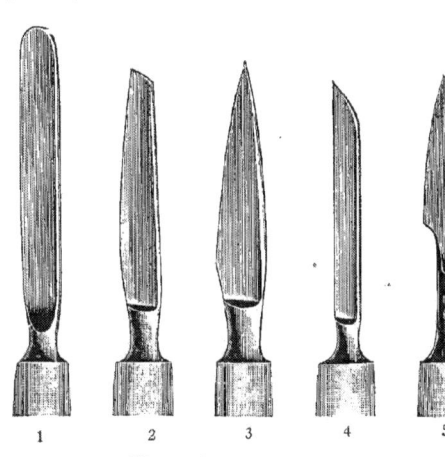

Fig. 1. SCALPELS

This has done much to standardize instruments and to-day men and women in all parts of the world are beginning to use similar instruments made from standard patterns.

The Scalpel. Several varieties of scalpel are used in podiatry to-day. Some of them have been developed from an absolute need and some from the personal desire of the practitioner. The scalpel should be about five-and-one-half inches long, having a blade length of from one-and-one-half inches to one-and-three-quarters inches. Made from these dimensions, the instrument is practical as to size and has a working surface sufficient for any purpose.

Fig. 1 shows several varieties of scalpel. No. 2 in this group is a practically shaped blade to be used for work on callositas or heloma. This instrument will maintain a good

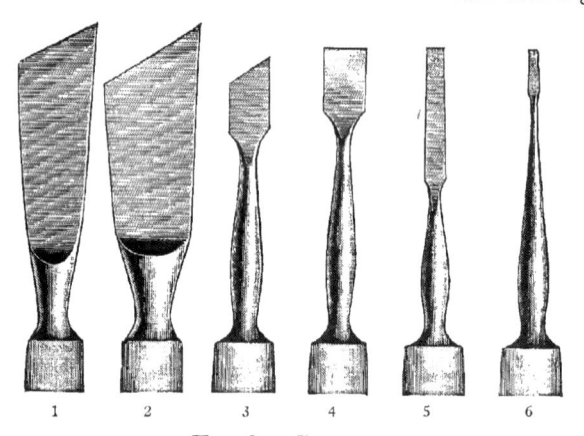

FIG. 2. CHISELS

shape with honing and is used by a great number of practitioners.

This No. 2 is used for the removal of heavy callous and general work. Nos. 3 and 5 may be successfully used for the dissection and removal of helomata. These pointed scalpels are indicated whenever delicate work on small surfaces is demanded.

The Chisel. The heloma and callosity chisels, Nos. 1, 2 of Fig. 2, are about five-and-one-half inches long with a blade length of one-and-one-quarter inches. Nos. 5 and 6 are nail chisels and will be discussed under that heading.

A series of chisels which are advocated by Harry P. Kenison, of Boston, differ from those shown in Fig. 2 only in that the handles are one-quarter of an inch in diameter and are round, being corrugated to prevent slipping. These instruments are five-and-one-quarter inches long.

Fig. 3 shows heloma and callous chisels (helotomă) recommended by E. C. Rice, M.D., of Washington, D. C. This variety of instrument is used principally for dissection work, but is also useful for shaving or paring methods. No. 1 of this group is used principally for large calloused areas on the plantar surfaces of the foot. The handles of these instruments are hexagonal and are five-and-one-quarter inches long.

The Nail Chisel. Varieties of straight chisels for the removal of ingrown portions of nail are shown in Fig. 2, Nos. 5 and 6.

Curved nail chisels are shown by Nos. 1 and 2 in Fig. 4. Their use is described in the chapter on Ingrown Nails. Nos. 3, 5, 6, in this group, are nail packers used for packing gauze or cotton in the nail groove. No. 4 in this figure is a curette excavator used for the removal of nail splinters or callous from the nail groove.

There is a newer type of nail chisel with a guard along one edge. This is to prevent the instrument from

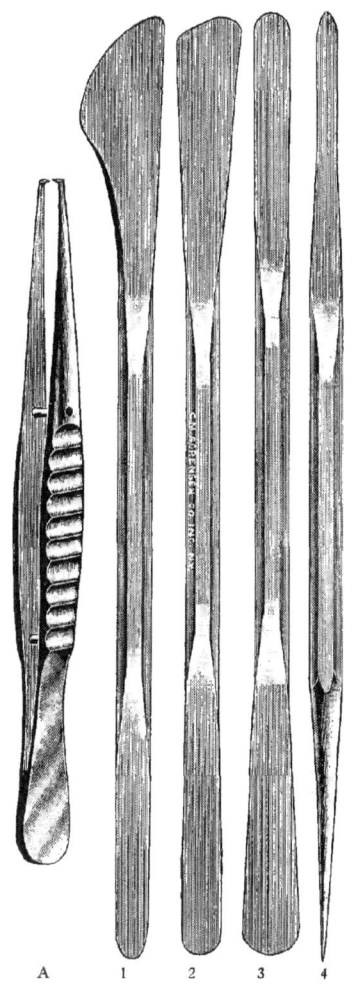

FIG. 3. HELOMA AND CALLOSITY CHISELS

penetrating the soft tissues of the nail bed while removing an imbedded portion of nail. This flange also aids in lifting the nail from its bed and in breaking up adhesions which may have formed in advanced cases.

No. 2, Fig. 5, is a nail groove gouge used for the removal of callous in that location.

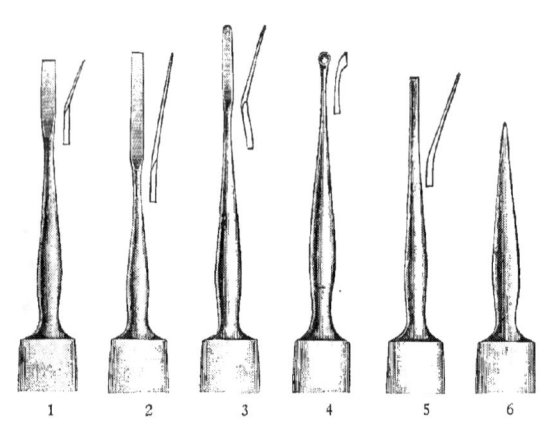

FIG. 4. NAIL CHISELS

Soft Corn Spoon. *(Podiatrist Curette.)* The soft corn spoon, Fig. 6, is in reality a shallow curette used for the purpose of dissecting an epithelial growth between the toes. The working edge of the instrument is sharp.

A modification of this spoon is shown in Fig. 5, No. 1. This instrument is commonly known as a "golf stick." It is used for the same purpose as the soft corn spoon. These instruments are of the same length, in

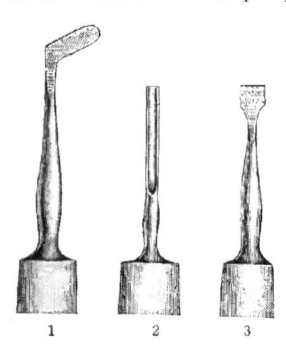

FIG. 5. MISCELLANEOUS INSTRUMENTS

FIG. 6. SOFT CORN SPOON

fact, are uniform in every way to the scalpel and nail chisel.

The Spatula. This is an instrument used almost entirely for the mixing of ointments and their application to a part. It is not sharp. (Fig. 7, No. 1.)

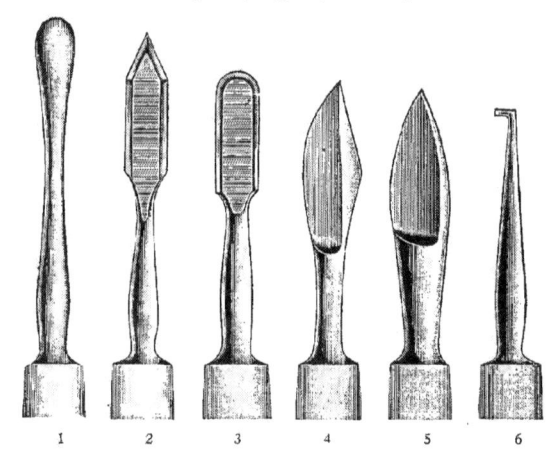

FIG. 7. MISCELLANEOUS INSTRUMENTS

The Nail Scraper. The scraper is used for cleaning around the nail, and for the removal of any callous which may be adherent to the nail body in or about the grooves. Two varieties are shown in Fig. 7, Nos. 2 and 3.

The Excavator. Excavators for use in the nail grooves

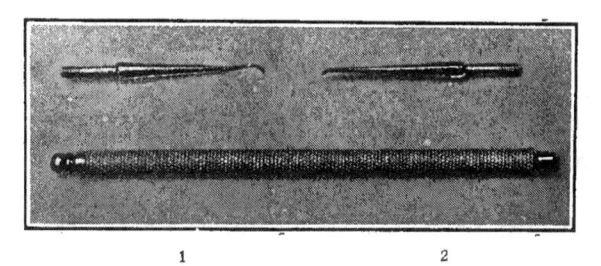

FIG. 8. EXCAVATORS WITH DETACHABLE HANDLE

are of great service to the podiatrist. Probably the most practical variety of this instrument is that borrowed from

INSTRUMENTS 85

the dentist. This form of excavator is composed of two parts, a handle, called commercially a cone socket handle, and an excavator point which screws into the hand piece. These points may be obtained in a great number of styles but the two shown in Fig. 8 are practical in all cases. No. 2 has a small semi-sharp point, while No. 1 has a larger point and is dull. These instruments can also be used as packers for placing gauze or cotton under the nail and in the grooves.

Other forms of excavators are shown in Fig. 9. No. 1 is a combination excavator and packer; No. 2, a packer; No. 3 an excavator; No. 4 a combination spatula and packer.

Special Ingrown Nail Instruments. A set of special instruments for use in

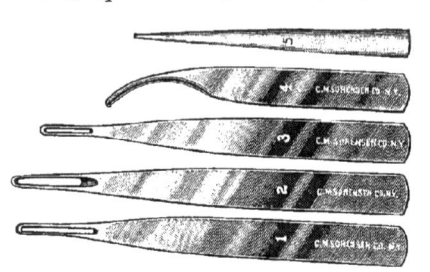

FIG. 10. INGROWING NAIL INSTRUMENTS

surgical procedures in ingrown nail cases is shown in Fig. 10. Nos. 1, 2, and 3 are used for the removal of ragged edges of nail. No. 4 is a nail elevator, used for pre-operative examination, and No. 5 is a special oil stone used for sharpening Nos. 1, 2, and 3.

Ingrown Nail Forceps. Two types of forceps for the removal of the im-

FIG. 9. EXCAVATORS

bedded portion of the nail after it has been loosened from the nail body, are in general use. One is of a curved variety and is particularly practical; the other has a straight point and a locking device and is in reality a small artery forceps.

Fig. 11 shows the straight point forceps.

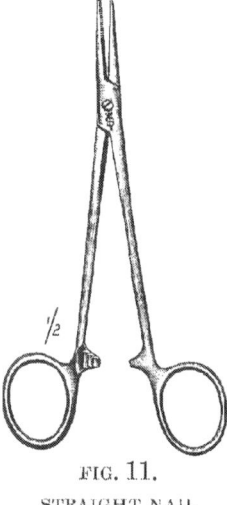

Ingrown Nail Clippers. The clipper shown in Fig. 12 is used almost entirely in ingrown nail operations. It is extremely light and if used in the general cutting of nails will surely be sprung. The clipper illustrated is more correctly a nail "splitter." These clippers may be obtained in two sizes, four and one-half and five inches.

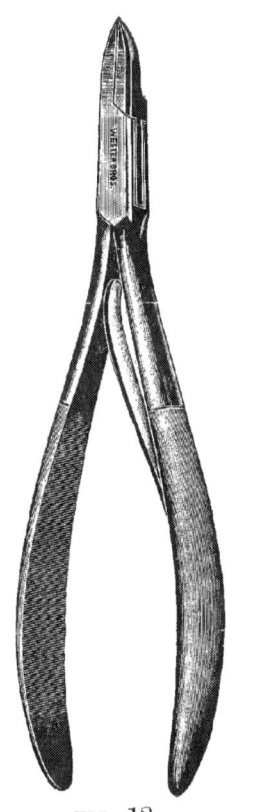

FIG. 11.
STRAIGHT NAIL FORCEPS

FIG. 12.
NAIL SPLITTER

Nail Clippers. The nail clipper should be of heavy stock so that all nails may be easily cut without injury to the instrument or pain to the patient. A heavy nail clip, even though it be dull, will do much more efficient work in general, than will a sharp light clipper.

Two styles of nail clippers are shown here. Fig. 13 is a clip for general work while Fig. 14 finds its particular efficacy in club nail cases. Notice the angle of the blade in this type of instrument.

Thumb Forceps. Thumb forceps are used extensively

in podiatry practice. All sterile dressings are handled with these instruments to insure immunity from the contamination of the hands.

Three varieties of thumb forceps are shown in Fig. 15. No. 1 has needle point corrugated jaws; No. 2 has curved,

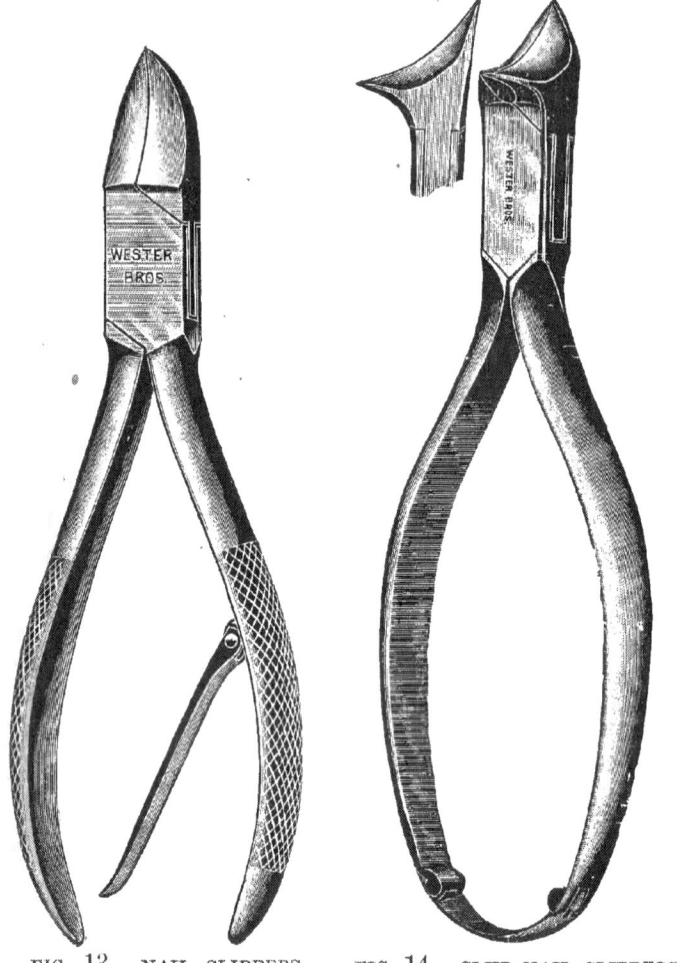

FIG. 13. NAIL CLIPPERS   FIG. 14. CLUB NAIL CLIPPERS

corrugated needle jaws; and No. 3 is a heavy pointed corrugated jawed instrument. These three styles are all four inches in length.

Iris Tooth Forceps. This instrument is used where the dissection method of treatment is employed. The sharp teeth at the end of the forcep jaws, grasp the thickened mass

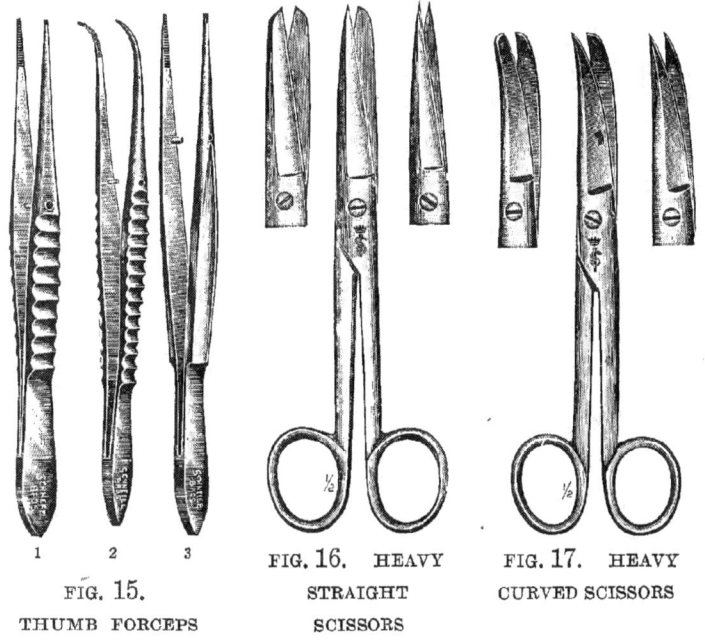

FIG. 15. THUMB FORCEPS

FIG. 16. HEAVY STRAIGHT SCISSORS

FIG. 17. HEAVY CURVED SCISSORS

as it is loosened from its bed. (Fig. 3-A.) The ordinary thumb forceps may also be used in this connection but they are much more liable to slip than are those of the iris tooth variety.

Scissors. The podiatrist needs at least four styles of scissors in his general practice.

For buckskin, felt and adhesive plaster a heavy scissors with straight blades is necessary. This scissors should be six or six and one-half inches in length and should preferably have round ends (Fig. 16).

INSTRUMENTS

A pair of heavy, curved scissors is also useful for shaping shields, cutting apertures and for other similar work. It is suggested that these be not too large for they are apt to be unwieldy. Four and one-half or five inches is ample size, and one point should be rounded, and one pointed (Fig. 17).

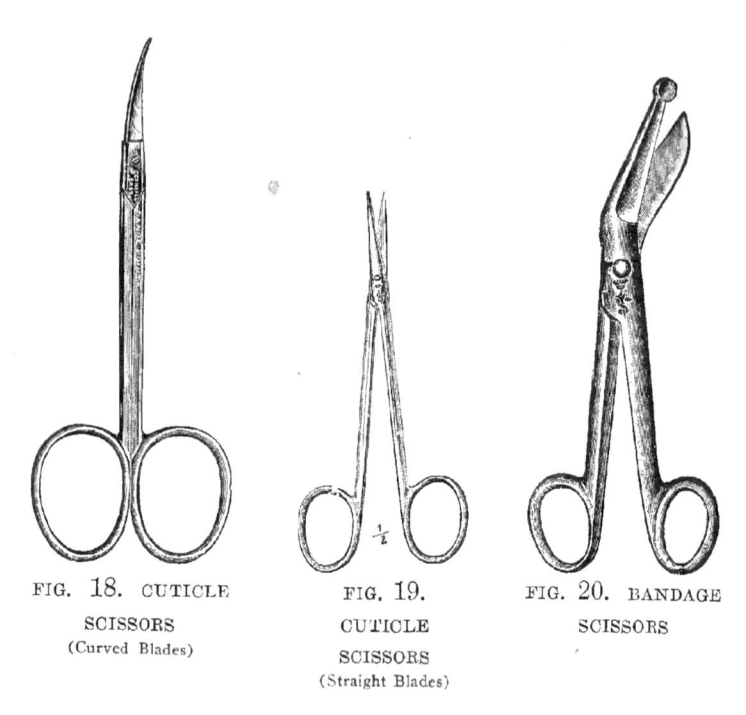

FIG. 18. CUTICLE SCISSORS (Curved Blades)

FIG. 19. CUTICLE SCISSORS (Straight Blades)

FIG. 20. BANDAGE SCISSORS

Cuticle scissors are useful in many chiropodical procedures. Fig. 18 shows a four-inch, lance point curved scissors. Fig. 19 shows a four and three-quarters inches straight pointed cuticle scissors.

A small bandage scissors, (Fig. 20) should be included among the podiatrists' instruments. It is not necessary to have a large pair, but one about four and one-half or five inches in size is very useful.

The Hypodermic Syringe. The choice of the hypodermic syringe is purely a matter of preference, but certainly an all-glass syringe (both barrel and piston) appears to be more practical from the standpoint of use and of sterilization. The metal barrel syringe is fast going out of use ex-

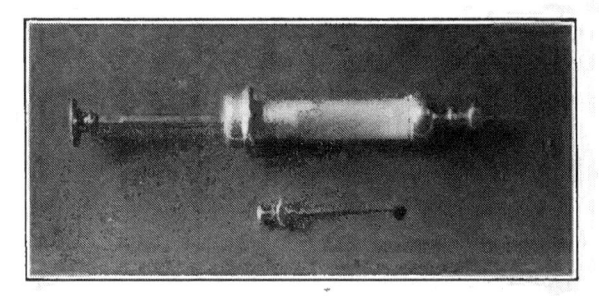

FIG. 21. HYPODERMIC SYRINGE

cepting of the type in which no washers are employed. A syringe having a capacity of 2 c.c. is ample for the use of the podiatrist (Fig. 21).

The Rotary Drill. One of the greatest boons to modern podiatry is the development of the rotary file or drill for their use. This instrument has become so all important in

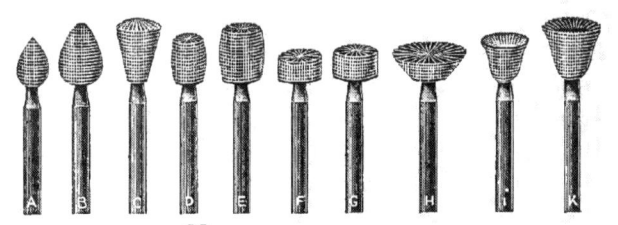

FIG. 22. ROUGH CUTTING BURS

the treatment of many nail diseases, and, in fact, in the prophylactic treatment of the normal nail, that we may well wonder how any results were obtained before its advent.

It is not the purpose of this chapter to go into the mechanism of the drill, but the selection of burrs is a subject which is of such importance as to merit mention.

INSTRUMENTS 91

Fig. 22 shows several varieties of rough or "cutting" burs for use in grinding down club nails. In this group "B," "D" and "E" are particularly practical.

Finishing burs are those used to smooth off the nail after the use of a cutting bur, for filing the edges of a normal nail, or for thinning the nail in prophylactic treatments (Fig. 23).

The Nail File. The hand file, for smoothing the edge of a nail after clipping (Fig. 24), should have a smooth and a rough side. The rough side is used in cases where the use of a drill is impossible.

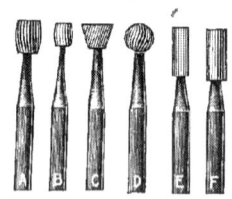

FIG. 23.
FINISHING BURS

Toe Separators. These are appliances used for the purpose of holding the toes apart while operating between them. The implement shown in Fig. 25, depends upon the tension of the heavy wire for its efficacy.

FIG. 24. HAND FILE (SHOWING ROUGH SURFACE)

There is also an appliance used for similar purposes which is dependent upon a screw adjustment.

Applicators. Applicators, used for solutions, may be obtained in metal and in wood. Those of metal have a short hexagonal handle and are corrugated at the distal end so that cotton may be wound about them.

The wooden applicator is a small round stick about six inches long. Such applicators are more practical than those of metal, for they may be thrown away after use. The metal applicators corrode after several applications of a corrosive drug and soon become useless.

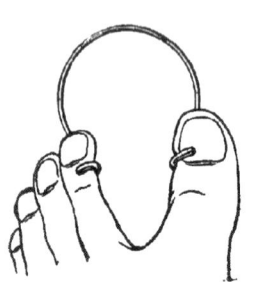

FIG. 25. TOE SPREADER

The Skiving Knife. The choice of a knife for the manufacture of shields of felt or buckskin depends principally upon the fancy of the user. Some prefer an all-metal, flat-handled knife similar to those used by leather workers (Fig. 26); others find it more practical to employ a blade set in a larger wooden handle, claiming that more purchase can be brought to bear upon the material to be cut, and consequently more accuracy is obtained. An instrument, known commercially as the "Murphy" knife, is a practical example of this latter variety. It has a wooden handle about four inches long, and a blade of similar length. The cutting edge is narrow toward the point and gives the operator a bias edge with which to do his cutting. The all-metal knife blade is similarly slanted. Skiving knives need not be made of the finest, highly tempered steel, and the edge placed upon them, when honed, need by no means be a "razor" edge.

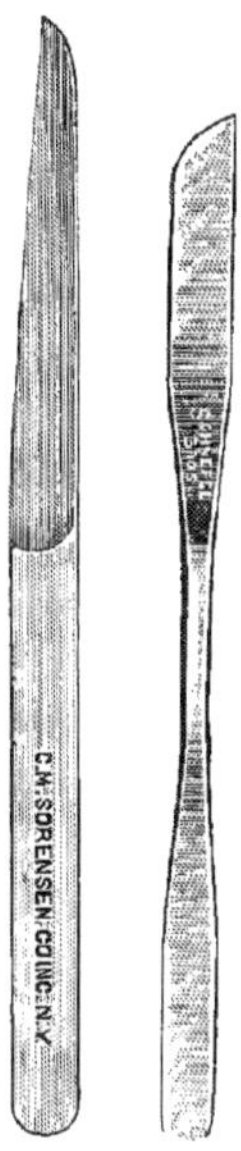

CARE OF INSTRUMENTS

Instruments need care just as do any fine machine. Knives and other pieces of fine metal will rapidly lose their usefulness unless proper and unceasing care is taken of them.

FIG. 26.
SKIVING
KNIVES

Honing. Nearly every chiropodist at the present time hones his own knives or chisels. This is an art which comes naturally to some but usually is only developed through constant practice. The first important point that needs to be considered in this connection is the selection of a hone. A hone is a plane true block of fine compact stone for sharpening edged tools, and there are a number of these which may be used for podiatry instruments.

The Belgian Hone is in all probability the most popular of the sharpening stones and when genuine and of fine quality, they are superior to all other forms of stone. One of the principal drawbacks in the purchase of a hone of this variety is the fact that many are manufactured of a composite substance which is extremely hard and upon whose surface no impression can be made with the instrument. All hones should be fairly soft, so that the knife blade, as it is drawn across the surface, will take hold, and not "rough" or "gritty." Any stone which has a tendency to roughness or coarseness will never put a real fine "razor" edge on a delicate instrument.

The Swatty Hone has been popular for years among barbers and others who are called upon to use razor-like blades. The one disadvantage in the use of this variety of stone is that they are hard, and considerable honing is needed to place a proper edge upon the instrument.

The Oil Stone is used more particularly for heavy instruments not demanding a fine surface for finishing. Skiving knives and the like may be successfully sharpened on stones of this kind. Some practitioners prefer to "rub down" an instrument on an oil stone or a "carborundum" stone and then smooth the edge or "finish" it on a genuine old rock Belgian hone. Carborundum hones cannot be obtained, as a rule, fine or smooth enough for real delicate work on podiatry instruments, but they are efficient for heavier instruments.

Technic of Honing. Having selected a stone the block is placed before you on a table. The knife is grasped firmly by the handle with the thumb and the third, fourth and fifth fingers. The second or index finger is placed at the junction of the blade with the handle on the upper surface. The blade of the knife is now laid upon the hone in such a manner that it is flat upon the stone's surface, and, using the whole forearm, the fingers and wrist remaining stationary so that the angle of the blade remains unchanged, the blade is drawn in an oblique (right to left) direction toward the operator's body. It must be remembered that the blade be drawn *obliquely* for if it be drawn straight no edge will be placed upon the instrument.

Having completed this oblique stroke, the whole instrument is turned in the hand and laid upon the stone so that the other side of the blade is now upon its surface. An oblique (left to right) stroke is then made toward the operator using, as before, the whole forearm. This stroke having been completed the whole procedure is recommenced.

The marks appearing on the blade of the knife caused by contact with the hone, plainly tell the operator whether or not he has the proper angle or whether he is holding the blade at the proper level through its long axis. Testing the sharpness of the blade on the finger nail or skin, or judging from the appearance of the contact marks, tells the operator whether or not the instrument be sufficiently sharp.

Do not overhone! This is a bad fault and will develop a "wire" edge on the instrument which may take hours to remove. An edge may be "wired" also by continued heavy pressure during the honing process. This should also be avoided. Usually several heavy strokes on either side of the blade, followed by a series of lighter ones, is sufficient to place an instrument in serviceable condition for a considerable period of time.

Polishing. Instruments which are subjected to boiling sterilization are bound to become discolored (not rusted) no matter what chemical may be put in the water to prevent this condition. For this reason it is found necessary, if the brightness of an instrument is to be retained, to clean or polish it from time to time.

Scrubbing with sapolio or some similar substance, not too gritty, will serve to remove most of the stains but the labor occasioned by a procedure of this kind is considerable and is greatly lessened by the use of a motor buffer or polisher. In cases where rust stains are present, this machine is indispensable, for no amount of manual rubbing will remove these marks. The buffer wheel should be of some soft material, usually chamois, bound firmly. Machine buffing can never be used on delicate, sharp blades, as it will ruin whatever edge may be present. Handles may be cleaned efficiently as can scissors, thumb forceps, and similar instruments by this method.

Wiping. After an instrument is removed from boiling water it must be thoroughly dried if it is to be kept in good condition. The ideal sterilizer is one combining a superheated steam chamber, or a water boiling receptacle, and a dry hot air chamber for drying the instruments after sterilization. If such an apparatus is not included in the podiatrist's equipment, the instruments must be thoroughly wiped until dry. This must be done with a sterile wipe to maintain surgical cleanliness and the process must be thorough.

Care must be exercised in using superheated steam as a sterilizing agent that the instrument does not remain for too great a length of time in the vapor. Boiling water can only reach 212° F., and an instrument will stand subjection to this degree of heat for a considerable time, but steam is often heated to twice this degree and this terrific temperature is bound to untemper an instrument which is allowed to remain in the vapor over 30 or 40 seconds.

CHAPTER VIII

SHIELDS AND SHIELDING

Shielding is one of the most important branches of practical podiatry. A great amount of study must be given to this work, and to afford his patient relief and comfort through the application of shields and strappings, the operator is continuously called upon to exercise his mechanical ingenuity or to develop this trait if it be not already existent.

The surgical treatment of a condition may be faultless, and yet upon the application of an ill-fashioned or poorly-fitted shield, the patient will experience even a greater amount of discomfort or pain than before the treatment was commenced, and the operator's previous good work is thus undone.

Definition. A shield is an appliance fashioned from some skin or fabric and used for the purpose of relieving pressure or friction, or to protect a tender part upon the foot. The nomenclature which is adhered to under this heading is comparatively a simple one. The various forms and varieties of shields mentioned and discussed are named either for their shape or for the particular parts of the foot to which they are applied. In some instances the two are combined. Thus a "lateral plantar half moon or crescent shield" has a crescent shaped body and is used for the protection of an area on the lateral part of the plantar surface.

MATERIALS

Various materials are in general use today in the practice of podiatry for padding or shielding. The object is to give here a brief yet comprehensive description of each in its turn, together with a general survey of when, where and how they may be used.

Chamois. This skin presents a material which may be used in shielding parts where a pad of great thickness is not required. Chamois skin is quite thin and has not a great deal of stability or "body" in its make-up, and skins of a uniform thickness throughout are seldom obtainable. The hide thins out considerably toward the belly of the animal and for this reason there is a great amount of waste. However, in many cases chamois may be used with success in connection with helomata on the dorsal or outer lateral surfaces of the fifth toe, the dorsal surfaces of the intermediate, and the ends of all the toes. For heloma molle, shields of chamois may also be used to good advantage, as they are soft and pliable and when placed between the digits they readily take the shape of the toes without causing the irritation following the use of shields of a coarser or stiffer "body" in like positions.

Buckskin. Buckskin is probably the most generally used material for shielding in practice today. This hide has good "body" and even when skived to paper thinness retains a great amount of its stability. Buckskin can be obtained in thicknesses ranging from one-sixteenth to one-quarter or even three-eighths of an inch, but care should be exercised in its selection that no pieces of coarse grained skin be chosen. This is noted because the coarse or "pebbled" skin does not skive readily, and when bevelled off, the edges remain ragged and uneven. There are several firms manufacturing excellent grades of buckskin. Shields of buckskin may be generally used in all conditions and locations, the thinner skins on the toes and dorsal surfaces and the thicker on the plantar surfaces and on the metatarsophalangeal joints of the great and fifth toes.

Adhesive Moleskin. A so-called moleskin having a prepared medicated adhesive substance on one side is becoming very popular with the profession. It may be obtained in rolls of from one to ten yards long, and from seven to twelve inches wide. It is very thin but has good "body," and under the pressure to which it would be ordinarily subjected as a shielding material, does not stretch nor pull out of shape. Because of this thinness and its pliability and softness, no skiving of its edges is necessary, and it makes a neat, clean, practical material from which thin shields may be fashioned. Adhesive moleskin may be employed wherever chamois or the thinner grades of felt or buckskin are used.

Sheep Skin. Sheep skin is one of the lesser used but, nevertheless, practical shielding agents. Its one disadvantage is that the finished surface is smooth and shiny and an adhesive substance does not remain intact unless applied at the time the shield is to be used. This, however, does not present any serious objection to the use of the skin, as it is easily skived, has good "body" and presents a neat, clean appearance on the foot. It is employed wherever chamois may be used.

Felt. Plain white piano felting, of the softer and more pliable grades, is largely used at the present time. This felt can be obtained in thicknesses of from one-sixth to three-eighths or even one-half inch. The last mentioned thickness is very seldom used, and then only in cases where a slight support is needed for the longitudinal arch or as a pad in cases of painful heel. In both these instances the felt is pasted in the shoe rather than adhered to the foot. The one-sixteenth inch grade is used (1) between the toes (applied usually without adhesive); (2) as a substitute for chamois, kid or buckskin in all places where these latter may be used. The thicknesses ranging from one-eighth to three-eighth inch are used generally on the lateral surfaces of the first and fifth metatarsophalangeal articulations, on the plantar surface under the prominences of the same joints, and for protecting painful areas on the dorsum of the foot (its lateral borders), or in the region of the heel and the tendo Achillis Felt shields may be applied with or without adhesive, and strapping should be done dependent upon the length of time the shields are required to remain.

For badly inflamed or tender helomata, felt presents an ideal material for shielding. Shields of this material are softer and more yielding, and while they cannot be expected to stand the same amount of usage as those of buckskin they are, nevertheless, strongly recommended in the above named condition. After the aperture is cut to fit the part to be protected, its (the aperture's) edges are nicked with scissors so that when applied they will expand and readily take the shape of the indurated areas While they naturally pack down and become of denser consistency than at the time of application, felt shields never become as hard as those made of buckskin

Adhesive Felt. This is the ordinary prepared felt manufactured by several firms, one side of which is covered with a preparation of dry gum arabic. Upon moistening this adhesive, the shield may be adhered to any part. Shields of adhesive felt are very handy to use when protection is desired for a short time and are very seldom strapped unless they are to be applied to the plantar surfaces. They have no specific use and may be applied wherever shields of other materials are used.

Lamb's Wool. This material is used principally for insoles in shoes in cases of painful heel or severe callosities on the plantar surfaces, and in conditions where the integument of the foot is thin and the patient experiences pain or burning sensations when walking The wool is left on the hide, so that there is ample body for the application of adhesive substances. This material, in the uses mentioned above, is seldom adhered to the foot itself, but is, rather, placed in the shoe.

PREPARATION OR MANUFACTURE OF SHIELDS.

The definite points to be considered in the making of a proper fitting are not many; these are important:

1. Location of the part to be protected so that the size and shape of the shield may be determined.

2. Thickness of the shield.

3. Skiving.

4. Aperture.

Location of the Parts to Be Protected. Extreme care should be exercised in deciding upon the size and shape of the shield. The location and size of the area to be protected should be taken into consideration and the shield should be so fashioned that no part of it extends on the tissue upon which its presence might cause irritation. For instance, a shield is to be applied on the dorsal surface of one of the intermediate toes, it should be wide enough to cover the surface of that toe, but should not be allowed to curl downward upon the digit's lateral surfaces or to lap over or extend upon the adjoining toes. Again, a shield applied on the plantar surface should never be allowed to extend forward to a point where it might crowd under the toes and come in contact with their webs.

No shield applied for the protection of one area should be allowed to extend over and press upon another area which is not normal integument. The reason for this is obvious, for in covering an heloma, for instance, a greater amount of pressure is brought to bear upon that excrescence, with the result that it is subjected to a greater amount of irritation and pressure than would be caused by the shoe itself.

Thickness of the Shield. Just as great harm is brought about by using a shield that is too thick or too thin as follows the absence of the protection which a shield provides. If it be too thick, the great amount of pressure put upon the surrounding area will depress those tissues to such an extent that severe congestion, with its accompanying pain and discomfort, is liable to ensue. In making a shield too thin, no protection is afforded to the area where it is desired and at the same time the toe is bundled up with a lot of padding and plaster which is entirely unnecessary, in that it does no good. The use of a shield should be avoided in all cases, when possible, but there are many situations in which a shield is indicated and which, when applied, proves highly effective. Shields naturally pack down more quickly when the weight of the whole body is constantly being applied, and so, naturally, the thicker varieties of shielding are used on the plantar surfaces. This applies to all shielding materials and in particular to felt.

Skiving. Skiving is a process by which the edges of a shield are thinned or bevelled to a "feather" edge. This is done for three principal reasons:

(1) When a shield's outer edges are skived to a "feather" edge, it no doubt adheres to the integument in a much more satisfactory and lasting manner than if those edges were allowed to retain a uniform thickness with the main body of the shield.

(2) By thinning the shield down at the edges any danger of unneeded and detrimental pressure upon the underlying and surrounding areas is removed. The object is merely to protect a certain part, and, therefore, if a pad is used which is of sufficient thickness around the painful area to protect the diseased tissue, the aim is accomplished, and to have any considerable thickness to the shield, except as it is immediately adjacent to the area to be treated, is entirely unnecessary.

(3) Skiving a shield at its outer extremities does away with, or at least minimizes, the danger of the shield being loosened or shifted, and consequently it will remain longer in place and with better results

The inner edges of the aperture made in the shield for the protection of the diseased part should also be skived. This is done with the idea of conforming the shield, as nearly as possible, to the shape of the indurated integument and does away with any irritation to the part which might be caused were these edges left perpendicular.

Aperture. For the purpose of protecting a diseased

part from the pressure of footgear, an aperture or opening is made in the body of the shield. The size of this aperture is so fashioned as to be slightly larger than the part to be protected. Many mistakes are made in shielding, due to the aperture not being cut in the proper place, and care should be taken in this connection. This opening is not always

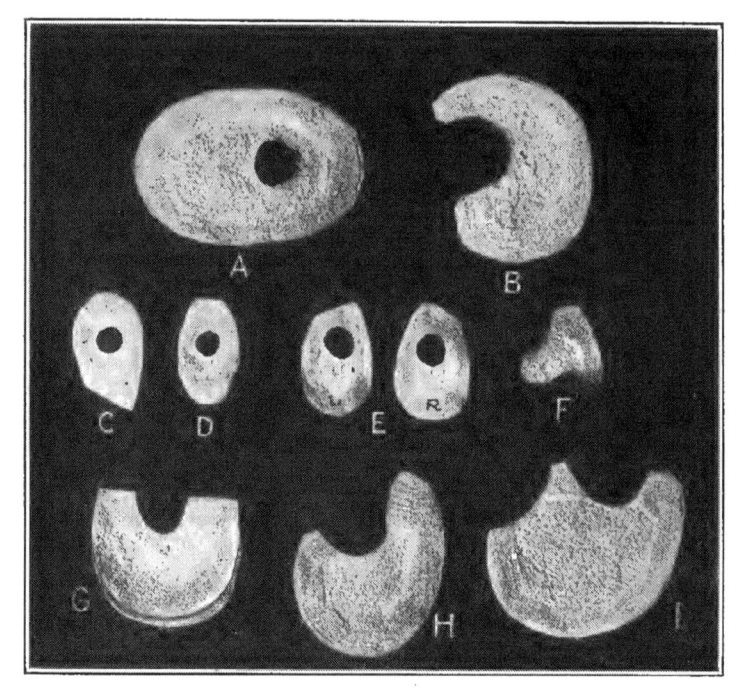

FIG. 1.

A. Oval
B. Half-moon or Crescent
C. Interdigital
D. Dorsal (Intermediate Toes)
E. Fifth Toe (Right and Left)
F. Boot Shield
G. Dorso-digital Half-moon (Built Up)
H. Modified Half-moon
I. Medio-plantar Crescent (With Cut-out for 1st or 5th Joint)

made in the centre of the shield; in many instances it must be placed either to one or to the other side of the median line, running anterio-posteriorly, and in other cases it should be nearer the front rather than the back of the shield, and vice versa.

For example: we are to shield an heloma on the fifth toe. Upon examination of the part we find that the growth occurs on the dorsal ridge of the digit and that while there is a considerable area of the normal integument on the toe's outer lateral side, the space between the inner edge of the growth and the fourth toe is very narrow. The aperture must then be so made in the shield that a very narrow portion of the skin or fabric rests upon the strip of normal tissue toward the fourth toe and that the wider edge extends down the side of the fifth digit. Again: in some instances we find that the spot to be protected is much nearer the distal end of the toe and the nail than the proximal part. The opening should then be made much nearer the anterior part of the shield than the posterior, so that when applied, the anterior part of the shield will not cover the nail or overlap the distal end of the toe. Too much stress cannot be laid upon this particular feature of shield-making and their application, and the student and practitioner alike will do well to give these points great consideration.

Method of Skiving. The most generally used and in all probability the most efficient method of skiving a shield is as follows: the material used, after being cut to the shape and size desired, is placed with the left hand. The skiving knife is then taken firmly in the right hand and with an oblique stroke away from the operator, the edges of the shield are cut away and thinned to a "feather" edge. This is continued around the whole outer circumference of the shield until a uniform thickness is obtained. After this procedure, should the centre of the shield present any inequalities or uneven ridges, these are pared away in a like manner until the whole surface is uniformly smooth.

One side of all pieces of buckskin will be found to be firmer and have a better body than the other. This is the surface to be allowed to remain intact, the bevelling being done on the reverse side. This insures a firm surface for the application of an adhesive substance.

The Skiving Knife. The knife which seems to be most

practical for our purpose in this procedure should have a blade from three and one-half to five inches long, about three-quarters of an inch wide at its base and tapering gradually until, at the end, the width of the blade is about three-eighths of an inch. This insures a large cutting surface and the blade, being tapered instead of an even width from point to base, allows the operator to employ an oblique movement in skiving the shield

The handle of this instrument should be fairly large and round, so that it will admit of a firm hold. A so-called "Murphy knife" is found to be a very practical and inexpensive instrument for skiving.

APPLICATION AND STRAPPING OF SHIELDS

In applying a shield, care should always be taken that the aperture is of sufficient size to protect all of the affected area. If this is not done, great inconvenience and perhaps severe pain is caused to the patient, in that the shield rests upon tender tissue which should be protected. It is also good policy to allow for any shifting which may take place. As for example, in the instance of an heloma: the shield should be applied so as to leave some space between the anterior edge of the indurated integument and the anterior edge of the shield's aperture. The foot in the process of walking (and particularly if the patient wears high heeled shoes) is being constantly pushed towards the forward part of the shoe, and, therefore, a shield protecting an heloma on the dorsum of any of the toes will be pushed back rather than forward. By taking this into consideration the shield, if it does shift, will still have a sufficient amount of sound integument to rest upon before it pushes back on the growth itself.

Adhesive Substances. Adhesive substances for adhering the shield to the integument should have no irritating properties whatsoever. The late George Erff perfected a small, neat alcohol lamp with a "sauce pan" attachment in which these adhesive substances, usually sold in stick form, are easily and quickly melted to a fluid consistency when they may be easily applied to a shield by means of a fine camel's hair brush. This enables the operator to spread the adhesive substance in a thin and even coat over the whole surface and is a much superior method to the older way of applying it directly from the heated stick.

Strapping. In adhesive plasters, by means of which shields may be securely held in place, we have a great assortment from which to choose. Plain rubber adhesive plasters are manufactured by many firms, as is the zinc oxide (medicated) adhesive plaster. Special plasters, medicated in various ways, are also on the market in abundance and no doubt find their use in special cases. It is found, however, that the zinc oxide plaster is perhaps the most practical in all instances, although by no means the cheapest. This plaster retains its adhesive properties much longer than the numerous other plasters which have been experimented with from time to time, and, being at the same time medicated with zinc oxide, an antiseptic, it makes a practical, cleanly and non-irritating adhesive plaster.

There are several important points to take into consideration in applying adhesive plasters for fastening shields more firmly on the surfaces of the foot.

(1) **No Strapping Should be Applied Too Tightly.** Too much cannot be said or written relative to allowance being made in strapping a shield for the natural movements of the foot. It must always be remembered, in the first place, that a patient's foot, elevated on the support of the operating chair, is at rest There is no weight upon it, and consequently the tissues of the foot are not expanded to their fullest extent For this reason circular strapping placed around a toe to hold a shield in place may seem sufficiently loose to allow perfect comfort; but when the patient steps down and walks for a few minutes, this same toe is expanded to a considerable extent, with the consequence that the plaster either cuts into the tender integument between or under the digit, or if not that, at least causes a severe enough

irritation to occasion great annoyance every time a step is taken. Therefore, one of the first important points to be taken into consideration in applying a shield is the tightness with which the adhesive strips may be drawn.

This is equally important in applying shields to the plantar surfaces, because, here also, allowance must be made for a great amount of expansion. In applying shields to these surfaces the toes should be extended as far as possible (drawn back toward the dorsum of the foot), the strapping to be applied while the toes are held in this position Were the adhesive strapping applied whilst the toes are in a flexed position, the integument on the plantar surfaces would be found in a series of folds or wrinkles. This integument is not always in that condition, however, and, consequently, when the patient allows the weight of his body to come upon the foot, in taking a step, and the toes are extended to their fullest, the tissues covering the plantar surfaces would be drawn and the strapping will pull on the skin, making the patient decidedly uncomfortable, or it will tear away altogether and so become useless.

(2) **Allowance Made for a Swollen Toe.** In this connection particular attention must be paid to the strappings of a shield. In many cases of helomata, or more particularly in acute conditions of interphalangeal bursitis, the integument immediately adjacent to the induration is not alone inflamed, but the whole toe is ordinarily swollen. In cases of this nature it will be found advantageous not to carry the strappings completely around the digit, but rather to place them so that, while they will hold the shield in place, they do not cover or come in contact with more of the swollen areas than is absolutely necessary to secure adhesion. This applies, of course, more particularly to the dorsal and lateral surfaces of the four lesser digits. To accomplish this two strips of half-inch plaster, each about one inch in length, are placed parallel to each other, one over the anterior and one over the posterior end, and adhered to the integument on each side of the shield. In many in-

stances it will be found advisable to do away with adhesive straps entirely and merely allow the shield to remain on for a day or two, when, the inflammation and swelling having subsided, a shield may be applied and strapped if necessary.

(3) **Edges of the Shield to Be Covered as Much as Possible.** It should always be the endeavor of the operator to cover the anterior and posterior edges of the shield and as much of the lateral surfaces as is possible. This minimizes the danger of those edges being raised from the integument during the normal movements of the foot. With this in view, it is perhaps wise to use as wide plaster as possible on the plantar, and, in many instances, on the dorsal surfaces as well.

There are five widths of plaster generally used in chiropody for the purpose of adhering shields. The narrow strip, manufactured by Johnson & Johnson expressly for chiropodists, the one-half-inch strip, the one-inch strip, the inch-and-a-half strip and the two-inch strip. The two-inch width is seldom used, and then never in connection with shielding, but rather for strapping weak ankles and arches.

(4) **End of the Plaster to Be Rounded.** This is for the purpose of preventing the tendency of the plaster to loosen up at the ends. By doing away with as many "corners" as possible and instead making rounded ends, the plaster is found to adhere much more firmly and the tendency to curl is reduced to a minimum.

SPECIFIC SHIELDING

Great Toe. The shields necessary in connection with affections of the hallux are four in number:

1. Those used in connection with bunions or metatarsophalangeal joint affections.

2. Those used in connection with corneus developments over the extensor tendon on the dorsum.

3. Those used in connection with corneous developments along the inner border or on the plantar surface.

4. Those used in connection with corneous developments on the adjacent sides of the great and second toes.

Location 1. Affections of the first metatarsophalangeal articulation or of the superadjacent tissues, usually require shields of considerable size, thickness and "body." Buckskin or felt are the materials to be used in this situation, as they can be skived to considerable thinness at the edge where pressure is unnecessary and often detrimental.

There are two forms of shields which may be used in this connection, viz. the metatarsophalangeal oval or the metatarsophalangeal half-moon. In a majority of cases the half-moon shield is the most practical, but the full oval may be used at times with equal or even better results.

The metatarsophalangeal oval (Fig. 1-A), is an oval shield about three inches long and two inches wide, which is used principally where the pressure causing the painful affection comes from the under lateral side of the joint. The aperture is so placed that it is much nearer the edge of the shield which goes under the joint, for it must be remembered that this shield should not extend down and to the plantar surface of the foot, where it might cause an inequality and undue pressure. The greatest amount of protection should come from the position of the shield, and for this purpose that portion of the skin or fabric is left thick, so that its elevation will equal at least, if not exceed, that of the affected part.

In strapping a shield in this location the half-inch, one-inch, or inch-and-a-half strips may be used. The inch plaster is probably the most practical, as it is of sufficient width to bind down the anterior and posterior edges of the shield and still will not extend over on the affected part in the aperture. These strips should each be about four inches in length and should be so arranged as to cross each other on the dorsum, one binding down the other. Thus the anterior and posterior edges of the shield, as well as the lateral surface on the dorsum of the foot, are covered. Some practitioners even advocate the use of strips of sufficient length to "criss-cross" both on the dorsum and on the plantar surfaces. It will sometimes be found that the anterior strips of adhesive plaster will extend too far up on the dorsal surface of the great toe and thus may interfere with its proper movement. In these instances it is advisable to cut out a curved portion of the strip so as to allow normal extension of the toe, without irritation from the plaster. The same holds good if the plaster should for any reason extend over the affected part in the aperture. The plaster should be cut away with curved scissors so that it remains only on the body of the shield. The half-inch plaster is sometimes used in strapping the metatarsophalangeal oval shield and is most generally adhered in the form of a triangle, the strips to be of sufficient length to cover each other on the sound integument, and so applied as to bind down all edges of the shield. The inch-and-a-half plaster is generally used in this manner in cases where it is desirable to cover the affected part of the joint as well as the shield, making the whole dressing practically waterproof. Then two strips of the inch-and-a-half plaster are used; each strip is split on both ends and lapped over so that it may be drawn down tightly on all sides of the shield. Three strips of the inch width would answer the same purpose but would make a larger and more bulky dressing.

The metatarsophalangeal half-moon (Fig. 1-B) is used in all cases where the pressure or friction comes upon the dorsum or the dorso-lateral part of the affected joint. The reason for its use in these instances is obvious If the pressure comes only upon one or both of these locations, there is surely no need of protecting the joint from plantar-lateral pressure, and the use of the full oval shield is contraindicated in that its one lateral surface, resting on tissue upon which there is already much pressure, might become uncomfortable and detrimental to the general condition of the joint.

The shield is adhered to the dorsal surface in such a manner that its two points are anterior and posterior to the affected part, with the broad lateral portion resting alongside on the dorsal surface. It will generally be found advisable and necessary to fashion the "anterior point" of the shield somewhat narrower and thinner than the posterior, as the former usually extends over upon the dorsum of the great toe and interferes with its movement if allowed to remain thick and bulky. In any event the greatest amount of protection is derived from the "posterior point" and the broad lateral surface of the shield, and this anterior point may be safely thinned or entirely eliminated (see *Modified Half-moon Shield*). In strapping the metatarsophalangeal "half-moon" shield, three strips of the inch width plaster, each four inches long, are adhered, one over the anterior tip of the crescent and extending well upon the dorsal and plantar surfaces, and the remaining two strips across the posterior part of the shield, overlapping each other and the two ends of the first applied strip (Fig. 2).

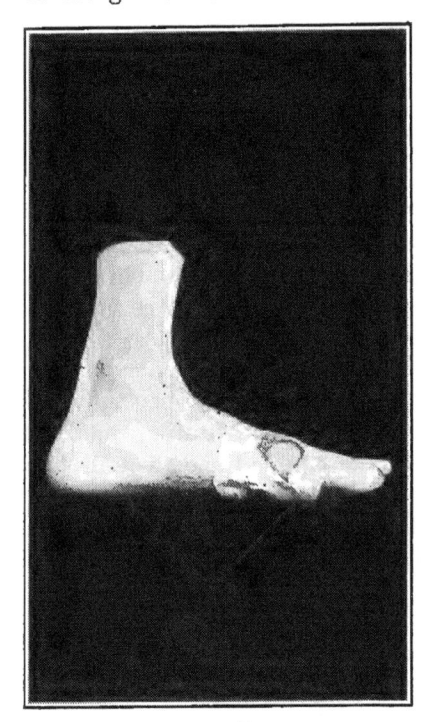

FIG. 2.
STRAPPING FOR METATARSOPHALANGEAL HALF-MOON SHIELD

Location 2. Shields are often required on the dorsum over the tendon of the extensor muscle for the protection of corneous formations or denuded spots due to rubbing of a new shoe on this prominence. Felt shields of considerable thickness are most generally used in these instances, as they are more pliable than those of buckskin and, in consequence, are not so harsh. They are usually cut in oval shape (though not so large as those described under *Location* 1), and are strapped in triangular arrangement with half-inch strips. In some instances, where pressure upon those portions of the tendon anterior and posterior to the affected area is undesirable, two straight pieces of felt of considerable thickness (so as to be of higher elevation than the prominence of the tendon) may be substituted with good results. They are placed on each side of the tendon and parallel with it. The strapping in this case consists of two half-inch strips placed across the felt shield at right angles to the long axis of the toe. A very practical protection of tender areas in this location is a half-moon shield whose opening is only of sufficient width to protect the affected spot. This shield is made from adhesive felt, and after it is fashioned and skived, a strip of the glazed adhesive, slightly wider than the tender prominence, is removed without disturbing the balance of the felt constituting the body of the shield. The shield is then applied and the adhesive substance thus comes only in contact with integument on each side of the tendon, allowing that cord to move at will without interference; at the same time ample protection is given the affected part.

This shield is usually strapped by using two strips of one-inch width plaster, each about three inches long. They are adhered, each overlapping the other, on the body of the shield, thus binding down its posterior and two lateral edges to the sound integument. Where a strapping of this nature would interfere with the normal movements of the tissues of the toes or of the great toe, one strip, three inches long and an inch-and-a-half wide, may be substituted and placed across the body of the shield (at right angles to the toes), thus binding down its posterior and a portion of its lateral edges.

Location 3. In cases of tyloma or heloma on the plantar or inner lateral border of the great toe, oval shields of buckskin are almost entirely used (same as Fig. 1-B, only smaller, to accommodate the smaller surfaces). There are two impractical points to be considered and avoided in this connection: (a) on shielding a part on the inner border of the great toe, the shield should never be allowed to extend up on the dorsum of the toe and lap over or cover the lateral and posterior nail folds. The tissues about the nail are sensitive to a degree, and any untoward pressure will in most instances start new troubles in this region. The adhesive strappings will, of course, cover a greater portion of the nail; but as the plaster is unusually thin, a great amount of trouble from the strips is seldom experienced. (b) In shielding the plantar surface of the hallux, the pad should never be fashioned to such length as to interfere with the natural bending of the toe at the web. If this be allowed the patient will experience a feeling of "fullness" at that point which may seriously interfere with his natural gait and comfort, besides which, irritation may be caused in these parts.

The strapping of shields applied to the plantar or to the inner border of the great toe is of necessity similar, as the pad is merely in a different position and the strips must practically cover the same territory. One-half-inch plaster answers most purposes and two strips are cut of sufficient length to encircle the toe and overlap each other on the side of the digit opposite the shield. Too many thicknesses of plaster between the toes should always be avoided, and to make this effective many practitioners prefer the narrow chiropodist strip, using one strip to encircle the toe twice, once on the posterior and once on the anterior edge of the shield. This is a matter of preference, but the writer favors the half-inch strip, as it has more adhesive surface and will consequently fasten the shield more firmly to the integument

Location 4. Corneous excrescences, whether hard or soft, are not commonly found between the great and second toe but, when so located, a shield is generally needed as an aid to treatment. A shield for this condition may be of buckskin or chamois, if intended to last for any time, and should be strapped in place. Felt shields are often used, minus adhesive and strapping, where temporary protection is needed. Using a shield without adhesive in any interdigital disturbance enables the patient to remove it and set it back at will, in this way avoiding the hardening or shifting when the shield is allowed to remain in place during and after a bath.

In fashioning any shield to be used in an interdigital location, the lower edge (that applied next to the web of the toe) should be cut on a slant (Fig. 1-C), to conform with the angle of the toe web. This procedure not alone makes the wearing of the shield more comfortable, but also gives it a steady base to rest upon, whether adhesive be used or not. In shielding an heloma between the great and the second toes, and particularly if the heloma be of any size or on either toe, it will usually be found advantageous to adhere the shield to the great toe. The second toe is uncommonly long and slender, and in most instances presents a very small surface around the heloma, to which a shield may be made to adhere.

The strapping of a shield in this location is similar to that applied on the opposite side (inner border) of the great toe; in most cases the half-inch plaster is employed and the ends are fashioned to overlap each other on the plantar or inner lateral surfaces of the digit.

Intermediate Toes (2d, 3d, 4th): Dorsal Surfaces. In shielding the dorsal surfaces of the intermediate digits, pads of buckskin, adhesive moleskin or chamois are exclusively used. On most feet the dorsal surfaces of these toes are quite narrow and care should be taken that the shield is not so wide as to interfere or rub against the toes adjoining or to lap around the toes on their interdigital surfaces. The shield should be wide in the centre (in which location the aperture is cut) and should taper slightly toward each end.

"Tapering slightly" does not in any sense mean to a point, but merely sufficient to conform to the general shape of the toe. Proper skiving is essential to a well fitting shield in this location, as it must adhere firmly on all sides and must not act as an irritant to the underlying and surrounding areas nor to the adjacent toes. For a sample of this shield see Fig. 1-D.

In strapping a shield to the dorsal surfaces of the three intermediate toes, the narrow chiropodist strip is generally found to be the most practical and probably the most generally used. It is best made to adhere in the following manner: strip to be six inches in length; with one end of the strip start on the side of the toe carrying the plaster downward on a tangent to a point opposite the rear portion of the shield, then crossing this posterior part of the shield, so bringing it (the strip) completely around the toe to the place of beginning. Cover the beginning "end" with the strip and carry it over the anterior portion of the shield; complete the dressing by adhering the remaining end of the plaster to the side of the toe opposite the beginning. We thus have two strips of plaster over the anterior of the shield lying next to each other and making approximately a quarter-of-an-inch of

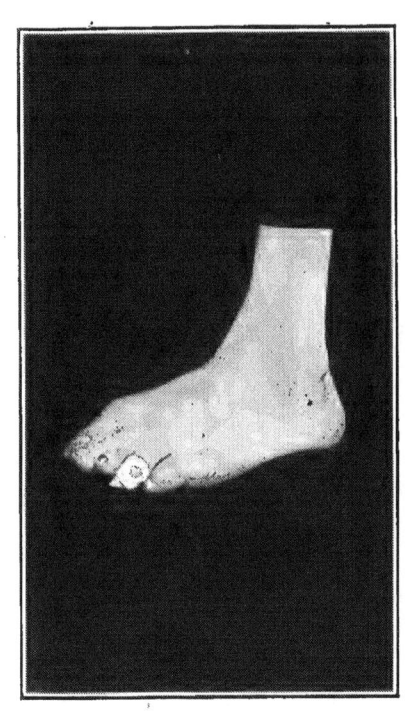

FIG. 3.
SHIELD APPLIED TO DORSUM OF FOURTH TOE

adhesive surface and only one strip over the posterior portion. In this way the anterior portion, which is most liable to loosen up from the constant rubbing of the stocking and shoe in walking, is doubly bound to the toe (Fig. 3).

In many instances where a shield is to remain for a day or so only, glazed felt will admirably answer all purposes. It is cut similar in size and design to the buckskin or chamois shield, but is most generally applied without strapping.

The Dorso-Digital Oval Shield. One more practical method of shielding an heloma on the dorsum of any of the intermediate toes may be described. In many instances, whether distinct hammer toe be present or not, the first interphalangeal articulation will be found decidedly prominent, and enlarged to such an extent as to make the application of an individual shield impractical. A large oval shield of buckskin or eighth-inch felt (Fig. 4) should then be used. The aperture is fashioned to fit the part to be protected and the long axis of the shield is allowed to rest across and upon the adjacent toes. A shield of this nature is seldom if ever strapped, and is removable by the patient while at rest or during the bath, to be replaced when the shoe

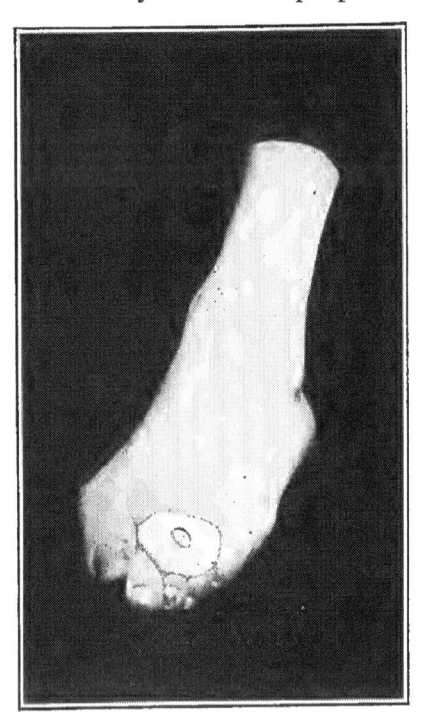

FIG. 4.
DORSO-DIGITAL OVAL SHIELD APPLIED TO THIRD TOE

is worn. The writer has observed many cases where the proximal phalanges of the intermediate toes were in a state of constant extension due to the contraction of the extensor tendons, and leaving a decided hollow in the dorsum of the foot directly over their metatarsophalangeal joints. In a condition of this nature a thick shield of this pattern is particularly practical and may be used not alone to protect a tender part, but also to fill up this hollow and allow the shoe to fit more firmly.

Where helomata are present on the dorsum of all of the phalangeal joints, this variety of shield is, of course, contra-indicated, as undue pressure would be brought to bear upon the already troublesome excrescences and a great amount of trouble would in this way be invited. In some instances a full oval shield is not used, but a dorso-digital half-moon, as shown in Fig. 1-G, is substituted. No definite ruling can be made as to which form of shield should be used, as each case presents a different aspect and the mechanical work must be applied accordingly.

End of the Intermediate Toes. Shielding is often necessary on the ends of the toes, and in such instances the padding should, as a rule, be made very thin and the subsequent dressing not bulky. This is advisable for several reasons: first, helomata in this locality are usually under or immediately adjacent to the nails and too great an amount of pressure cannot be put upon these structures; second, that there is trouble on the end of the digit is proof positive of the shoe being too short and, therefore, if too thick a shield be used, the pressure on the surrounding tissues will be too great to be comfortable; third, helomata in these locations are seldom found to be elevated to any extent above the normal surface of the integument and when removed, the tissues are usually at their normal elevation, so that shields of material as heavy as those used in connection with helomata in other localities are unnecessary.

A shield of thin buckskin, adhesive moleskin or chamois is best in these cases. It is applied, generally, so that the long axis is across the end of the toe and seldom so that the ends of the padding overlap the free edge of the nail or compress the plantar surface of the digit. Where the heloma to be protected is situated close to the nail, and it is advisable that the padding extend over that structure, by clipping the nail closely and filing it down and at the same time using an exceedingly thin shield, successful protection can be secured without unfavorable results. Such shortening of the nail is, however, not advisable in all cases. This article deals entirely with shielding, but attention must be here drawn to the fact that there are many instances of an heloma occurring on the end of one of the lesser toes, when a shield is contra-indicated. There are many cases where the toe nail, if allowed to grow long, will protect the tender part far more successfully than will a shield. Therefore, it is always well to consider if protection can be obtained from the nail itself before applying a shield in this location.

Strappings. The application of adhesive strips to a shield in this locality demands considerable ingenuity on the part of the operator, but there is no stereotyped method to be employed. One general method may, however, be explained: cut two pieces of chiropodist strip, each about two-and-one-half or three inches long. Apply the centre of one strip over one end of the shield, lateral to the aperture, and carry one end of the strip on a line running toward the proximal end of the toe and in a manner so as to cover as much of the edges of the shield on that side as possible.

Overlap these plaster ends on the interdigital surface of the toe opposite to the place of beginning. Adhere the second in like manner to the other surface of the shield on the side of the aperture, and carry the plaster ends in such a way as to cause them to overlap each other on the interdigital surface of the toe opposite the place of beginning. In this way both lateral and nearly all of the plantar edges of the shield will be covered and bound down with adhesive plaster. It will be found generally that the edge of the shield coming under the free edge of the nail needs no reenforcement by adhesive strips, as the length of the nail will prevent any tendency to loosen up the plaster in that location. Cut a third strip about two inches long and with it circle the toe, binding down all four ends of the two strips already applied. Trim off the ends of the plaster, which extend from under this last applied strip, and the whole makes a neat practical shielding for trouble in this situation. (Fig. 5).

There are many ways in which a shield in this location may be strapped, but as always, and particularly in this instance, there are so many circumstances which go to alter the mode of strapping that it would be well-nigh impossible to explain them all or to outline a set method of procedure.

Interdigital Surfaces. Helomata, both hard and soft, often occur between the toes and, in these cases, to insure complete relief to the patient, a s h i e l d is usually an absolute necessity.

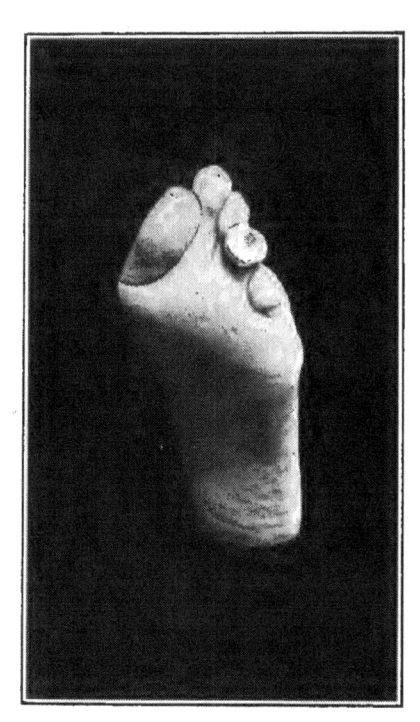

FIG. 5.
SHOWING SHIELD APPLIED TO END OF FOURTH TOE

Buckskin, sheepskin, adhesive moleskin, and chamois are the materials most generally used for interdigital shields although the thinner varieties of white felting, with or without adhesive, may be substituted in some instances.

The shield should be fashioned of equal length to the surface of the toe, from the web to the distal end, and should be only wide enough to correspond to the thickness of the toe. If the shield be allowed to lap over on the dorsum of the toe or under on its plantar surface, new pressure is brought to bear on these parts, to the discomfort of the patient It must always be remembered that the toes bend during the various movements in walking, and that if a shield be allowed to curl under the toe, the thickness of the material used will interfere, to a great extent, with the normal flexing and extending of the toe, even to such a degree in some instances as to cause lesions of more or less severe character on the skin.

To allow any shield to cover or to press upon the tissues directly adjacent to the nail is always to the discomfort of those parts, and in this, as in all other instances, should be avoided.

The bottom of the shield (Fig 1-C) should be cut on a tangent, so as to conform to the corresponding slant of the toe web. This insures not only the minimum danger of irritation on those tender parts, but also allows the shield a firm base upon which to rest, and prevents any possible tilting or shifting.

Shields for application to the interdigital surfaces seldom need to be of great thickness, and the thinner the shield used the more flexible it is, and the less pressure is brought to bear on the outer surfaces of the toes. It must be remembered that everything placed between the toes, of necessity, spreads those members further apart, and naturally this causes a greater amount of pressure from the boot on the outer surfaces Skiving is an essential requirement in interdigital shields, although in some instances where they are to be used between the great and second toes, this (skiving) may be omitted.

Thin felt shields, minus adhesive, are often employed between the toes for transient protection, a fresh one being usually placed in position daily.

Strapping. The most practical method of strapping an interdigital shield is by means of the narrow chiropodist strip. The method used is similar in every particular to that employed in the use of the same width strip in applying a shield to the dorsum of the intermediate toes.

Another less used method is as follows: take a six-inch chiropodist strip; at its centre adhere it to the upper end of the shield (that nearer the distal extremity of the toe), and carry both ends around the toe, crossing them on the side opposite to the starting point. Then bring the loose ends around the toe again to the side upon which the shield is adhered and overlap them over the bottom of the shield, allowing the ends to run for attachment on the sound integument.

Fifth Toe: Dorsal Surface. There are more corneous developments on this digit than on any of the others, and as this toe presents a free surface on its outer side, which is not the case with any of the other lesser digits, many varieties of shielding and of strapping are used.

As with the dorsal surfaces of the intermediate toes, buckskin and adhesive moleskin are the most generally used shielding materials, and pads of the thinner varieties are in most cases sufficient for the needs. But, as this toe is probably the most abused of any and is often found distorted into positions of extreme flexion or extension and is sometimes lapped over the fourth toe, shields of a greater thickness, or "built up" pads, are very often indicated. The ordinary buckskin or adhesive moleskin shield is fashioned oval in shape, but the anterior end is cut either straight across or slanted toward the outer lateral edge, so that we have a shield, round at its posterior extremity and tapering toward the anterior end, having a straight edge (Fig. 1-E). Shields for the fifth toe must be carefully skived, especially at the anterior end which goes toward the nail. The writer has often seen cases in which new helomata, sometimes as many as three or four, have developed on the dorsum of this toe anterior to the original callosity, exclusively caused by the habitual wearing of thick shields.

The size of the shield depends wholly upon the size of the toe and the area to be protected, but the length of the shield should never be allowed to interfere with the bending of the toe at its metatarsophalangeal articulation. If this precaution is not observed, in walking the shield rubs against the dorsum of the foot and is not alone loosened at its posterior edge, but causes irritation to the skin in that region. As with those used on the dorsum of the intermediate toes, the aperture of a shield for the fifth toe should be cut of sufficient size to allow a space between its (the aperture) anterior edge, and that of the calloused area; this is to allow for backward shifting.

Another form of shield used in cases where the small toe is flexed to a degree and an heloma has developed on its apex, is what may be called the fifth digital half-moon (Fig. 1-B). It is usually necessary to build up a shield of this variety. By "built up" is meant that two thicknesses of material are used, one pasted upon the other, to give the shield greater thickness and stability. The upper thickness is formed so as to protect the rear and lateral sides of the corneous area, but not the front. The second, or under thickness, is fashioned round at its posterior edge and straight at its anterior surface. This, being placed under the upper layer, gives the shield sufficient thickness to be of equal height to the elevation of the heloma or even higher, thereby avoiding all undesirable pressure upon the painful area, and at the same time filling out whatever hollow there may be in the foot at this point.

Strapping. There are five general methods of strapping to adhere a shield to the dorsal surface of the fifth toe. Some conditions demand the use of one of these and none other, but in most instances any method may be used with good effect. These five methods are as follows:

1. Narrow chiropodist strip.
2. Combination narrow and half-inch strip.
3. Half-inch strip (using one strip).
4. Half-inch strip (using two strips).
5. Inch strip.

Number 1. In using the narrow chiropodist plaster, the strip is applied in a similar manner to that already described for toes, arranging the plaster so as to cover the anterior of the shield with two widths of the strip and the posterior surface with but one (Fig. 6). As an alternative for this, the method described in the second instance in connection with interdigital shields may be utilized.

Number 2. The narrow strip and the half-inch combination consists of a narrow strip, about four inches in length, adhered to the inner surface of the toe and carried twice around the toe across the surface of the shield, anterior to the aperture. This, as will be seen, binds down the distal end of the shield. The half-inch strip, about three inches in length, is then cut as shown in Fig. 7-B.

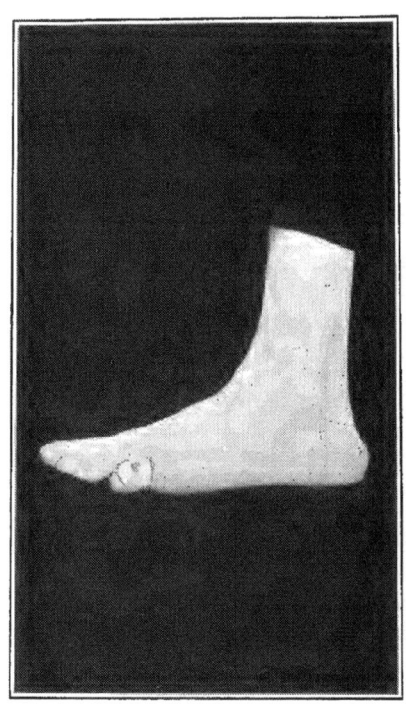

FIG. 6.
STRAPPING OF 5TH TOE SHIELD WITH CHIROPODIST STRIP

Taking this strip in both hands, insert it between the toes in such a manner as to allow the narrow portion of the plaster to fit into the narrowest part of the toe web. Then carry the outer broad end of the strip around on the dorsum of the toe and adhere it across that part of the shield posterior to the aperture, taking care, however, that the adhesive plaster is half on the shield and half on the integument adjoining it. Adhere the remaining broad end of the plaster (that coming from between the toes) over the first applied posterior strips, taking the same care that shield and skin are both covered by the plaster (Fig. 8).

This alternate style of strapping is particularly useful in cases where the narrow strips of method No. 1 are found to irritate the skin of the toe web, or if there be a corneous excrescence developed there which cannot be covered by the plaster; instead of using the half-inch strip, as just described, a half-inch or inch strip, about two inches in length, is cut and placed across the

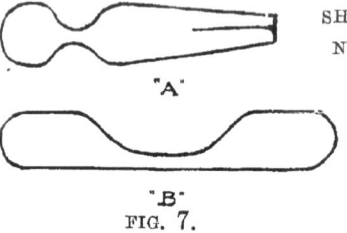

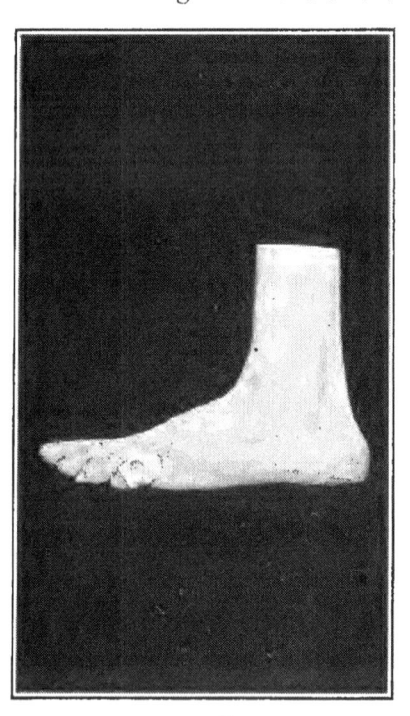

FIG. 8.
SHOWING SHIELD STRAPPED WITH NARROW AND HALF-INCH STRIP

FIG. 7.

posterior of the shield and is adhered to the integument on the dorsum and plantar of the foot. Should any portion of this poste-

124 PODIATRY

rior strip lap over the aperture, it should, of course, be cut away.

Number 3. In this manner of strapping (using one one-half-inch strip) we have one of the most practical methods in vogue today. A strip about six inches in length is fashioned in the manner of Fig. 9. The wide portion in the strip's centre is then adhered to the anterior surface of the shield and the ends are carried around, one on each side of the toe, in such a manner as to allow the narrowest portions to crisscross in the narrow part of the toe web on the plantar surface. The wide ends are then carried around the dorsum of the toe and are overlapped on the posterior portion of the shield. This method of applying the plaster supplies a greater amount of adhesive surface than by the use of the narrow strip and is just as practical, or more so, in many ways.

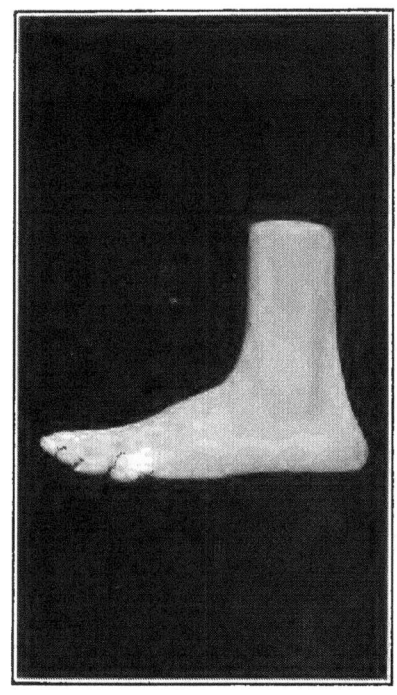

FIG. 8.
SHOWING DRESSING COMPLETE WITH COCOON OVER APERTURE

Number 4. In using two one-half-inch strips to adhere a shield to the dorsum of the fifth toe, the plaster is fashioned as shown in A and B (Fig. 7). The strip marked "A" is cut about two inches in length and split on

FIG. 9.

the square end. That marked "B" is about three or three and one-half inches in length. The strip "A" is laid over the anterior surface of the shield with the split end toward the inner side of the toe. The anterior one of the two split ends is then drawn tightly over the anterior edge of the shield and adhered to the inner surface of the toe; the remaining split end is adhered over the first and should also be drawn tightly, so that the anterior portion of the shield is closely bound to the dorsum of the toe. The rounded end of the plaster strip is then carried around the outer side of the toe in such a manner as to allow the narrow portion of the plaster to rest over the corresponding narrow part of the toe on its plantar surface. The wide extremity is brought around to the inner side of the toe and is placed over the split ends already adhered. This binds them securely to the interdigital surface of the toe. Any loose ends showing after the foregoing is completed should be clipped off. One wide end of the strip "B" is then adhered

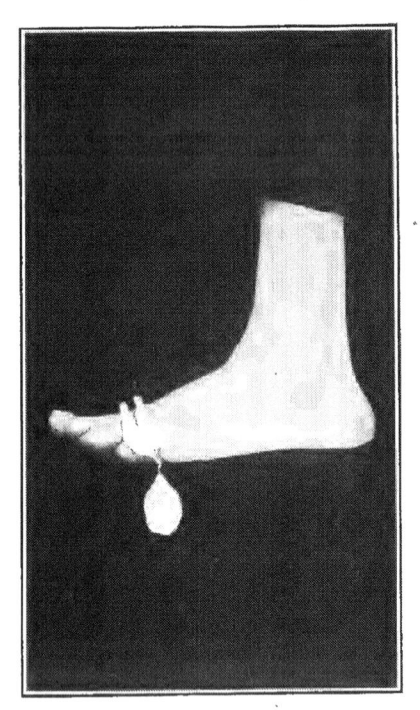

FIG. 11.
SHOWING ANTERIOR PORTION OF ADHESIVE STRIP APPLIED

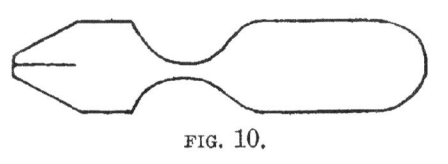

FIG. 10.

across the posterior surface of the shield and the plaster carried around the toe (the narrow portion of the plaster fitting in the narrow part of the toe web) and the remaining wide end is overlapped on the posterior portion of the shield, thus securing the other wide end already adhered to the shield.

Another method, differing merely in the position of the last wide end of the strip "B," is as follows: instead of adhering this end crisscross over the posterior portion of the shield, bring it further toward the anterior of the toe and adhere it directly across and over the aperture, fastening the end upon the inner side of the toe. This makes a waterproof dressing with none of the shield showing when the dressing is complete; it is contraindicated when a soft dressing is desired over the inflamed parts.

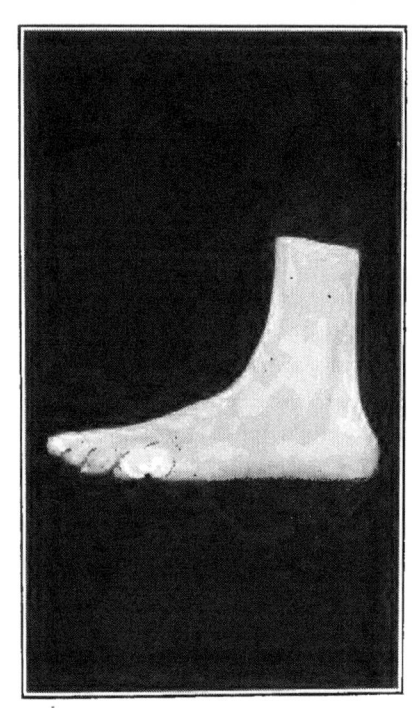

FIG. 11
SHOWING DRESSING COMPLETED

Number 5. The other method which may be used is to cut off about six inches of one-inch plaster (although the length used depends upon the size of the toe), and fashion it as shown in Fig. 10. The split ends are then adhered on the inner side of the toe, so that the wide portion next to them is drawn tightly over the anterior surface of the shield. The narrow portion is then carried around the outer side of the toe and is placed, as previously described, on the corresponding narrow surface of the toe web, and the remaining wide end is brought between the toes and over the posterior surface of the shield, entirely covering the pad and adhering it to the integument on the outer surface of the shield, over the metatarsophalangeal joint. This also makes a practically waterproof dressing (Fig. 11).

Fifth Digital, Built Up, Half-Moon Shield. In strapping a "built up" half-moon shield in this connection there are one or two methods which will answer in all cases. The first method is the use of but one strip of plaster, either of one-inch or of one-and-a-half inch width. This is placed transversely across the body of the shield so that no plaster extends over into the aperture, and it is adhered to the integument on the dorsal and plantar surfaces of the foot. As this shield is so much wider than the toe, it is not practical to encircle the toe with adhesive strips in fastening it. The other method at times employed, and the one that is advocated, in that it binds down the "points of the crescent," situated laterally to the corn when the shield is in place, consists in the use of two strips of the one-inch plaster. These are each cut about two inches in length, one being placed diagonally across the body of the shield in such a manner as to cover the outer lateral point of the shield, and the other in a like manner, so as to cover the inner lateral point of the shield and overlapping the first applied strip on the body of the shield. In many instances, however, this variety of shield is not strapped and is removed and re-applied by the wearer at will.

It may sometimes be found advisable, when a small shield cannot be used and where the spot to be protected is nearer the distal part of the toe, and in consequence would not receive sufficient protection from a half-moon shield placed at its proximal end, to apply to the part a full oval shield, slightly modified as to its anterior edge. This shield is of the same shape as that shown in Fig 1-E, except that it is larger. It is made from the thicker grades of buckskin and is fashioned so as to rest on the fourth toe and over the fifth nail, and for this reason these two contact surfaces of the shield must be well skived. This shield is seldom strapped and then only at its posterior surface, and in like manner to the strappings described for the fifth digital half-moon. A large shield of this kind evens up the whole surface of that part of the foot and so equalizes the pressure that it is distributed generally.

Lateral Surfaces. Helomata on the outer lateral surface of the fifth toe are generally shielded in a manner similar to those occurring on the dorsum; the shield in the lateral location, however, should never be of great thickness. In most instances corneous developments of the small digit on these surfaces are situated adjacent to the nail and the shield, and to be comfortable, should not be allowed to overlap the nail structures. If, however, to obtain proper protection, overlapping must be allowed in order to cover these areas, the shield should be of paper thinness, especially at its anterior end.

In this situation a shield is often used which gives protection from the anterior, posterior and outer lateral but not from the inner lateral surface, which would of necessity have to be adhered over the dorsum of the toe and the nail.

This form of shield is practically of the same shape as the ordinary fifth toe protector but with the inner lateral surface next to the cut away aperture It is particularly practical in cases where the spot to be protected is directly next to or in the corner of the nail. By a shield so fashioned, the protection of the part is derived from all but the nail.

Strapping. The narrow chiropodist strip affords the most practical method of strapping a shield in this location, and the method is similar to that employed on the dorsum of the fifth or intermediate toes.

In strapping the last mentioned form of shield, the strips are applied in a similar manner. Care is taken to adhere the plaster over both points of the shield, anterior and posterior to the affected part.

Interdigital Surfaces. The shielding of helomata occurring on the inner surface of the fifth toe is similar in method to that employed in shielding like parts on the intermediate toes. This applies to the strapping as well. Thick shields are contra-indicated, as they force the fifth toe out against the shoe; if used on that part they will undoubtedly create trouble to the toe in question. Both hard and soft helomata often occur in this connection; they are located, not on the sides, but rather well down in the web of the toe In such cases a specially fashioned shield is required which, from its shape, is known as a "boot shield" (Fig. 1-F). This shield is of material such as is used in making the ordinary interdigital pad, being the thinner grades of adhesive moleskin, buckskin, or chamois. It is applied usually on the adjacent side of the fourth toe, the narrow portion uppermost and the wider part with its concaved surface directly above the uppermost ridge of the corneous area. This not alone prevents lateral pressure, but, by means of the tongue-like shape at one side of its base, it also prevents pressure on the part from the plantar surface.

It is often found that helomata, developing in the interdigital web of these toes, are caused by pressure on the part, due to the dropping of the fourth metatarsal bone. To bring the head of this bone up into position, and in that way relieve the pressure, it is often found necessary to apply a felt or buckskin shield on the plantar surface of the foot under this articulation. This may be done in addition to applying a shield between the toes or each may be used separately, as experience dictates. Alfred Ahrens, of New York, one of the teaching staff of The First Institute of Podiatry, has devised a shield, known by its shape as the "duck shield," which is so fashioned as to present a shielding surface between the fourth and fifth toes, as well as an expanded end which extends down upon the plantar surface and throws the head of the fourth metatarsal up into normal position.

Strapping. The narrow strip is the most practical means of strapping a "boot shield" to the fourth toe. Two turns of the plaster are carried around the digit, the first covering the shield about at its centre and the second crossing near its uppermost end. One half-inch strip may also be used, its two ends crossing each other on the side of the fourth toe, opposite the shield; or in some instances, if the shape of the toe permits, the ends may be adhered to the dorsal and plantar surfaces of the foot.

Metatarsophalangeal Articulation. In protecting a part in this location three styles of shield may be employed.

1. Oval.
2 Half-moon
3. Modified half-moon.

Number 1. The thicker grades of buckskin or felt are generally used for this protection, as the part, if affected, is usually considerably elevated above the surrounding integument. As in connection with the first metatarsophalangeal articulation, the oval shield is so fashioned that the principal protection will be derived from the upper lateral and posterior surfaces. The anterior and under lateral surfaces are made correspondingly thin and narrow, so that no undesirable pressure is brought to bear on the integument beneath these surfaces. In this instance, two reasons may be given for such a course: first, all unnecessary pressure is naturally contra-indicated; second, the protection from these sides is, in nearly every instance, useless and unproductive of results. Usually, if the point to be protected be near the band of the fifth toe, the shield must be scalloped so as to allow for the backward movement of this digit when in an extended position. Great care must be taken in applying all shields to allow for the natural movements of the parts in walking In this position, more particularly, a cumbersome, ill-fashioned shield may become a source of irritation during the movements of the foot in exercise. Ninety per cent. of shield troubles are due to their being improperly fitted or to their imperfect fashioning.

If a shield used in protecting the fifth metatarsophalangeal articulation is not scalloped, as previously mentioned, to allow for the backward movement of the proximal phalanges of this digit, irritation is not only bound to occur, but the movement of the toe will loosen up the anterior rim of the shield (despite strapping), and consequently shifting of the shield is sure to occur.

In strapping an oval shield to this part, two strips about four or five inches long are cut from the one-inch width plaster. They are adhered so as to cover the anterior and posterior portions of the shield and the upper loose ends, made to overlap on the dorsum of the foot, are carried firmly over the side to the plantar surface, overlapping also on the sole of the foot.

From experience, the writer much prefers the substitution of the so-called half-moon, or the modified half-moon shields (Fig. 1-II) in place of the oval just described.

Number 2. The metatarsophalangeal half-moon shield supplies all the necessary protection from its upper lateral and posterior surfaces without extending down around and under the plantar surface of the joint. It must always be remembered that the insole of the shoe joins its shank at this point and, in many instances, particularly if the shoe has been worn to any extent, the insole is inclined to curl up and to thicken, and in nearly every case where the shield is allowed to run over the edge of the foot, undue pressure, with its train of bad effects, is made on the parts.

The half-moon shield is placed on the dorsum of the foot, the "points of the crescent" extending anteriorly and posteriorly to the part to be protected. The anterior is made narrower and thinner than the posterior point for, as is the case with the oval shield, the greatest amount of protection must come from the wide lateral surface (the main body of the shield) and from that portion lying posterior to the protected part.

As is the case in any shield, the anterior part of the crescent or half-moon variety must be placed far enough forward so that if it does shift, there will still be sufficient normal integument for it to rest upon before it comes in direct contact with the anterior edge of the calloused area. However, care must also be taken and allowance made so that backward movement of the fifth toe does not tend to loosen up this anterior edge

In strapping the half-moon shield, two strips, four inches long and one inch wide, are used in like manner as that described in the strapping of the oval shield In some instances the anterior point of the crescent is found to be narrow enough so that a strip of the half-inch plaster, cut the same length, may be substituted with equally good results. The inch width, or in some cases the inch-and-a-half width, is used across the posterior portion of the shield.

Number 3. The modified metatarsophalangeal half-moon shield is practically the regular half-moon minus its anterior point. Many practitioners have suggested a shield of this nature for protection of the first and fifth metatarsophalangeal joints for the reason that the anterior point is of little or of no use and may become a decidedly detrimental feature should the shield shift in any way. Its application and strapping is similar in every particular to that of the half-moon. The writer, however, has often used two strips of one-inch width plaster, each about three inches long, and has adhered them in criss-cross fashion over the posterior of the shield so as to cover the entire posterior portion and some part of the lateral edge, and has also found this method entirely satisfactory.

Plantar Surfaces. The plantar surfaces of the foot. being subject to continued pressure and at times to considerable friction, are prone to develop many calloused and corneous areas. In many of these cases shielding is absolutely imperative to successful treatment.

It must always be remembered that these excrescences are, in a measure at least, a protection to the underlying parts, and their removal often makes the patient conscious of their loss. Ofttimes the tissues so exposed become congested and decidedly tender. This, of course, is to be considered at all times, but particularly so on the plantar surfaces of the foot. Another point which must be taken into consideration in this connection is that the normal tissue padding (fat and muscles) of some people's feet is very thin; in consequence, the heads of the metatarsal bones are unprotected. In most cases of this kind shields must be applied to take the place of nature in order to insure any degree of comfort to the patient.

Shields to be placed on the plantar surfaces, and particularly those to be applied to the metatarsophalangeal regions on the "ball" of the foot, must of necessity be of decidedly heavier quality and contain more "body" than those applied to the dorsal or lateral regions. The reason is that the constant weight of the body quickly flattens the shields out to such an extent as to render them useless as far as protection is concerned.

The full oval shield (Fig. 1-A) is the agent best calculated to protect sensitive areas on the plantar surfaces, and it can be safely said that it may be and is used in almost every case of this kind. Naturally the most general locality for the formation of helomata is under the metatarsophalangeal articulations. These areas, particularly in persons whose feet are thin and lack the proper natural padding, become the seats of severe callosities and helomata. The shield to be used should always be of sufficient size to allow surface enough so that the patient will rest upon the shield rather than on the integument; but they should never be allowed to extend up under the toes or be placed in any way so as to irritate the tender tissues surrounding the diseased area. For this reason many practitioners have advocated the use of the medio-plantar crescent shield (Fig. 1-I), so placed that the greater body of the shield is posterior to the heloma and the "points of the crescent" extend forward laterally to the heloma and point toward the toes. This variety of shielding is particularly efficient when the part to be protected is located rather anterior to the metatarsophalangeal articulations, as is often found in cases of blisters and veruccæ.

However, in most instances where the trouble is situated directly over these joints, an oval shield may be used with perfect impunity and good results will usually follow.

The long axis of the oval shield is placed, as a rule, crosswise on the foot, as the greater amount of protection is derived from the surfaces immediately adjoining the affected area, laterally rather than anteriorly and posteriorly. In cases of excessively arched feet (not necessarily *pes cavus*) and when the integument is quite thin, a great deal of protection may be afforded by "building up" the shield on its surfaces, which are to be posterior to the areas to be protected. This fills up, to some extent, the hollow caused by the high longitudinal arch and gives the patient a larger surface upon which to stand or walk. This same theory of shielding may be successfully applied in cases where the calloused area covers the whole "ball" of the foot, making it impractical to shield any one spot without jeopardizing the comfort of the rest of the integument by placing a shield over it. A large piece of felt may then be applied directly posterior to the callosity, the felt to be of sufficient thickness to allow the patient to rest upon the shield rather than upon the painful calloused area.

Strapping. In strapping the plantar oval shield, the one-inch width plaster is most generally used. Three strips are cut, one about two inches and the remaining ones approximately three or four inches in length. The short strip is then placed over the anterior edge of the shield and is adhered to the integument, adjacent laterally to the shield. One of the longer strips, placed diagonally over the shield's lateral edge, starting from and covering the plaster strip already adhered transversely across the anterior end and running backwards and covering the whole lateral surface of the shield, is adhered to the integument immediately posterior. The remaining long plaster strip is then placed in like manner over the other lateral surface of the shield and is adhered so as to cover the posterior end of the first placed lateral strip. This lapping of the plaster ends lends reenforcement to the strapping and undoubtedly minimizes the danger of the plaster loosening and at the same time all the edges of the shield are bound down to the integument (Fig. 12).

It should be remembered that when applying adhesive strips in the strapping of a plantar shield, the toes should always be drawn backward towards the dorsum of the foot to their fullest extent, the straps to be applied whilst the toes are held in this position. This is to allow for the extension of the toes in the last position of walking and prevents the plaster from pulling on the sound integument.

In several instances it has been advocated that but two one-inch width strips be used on a shield of this nature, and the same method may well be applied to the strapping of the medio-plantar crescent shield previously described. These strips are cut of equal length, each about four-and-a-half or five inches.

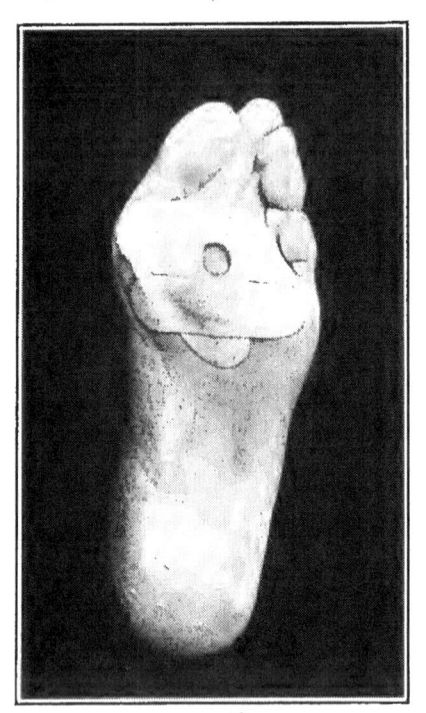

FIG. 12.
SHOWING COMPLETE STRAPPING FOR MEDIO-PLANTAR OVAL SHIELD

About one inch from one end, each strip is narrowed from the sides so as to allow the admission of the plaster between the toes. This one end is then adhered to the integument on the dorsum of the foot, the narrow portion being carried between the third and fourth or the fourth and fifth toes (as the size of the shield may indicate) and the remaining portion of plaster is adhered diagonally across the outer lateral surface of the shield. The other strip, adhered in like manner on the dorsal surface, is carried between the toes (usually the great and second) over the inner lateral surface of the shield, lapping over the end of the first strip applied. This method of strapping covers, to a considerable extent, the anterior portion of the shield and does away with the transverse strip which in many cases becomes an irritating agent to the tender integument under the toes.

The argument against this method of strapping may be the danger of irritation between the toes. From the experience had in using this method, the writer has had no bad results, and if the strips are properly adhered, the normal movements of the foot being taken into consideration and the plaster lying between the toes cut sufficiently narrow, no bad results can take place and there is no doubt of the greater efficiency and lasting power of the strapping.

The Lateral Plantar Half-moon. When the area to be protected is situated on the extreme lateral edges of the plantar surface, as often found in these locations, and the callosity extends to or sometimes over the lateral border of the foot, the full oval shield is contra-indicated. In its place the lateral plantar half-moon is substituted with better results in all cases.

This variety is identical with the dorsal half-moon shield and is applied so that the main body of the shield lies laterally on the plantar surface, while the "points" are allowed to extend somewhat over the lateral border of the foot so that some protection is afforded from this source. The major protection, however, is, of course, obtained from the main body of the shield on the plantar surface.

The anterior "point of the crescent" is generally fashioned so as to be narrower and thinner than the posterior, for in nearly every instance this must extend near the under surface of the great toe and of the small digit, and must in no way be allowed to interfere with their movements. Two strips of one inch width plaster are generally used in strapping the lateral plantar half-moon, although in some instances it will be found necessary (due to the close proximity of the digital webs) to substitute a strip one-half inch in width for the anterior strapping.

The straps are so placed as to overlap both on the dorsal and plantar surfaces and to bind down the anterior and posterior edges of the pad. In all strapping the result to be obtained is the binding down of the edges of the shield rather than merely binding down the main body.

Lateral Borders. Practically the only spot on the lateral borders of the foot where callous formations may be met is over the expanded base of the fifth metatarsal bone, although blister formations or other tender areas may develop anywhere along the edges.

The full oval shield is almost entirely used in connection with protection in these locations and is usually strapped with three strips of the inch width plaster or, if the shield be small, three strips of one-half inch width plaster will answer.

These are placed as follows one strip slightly shorter than the other two is adhered transversely across one end of the shield and the other two are applied diagonally from the ends of the first, so as to completely cover the lateral edges of the shield and overlap each other on the sound integument beyond its end.

Os Calcis Region. Many cases coming to the notice of the podiatrist require the application of a shield in the region of the os calcis, either on the plantar, lateral and posterior surfaces of the heel itself, or further upward on the prominence of the tendo Achillis. The oval shield is most generally used in these instances, and felt will usually be found to be the most practical shielding material. Felt, in particular, is advocated because it is softer and more yielding than most other materials, and in shielding a tender area on the tendo Achillis, nothing harsh can be used without danger of causing irritation to the surrounding and underlying soft parts.

Strapping is similar to that used in adhering the oval shield to the lateral border, but naturally the operator must exercise his own ingenuity in the method of strapping to meet the conditions present.

The art of applying a shield is not one to which any set rules can be applied. Each case is individual and the operator who goes about this branch of his work in a stereotyped manner will find his efforts devoid of results.

Often a half-moon shield is used where the part to be protected is so located that a full oval shield may not be applied. Sometimes the "points" are applied upward and sometimes the main body of the shield lies above the protected area and the "points" are downward The strapping is similar to a strapping for any such shield and the strips are applied in such a way as not to interfere with normal movements of the heel or of the tendon.

There are many instances in which incipient bursal inflammations are developed adjacent to the tendo Achillis, due to the wearing of a new or stiff pump or boot Many cases of this nature were found among the militiamen preparing to go to the "border" last Spring. The constant marching in new and stiff shoes, which was part of their training, caused a great amount of trouble just above and at the insertion of this tendon. In these cases two pieces of felt, shaped to the tendon and thick enough to fill up the hollows at its sides, were applied and then strapped securely in place by strips of adhesive plaster, one inch in width, which covered felt, tendon and all This strapping served not alone to secure the felt shielding in place, but also to immobilize the part so that these deeper inflammations had a chance to subside.

Dorsal Surfaces. On the dorsal surfaces of the foot, over the articulations of the metatarsal bone with the internal cuneiform and the cuneiform with the navicular, small and seemingly insignificant, helomata miliare (seed corns) are found to develop. In many instances the removal of these growths will not bring relief unless a shield is applied with the final dressing. This is due to the lack of muscular padding over these bones and the skin becomes irritated by tight lacing of the shoes.

A small oval shield, not too thick and usually of thin buckskin, kid or adhesive moleskin, is usually applied, although the thinner varieties of felt may be used with good results. The shield is generally strapped in a manner similar to those applied to the lateral borders or to the os calcis region, that is, with three strips of one-half inch width plaster applied to cover all edges of the shield in triangular form.

MORTON'S TOE AND METATARSALGIA

The treatment of anterior arch trouble is usually and wisely recommended to the orthopedic specialist, but there are numerous incipient and advanced cases for which the podiatrist must necessarily give at least temporary relief. Shields, as well as strapping, play an important part in the rectification of these annoying conditions, and under this heading the shielding in particular will be discussed

The heads of the metatarsal bones forming the anterior metatarsal arch, having dropped from their normal positions, cause pressure upon the digital nerves and bring on the varities of pain which are found in these conditions. It seems a logical theory that in order to alleviate these painful manifestations, support so designed as to return these bones to their normal position and hold them there would constitute a practical and efficient treatment

From the podiatrist's standpoint, this may be accomplished by means of shields of felt or buckskin, adhered to the plantar surface of the foot in this region or by placing such supports in the shoe These methods may at least afford temporary relief and in some instances, if their use be persisted in, permanent cures have been effected The cure, however, is usually attempted by means of metal appliances which are worn in the shoe and which have a raised portion or "button" just posterior to the metatarsal heads.

There are several forms of shields (or rather in this instance pads or supports) which are in general use for the correction of anterior arch trouble. These vary in size, shape, and thickness according to the number of bones involved in the displacement. Varying success is met with in the use of these supports and each individual case is usually found to demand changes or modifications in the support, so that the following description should be taken for the general points alone:

Morton's Toe. This affection, being limited to a displacement of the head of the fourth metatarsal bone with the lateral pressure from it upon the digital nerve, naturally does not need so large a shield as would be demanded were the bones of the whole anterior arch out of alignment.

A pad of felt, about two-and-one-half inches long, an inch-and-a-half wide at the anterior point, made to taper slightly towards the posterior end, and three-eighths-of-an-inch thick, will be found to give relief in most cases. The felt is skived at the posterior end so that its thickness lessens gradually as it extends posteriorly along the metatarsal bone. The pad is applied directly to the rear of the head of the fourth metatarsal bone, and the thickness of the pad serves to force the depressed bone upwards and thus into proper alignment. It may be found necessary at times to use even thicker material in the manufacture of the pad or to place a small piece of felt upon its upper surface, so that as it is adhered to the part, this elevated area will come directly posterior to the depressed metatarsal head and thus elevate it.

In strapping the piece of felt, two or three strips of one inch plaster are used. These are long enough to cover the width of the plantar surface and to extend upon the dorsal surface on each side. One end of the plaster is firmly adhered to the dorsum of the foot, the plaster being carried around under the foot over the pad, to be then adhered to the inner dorsum of the foot. Sufficient tension should be put on the adhesive strips to pull both borders of the foot down, thus aiding the pad in pushing the heads of the affected metatarsal bones up in place. In fact, in some cases a strapping of this nature with adhesive plaster will serve to give at least temporary relief to the patient without the use of a pad. Some practitioners advocate a pad of sufficient length to cover a greater portion of the metatarsal bone.

If the pad is entirely covered by the three lengths of adhesive plaster, it will not alone last longer but the danger of its slipping out of place is minimized

Metatarsalgia. When the whole anterior arch is involved in a displacement, a pad of sufficient size and thickness to support the heads of all the metatarsals is necessary. There are two principal forms of support in general use. A strip of buckskin or felt of sufficient length (which will, of course, vary in different feet) to cover the four lesser metatarsal heads and about one-and-one-half to two inches in width, is adhered to the foot just posterior to the depressed parts. This is covered with adhesive plaster and serves as a support to the whole anterior arch region.

In the writer's experience, however, the fifth metatarsal bone is rarely involved in this general depression, and this seems natural when it is considered that the first and the fifth metatarsal bones act as pillars for this arch in the normal foot.

Should complaint be made of a pain coming from the anterior arch trouble and occurring between the fourth and fifth toes, it usually will be found to emanate from the depression of the fourth metatarsal head. Keeping this in mind, a pad or support, which has found great favor, is fashioned from thick felt or buckskin (one-quarter to three-eighths) in such a way as to allow its anterior edge to come just behind the metatarsal heads. This pad should be about four or five inches long and the portion that extends back under the longitudinal arch should be skived so that it easily conforms to the contours of the foot in that region. In order to obtain support to the three middle metatarsal heads, the corners of this pad, which would extend over those of the first and fifth, are to be cut away; otherwise the pad would cause undue pressure upon parts requiring no support and thus prove detrimental.

The pad is held in place with adhesive strips extending from the outer to the inner dorsum, applied in the same manner as described for the Morton's toe pad.

This pad practically gives the patient a new sole to walk on, and at the same time holds the depressed bones up in place. It will often be found advantageous to apply a pad of this kind, about one-eighth or one-quarter of an inch thick, in conditions where the patient complains of a burning sensation in the soles of the feet, even though there be no apparent lesion or displacement of the metatarsal bones.

A number of devices are on the market for the relief of all forms of affections common to the arches of the foot The relative merits of such contrivances will be fully discussed in the forthcoming volume on Podiatry Orthopedics (Schuster and Stafford), to be published under the auspices of The First Institute of Podiatry.

CHAPTER IX

LOCAL ANESTHESIA

Local anesthesia is a condition of insensibility brought about in a part of the body by the use of agents called local anesthetics. The person in whom the local anesthesia is produced does not lose consciousness as in general anesthesia, the part alone being made insensible.

There are many agents which, when applied to a part, by one means or another, cause that part to become insensible to pain, but for the podiatrist the following agents are best calculated to serve his purposes: cocaine, novocaine, alypin and urea hydrochloride, ethyl chloride, ethyl bromide, carbon dioxide snow, apothesine and ice. (See footnote page 148.)

Cocaine is an alkaloid extracted from coca leaves. These latter are not to be confused with cocoa, the seed of the chocolate tree. When cocaine is treated with hydrochloric acid, hydrochloride of cocaine is produced which occurs in a white crystalline powder, soluble in water and alcohol. When injected into the skin, or applied to an open wound, it acts as a paralyzant to the vaso-dilators and as a stimulant to the vaso-constrictors When applying this drug, a tourniquet should be used wherever possible, so as to prevent absorption This precaution is essential, as cocaine* is very toxic, and even small quantities may produce bad effects in some persons. There are cases on record in which 1/100 of a grain of this drug has produced all the symptoms of toxemia. whereas there are persons who can stand doses up to one grain. It is therefore essential to use judgment and care in administering a drug which on account of the idiosyncrasies of some people, is likely, even in minute doses, to produce serious, if not fatal symptoms.

---

*Podiatrists are advised to refrain from using cocaine on account of its dangers

In podiatry, a ½% solution is strong enough for general use, provided that time enough is allowed for the drug to be diffused. For an ordinary ingrown toe nail, two cubic centimeters of the above solution is usually sufficient to produce anesthesia of the part.

Novocaine is a synthetic preparation and occurs in colorless needles. It can be heated to 120 degrees Centigrade, without undergoing decomposition, which is not the case with cocaine hydrochloride. Although not quite as efficient as an anesthetic, novocaine is only 1/7 as toxic as cocaine and therefore can be used with greater safety and podiatrists generally have abandoned cocaine for novocaine. It has a slightly irritating action while being injected, but on the whole it is preferable to cocaine for podiatry practice. Physiologically, it has the same action as cocaine, and is indicated wherever the latter drug is used. It is usually injected in one per cent. solutions

Alypin occurs as a crystallin powder. It is a most efficient anesthetic and because of its non-toxic action, it is to be preferred in cases in which there is a fear of toxemia. Maximillian Stein, M.D., Professor of Surgery at the First Institute of Podiatry, has used this drug extensively for producing local anesthesia, and his results have been very satisfactory. For use in podiatry, a 1/4 to 1/8 per cent. solution is often sufficient It may be used freely in 1/4 per cent strength without danger of toxemia When injected, it produces no anemia, and consequently there is no danger of subsequent hemorrhage, such as might accompany the use of either cocaine or novocaine.

Quinine and urea hydrochloride is one of the quinine salts, consisting of one molecule of quinine hydrochloride and one molecule of urea. It has no toxic action when injected into the tissues, but it retards healing, and scar tissue forms over operated areas where it has been used. Many operators prefer this drug on account of its non-toxic action when used in large quantities, despite the likelihood of a scar and slow union. In parts of the body where contraction of the tissues is a desirable after-effect (such as would be the case in hemorrhoids), quinine and urea hydrochloride is to be preferred over other local anesthetics. David H. Levy, M.D., a well known surgeon of New York City, prefers it to all other local anesthetics.

Ethyl chloride and *ethyl bromide* are clear volatile liquids, and upon their rapid evaporation depend their anesthetic qualities. When a substance evaporates rapidly, it extracts the heat from surrounding bodies in doing so, and, consequently, when such a substance is applied to the skin, it soon extracts the heat from the part and with the local anemia thus produced, sensation is lost. Ethyl chloride and ethyl bromide are manufactured in tubes so arranged as to eject a fine stream of the liquid. When this stream comes in contact with the skin, evaporation is rapid and gradually the part becomes numb; continued, it becomes frozen. This method is not as efficient as the hypodermic injection because the anesthesia is not so lasting, moreover, the reaction is severe and painful. Otto Sjogren and Fred Schmitt, practitioners of known repute, have entirely discarded both of these drugs from their list of local anesthetics, for reasons above mentioned.

Carbon dioxide snow is prepared by allowing liquified carbon dioxide gas to slowly escape from its container into a glove finger, where it solidifies into a mass, assuming the shape and form of the receptacle; it is called the *carbon dioxide pencil*. When this mass or pencil is applied to a part, it extracts the heat and anesthetizes by freezing. The dangers attending the use of the carbon dioxide pencil are the same as with ethyl chloride or ethyl bromide and, due to its extremely low temperature, there is danger of causing death of the tissues and of producing conditions giving rise to subsequent ulcerations that are slow to heal. As an anesthetic, it is not advised for podiatry.

Technic of Producing Local Anesthesia. There are three methods of producing local anesthesia: (1) the hypodermatic method: (2) the pressure method (3) freezing.

The freezing method is of no great value to the podiatrist, and having been already briefly described, further comment is deemed unnecessary.

The pressure method of producing local anesthesia is new, and although extensively employed in the practice of dentistry, podiatry offers but little opportunity for its free use. It is necessary to have an exposed nerve, such as is found in the cavities of painful teeth, or an open wound into which the drug can be absorbed, before this method can be used. In cases of ingrown toe nail, in which the groove is lacerated, either by the patient or by the nail itself, pressure anesthesia is often efficacious. Small pellets containing cocaine or novocaine, with adrenalin, are put on the market for this purpose. One of these pellets is placed in the nail groove, and a drop of alcohol is made to fall on it. The contents of the pellet are promptly dissolved by the alcohol, whereupon the operator places his thumb over the nail groove between the nail and the nail flap and exerts downward pressure. This forces the dissolved fluid into the tissues, where it acts the same as if it were injected. This procedure is painful for just a moment while the pressure is being applied, but the pain soon ceases and nerve sensibility is lost.

The most generally used method of applying local anesthetics is by means of the hypodermic syringe and is called the *hypodermatic method. This is preferable to all other forms of inducing local insensibility, and if the technic is mastered, operations will be painless with the exception of the initial prick of the needle.

The Hypodermic Syringe should be so constructed that it may be sterilized by boiling. There are many types of such instruments sold, and in making a selection, only those which will permit such boiling should be considered. The all glass syringe or the glass and metal syringe with the metal piston are best, because the fluid contained therein is

---
*Hypodermic and hypodermatic are synonymous terms although medical lexicographers, as a rule, give preference to the latter.

visible, thus preventing the injection of air. Needles should be of the rust-proof variety and for use in podiatry, they should be one-half or one inch long and have a twenty or twenty-two gauge lumen.

After the syringe has been sterilized, it should be adjusted and the fluid drawn into it after the needle is attached to the barrel. The entire instrument is then turned, needle up, and the air that may be in the barrel is expelled by pressure on the piston. When this is done, the syringe is ready for use.

If the needle is sterile, the only preparation necessary for the skin is to paint it with tincture of iodine, and then the injection of the anesthetic may be commenced. The area to be anesthetized is determined, and then at the most proximal portion, the skin is grasped between the thumb and forefinger of the left hand. The syringe should be held in the right hand with the barrel between the first and middle fingers, and the thumb on the piston. When the skin has been blanched by the pressure of the fingers of the left hand, the point of the needle, lumen downward, is thrust into the skin with a quick movement and immediately after, pressure is brought to bear upon the piston. As the fluid enters the tissues, it produces a blanched area which is called a wheal. As the wheal is formed, the needle is gradually moved forward in the derma until it is inserted as far as the base. It is then withdrawn, and a second injection is commenced, a little back of the distal end of the wheal. This second injection, being started in a part already anesthetized, will cause no pain. So the needle is gradually moved forward in the derma until the desired area has been covered.

When the deeper tissues are to be anesthetized, the needle may be directed at an angle to the surface, pressure being borne on the piston of the syringe as the needle gradually moves deeper into the flesh. It must be remembered that if the needle is re-inserted into an area that is already deadened, there will be no pain The fluid should be ejected from the syringe slowly, which insures an even distribution of the drug, as well as comfort to the patient, while the anesthetic is being administered. Most drugs cause a burning sensation if injected too rapidly.

The most common lesion for which local anesthetics are used in podiatry is the ingrown toe nail, and to get good results in these cases, the technic must be followed in detail. After the derma has been anesthetized over the region of the nail root and groove, one deep injection should be made at the root, and vertically to the skin. This will insure loss of sensation when the root is cut and when the matrix at this point is curetted.

To prevent the absorption of toxic drugs into the system, some means should be devised to cut off the circulation during the operation. This is accomplished by the tourniquet, which is usually made of flexible, solid rubber, about one-sixteenth or one-eighth inch-in diameter and about a foot long. When this band is tied around the base of the toe, and pulled tight, it cuts off the circulation. Tourniquets cannot be used when operating upon the foot proper, and in these cases it is necessary to be guarded in the use of toxic drugs.

After the use of cocaine or novocaine there is a reaction, and occasionally the pains produced by this reaction are severe. These pains may be alleviated to some extent by the use of wet dressings, but they last only for a short time so that it is often unnecessary to treat them. The patient should be warned of the reaction. The local anemia produced by the injection of these drugs is subsequently followed by hyperemia, and it is therefore necessary to guard against hemorrhage in cases in which free incisions have been made. Wounds should be packed, and proper bandages should be applied to prevent any such possibilities.

Apothesine (Parke Davis & Co.) is a new synthetic preparation of definite chemical composition. It is 1/8 as toxic as cocaine, is very soluble in water and alcohol, and may be sterilized by boiling for five or ten minutes. It is used in a one per cent solution and came into favor during the war, by reason of the scarcity of cocaine and novocaine. Apothesine is not a habit forming drug and is therefore easily obtainable. At The First Institute of Podiatry this preparation and novocaine are almost exclusively used for producing local anesthesias.

CHAPTER X

HELOMA

Derivation. The word has its origin in the Greek *"helos,"* meaning corn; (plural: *helomata*).

In the accompanying cut will be found a photograph of two building nails bearing the name and time of the reign

BUILDING NAILS (HELOS) USED IN PRE-HISTORIC TIMES

of King Gudea in Ur, Chaldea, about 2500 B.C. Plaster casts of the above were presented to The First Institute of Podiatry by Fridtjov Anderson, Colonel in the Norwegian Artillery. These nails were called helos and because of their semblance to the foot excrescences, commonly called corns, the latter were therefore named helomata.

Synonyms. Corn, clavus, horn

Definition. An heloma is a circumscribed, conical, deep seated overgrowth of the epidermis, the apex of which presses down upon the derma. Corns usually occur about the toes, but may appear upon any part of the body subject to friction or pressure They range in size from a pin head to a ten cent piece.

According to their appearance, texture or composition, helomata are classified as follows:

> Heloma durum, or hard corn
> Heloma molle, or soft corn
> Heloma vasculare, or vascular corn
> Heloma miliare, or seed corn

HELOMA DURUM

Heloma durum is a hard circumscribed overgrowth of the epidermis and may occur as above stated, but is usually found on the outer side of the fifth toe, the dorsum of the second, third and fourth toes, and on the plantar surface of the inter-phalangeal joint of the great toe

Symptoms. The symptoms of an heloma durum may be classified as subjective and objective. The chief subjective symptom is pain in varying degrees. The formation of the growth produces a pressure upon the nerves which, in turn, gives rise to pain varying from a dull and mild sensation to a sharp and intense excitation. These pains are increased when the part affected is further irritated by ill-fitting shoes, by friction or by other pressure.

It is a well known fact that the pain in a corn is increased when the weather is about to change. Helomata, which at other times cause no inconvenience, will prove a source of annoyance at this time. This is due to certain physiologic changes that take place in the body as follows: the atmosphere preceding a storm becomes more and more charged with moisture. As this increases, the function of the skin, namely the elimination of liquid waste, is gradually diminished. This function is taken up and performed by the kidneys, and as the air becomes fully charged with moisture, the entire work of elimination is carried on by these latter organs This physiologic change requires a readjustment of the blood supply and the nerves which control it, so as to bring about a proper equilibrium. In this latter procedure the little nerve fibres are unfavorably influenced, and pain results. The gradually increased uncomfortableness that is experienced is due to gradual increase in the humidity and when precipitation takes place and the air is freed from this atmospheric pressure, relief is afforded.

The patient will complain of pain while shoes and stockings are worn, but will feel relieved when they are removed, except in cases where inflammatory processes have commenced. The pains at these times are of the throbbing, pulsating variety, such as accompany all inflammations.

A clinical examination of an heloma durum shows a horny mass of epidermic cells crowded together with no regular formation within the growth. There is a sharp line of demarcation between it and the surrounding tissues and it is also distinguished by its darker, yellowish color in contradistinction to the healthy pink of the normal skin. Within the growth, and usually at its centre, may be seen a darker, more compact mass, which penetrates deeper into the tissues This is the radix or nucleus, incorrectly termed the root, or the eye, of the corn. The skin immediately surrounding the heloma usually presents a red line, due to the somewhat lessened irritation that originally produced the corn. The color is due to congestion in the derma.

Etiology. Helomata dura are commonly caused by direct intermittent friction or pressure of ill fitting shoes. The shoes may be too tight, thereby causing pressure, or they may be too loose, thereby causing friction. Helomata that appear on the plantar surface of the foot may be caused either by some roughness in the finish of the shoe or by soles which are too thin, or by downward displacement of the heads of the metatarsal bones beneath, caused by wearing shoes that are not anatomically correct.

Imperfections in the stockings, such as knots in the worsted or poor workmanship in darning, are also factors in producing helomata. Any concentrated or undue local pressure is capable of causing this overgrowth, provided, however, that the pressure is not primarily of sufficient intensity to set up such an amount of congestion and consequent inflammation as to lead at once to an ulceration of the part.

The same principle of intermittent friction and pressure, with counter-pressure, as a cause for helomata holds good on any part of the body surface.

Pathology. The pathologic changes accompanying the development of an heloma are mostly morphologic. The intermittent friction and pressure produce first an irritation or excitation of the cutaneous nerves, this causes an increased blood supply to the part and congestion takes place in the derma immediately beneath.

Were this pressure or friction to cease at this time, nature would restore the tissues to their normal condition in a very short time; but, as this pressure or friction is continued from day to day, the habitual congestion produces a chronic enlargement or hypertrophy of the papillae of the derma.

The epidermic cells originate from the material supplied by the blood plasma, which is conveyed through the walls of the capillaries to the surface of the basement membrane by endosomis, where it forms into granules which contain nuclei of unusual size. These granules, the first organic shape of the future cells, gradually develop into nucleated cells.

Bearing in mind the development of the cells in the normal skin, with an increased blood supply, there will naturally be a more rapid proliferation or development of cells taking place over the enlarged papillæ than over the surrounding normal ones. This excessive development of cells causes an abnormal upward crowding of the preceding cells, with the result that the horny layer gradually becomes thickened. With this thickened layer acting as a counterpressure from above, cornification of the tender cells takes place more rapidly with each succeeding new layer that is added to the under portion of that already formed. The growth at this time takes place at the interior and lateral portions of the heloma, principally the former

This process in due time causes the epidermis to become transformed into a dense homogeneous mass of cells which is called a *callosity* The size of the callosity is determined by the area of the papillæ affected.

The etiologic factors which cause the enlargement of the papillæ and the overgrowth of the epidermic cells continue, and that part of the growth which was first formed and is most usually central, becomes more dense than the surrounding callosity. This is due to the greater irritation to which it is subjected, and eventually this extends downward and penetrates the derma. The pressure of this new development, known as a "radix," against the papillæ, causes these organisms to undergo progressive atrophy with the result that they are at times completely absorbed. Thus, we have the common heloma durum. The heloma now receives its nourishment from the lateral portions, which still continue to maintain their increased vascularity.

It often happens that an heloma is subjected to unusual pressure during its formation, which causes serous effusion or even subcutaneous hemorrhage in minute quantities This effusion is absorbed by the soft cells which are in the process of transition into horny tissue. These cells take on a laminated appearance which present different tints, from a light yellow to a dark red

The nerve filaments of the skin are also affected during the development of an heloma, and when this process is marked, the condition known as neuro-fibrous heloma is the result. These little neuromata very often become quite enlarged. The favorite location for this condition is the inner plantar edge of the great toe, and sometimes the outer plantar edge of the metatarsophalangeal joint of the fifth toe.

These helomata consist of two or three little irregularly shaped structures extending downward into the derma and in juxtaposition to each other, the septum dividing these structures being made up of one or more rows of enlarged papillæ which have become highly vitalized through the enlargement of the nerve fibres contained in them. The condition is very painful and great care must be exercised when operating upon them. The most logical reason for their appearance upon the plantar edges seems to be the fact that the long papillæ of the plantar surface leave off abruptly and are joined by the shorter ones of the dorsum. The line of junction is undoubtedly subjected to a greater degree of irritation than where the size of the papillæ is uniform.

Diagnosis. A typical heloma durum is a mass of epidermic cells, round in shape and varying in size. The color is usually yellow, but in cases where serous or bloody infiltration has taken place, the color may increase to red or even to dark purple.

Heloma durum may be mistaken for heloma vasculare or verruca, on account of the dark blood stains which are often in evidence, but when the top layers of the heloma are removed, the dark spots which were mistaken for blood vessels are not found in the growth proper, but are deep in the structure resting against the derma. When these spots, which are clots, are cut with the knife, no bleeding occurs; whereas, if the condition were one of heloma vasculare or verruca, hemorrhage would be produced.

Lesions of several skin diseases, such as eczema and psoriasis, very often produce scales or crusts on the feet which might be mistaken for helomata, for when the fingers are passed over them they feel as if they were an overgrowth of the skin. These scales or crusts, however, are usually loosened at the edges and the color is quite different, being red or white. Other indications of the presence of a skin affection will usually be found on other parts of the foot.

The radix, or nucleus, of the heloma is a characteristic which differentiates it from the ordinary callosity. The radix is a dark solid mass of epidermic cells which has an almost transparent appearance. When cutting an heloma, the radix may be felt by the tension produced as the knife passes through it.

Helomata dura found on the plantar surface of the foot over the heads of the metatarsal bones are not readily distinguished, due to the fact that they are covered by a layer of callous, which, when removed, exposes the nuclei to view.

Prognosis. The prognosis of heloma durum is uncertain. There are many cases on record which have disappeared after the first treatment and, on the other hand, some

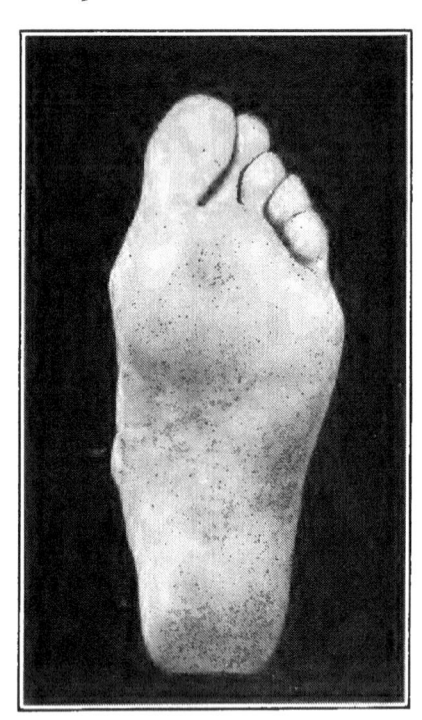

HELOMA DURUM ON PLANTAR SURFACE

cases regularly recur notwithstanding many years of regular attention. This is due to two conditions: first, the cause of the heloma, namely, the continued wearing of the shoe, and, second, the papillæ beneath the growth remain enlarged and continue their function of excessive cell proliferation. The latter reason is more important than the first, for, even in cases where proper foot gear is provided and no friction or pressure is permitted, the heloma may continue to grow The only way to account for the total disappearance of some helomata, after treatment, is, that when the growth is removed, the size of the papillæ diminishes and normal function is restored. The situation of heloma durum is very important in considering the ultimate cure of the growth Those on the outer aspect of the little toe rarely get well, due to the prominent position of that digit, while those on the plantar surface over the heads of the metatarsals are often completely cured after the proper treatment has been applied When the heads of the metatarsal bones have been properly adjusted, the helomata produced by their downward displacement gradually disappear.

Treatment. The treatment of heloma durum is divided into three classes, viz.: preventive, palliative and operative

Preventive treatment consists in securing freedom from friction of or pressure on the parts affected. Foot gear of proper size and shape is essential The shoes should be neither too tight nor too loose; they should fit snugly in the heel, and the toe box and front of the shoe should be broad enough to allow of freedom for the toes. The quality and kind of leather used for the shoe should also be considered This should be soft and well seasoned, vici kid and calf skin being preferred. Patent leather and colt skin are undesirable, in that they are hard and almost air tight Shoes made to measure on a last constructed from a plaster of Paris cast of the foot, are the best. In making a shoe, consideration should be given to other deformities, such as flat foot, metatarsalgia, etc, and means for correcting these ailments should be taken.

The stocking should be large enough to prevent pressure on either lateral side of the foot. There are stockings on the market which are cut for each foot and are known as right and left stockings. These are very desirable, as they prevent distortion of the toes, which is often produced by the regular stocking cut to a point at the third toe. The material is of little consequence, except that wool or cotton absorbs moisture excreted by the glands better than silk

Palliative treatment includes the application of palliative agents, among which silver nitrate and salicylic acid are most serviceable. These remedies cause dessication and shrinkage of the horny growth, which is thus made to shell out from the bed in which it lies. This method of treating an heloma durum is long and tedious, as many applications of the drugs are required to obtain a result. Great care must be exercised to prevent the applications from touching the surrounding normal skin. The virtue of so-called corn cures, which are very plentiful and are given artistic names, all depend upon some drug or chemical, chief among which is salicylic acid. The danger to the layman is readily seen, for when these agents are applied carelessly or in large quantities, the action is too severe, and ulceration and infection is the result.

When the practitioner finds it necessary to resort to palliative measures in the treatment of an heloma durum the following procedure is advised: the tissues surrounding the horny growth are protected by painting with several layers of collodion or glycerine jelly (Unna) A piece of salicylic acid plaster is cut to the size of the heloma and placed over it and a proper protection applied. Or, a shield can be fitted around the part and in the aperture is placed a 25% salicylic ointment, and the entire dressing is covered with adhesive plaster This dressing is allowed to remain in contact with the part for two or three days, when the dressing is removed and the white, macerated tissues are scraped or cut away. The treatment is again applied and repeated as often as necessary (See chapter, *Shields and Shielding.*)

Operative treatment may be divided into two classes, the radical and the non-radical. The *radical* method is painful, but with the use of local anesthetics, good results are obtained without discomfort to the patient. Alypin, 1:2%, quinine and urea hydrochloride, 2%, or novocaine, 1% (the latter being preferred by the writer) may be used to produce local anesthesia*. The parts are thoroughly cleansed and made aseptic by washing with the tincture of green soap, followed by alcohol, 60%, and finally painting the entire surface, including the surrounding parts with tincture of iodine. The hypodermic needle and syringe and all the instruments to be used in the operation are boiled in water for at least ten minutes. A spot is selected for the injection of the anesthetic, and ethyl chloride is sprayed on it, to make the primary injection of the needle painless. The needle is forced into the derma and pressure brought to bear on the piston of the syringe, as it moves forward into the tissues. By following the wheal thus produced, the entire area surrounding the heloma can be anesthetized.

When the anesthesia is complete, two semi-eliptic incisions, meeting at their extremities, are made through the skin, care being taken that they penetrate the subcutaneous tissue. These incisions should completely envelop the growth The tissues between the incisions are seized with an artery forceps, and the entire wedge, including the derma and subcutaneous tissue, is dissected out This produces free oozing, and it may be necessary to twist a small vessel. Hemorrhage is never severe. The edges of the wound are brought together (apposition should be perfect) by one or two fine sutures and primary union takes place in a few days, or, if the wound is not large, the part may be dressed and allowed to heal by granulation. Subsequent dressings should include shields for the prevention of friction or pressure.

Dr. Robert T. Morris, of New York City, recommends skin grafting with this operation, in order to prevent the formation of scar tissue, a very desirable consideration. After the tissue has been dissected out, some skin is taken from the fleshy part of the leg and is attached over the wound. This eliminates drawing the edges of the wound together, which procedure often causes harmful after-effects.

*Apothesine, lately introduced, is proving efficacious and reliable (see page 148)

The *non-radical operative* treatment of heloma durum is the most popular and practical method employed by chiropodists today. The growth is removed down to the true skin, care being taken that this layer is not punctured and bleeding thus produced.

There are two general methods of procedure for the surgical treatment of callositas and helomata in vogue today. These are known as the paring or shaving method and the dissection or excision method. This nomenclature is derived from the operations themselves.

As the term implies, the paring method consists of removing the callouses with the chisel, knife or scalpel by shaving away the growth with a series of knife strokes or cuts, and the subsequent removal of the cone body or radix with the point of the same or a similar instrument.

Technic of the Shaving Method. The part is thoroughly cleansed with a standard antiseptic, such as phenol, 5%, lysol, 1%, or cresol, 1%, and this is followed by alcohol, 60%, which is allowed to remain in contact with the heloma for a few minutes. The instrument employed should be sterilized by boiling in water for at least fifteen minutes or by placing it in phenol, 95%, until the liquid clings to the blade, followed by alcohol, 95%.

After thorough asepsis has been obtained, the tissues adjoining the area to be removed are held firmly between the thumb and index finger of the left hand and the knife is grasped firmly with the fingers of the right hand.

By holding the tissues of the part firmly so that they may not move, the pain to the patient and the danger of invading the vascular tissues is minimized. A knife, no matter how sharp, is bound to pull the tissues overlying a tender and inflamed part unless these tissues are in some way prevented from moving.

After the overlying callouses have been thoroughly pared away, and the part is found to be soft and flexible, the nuclei are removed. In removing these hard bodies the operator who shaves or pares, practically becomes a dissector. With a sharp pointed knife the heloma is loosened from the surrounding soft parts until entirely freed, when it is lifted out Should there be two or more helomata under one callous, the same procedure is adopted for each individual growth until all are removed and the whole area is found flexible.

The stroke of the knife in the shaving method is usually toward the operator, his fingers and thumbs being so arranged as to limit the distance which the blade may travel and so prevent cutting the patient or himself

In shaving an heloma on the dorsum of the intermediate toes, the index finger of the left hand is placed anterior to the hardened area and the thumb, posterior. The knife is then held as a penholder and the strokes are made toward the operator, the toe being moved or rotated to bring all the surfaces of the growth under the blade of the knife

On the plantar surface the operator, at times, is forced to work away from himself, but in most cases the blade is directed toward himself.

For operating on helomata between the toes, the knife is held as a penholder and the blade is directed toward the toe or web. Many of the practitioners who "shave" use a distinct dissection method for the removal of helomata in this location. They employ what is known as a "spoon" —a shallow flattened curette—and starting from the outer edge of the calloused area, work under the hardened layers until the entire growth is loosened, whereupon it is deftly removed.

The stroke of the chisel in the shaving method is usually away from the operator. This is in contra-distinction to the stroke of the knife or scalpel. When operating on the dorsum of the toes, however, most operators using the chisel direct the blade toward themselves, unless, as is common, the operator moves around in front of the patient, when the cutting is done away from the operator.

Technic of the Dissection Method. One of the oldest, yet one of the most popular methods of operation is that known as dissection. As will be understood by the term, this method is a procedure whereby the growth is excised by the helotomon, as a whole, from the underlying tissues This is in contra-distinction to the paring or shaving method.

Two of the best known practitioners who use this method of procedure are E. C. Rice, M.D., of Washington, D. C., and Charles F. Stevens, of Elmira, N. Y Dr. E. C Rice has this to say on the subject·

"The limited knowledge of the chiropodists of earlier years did not apply to their handling of instruments, which was professionally scientific to the highest degree The dissecting method was the method of operating in the early days.

"In the late fifties a practitioner by the name of Josiah Briggs taught many young men, among them Elliot W. Johnson, and the writer's father, W. E. Rice A Scotchman also instructed Nehemiah Kenison. They in turn taught others the dissection method. There will always be two professional methods of operating on helomata, the shaving (exfoliating) and the dissecting (excision) methods, and practitioners should understand both

"Those who have a light touch, if determined to learn, can become skillful in the art of dissecting, and, when acquired, their life's work will become a daily fascination The procedure calls for skill that compares with that employed by the eye, nose and throat specialists and is appreciated by the most eminent surgeons

"The word 'dissect' implies a separation, and this method permits the operator to separate the heloma from the normal tissue in one piece so that classification is made simple. In removing the growth in its entirety, it is possible to observe the various forms the nuclei take, and the classification the writer would make is as follows: granular, grain-like in appearance, sometimes called 'surface corn'; crescent, forming a semi-circle about the joint, wedge, having a wedge-shaped nucleus, commonly found on the plantar surface; cone, from its shape, thumb tack, also named from its shape; multiple nuclei, resembling any of the above named and having numerous central points; soft, the gristly tissue between the toes; elevated, protruding, horn shaped; circular, because of the form of the nucleus

"The instruments used in this method of operating are the chisel (helotomon—Dr. F. Oefele (editor,) and the iris mouse-toothed forceps.

"The original chiropodist's instrument in this country was a cross between the surgeon's scalpel and a chisel. The blade was shaped much like the human foot and was on a handle such as is used on the standard razor. From this first instrument of chiropody was evolved the only distinctive instrument of our profession, the chisel, which has been successfully used for more than half a century.

"It is distinctly a chiropodist's instrument, as much as the plane is the tool of the carpenter With this chisel the dissecting method is made possible, for its cutting edge, as its name suggests, is on the end of the instrument, and permits of the most delicate work. The chisel should be five and one-half inches long and should have a rough hexagon handle. The round or oval handles do not permit perfect finger control The blade or cutting edge may be oblique, straight or oval, as the operator desirs.

"The technic of the dissecting method of operating is as follows:

"The chisel is held in the right hand and the forceps in the left. Hold each as you would a correctly held penholder; to support and to steady the hands, let them rest gently on the fourth and fifth fingers; when operating between the toes, the supporting fingers rest upon and press aside the toes so as to give plenty of room for operating.

"The tissues at the periphery of the heloma are separated; with the forceps grasp the free edge and raise sufficiently to see the line of demarcation and use enough traction on the forceps to overcome the pressure of the chisel, not enough, however, to produce the sensation of pulling.

"When properly performed, the gentle lifting of the tissue prevents the nerve being pressed upon or pinched between the blade of the instrument and the underlying bone. The line of demarcation is made by the union of the light and dark shades of tissue, the normal being the light and the darker shade belonging to the heloma.

"Those who use the oval chisel find they can do more work and have fewer hemorrhages, and only occasionally do they find it necessary to use the nucleus dissector, which is required to remove an heloma of the thumb tack variety, as its shaft may extend to a depth of a fourth or a third of an inch. In dissecting this type of heloma, when the head of the same has been separated back to its shaft, the traction on the forceps is increased, the tissue being gently lifted and turned back. This tends to present the shaft toward the blade, and as cutting proceeds the shaft seems to be lifted up and out of the soft tissue into which it is embedded.

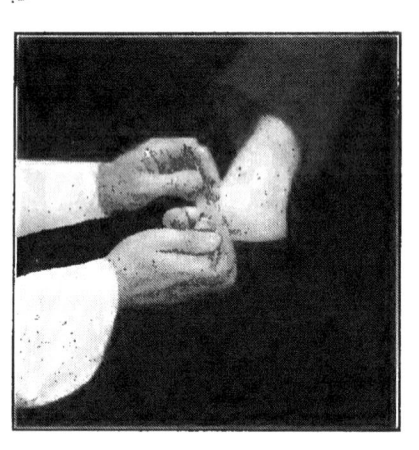

ILLUSTRATING METHOD OF SPREADING TOES APART BY USING FOURTH FINGER OF EACH HAND, MAKING OPERATION EASY

"To beginners, the writer would suggest the oval-shaped chisel and would advise practising first on the plantar surface."

C. F. Stevens contributes the following:

"Speaking generally and taking the average heloma as an example, my method of procedure would be somewhat as follows:

"These growths are hardly ever deep, and are removed

by the following process more easily than to chisel or pare. After the usual antiseptic precautions as to the operator's hands, instruments and the patient's foot have been taken, the operator grasps a sharp, pointed, slim instrument.

"Holding this knife with the right hand and with a small forceps in the left, he grasps the free part of the growth with the forceps, carefully raising this part to determine if possible how much is free and how much is attached to the deeper tissues.

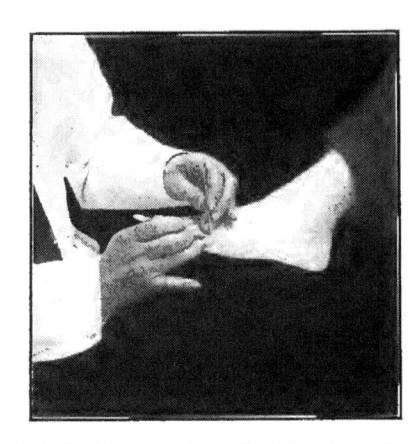

PROPER USE OF FINGERS ELIMINATES NECESSITY OF TOE SPREADERS

"With a sharp blade he makes a series of slight strokes, cutting but little at a time, on a line between the growth and the skin (the growth being darker than the skin), thus separating the excess deposit of horny cuticle from the skin, following every curve, deep part or point, until all is separated in the one mass. In this manner he is enabled to remove all in one piece. Dressings vary, according to the prominence of the part and the shoe worn.

"Since the writer was taught this method of procedure he has found it to be much easier to separate such a horny growth from its bed, than to try to pare it off in bits or shave it as the patient himself tries to do. Helomata being hard, very naturally resist the cutting of a knife, and the blade, therefore, when trying to pierce the hard mass, pulls on the sensitive tissues beneath, thus causing pain. Following the line between the normal and the abnormal tissues in operating, much softer integument is encountered; therefore, the cutting is easier and can be done with practically no pain.

"The cautious, careful operator will seldom invade the healthy tissues beneath sufficiently to cause capillary hemorrhage. A paring or shaving process could, of course, first be employed to remove the indurated callous, then proceed to carefully separate the deep parts as described in the case of heloma. Simply raising gently with the thumb forceps and cutting a very little at each stroke with a sharp pointed blade, following each wave or indentation indicated, as the work progresses, until each piece or mass is separated and removed, will be found a preferable procedure. However, we have found it as simple and easy to dissect the mass as a whole as to operate by paring and then removing the deeper parts

"In case of a deep-seated hard corn where the toe is red, inflamed and very sensitive, the first described method (as in heloma) is usually best. Often upon reaching the lowermost layers, one finds a quantity of pus. When this escapes, as it does, the pressure on the inflamed tissues is lessened, and the patient will allow the operator to proceed faster.

"With a deep-seated heloma on the sole of the foot, the same method is followed, no matter how deep or seriated. The operator (after one or two small cuts) gently raises the edge with the forceps, while with the same style of blade he cuts down and around the growth, until the whole piece with its radix is lifted out.

"In connection with this the writer hears some one say, 'even though you do remove the growth scientifically and without pain, severe pain will follow in an attempt to walk.'

"Of course, comfort depends in many instances on the dressing. The writer is not a great believer in heavy shielding and the method of dressing he employs is as follows: take a pledget of cotton which, when rolled, is about as large as the heloma just removed; place thereon a small amount of sedative in ointment form; place this in the cavity left by the removal of the growth, then cover all with a goodly sized piece of adhesive plaster. Instruct the patient to wear this for twenty-four hours, when he may remove the plaster. By this dressing the tissues that had been held up by the large heloma, are still held up by the rolled pledget of cotton, at the same time the cotton gradually flattens down with the patient's weight Thus the tissues are allowed to resume their normal position slowly and easily

"When the adhesive plaster is removed, the cotton dressing comes with it. The tissues adjust themselves in from twelve to twenty hours and thus an equilibrium is painlessly established.

"Several years ago the writer chanced on to this method of dressing and since then he has used it and found it to be very efficacious in a large majority of cases; he has termed it the 'filling dressing.'

"In operations on heloma molle the same surgical procedure is employed. It matters not whether the growth be on the side of the toe, or deep down between the toes on the web. The sharp, fine pointed, narrow blade enables one to operate in a closely contracted space, and when used with short little cuts the blade reaches down, around and under the growth, thus loosening it completely and leaving its usually deep seat, clear and free from any parts which might remain, if chiseling or gouging were employed "

(The authors of this work all operate with the knife or scalpel and have found that form of instrument very satisfactory. The beginner is advised to study and learn both methods so that he may be able to use both at any time The fact that there are two methods does not mean that one is better than the other. There are many successful practitioners of both classes.)

Some persons have a great amount of dorsi-flexion of the toes, due to hammer toe or hallux flexus, and they usually develop an heloma on the distal end of the toe, under the nail. This is treated by cutting away the nail over the growth, and when the heloma is exposed to view it is treated in the same way as other helomata dura

The subsequent dressings for helomata depend upon

the state of the tissues beneath. Care should be exercised in operating so as not to cut too close to the normal skin, otherwise the parts become extremely sensitive.

The epidermis is a storehouse for bacteria, and when an heloma is removed, there is always a possibility that some of these bacteria may enter the body through some slight and invisible abrasion which does not necessarily bleed. It is, therefore, necessary to take precautions against this danger, and this is best done by painting all surfaces operated upon with a 4% solution of tincture of iodine (this may be made by diluting the official tincture with an equal amount of grain alcohol). This should be followed by painting these same surfaces with icthyolated collodion or nafalan collodion.

If the toe is inflamed it is treated with an agent that has the power to reduce inflammation. In severe inflammations, a wet dressing of Burow's solution may be used to good advantage. The principal ingredient of this solution is aluminum acetate, which is astringent in its action, and a wet dressing applied for twenty-four hours will usually reduce the condition In milder cases of inflammation, ointments of icthyol, 10 or 15%, may be applied This means of medication is very desirable whenever the application of a shield is indicated, because the aperture of the shield is a suitable place for ointment dressings.

When an heloma is found to be infected, the growth should be removed and the pus present evacuated. This should be followed by the application of hydrogen peroxide and the parts should then be irrigated with bichloride of mercury solution (1/4000). The wound may now be treated with a wet dressing of Burow's solution or, in severe cases in which there is an indication of the presence of cellulitis, bichloride of mercury solution (1/5000) for twenty-four to forty-eight hours, should be similarly applied

Subsequent dressings to stimulate granulation and promote healing may be applied, balsam of Peru or silver nitrate ointment or colloidal iodine being very efficacious.

The latest medication for infected areas, either great or small, and one of the many discoveries in surgical treatment since the beginning of the present war, is the Dakin solution. The worth of the application of this solution is based upon the helpful influence of free chlorine in small quantities, to tissues that have been mutilated either by injury or infection. Chlorazene tablets, purchasable in all drug stores, contain the elements desired for this treatment. Liquid chlorine ampules (J & J) also make an accurate Dakin solution.

If, upon examination, an infection shows that the deeper tissues, such as the periosteum or the bone, are involved, the patient should be sent to the surgeon, whose function it is to treat such cases, who will make incisions into the soft tissues so as to establish free drainage. The wound thus produced is packed with sterile gauze, and often with the aid of wet dressings, and nothing more, the wound is allowed to drain and heal.

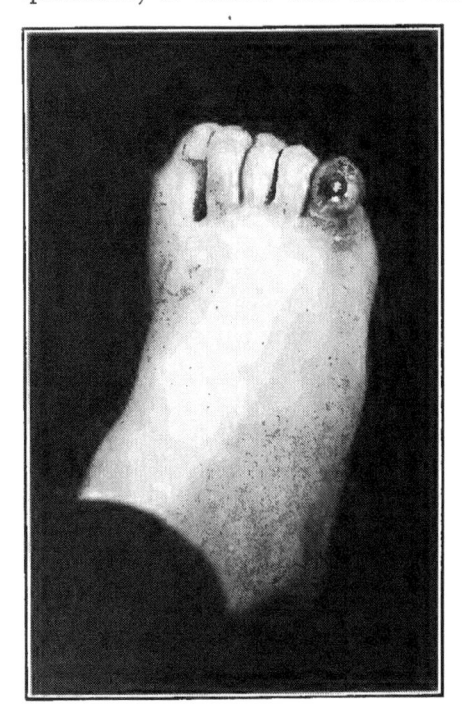

INFECTED HELOMA

The protection of the parts after an heloma has been removed, so as to insure comfort to the patient, is an all important part of the treatment of this ailment and a special chapter has been devoted to this feature of chiropody practice. (See Chapter *Shields and Shielding*.) There are certain types of helomata dura that are never relieved of pain, even after operation, unless a well-fitted shield has been applied.

HELOMA MOLLE

Definition. Heloma molle is a soft, white, macerated growth found between the toes, principally in the web of the fourth interosseous space and on the lateral sides of the interphalangeal joints of the toes.

Symptoms. The pain accompanying heloma molle varies with the degree of pressure brought to bear upon the toes. Where the heloma is situated in the web of the fourth and fifth toes, there is a sensation as if there were some foreign body, such as a pebble, between the toes, and as the growth develops the pain becomes gradually worse. The pain of an heloma molle, in other parts, is similar to the pain of heloma durum, and usually ceases when the foot is not encased in a shoe.

Upon examination, an heloma molle presents a white soft mass, having the consistency of rubber. There is no sharp line of demarcation between the lesion and the healthy skin. This is due to the blanching of all the tissues that come in contact with the excretions. In some instances there is a yellow ridge surrounding the neoplasm. The growth is superficial, due to its anatomic position. There is very little soft tissue between the epidermis and the lateral sides of the extremities of the phalanges, and therefore there is no possibility of the growth becoming deep seated, as in heloma durum. The radix, or nucleus, when present, is of a dirty white color.

Helomata mollia found in the web of the fourth and fifth toes, have well-defined nuclei which penetrate into the interosseous space between the metatarsal bones. These are easily distinguished since, as the surrounding callous is removed, they appear as a dirty white spot in an area of healthy pink skin.

Etiology. Helomata mollia are caused by shoes, the same as other types of helomata, but in this case the foot gear acts as a secondary cause. Normally the phalanges are placed so that the base of one bone is opposite the head of another. When lateral pressure is brought to bear upon the toes, these bones press upon each other and thus produce an overgrowth of skin cells.

The sweat glands continue to functionate, but the parts being pressed together, do not allow the perspiration to evaporate; hence, there is an accumulation of moisture which acts upon the skin, producing a soft, white, macerated mass, with a rubber-like texture.

In the case of helomata mollia found in the web of the fourth and fifth toes, there is an outward rotation of the head of the fourth metatarsal bone, due to the lateral pressure on this region, causing the bone to drop and rotate outward; this in turn presses upon the base of the fifth proximal phalanx.

Pathology. The pathology of heloma molle is identical with that of heloma durum, except that the nucleus is rarely deep-seated. The epidermis composing heloma molle has no distinct cell formation, because of the macerated condition of the mass, but occasionally the nucleus of such a lesion, found in the web of the fourth and fifth toes, shows some of the original cell formation. Inflammation, terminating in suppuration, is very often encountered in this condition. Because of uncleanliness of the parts, bacteria thrive in this locality and the acidity of the moisture very often produces a fissure or abrasion in the tissues which may lead to infection and subsequent suppuration.

Diagnosis. The typical heloma molle is a mass of epidermic cells rarely larger than half the size of a dime. The color is white, with a dark grey centre, denoting the radix.

Very often an ordinary exfoliation of the epidermis between the toes may take on the appearance of an heloma molle, but careful examination will show that there is no overgrowth of epidermis. This exfoliation is easily loosened with a pair of forceps.

Fissured toe webs, accompanied by exudation and exfoliation of skin, may be mistaken for heloma molle, and treatment inaugurated for the latter condition will produce bad results, particularly if chemicals are used.

There need be no doubt about making a positive diagnosis if the color and texture of the growth be borne in mind. The finger passed over the affected surface will give the sensation of increased tissue.

Prognosis. The possibilities of the ultimate disappearance of helomata mollia is good. If the proper shoes are worn and the proper treatment be installed, the growths will gradually become smaller and will finally disappear.

The helomata that appear between the toes on the interphalangeal joints are most easily cured, by simply keeping the adjacent sides of the toes separated. Those that appear on the outer lateral side of the great toe do not respond to treatment as readily as the other types, for there is more soft tissue over this joint and usually the great toe is in a fixed position and does not easily straighten.

Helomata mollia that appear in the web of the fourth and fifth toes can also be permanently cured, but it is neces-

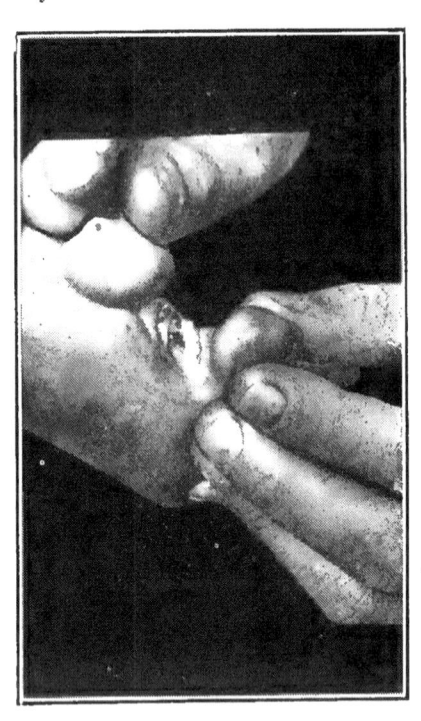

HELOMA MOLLE

sary to raise the head of the offending metatarsal bone, as well as to separate the toes.

Bearing in mind the etiology of heloma molle, and installing treatment which will correct or remove these causes, time and conscientious treatment will ordinarily insure a favorable outcome.

Treatment. Treatment of helomata mollia is divided into two classes: the non-radical surgical and the therapeutic. The latter method is the most popular, as it is very often impossible to use the knife. The texture of the skin, and the anatomic position of the growth often make it impossible to use an instrument with a cutting edge with a view to obtaining good results.

The *non-radical surgical* method consists of removing the corn in much the same way that an heloma durum is removed. The long cutting edges of knives and chisels are not well adapted for work between the toes, and for this purpose the "golf stick" and the "soft corn spoon" have been devised and are used extensively. The "golf stick" is an instrument which, as its name indicates, resembles the stick used by the golfer. Its cutting edge is almost at right angles to the handle and is about three-eighths of an inch long. This makes a very desirable instrument for removing helomata mollia on the lateral sides of the interphalangeal joints. The end of the instrument is rounded so as to allow for the removal of nuclei, if present. The cutting edge of the "soft corn spoon" extends almost around the entire instrument, and admits of a circular movement such as is employed in dissecting helomata dura. This instrument is used for removing soft corns that appear in the web of the toes, and is very efficient, inasmuch as by its use the operator is enabled to remove the growth without cutting into the tissues, as is often done with a knife or a chisel having a long straight edge.

The *therapeutic* method of treating heloma molle depends upon the caustic action of several drugs, among which may be mentioned salicylic acid, trichloracetic acid and silver nitrate. The two latter are used only occasionally, as they are powerful caustics, and unless applied with great caution they may produce harmful results.

Salicylic acid finds great favor among practitioners of podiatry, and the usual technic is as follows: after asepsis has been practised and the growth cannot be removed by the use of the knife, an ointment of salicylic acid, 15%, is applied over the growth, care being taken that the medication does not come in contact with the surrounding normal tissues. This is covered with a protective cocoon dressing, or the ointment may be applied into the aperture of the shield, if one is used. The dressing is allowed to remain in contact with the part for from four to seven days, depending upon the thickness of the skin. When the dressing is removed, the entire mass will be found, as a rule, to b loosened from the tissues beneath. If all of the growth is not thus loosed, the treatment is repeated and the patient is instructed to return in the prescribed length of time.

Shielding plays an important part in the treatment of heloma molle. For the type that forms on the lateral sides of the interphalangeal joints, a shield of the oval type with the aperture over the affected part, is most efficient, while for those that appear in the web of the toes, an oval shield with a semi-circular opening on the proximal end, which sets between the toes and protects the growth, is most desirable. In connection with a shield to protect the growth and separate the toes, it is necessary to raise the head of the affected metatarsal bone, which is the cause of this type of heloma molle. For this purpose, Alfred Ahrens, of New York City, has devised a dressing which he terms the "duck shield," because of its resemblance to that animal. This shield has a dual function. It separates the toes and then passes down to the plantar surface of the foot over the metatarsal bone, and acts as a pad to raise the bone. The continuous application of this device to helomata mollia of this variety will produce good results.

HELOMA VASCULARE

Definition. Heloma vasculare, or vascular corn, is an overgrowth of the epidermis in which enlarged and elongated blood vessels are found.

Symptoms. The growths usually appear on the plantar surface of the foot, but occasionally they may develop in old callouses and helomata situated on the dorsal surface of the fifth toe. Pain is more severe than in other forms of helomata, the patient complaining of a burning sensation when not in a standing position. This form of growth is similar in appearance to heloma durum, having in addition small dark-red spots scattered throughout it, which bleed upon being cut. These spots are not blood clots, such as are found in helomata dura as the result of injury, but are distinct blood vessels. The composition of the tissues is very dense, particularly when the growth is situated over the head of a bone, as is ordinarily the case when it appears on the plantar surface. The color of the entire mass is somewhat darker than in heloma durum, being grayish, or sometimes brownish, in appearance.

Etiology. As previously stated, helomata of all types are due to intermittent friction and pressure. The blood vessels that are found in this particular form are forced into the epidermis owing to lateral pressure of the shoes, or to the pinching of tight stockings. Why the blood vessels should be forced up into the epidermis is most peculiar, but helomata vasculare appear where the normal papillae are longest, and this increased length of the vessels tends to force them up into the dead skin. Athletes, particularly runners and jumpers, are most commonly afflicted.

Pathology. Heloma vasculare consists of an overgrowth of epidermic cells in which are found the elongated vessels. There is an increase in epithelial tissue, but there is no increase in the quantity of the connective tissue and blood vessels, as in verruca. The blood vessels leave the papillary layer of the derma and enter directly into the epidermis, without any elevation of the surrounding connective tissue. On some occasions a nerve ending is found embedded in the callous mass. This adds considerably to the pain, but is not the true neuro-fibrous corn described under heloma durum, which has no accompanying blood vessels. The area surrounding an heloma vasculare is usually inflamed, but the inflammation rarely terminates in suppuration.

Diagnosis. The true heloma vasculare may be easily distinguished from verruca when the two conditions appear on the dorsal surface or any surface not subjected to extreme pressure, in that the latter is an overgrowth of all the layers of the skin, including the derma, and has a characteristic cauliflower appearance. However, when verrucæ appear on the plantar surface, they lose their cauliflower appearance and become flattened; they then resemble heloma vasculare, except that they are somewhat darker.

The blood vessels in heloma vasculare are not so numerous as in verruca, but this diagnostic point may not always manifest itself to the naked eye. A differential diagnosis between these two conditions is of no great importance, as the treatment is practically identical.

Heloma vasculare may be readily distinguished from heloma durum by the small red spots found therein which bleed when cut. Very often an heloma durum has a dark red spot at the base of the mass, due to the rupture of a small vessel and consequent clotting of the blood. This dark red spot does not bleed when the knife is passed through it, denoting the absence of blood vessels.

Prognosis. Heloma vasculare will always respond when the treatment is thorough. There may be a recurrence of heloma durum over the spot where the original growth was located, but the vascular condition, when once eradicated, should not return.

Treatment. The treatment of heloma vasculare may be divided into three classes, viz.: surgical, medicinal and mechanical.

The technic of the *surgical* method is as follows: the

part is cleansed with tincture of green soap, followed by the application of tincture of iodine, 4%. The instruments having been sterilized, the part is anesthetized by the hypodermic method and a semi-eliptic incision is made a little to the outside of one-half the growth. The flap thus produced is seized with an artery forceps. The forceps are then raised and the rest of the growth is dissected out with a sharp knife or with a heavy pointed scissors. When the entire growth has thus been eradicated, a few layers of gauze should be placed over the part to produce pressure. A bandage should be applied over all to hold the dressing in place. This may be removed in three or four days, provided no inflammation is present, and the subsequent dressing should contain balsam of Peru or some other stimulant.

The *medicinal* or *chemical* treatment of heloma vasculare consists of the gradual destruction of the growth by means of chemicals, chief among which are nitric acid, potassium hydroxide and salicylic acid. If nitric acid is employed, the callous is removed so as to produce a slight oozing of blood, and a drop of the acid is allowed to fall in the centre of the mass. This is allowed to remain in contact with the part for two days, when the eschar produced is removed, and the acid is again applied. This treatment is continued as long as necessary to completely destroy the growth; when a slight exudation of pus is noticed, the application of the acid should cease. The subsequent ulcer thus produced is treated in the same manner as any other ulcer (see chapter *Ulcers*).

The salicylic acid method of treating heloma vasculare varies greatly depending upon the strength of the acid employed. If a weaker percentage is used, the treatment is practically the same as that with nitric acid. Several applications are necessary to completely remove the entire excrescence. The weaker solutions of this drug are the 10 to 15% ointments. The stronger ointments contain from 50 to 60% of the acid. The treatment with the 60% salicylic acid is preceded by cleansing the parts and removing the superfluous callous The acid is then applied and the part protected. The dressing is allowed to remain in contact with the part for from ten days to two weeks, and when removed, the entire mass may be easily scooped out. When the stronger acid is used, it is often necessary to warn the patient that if there should be any throbbing pain experienced, he must return for treatment at once. This pain is due to the rapid action of the drug, and to a mechanical inflammation which ensues. Examination will usually reveal a newly formed ulcer, which must be cleansed and treated in the usual manner. The salicylic ointment method is finding great favor, particularly on account of the few treatments necessary. Those inclined to nervousness and imaginary fears, regarding chiropodical or any other operations, are also usually highly pleased with this non-surgical method of treatment because the use of the knife is avoided and cure is not long delayed

In treating these cases medically, it is well to remember that the chemicals employed have a destructive action on the healthy tissue beneath the heloma as well as upon the heloma itself, and caution should be exercised in applying them. The case should be carefully watched and at no time should the operator allow the patient to remain away from the office for a greater length of time than above specified. It is also well to remember to warn the patient of the dull throbbing so characteristic of inflammation, which gradually increases as the pains become worse These pains are due to a chemic inflammation produced by the action of the drug upon the normal tissue beneath the growth, and are always an indication to discontinue treatment, remove what is left of the destroyed tissue, and direct treatment to the healing of the parts.

The *mechanical* treatment of heloma vasculare consists of the removal of the growth by means of electricity. The fulguration spark and electrolysis are the two methods employed.

The fulguration spark is a concentrated violet ray, or

high frequency current. The current is concentrated by passing it from the coil through a narrow glass electrode, at the far end of which is inserted a small piece of platinum or copper wire. As the current passes through the tube and the charged wire is brought in apposition to the excrescence, instead of the usual blue spark that is produced by the high frequency current in an ordinary vacuum electrode, there is a yellow spark produced which is quite painful to the body tissues. This spark has a caustic action, and after penetrating the superficial layers it enters into the deeper structures and there causes a destruction of the tissues.

Two, or at the most three, applications of this current, each of thirty seconds duration, will suffice for helomata vasculare which are situated on the dorsum of the foot. On the plantar surface, however, the tissues are more dense and many more treatments are required. It is on account of this density of the tissues that fulguration or any other form of electricity for the treatment of plantar growths is inadvisable

Electrolysis consists of inserting a needle or other sharply pointed instrument to which the negative pole of a galvanic cell has been attached, beneath and around the growth. The positive pole is attached to a spot near where the condition is found, usually the calf of the leg. As the current is passing through the foot, the water in the tissues undergoes electrolysis, and after a time, as the hydrogen goes to the negative pole, bubbles of this gas are noticed around the free surface of the needles. This is an evidence that the decomposition has gone on sufficiently and the needle may be withdrawn If the growth is a large one, the needle should be re-inserted at right angles to the original insertion, and the process repeated. If this is done properly, after two or three days, the entire mass will separate from the surrounding tissues. The greatest care must be observed in practising asepsis, as the electrolysis method is not an antiseptic one. The needle must be thoroughly boiled, and the part cleansed in the same manner as if a surgical operation were to be performed. This method, as well as the previous one, is not practical for helomata vasculare that appear on the plantar surface of the foot.

The carbon dioxide pencil may also be used in the treatment of this condition. This method, however, is not advised, as the parts become frozen from the contact and the pain of reaction is severe.

As previously stated, the treatment of heloma vasculare is almost identical with that of verruca and the reader is advised to consult the chapter on verruca for further knowledge along this line of treatment.

HELOMA MILIARE

Definition. Heloma miliare, or heloma disseminatum, or seed corn, is a small excrescence usually found in large numbers on the plantar surface of the foot, around the heel, or over the dorsal and inner lateral surface of the great toe joint The growth is about the size of a millet seed

Symptoms. This form of heloma does not produce the extreme pains caused by the other types of this growth, and only when they develop in great numbers do they become annoying. The patient then complains of an uncomfortable feeling, as if there were a foreign body in the shoe or stocking. Upon examination, several small helomata are seen. which appear to be all nuclei.

Etiology. Wrinkles produced by wearing loose stockings are a factor in producing helomata miliare; nails which protrude from the plantar surface of the shoe are also a fruitful cause of this condition The wrinkling of the stockings produces an uneven surface over the length of the wrinkle and the weave of the material, usually wool, causes these helomata to develop. The nails found in shoes are usually caused by imperfect repairing. They do not extend out more than just the smallest fraction; in fact they protrude just enough to allow the patient to go along for several days or weeks without noticing that something is wrong.

Pathology. Hypertrophy of the epidermis takes place at the nucleus only, but the area immediately surrounding the heloma miliare feels hard and congested to the touch. Hypertrophy of the papillae occurs, but only a small number are involved. There is no disturbance in the skin between the individual growths, each of the neoplasms having a distinct etiologic factor in its production.

Diagnosis. The heloma miliare is characteristic and cannot be mistaken for any other condition. As stated, the growth is rarely larger than a millet seed and appears to be all nucleus. There is an area of normal skin between these helomata, when they occur in numbers.

Prognosis. Careful operating and intelligent after-care will produce a cure in from four to five treatments. There are cases on record that have entirely disappeared after one treatment, but these are rare. The footgear, both shoes and stockings, should be examined and if found faulty should be corrected. This aids in a rapid cure and will, as well, prove a preventive.

Treatment. The removal of these helomata may be accomplished with the knife, but the ordinary scalpel is useless. It is necessary to have a very finely pointed small knife, and the procedure is the same as that followed in the treatment of the nucleus of heloma durum, except that more care must be practised, because of the smallness of the growth. The helomata miliare occur in groups containing as many as twenty or even thirty distinct minute growths, and it is necessary to take as much care with each one of them as with the first one removed. This is trying both to the patient and to the operator, but as it is essential to the successful cure to have the growths removed individually and carefully, patience is necessary. The after dressings may consist of ichthyol ointment, 15%, applied on a piece of lint, or balsam of Peru painted on after the helomata have been removed, and covered by a lint or cocoon dressing.

Some practitioners apply tincture of iodine to the part without further dressing.

The therapeutic method of treatment consists of applying salicylic acid plaster, cut so as to fit over the affected area, and allowing this to remain in contact with the part for several days. This softens the tissues, so that the small growths may be easily removed, but care must be taken, as the acid will destroy the healthy tissue between the helomata unless each growth is isolated in treatment. The disintegrating process must not be allowed to continue to the extent that it does in the treatment of heloma molle or in the other conditions in which salicylic acid is employed It is then often necessary to use the knife to remove the remaining tissue.

Recurrence is the rule in helomata miliare, but after persistent treatment the condition usually disappears It must be borne in mind, however, that the footgear of the patient must be carefully examined and necessary corrections made. This, in itself, without the thorough treatment prescribed above, will often result in a cure of the most annoying cases of heloma miliare

CHAPTER XI

CALLOSITAS

Derivation. The word callositas is derived from the Latin "callus," meaning horn

Synonyms. Callus, callosity, callous, tyloma, tylosis.

Definition. Callositas, or callouses, are a thickening of the epidermis, usually found on the plantar surface of the foot. They also occur on the dorsum of the toes, and are found on the hands of mechanics who continuously use hand tools involving pressure on the parts. Coachmen develop callouses between their fingers on account of the manner in which they hold the reins while driving. In rare instances, women have been known to have callouses on their hips, due to the pressure of the steel in their corsets, and cavalry men who sit in the saddle for long periods develop callous on the parts exposed to irritation.

Symptoms. Callosities are composed of variously sized areas of yellowish or grayish, horny excrescences of epidermic cells. They are hard, dry and horn-like, thicker in the centre of the growth and gradually becoming thinner at the periphery. There is no sharp line of demarcation between a callous and the surrounding skin, such as is found in helomata, but the thickened cuticle gradually blends with the surrounding skin.

Etiology. A callosity is the result of an irritation of some form and is nature's way of protecting the delicate structures beneath the skin from the direct pressure or friction to the parts. The outer layers of the skin become thickened and act as a buffer, which absorbs shock and prevents inflammation and tissue destruction When found on the soles of the feet, callouses are due to standing or walking in improper footgear. The ball of the great toe is a very common site for callosities; also the region over the heads of the metatarsal bones, due to high heels which force one to walk directly on these parts without equal weight distribution, is subject to them.

Callosities may occur as the result of chronic skin lesions such as eczema, psoriasis, lichen planus and icthyosis and after the prolonged use of arsenic.

Callosities occurring on the dorsum of the toes are caused by the pressure of the skin against the top of the shoe. The parts beneath the callous at this point usually show the presence of bursitis, which causes a swelling and subsequent pressure on the skin

Pathology. The changes that take place in the formation of callosities are the same as those which arise in heloma, except that the deeper layers of the epidermis and the true skin are not affected unless accidentally infected or injured

There is no inflammation present except in cases of infection or injury. The upper layers of the epidermis are the only ones involved, and the condition is really a physiologic rather than a pathologic one. It is more of a protection than a true hypertrophy. The overgrowth may continue to a greater extent, and then even helomata may develop

Diagnosis. The callosity is yellow to grey in color and is composed of a horn-like mass of epidermic cells. It is easily distinguished from an heloma in that there is no nucleus present, and the part is not severely painful on pressure. It may be mistaken for some of the chronic skin lesions, previously mentioned, but the skin eruption presents a scale or crust which readily peels off, en masse, leaving the bare rete Malpighii exposed. The callosity comes off in layers and, as the deeper structures are reached, a healthy pink color is noticed

Prognosis. A change in occupation or a change of footgear often results in the disappearance of this condition. Unless the direct cause is removed there will be a recurrence, which is an indication that the part again needs protection and care. Persons who have been accustomed to standing or walking for protracted periods of time, such as policemen, floor walkers, etc., soon lose the callouses they developed, after they change their occupation.

Treatment. If the growth becomes thick enough to cause discomfort, it may be easily removed, by softening it and then scraping or paring it. The foot may be soaked in an alkaline foot bath composed of one-half ounce of sodium bicarbonate to two quarts of hot water, or painting the part with a dilute solution of potassium hydroxide (caustic potash), 5%, several applications every few minutes, the softened area being scraped away after each application. Salicylic acid plaster, 25%, placed over the affected area and allowed to remain in contact for forty-eight hours, will usually loosen the redundant mass. If the callosity appears over the head of the first or fourth metatarsal bone, mechanical adjustment should be made, whereby the pressure in walking is thrown upon the entire surface of the anterior part of the foot. Pads of felt or buckskin, properly skived and fitted, will accomplish this result.

Care must be taken that too much of the induration is not removed when treating this condition. As previously stated, the calloused mass acts as a protective for the parts beneath and is nature's way of preventing serious trouble, and if too much is removed, pain will be experienced when the foot is used in walking. If this should occur, the part should be painted with tincture of iodine, 4%, and covered with moleskin or adhesive plaster. If an abrasion has been made, it is important to dress the part with an antiseptic, followed by a stimulating agent, all of this to be covered with a cocoon dressing or a lint shield.

Where callosities are caused by a displacement of the anterior metatarsal arch, or by any of its bony constituents, the bony lesion must be corrected before the callosities will respond to treatment.

CHAPTER XII

VERRUCA

Verruca, sometimes called papilloma, is an innocent or benign tumor, containing many blood vessels, and is an overgrowth of all the layers of the skin including the derma. It is usually found on the hands and feet, but other parts of the body may become affected, particularly the face.

Verruca, like other innocent or benign tumors, does not penetrate into the surrounding tissues, and is encapsulated. Those found on the foot are divided into two classes, (1) the verruca arida, or dry wart, and (2) the verruca humida, or moist wart.

The common wart found on the hands and fingers, is a form of verruca arida and is called verruca vulgaris. There are many other names used to designate verruca, but these are only indicative of the location, shape or consistency of the growth, which, as stated, is either of the arida or humida variety, and additional nomenclature tends to confuse the student. Among these are the verruca plantaris, verruca calcis, verruca metatarsalis, verruca lobosa, verruca fibrosa, verruca digita, etc.

Synonyms. Papilloma, Wart. Fr. verrue.

Derivation. Verruca is derived from the Latin, meaning wart.

Etiology. There is no general agreement among pathologists as to the cause of verruca. The older theory held that verruca was due to want of normal power within the integument. Some claim it to be due to a microorganism, while others assert that it is caused by irritation or injury. The latter reason seems to be the most reasonable one, since the patients who have been questioned thoroughly, all seem to give a history of trauma or of some chronic irritation.

Some verrucae seem to occur spontaneously and it becomes difficult to draw a line between those that grow in this manner and those that develop from an injury or from a chronic irritation. Predisposition seems to play an im-

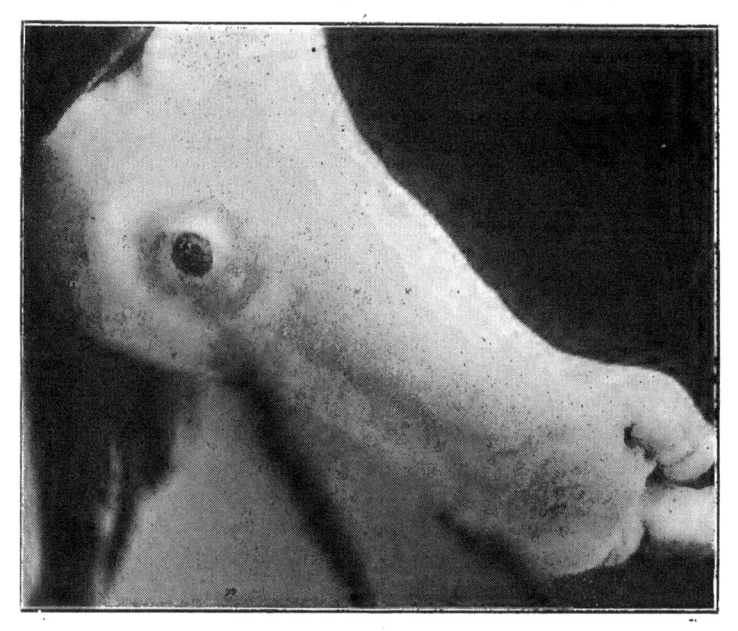

VERRUCA HUMIDA OR CALCIS

portant part in the etiology of verruca, but irritation is surely a factor in most if not in all cases. This predisposition may lie in the peculiar structure of the tissues, which is of course, difficult to determine.

The fall and early winter, seem to be the time at which most cases appear, and their history seems to indicate that either there has been an injury or an irritation, such for instance as is produced in walking barefooted on the beaches, which occurred during the previous summer. Those who walk distances over rough roads in the mountains, or who wear thin-soled shoes and sneakers or hob-nail shoes, or who have stepped on a sharp stone, are most likely to develop verrucæ.

Verruca is found on the hands of young persons, and on the feet of adults, but only occasionally is this growth seen on the feet of children. This is undoubtedly due to the fact that young people use the hands in playing to a great extent, and in that way are subjected to irritation, whereas the shoes of adults, and the rigidity of the tissues in older persons cause the development of verrucæ on the feet.

Observation has shown that those of athletic bent, such as golfers, tennis players, base ball players, etc., are affected to a greater extent than those who follow a sedentary occupation

Pathology. Verrucæ of all types are overgrowths of the derma covered with a somewhat hypertrophied epidermis, which is more granular and rougher than the normal skin. The wart may be only a simple, smooth, hemi-spherical elevation, or it may have a rough cauliflowerlike appearance, sessile or pedunculated. These latter may be dry or moist and may be elevated above the level of the skin or flattened to the level of the normal surrounding tissue. The size varies from minute points to growths as large as a nut. They are somewhat pigmented and bleed easily.

Verruca may occur singly, as it usually does on the foot, or it may occur in groups, and there may be several such groups in widely scattered parts of the body. The most common sites are the hands, feet, neck, back and face. Warts also occur on the mucous membrane, particularly in the bladder, larynx, nasal chamber and the gastro-intestinal tract, in which locations they are commonly termed papilloma.

The structural essentials of verrucæ are the centre or ground work containing blood vessels and an epithelial covering. In the skin, the growth resembles the normal papillae, all of these latter however, being greatly enlarged. There is hypertrophy of all the connective tissue cells, and in the growths that have a cauliflower appearance, a vertical section shows a branching arrangement. Each of the branches has a connective tissue frame work with an epithelial covering The epithelium is of the striated-squamous type and shows a decided tendency to hornification Distinct concentric whorls of horny epithelium, such as are seen in epithelioma of the skin, may be found in verruca The amount of connective tissue ground work varies, in some cases being excessive, while in others the growth appears to consist entirely of proliferated epithelium. In these latter cases the resemblance to epithelioma is rather marked, but a distinction can be made by observing that the tumor grows outward while the malignant tumor grows into the deeper structures and there is always some connective tissue stroma present. This is important for the podiatrist to remember as it may often be necessary to distinguish between the benign and the malignant tumors of this type.

VARIETIES OF VERRUCA

Verrucæ of the hands and feet vary to a greater or lesser extent depending upon the location of the lesion. The shape of the growth differs with the amount of pressure brought to bear upon it, those of the hands being better defined than those of the feet.

The Verruca Vulgaris, or common wart of the hand, is found on the palmar and dorsal surfaces, more usually in children than in adults. They often appear in large numbers, and very often the forearms and elbows are effected. The lesion is an elevated, rounded, conical hypertrophy having an uneven top and resembling a cauliflower. The growth develops slowly, and in its beginning has the same color as the surrounding skin. Later in its formation it becomes darker and takes on a cracked, rough cauliflower-like shape. There is no pain manifested, but the growth bleeds easily upon being injured, due to its great vascularity.

The Verruca Arida, or dry wart of the foot, usually

appears upon the plantar surface, over the metartarsals and on the ends of the toes. It is in reality a modification of the verruca vulgaris, which has been subjected to pressure. There is a distinct callous formation covering and surrounding the growth, and the entire mass has a flattened shape. At the ends of the toes on the dorsal surfaces and along the nail grooves, verrucæ which have a slight elevation often appear and are of the arida type.

The Verruca Humida, or moist wart, is found on the foot, usually on the heel and between the toes. It has a spongy, soft appearance, with a sharp line of demarcation separating it from the surrounding tissues; the centre of the growth is white and has a crater-like shape. It is sometimes covered by a layer of callous, which is spongy and blanched, much the same as that of an heloma molle. The sudoriferous excretions in those suffering with hyperidrosis or bromidrosis are the cause of the color and texture of these lesions.

Diagnosis. Verruca is an overgrowth of all the layers of the skin, and when it appears on places where it is not subjected to pressure of any great magnitude, its diagnosis is a simple matter. When, however, it appears on the foot, its true character is lost, and it may be confused with other lesions, notably epithelioma, syphilitic lesions and heloma vasculare.

The malignant epithelioma is occasionally seen as a warty growth, but it generally has adherent scabs, ulcerates superficially, and has a disagreeable odor. The surrounding tissues are infiltrated and severe and persistent pain is common. Innocent tumors of this type, after a long period, may become malignant; increase in the size of the growth, implication of neighboring glands, infiltration of adjacent tissues, plus the other symptoms of epithelioma, should be sufficient to arouse suspicion as they are indicative of the more serious developments.

Some lesions of syphilis taking on a papillary character, may be mistaken for verruca, but other indications of a specific condition are usually present so that when confusion as to diagnosis arises, the lesion may be readily distinguished if it be a luetic one. The smaller tertiary ulcers of syphilis that appear on the plantar surface of the foot often have cracked, uneven overgrowths around and on them, which upon superficial examination may be mistaken for verruca, but a negative Wasserman test (see Miscellaneous Foot Lesions—*Syphilis*) will make it possible for the practitioner to eliminate syphilis as a factor.

Venereal warts occur on the genitals only and need not be considered in this chapter.

Verruca and heloma vasculare are often confused, but inasmuch as the treatment is identical in both these lesions, an error in diagnosis is of no particular consequence. In heloma vasculare the affected papillæ, which are found in the hornified skin, are few in number and are confined to a limited area, whereas in verruca all the papillae are affected and the entire growth is vascular.

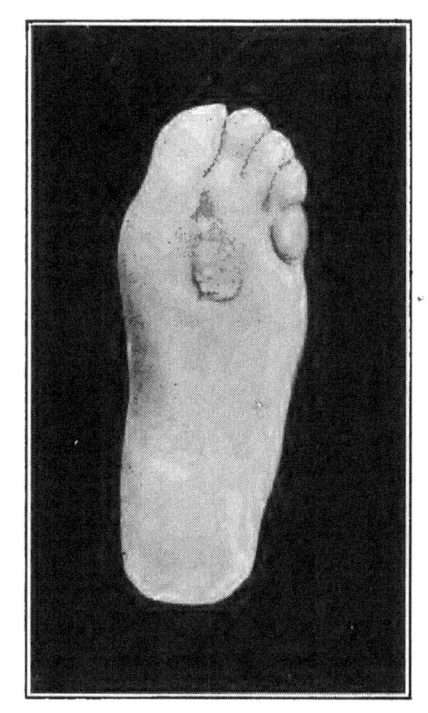

EPITHELIOMA

Prognosis. Some verrucæ disappear spontaneously, but those appearing upon the foot are persistent and painful, and require regular treatment to effect a cure. The growth will get well with proper attention and only when it changes its nature and becomes malignant, is the prognosis unfavorable.

Treatment. The treatment of verruca is more varied than the treatment of any other chiropodical lesion, and the practitioners using these different methods all seem to favor the one particular form with which they have had the most experience and the best results.

Treatment is generally effective, the percentage of failures being very small, notwithstanding the statement of those who expect immediate results, and not receiving them, claim failure on the part of the practitioner.

The various treatments are as follows:

Potential Cautery—including the following chemicals: Nitric Acid, Acetic Acid, Monochloracetic Acid, Trichloracetic Acid, Salicylic Acid, Silver Nitrate, Potassium Hydroxide, Sodium Hydroxide and Pyrogallic Acid.

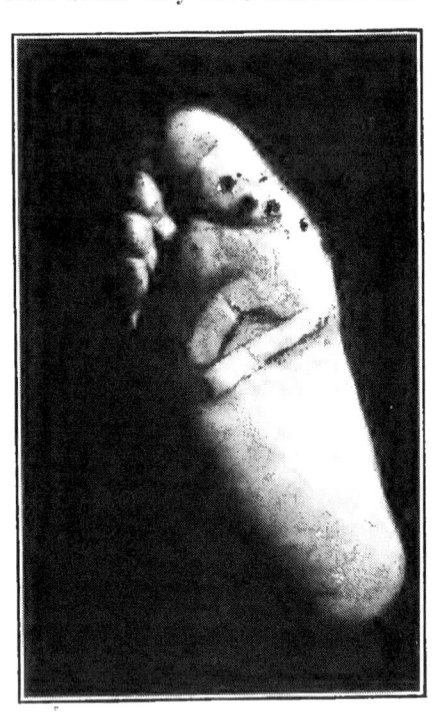

MULTIPLE VERRUCA

Excision.
Fulguration.
Electrolysis.
Direct Cautery.
Carbon Dioxide Pencil.

Potential Cautery. The treatment of verruca by the use of chemical agents which destroy the tissues to which they are applied, is unquestionably the most popular method of treating this lesion and is practised to a great extent by modern podiatrists. The tissues are destroyed in one of two ways, depending upon the chemical selected. The acid caustics destroy the tissues by oxidizing them, and the alkali caustics destroy the tissues by dehydrating them. Therefore the kind of tumor with which one has to deal is a factor in determining which caustic is best suited for rapid and certain cure. A verruca which is hard and dry will be easily destroyed by oxidation, whereas a verruca that is soft and moist will be easiest of removal by dehydration.

The selection of a particular chemical for removing a certain type of growth, is more or less a matter of individual choice on the part of the operator, as any one of the recognized remedies will suffice if the technic of its application be properly followed. A podiatrist who uses nitric acid for verruca arida, may just as well use trichloracetic acid and obtain equally good results.

Inasmuch as there are so many agents which one can use successfully, the authors have asked several well-known practitioners of podiatry to state their technic in the treatment of verruca, and later on in this chapter their views will be found quoted verbatim.

The method of procedure for the treatment of verruca by the use of acid caustics generally is as follows:

The field of operation is rendered aseptic by means of a solution of bi-chloride of mercury (1/2000) or a solution of alcohol, 60%. A sharp knife or chisel is employed to remove the callous that usually covers the growth. As soon as bleeding is observed, which is an indication that some of the capillaries of the tumor have been cut, a styptic, such as Monsel's solution or powdered alum, is applied and readily controls the hemorrhage. The part is then thoroughly dried with sterile gauze or cotton, and the caustic selected is applied to the part. If an acid is used, a single drop is usually employed at each treatment. The patient, as a result, will complain of a burning sensation in the growth which persists from a few minutes to an hour, depending upon the amount of the acid absorbed. If the growth is dense, the absorption is lessened and more frequent treatments become necessary.

A properly fitted and skived shield of felt is then applied, with a hole large enough to prevent pressure over the affected area No other medicament is required, nor is it necessary to cover the verruca. The acid forms an eschar which seals the lesion and prevents bacterial infection. The second treatment should take place forty-eight hours after the first, and the same procedure should be practised, including the asepsis. The treatments are continued every other day, daily, if possible, until the entire growth has been destroyed.

Unless great care is exercised, as the destruction of the growth continues and its size decreases, the acid coming in contact with the underlying healthy tissues creates pain of a throbbing character and later on pus is likely to form under the eschar. Some practitioners believe that both the pain and the pus are necessary precursors of the healing process, but neither is essential. They are both the usual concomitants of the later stages of this treatment merely because, as stated, it has been impossible to exercise the strict care desired.

When the growth has been destroyed, the eschar is entirely removed and if pus is present it is drained. Hydrogen peroxide is a most efficient agent for this purpose. The lesion is now treated much the same as any other ulceration, that is to say, by stimulants, balsam of Peru or ichthyol being the mediums usually preferred. The balsam of Peru used for this purpose should be diluted with an equal quantity of castor oil; the best method of applying ichthyol is in ointment form (25%) with vaseline as a base.

The treatment of verruca by means of the alkali caustics is much the same as with the acid caustics, except that the cauterization by the latter method may continue so as to destroy the entire growth at one treatment. This of course would prove even more painful than if done intermittently, therefore it is far better to treat the patient at several different times than to attempt anything quite so radical. The parts must be protected during the treatment and the subsequent ulcer invariably produced by this method, is treated the same as the ulcer frequently resulting from acid applications and previously described.

Nitric acid is extensively used in this condition in the pure state. The treatment of the eschar produced varies.

S. Rutherford Levy, of San Francisco, California, uses the nitric acid pure, and reports very favorable results. He removes the eschar after each treatment.

Alfred C. Moran, of Pawtucket, R. I., also favors nitric acid, but advises that the eschar be allowed to remain on the part until healing takes place or until signs of suppuration manifest themselves. He punctures the surface of the growth with a sharp instrument to assist the diffusion of the acid.

Albert E. Smallwood, a well-known and busy practitioner of podiatry, of Pittsburgh, Pa, reports good results with the use of trichloracetic acid (Merck) and his modus operandi follows:

"*Trichloracetic acid* is a safe caustic and should be used full strength. A tooth pick is wrapped with a small piece of cotton and the latter is saturated with the acid. (The crystals of the acid are permitted to stand exposed to the air for a few minutes when they will deliquesce.) Apply the cotton thus prepared directly over the verruca, allowing it (the cotton) to remain in situ; then cover the growth and the cotton with a thin felt shield and fasten it with adhesive plaster. To prevent the acid from coming in contact with the normal tissues, the latter should be protected with oil or vaseline. Have the patient return in two days for a second treatment, and if the pains were only of short duration, the same procedure is repeated. The white eschar produced is removed, care being taken that bleeding is avoided. It is better to remove only a little of the eschar, as this saves suffering in the interim of treatments.

"Treatment is continued every other day until the entire growth is eradicated, which is usually indicated by the presence of pus. The subsequent treatment is that for ulcerations in general."

F. S Sargent, of Providence, R. I., prefers *silver nitrate* to any other of the potential caustics. He uses the pulverized salt, applied directly to the verruca, protecting the surrounding tissue with adhesive plaster and using felt shields during the treatment. When the part has suppurated he cleanses the wound, dusts with some antiseptic powder such as aristol, and to stimulate granulations he applies balsam of Peru, 50%, in castor oil.

One of the best known practitioners on the pacific coast, Helen C. Sexton, has a very interesting technic for the destruction of verrucæ, which is as follows:

"Place a small wad of cotton soaked with a 5% solution of *potassium hydroxide* over the growth and apply the surface electrode of the high frequency current for five minutes, or until it is uncomfortable to the patient. Then dissect out as much of the dead tissue as possible and if bleeding should occur, do not attempt to check it for a few minutes The hemorrhage is then easily controlled by digital pressure. A piece of moleskin, about the size of a fifty cent piece, with a hole in its centre, the exact size of the verruca, is next applied, and in the aperture a sixty per cent. salycilic acid ointment is placed. The ointment is covered with fish skin and the entire dressing protected with a well skived and properly adjusted felt shield. The patient is instructed to return in one week unless pains develop, in which case he should return immediately. The treatment is continued every week until the growth is destroyed, and after the skin surface is again normal, the patient is instructed to wear a protective, such as a piece of moleskin, for at least one week. If a case does not respond to this treatment in a period of three weeks, electrolysis is resorted to."

James Parker Buntin, of Boston, Mass., calls the following his "antiquated" treatment, but says he has had very good results with it and with very little, if any discomfort to the patient:

"Take a small piece of caustic potash (*potassium hydroxide*) and allow it to stand in the open air until it slacks. Then thicken it to a paste with pulverized gum arabic, which will prevent it spreading to the surrounding tissues when applied Carefully remove the superficial layers of the verruca and apply the paste and let it remain for ten minutes. Soak the part in sharp vinegar or sweet oil, either of which will neutralize the action of the caustic potash. This treatment is continued every other day until the entire growth is removed."

Oscar Klotzbach, of Cleveland, Ohio, is using *methylene blue* for the treatment of verruca, applying the drug (once a week), and protecting the part with sterile dressings. This is a painless method.

Bertha DeWolfe, of Denver, Colo., is using *ethylate of soda* for verruca and reports gratifying results. The drug is dampened with a drop of absolute alcohol and placed in the centre of a piece of adhesive plaster, the size of a twenty-five cent piece, and then applied so that the sodium ethylate comes in direct contact with the warty growth. The treatment is repeated daily, at first, and then every other day, until a cure is affected. The pain is slight, being limited to one or two days of slight discomfort. If the ethylate of soda is employed for verrucæ of the dorsum of the foot or of the fingers, it should be diluted, varying from 15% to a saturated solution. The full strength of the drug should be used on the plantar surface of the foot only.

Anna Moyde Savage, of Syracuse, N. Y., who has had experience with many treatments for verruca, has been using and recommends *pyrogallol* for this lesion. Her statement follows:

"Pyrogallol is a white, lustrous, bitter crystalline substance soluble in water, alcohol and ether. It is used extensively in diseases of the skin, and in all the cases of verruca in which it was used, a 30% ointment in a vaseline base proved sufficiently strong to remove the growth. Most of the cases respond to one treatment, and no case has ever required more than five treatments to effect a cure.

"The treatments are given at intervals of from five to seven days, and at no time is it necessary for the patients to remain in bed or refrain from their usual occupations. A fairly thick pad of felt is applied with an opening large enough to protect the verruca. In this opening the 30% ointment of pyrogallic acid is applied, a cotton or gauze dressing being placed over it, and then the entire dressing is securely fastened with adhesive plaster. There is no pain or discomfort during the treatment, and only when the pyrogallol has destroyed the tumor and penetrates into the healthy tissues, is a drawing pain noticed This is mild and lasts but one day, and when the final dressing is removed, the verruca is eradicated. The subsequent ulceration may be treated with any stimulant, after aseptic precautions have been observed, some iodine preparation for example. The pad should be worn until the entire lesion is healed. No case so far treated with this method has shown any signs of recurrence."

Salicylic Acid is used to a great extent for the destruction of verrucæ, and is admirably adapted for this purpose, inasmuch as it is painless and does not require frequent changes of dressings A piece of adhesive plaster is fitted to the part with a hole cut in it exposing the verruca. A piece of felt of the required thickness is then applied to the foot, which acts as a shield In the holed-out portion of the felt, a 60% salicylic acid ointment is applied directly over the verruca. The adhesive plaster first applied prevents the acid spreading to the surrounding normal structures. The entire dressing is protected with adhesive plaster and the patient is instructed to return in a week or ten days. By this time the therapeutic action of the acid will have manifested itself, and a suppurative process will be noted at the base of the growth. The patient complains of throbbing in the part and when the dressing is removed, the part cleansed and a sharp knife inserted into the growth, oozing of pus will occur. The entire mass can be then removed, whereupon the abscess cavity should be thoroughly cleaned This can be done by means of peroxide of hydrogen. The pyogenic membrane can be destroyed by the use of pure phenol followed by alcohol, after which a stimulant, such as balsam of Peru or ichthyol, should be applied. These latter dressings should be changed every other day until the wound is healed This method is particularly adaptable for verrucæ around the nails.

Excision. The removal of verruca by surgical means is a very simple procedure and, if properly done, should result in an absolute cure in every case in which it is employed.

The part to be operated upon is rendered sterile by thoroughly cleansing with soap and water, and subsequently painting it with tincture of iodine. The instruments are boiled for at least fifteen minutes in water containing a little sodium carbonate and the hands of the operator are thoroughly cleaned and dipped in alcohol.

Local anesthesia is induced by the hypodermatic injection of any approved anesthetic, preferably novocaine, 1%, and when the tissues around and beneath the verruca are thoroughly anesthetized, the operator makes a semi-elliptical incision a little outside of and beneath the growth. The flap thus produced is grasped with an artery forceps and raised. This affords room to dissect out the growth with a scalpel or with a pair of heavy, pointed scissors.

The wound produced by the removal of the verruca should now be packed with sterile gauze and a bandage applied to prevent infection. If the gap is a large one it may be closed by taking one or two sutures (interrupted) and drawing the edges of the wound together in this manner.

To afford relief from the reaction of the anesthetic,

and as a precautionary measure against infection, a wet dressing of bichloride of mercury (1/5000) should be applied for from twenty-four to forty-eight hours immediately following the operation. This, however, is unnecessary if asepsis has been practised throughout the operation. If no complications arise, the dressing should be left undisturbed for four or five days, when the bandage can be softened and removed. (Tearing a dry bandage from a granulating wound will destroy some of the newly formed granulations). If sutures have been used, they should now be removed, and a mild stimulant such as balsam of Peru, 50%, or ichthyol, 10%, should be applied to stimulate further granulation. Dressings should be changed every other day until the area is completely healed, a process requiring from one to two weeks. With proper shielding, the patient should be able to walk comfortably after the first dressing has been removed.

Fulguration. The use of electricity in the treatment of disease has greatly increased in recent years. This is particularly true of the high frequency current, examples of which are the so-called violet ray and the X-ray. This form of electricity is quite different from the usual form encountered when using the faradic or galvanic currents, and although its voltage is expressed in the thousands, it is quite harmless when one knows just how to use it.

For the purposes of the podiatrist, a small coil generator with one or two electrodes, will usually suffice. The fulguration electrode is a glass rod through the centre of which passes a piece of fine copper or platinum wire, terminating a little beyond the end of the tube. This free end of the wire is protected by a small glass cup which fits over the end of the tube. The tube itself is a vacuum. The rear of the electrode is set in a brass cup, which fits into the handle of the apparatus and makes direct contact with the wire conducting the current from the generator.

For the destruction of verruca the part is cleansed with alcohol, and the electrode is placed directly over and in close contact with the growth. A small amount of current is then passed through the apparatus, and a yellow spark will be noticed leaving the free end of the wire and entering the verruca. If this is painful to the patient, the current must be reduced. When the entire area has turned white, the current is turned off. This takes from 20 to 40 seconds, depending upon the size of the tumor.

The part should be dressed with a well skived shield, to afford protection, and should then be covered with dry, sterile gauze. This dressing is left unmolested for a few days. The growth during this time dries up completely and when the dressing is removed the growth can easily be separated. If all of the neoplasm has not been destroyed, another application of the high frequency current should be made over the remaining portion. When the entire growth has been thus removed, the tissues are protected with a piece of moleskin for one or two weeks.

Rudolph Mertin, of Boston, Mass., has used the high frequency current extensively in the treatment of verruca and he says that two or three applications of from twenty to thirty seconds duration usually suffice to effect an absolute cure for even a large sized growth of this variety. He advises that, for nervous patients, the current be reduced and if necessary the treatment be extended to six or even ten different applications. This eliminates fright and nervousness.

Electrolysis. The use of the galvanic current in the treatment of verruca is finding great favor among podiatrists, and is especially adapted to verruca vulgaris of the hands. The current may be generated in a few small wet or dry cells, and by passing it through a rheostat with a milliamperemeter attached, it can easily be regulated and controlled. There are many such machines on the market today, any one of which will answer the purposes of the practitioner. Ordinary direct lighting current, if properly reduced, is admirable.

James R. Bennie, of Philadelphia, Pa., who uses

this method of treating verruca exclusively, has developed a technic that is fully described in the following:

"Eight years ago I began treating verruca with electricity and such was the success that invariably followed the use of this agent, that I quickly abandoned all other methods of treatment. I use the galvanic current, and the growth is destroyed by electrolysis. This is the quickest, the surest and the least painful method of treatment and is equally successful in treating helomata vasculare and moles.

"Electrolysis is accomplished by the use of the negative or active pole. Through the action of the negative current, caustic alkalies are formed. The action of these alkalies, in conjunction with the current itself, causes the growths to liquify and disintegrate. Any galvanic current which will give from two to ten milliamperes during the treatment, may be used. An essential point to remember is that the negative pole is the operating pole whenever tissue is to be liquified and disintegrated The positive pole contracts and hardens the tissues.

"The procedure in the treatment of growths by electrolysis is simple, but the greatest care should be observed in carrying out all antiseptic precautions. Remove all calloused tissue on or about the growth Saturate the positive pole, which should be a copper plate covered with felt, with an aqueous solution of common salt, then place the pole on the skin as near the seat of operation as possible. The negative pole should be a platinum needle or needles, as the case may demand. I have used as many as twelve needles at one time. The needles should be sharp, and platinum is the best metal for this work.

"With the field of operation properly prepared, transfix the growth through its base with the platinum needle, taking care not to penetrate too deeply into the true skin about the growth. The current is then turned on and applied in the strength of from one to five milliamperes. The application is continued until the verruca assumes a pearly hue. A frothy substance will form in and about the needles; this is hydrogen gas mixed with a serous exudate and is positive evidence that disintegration is completed. If the growth is exceptionally large and painful, local anesthesia may be induced by hypodermatic injection.

"The time required for each treatment varies with the character of the verruca. The more vascular the verruca, the quicker its disintegration. When the current is turned off and the needle removed, the part should be antiseptically dressed, and should be protected with a shield of felt or buckskin, properly fitted and fastened. At the expiration of one week the patient is requested to return for further treatment, when the dressing should be removed and the eschar cut away. If the verruca is not completely destroyed, the treatment is repeated.

"The appearance of the part after the verruca has been completely destroyed is not always the same; in some cases coagulation occurs; again there may be present a small quantity of purulent fluid. When the products of the destruction of the growth are removed, a healthy granulating ulcer remains, which yields readily to antiseptic treatment.

"When a large number of verruca are present, try to determine which is the original growth and treat it first. With the destruction of this lesion, the others will frequently disappear without further treatment, thus enabling the podiatrist to accomplish a brilliant result which will greatly impress the patient. I have frequently observed this singular result of the galvanic current and believe it to occur from the fact that the verruca develop within a definite nerve area, and that the current affects the enervation of this area and thus brings to completion the cure."

Direct Cautery. The destruction of verrucæ by means of heat is practised to a greater or lesser extent by a few practitioners of podiatry, but on the whole, other methods which are available are superior to it. Any implement which can be heated sufficiently hot, so that when applied it will burn the growth, may be used in this treatment. A small piece of carbon, pointed at one end, and small enough to be easily handled with the thumb forceps, is used by some practitioners. The pointed end is placed in an alcohol or other flame until the carbon is glowing. It is then applied directly to the verruca, and allowed to remain there until the pain becomes unbearable. One or two seconds should be the limit of each application. The carbon is again heated, and the application is repeated

For the convenience of the practitioner, an electric apparatus has been devised, which, with the aid of a platinum electrode, affords an opportunity to generate sufficient heat for this form of cautery. The platinum electrode is attached by two wires to the coil, and when the contact is made the fine metal end soon becomes red hot. The temperature is easily controlled by a little switch on the side of the handle of the electrode. The platinum point is brought in direct contact with the part to be destroyed, and after several short applications, this is easily accomplished.

This method has several disadvantages, because the pain during the operation is intense, and the smell of the burning tissue is very disagreeable to both the patient and the operator. Further, the sight of the red hot metal being applied to the foot usually frightens the patient, so that, all in all, other methods are desirable.

Carbon Dioxide Pencil. For the treatment of verruca by this method, the apparatus necessary is a small tank of liquified carbon dioxide gas, and some small cylindric receptacle in which the gas can be condensed into the solid form. A glove finger is very good for this purpose. The gas is allowed to escape into the glove finger, where it solidifies, forming carbon dioxide snow, or what is commonly called the carbon dioxide pencil. The temperature of this snow or pencil is very low, being much below the freezing point of water.

The pencil is applied directly over the verruca and is allowed to remain for a few minutes, until the entire tissue has been devitalized. The extreme cold causes the blood supply directly beneath and around the growth to cease, much the same as exposure causes local anemia in chilblains and frostbite. The tissues around the part become blanched and the growth separates from the normal structures in a few days. There is usually a slough which will respond to treatment.

Great care should be exercised, so that the application is not prolonged, as this will destroy normal tissue, and cause deeper ulcers which do not readily heal. This method is painless during the operation, but the pains of reaction are marked, varying with the duration of the application, and with the resistance of the individual. Wm. Golus considers this method of treatment extremely harsh Monroe Redell and Irvin Mayer are similarly minded. All of these practitioners state that they give the preference to any and all other procedures whenever called upon to treat verruca —they will not use the carbon dioxide pencil because they fear the after-effects.

CHAPTER XIII

CALLOUSED NAIL GROOVE

The formation of hardened, or calloused skin in the nail groove is, unhappily, a very common occurrence. In our present day of high-heeled and pointed shoes the nail grooves of all the nails, but particularly those of the great toe, are subject to a great amount of pressure and friction. This irritation develops conditions in these structures, ranging from a transient inflammation to the formation of distinct helomata, or the general callousing of the whole surface of the groove, both under and beside the nail.

In many cases where an heloma has developed in the inner lateral nail groove of the great toe, the condition is judged and treated as an ingrown nail.

Why this error in diagnosis should occur is hard to reason out, for, while the subjective symptoms of the two conditions may be and usually are similar, the objective symptoms are so entirely different that the only accountable reason for a mistaken diagnosis is carelessness or ignorance on the part of the practitioner. The true ingrown nail is not a particularly common occurrence and, as has been previously explained, a nail to be classified as ingrowing, must present an edge that has invaded and is imbedded in the softer tissues of the adjacent nail fold. In calloused nail groove, nothing of this nature has occurred and it is the maltreatment of cases of this kind that usually leads to true cases of ingrown nail.

Definition. A calloused nail groove is a condition in which a localized heloma (sometimes several disseminated helomata), or a general calloused condition has developed in a lateral nail groove.

Symptoms. *Subjective symptoms:* excruciating pain on the slightest pressure, heat, and throbbing in severe and neglected cases.

Objective symptoms: swelling, usually localized in the nail fold involved; redness and general inflammatory condition; upon close examination the heloma or the callous is easily demonstrated in the fold by reason of its unyielding qualities.

Etiology. This condition may be caused by irritation of the tender tissues of the nail-fold brought on by persons who persist and delight in "digging" about the edges of the nail with some instrument. In most instances, however, a short or narrow shoe or stocking will cause sufficient pressure of the edge of the nail upon the tissues of the groove to cause nature to provide a protection which tends to prevent the nail from piercing these softer tissues; the protection appears in the form of callous. This callous will appear as a hard development throughout the whole nail groove, and we find those tissues to be unyielding and to have lost nearly if not all of the pinkish tint which the great amount of vascularity underneath normally gives to the tissues about the nail. The color is yellowish or sometimes greyish white. Where a distinct heloma is present, it may be found covered by a thin sheet of callous which covers some part of the groove, or it may be distinctly independent and isolated from any such development. When this latter condition is met, the heloma will usually be found to be circumscribed, its edges regular and its shape circular. These latter instances are not so common as the general callousing of the entire groove. Where the helomata are found disseminated, they will usually occur on the inside of the flap next the nail, although in some cases they will be found under the edge of the nail itself. In these first mentioned instances the pain will be greatest upon lateral pressure and in the latter upon dorsal or plantar pressure

Treatment. Various methods of treatment are employed for the alleviation or cure of this painful ailment.

They may be divided, for discussion, into two general classes: surgical and medical.

Surgical Treatment. This method consists in removing the callous or the heloma by means of a fine-pointed scalpel or a small curette. The nail groove is first well softened by the application of small pledgets of cotton saturated with warm water, or by the use of some epidermic solvent such as liquor potassae, after which the parts are dried and the operation is begun. With a sterile nail chisel sufficient of the edge of the nail is cut away so that the heloma or the callous is exposed. This not only gives the patient instant relief but also allows room for the operation and the subsequent dressing.

With a pointed scalpel or bistoury, the growths are removed, much in the same manner as helomata in any location might be treated. If the calloused condition be general throughout the groove, a small curette is used and the callous is loosened from the anterior end of the fold and stripped backward toward the root of the nail.

The subsequent treatment consists in applying an ointment, such as ammoniated mercury (5%), and packing the nail groove with sterile gauze. Should the operator prefer a liquid, the gauze packing may be saturated with bichloride of mercury, 1/5000, or boric acid, saturated solution; but it will be generally found that the ointment is more effective in reducing the inflammatory symptoms present and also any irritation which may have been caused during the operation.

Whilst this operation is being constantly performed and seems to be genrally in vogue, much more satisfactory results are obtainable from local medical applications.

In the first place, in using a scalpel or curette in the nail fold, the operator must be very skillful in order not to cause a hemorrhage and subsequently a tender digit. In many instances, no matter how skillful the operator, or how much care be exercised in the operation, it will be found a practical impossibility to strip the callous from a nail groove without capillary rupture. This latter, of course, is undesirable and usually, no matter how the lesion is dressed, the groove remains tender for days.

In some cases the small helomata found in the nail fold should at once be at least partly removed, to give the patient relief. This may be done with a fine-pointed scalpel and local treatment may then be applied.

Medical Treatment. There are two methods of medical treatment employed. One finds its efficacy in the use of salicylic acid as an epidermic disintegrant, and the other in the application of liquor potassae (potass. hydrox. 5%) as a cuticle solvent.

Salicylic Acid. After a sufficient portion of the nail has been removed to give relief to the patient, the nail fold is thoroughly cleansed and dried and the following ointment applied in the groove:

```
        Acidi salicylici    . . . .   . . . .   8.
        Camphorae
        Chloral       . . . . aa .  . . . . . .  0.30
        Ceratum ......................  30.
        M. ft. unguentum
```

After a week or ten days has elapsed, the whole calloused area will be found to be entirely disintegrated and may be easily removed with a fine-pointed excavator. The groove is then packed with either gauze or cotton, and an appropriate ointment or solution is applied to alleviate the inflammatory condition.

The treatment with salicylic acid is easily combined with the surgical treatment, if it be found necessary to remove a portion of the corneous formation in order to afford relief to the patient.

In some cases it will be found efficacious, after the callous has been removed by means of the salicylic ointment, to apply silver nitrate (50%) to the groove. This will reduce the inflammatory conditions and at the same time act as an astringent to the underlying capillaries and as a sedative to the inflamed tissues. The alternate weekly use of the ointment and the silver salt is advocated, and gratifying results are usually obtained from this treatment in cases where it can be used.

Liquor Potassae. Potassium hydroxide solution is most generally used in cases where the callous is general in the nail fold rather than where there is simply a localized heloma.

An applicator is saturated in the solution and rubbed over the calloused area until the mass is softened, when it may be easily removed. While this mode of treatment is a popular one it has been the experience of many practitioners that the liquor potassae merely softens the calloused condition, failing to disintegrate it entirely, and allows the parts to harden, directly the application is discontinued Joseph Renk, a well known New York practitioner, reports the best of results from this treatment, when carefully used.

No doubt there are good features in both treatments and a wise practitioner, utilizing both, will adopt that from which he obtains the best results.

In no instance should the nail fold be packed tightly in these cases. The operator should remember that if he removes a sliver of nail one-sixteenth of an inch in width and then packs the resultant space with a pledget of cotton, gauze or lamb's wool one-eighth of an inch in thickness, he will cause more pressure to be brought to bear on the parts than there was originally present; this is, of course, to be avoided under all circumstances.

On the other hand it must be remembered that sufficient packing should be used to retain the normal line of the nail fold and to keep these softer tissues in the proper place. Under no circumstances should they be allowed to crowd up and over the nail, for if this does take place we are merely setting the stage for a possible ingrown nail. Jack Grossman, M.Cp., makes this a strong point in his talks to the students of The First Institute of Podiatry

CHAPTER XIV

ONYCHOCRYPTOSIS OR INGROWN TOE NAIL

Definition. Onychocryptosis, or ingrowing or ingrown toe nail, is a condition in which the lateral edge of a nail has penetrated through the epidermic layers and has become imbedded in the adjacent or subjacent soft parts of the lateral nail grove. This abnormal condition gives rise to a number of complications, viz: simple inflammation, ulceration, circumscribed or diffused cellulitis and the formation of proud flesh. These may occur singly or as is commonly found, the last three in unison. The unclean condition of people's footgear, the general unsanitary conditions of the foot, or mal-treatment of ingrown nail in its incipiency, often give rise to the still graver septic complications which ultimate in a general septicemia.

A nail then to be classed as an ingrowing nail must be specifically ingrowing. Mention is made of this fact, which many in their wisdom may deem superfluous, because so many conditions of callous or helomata in the nail groove are mistaken for ingrowing nail and their treatment as such is not only useless, so far as a cure is concerned, but is decidedly detrimental to the comfort of the patient and to the future general condition of the nail involved.

Etiology. A large percentage, perhaps larger than most people imagine, of ingrown nails arise from the injudicious cutting of the part by an inexperienced person. Directly after an amateur operation upon a painful nail, acute symptoms of ingrowing nail do not necessarily develop—although it does happen in many cases; but the etiology of a great number of acute and well defined cases of ingrown nail, as stated, can be traced primarily to self inflicted nail injury at some previous time.

The changes taking place in the nail and in the tissues of the nail groove after the removal of the lateral border of the nail, are pronounced. Take, for example, the great toe nail, as this is the most easily studied on account of its size and at the same time is the most general seat of troubles of this nature.

The nails are placed on the dorsal surfaces of the toes as a means of protection to the expanded extremities of the distal phalanges. Perhaps the Divine Providence in moulding his masterpiece, man, foresaw the advent of modern footgear and realizing its baneful effect upon the human extremity, developed upon the great toe a heavy nail from which a great deal of protection for the more tender tissues beneath might be obtained. At any rate, the great toe nail today bears the brunt of the pressure from our leather footgear and for that reason is probably the seat of so many painful afflictions.

The free edge of the normal great toe nail is found to be more flattened and expanded than the posterior portions of the nail nearer its root. This flattened expansion holds the softer tissues of the end of the toe and of the lateral border of the nail groove in place under the nail and also prevents them, if allowed to remain untouched, from crowding up or around the nail at any quarter. But allow the free edge and the lateral border of the nail to be removed, and particularly by inexperienced hands—and observe what takes place. These softer tissues which were normally held in place by the free borders of the nail, fill up the spaces left by the removal of the nail borders. Even this condition, were the nail to remain stationary and cease to grow, would not be conducive to great pain or inconvenience. But the nail is being continually pushed forward by the formation of new cells at its posterior extremity. This is embedded in the posterior nail fold, and when the newly formed portion of the same width as originally found arrives at the point where the softer tissues are crowded up and into the space left by the removal of the borders of the nail, instead of growing over them and forcing them back into their normal position, it finds this impossible, and grows into them.

From the foregoing we are not to take it for granted that all cases occur from injudicious cutting of the nail's lateral borders. Short and tight shoes and hose are in some cases the exciting causes of ingrowing nails and, from observation, we are led to believe that while the actual ingrowing nail is not hereditary, nevertheless the predisposition toward nail inversion is manifest through an entire family or even through a generation.

In the case of tight footgear or hosiery, the cause is the crowding of the great toe against its neighbor, forcing the softer tissues of the nail groove and flap to be crowded against the lateral edge of the nail. In these cases the principal site of occurrence will naturally be the outer sides of the great toe, in fact, in most cases, this groove will be found to be the most general site of occurrence. The soft tissues of the nail flap being crowded over and around the nail's lateral edge, there naturally follows an irritation in the groove, caused by the nail rubbing upon these tissues which, in time no doubt leads to ulceration of the parts with the accompanying inflammatory symptoms.

Uric acid diathesis may in one sense be said to be the cause of some cases of ingrown nail in that when patients so suffer, the nails are prone to chip off at the edges leaving the latter ragged and so allowing a chance for irritation from the saw-like projections, ultimating in an ulcerated condition of the wounded parts.

Complications. Other than the general inflammatory conditions brought about in connection with the ulceration caused by the edge of the nail penetrating the softer tissues, proud flesh is probably the complication most generally met with in these cases.

Proud flesh, thus produced, is due undoubtedly to the constant irritation of the nail upon the exposed surfaces of ulcerated area. It forms in many shapes and the mass developed depends largely upon the length of time the condition is allowed to progress without proper treatment. The excess growth is usually found covering the whole exposed area, or only forming in a teat-like prominence with a small circumscribed base and expanded extremity. The pain to the patient is undoubtedly augmented by the presence of proud flesh and the discharge from the ulcerated areas is thereby increased. Hemorrhage from the movement of the toe in walking is prone to occur and the general unwholesomeness of the part is thus exaggerated.

In some cases the production of these exuberant granulations takes place under the body of the nail as well as in the groove or on the flap and they are not clearly discernible until the imbedded portion of the nail is removed, when they will be seen to crowd upward into view.

Any open wound upon the surfaces of the foot is very liable to septic infection. Regardless of the cleanly care one may give his feet and regardless of the washing of hose, infection will still take place, and only naturally so. The feet are coming constantly in contact with septic surfaces and the inside of a shoe presents large areas for the resting place of countless microorganisms in that it combines the three elements which are best suited for the growth of bacteria, viz: heat, moisture and darkness.

Ingrown nails are even more prone to infection than is a lesion in connection with an heloma or a fissured toe web, and in many instances where cases have been allowed to run for some time before the surgeon or podiatrist is called into consultation, infection has already occurred.

In connection with septic cases, abscess cavities are often found immediately in the nail groove, under the body of the nail itself or with a suppurative sinus burrowing backward under the posterior nail fold and involving the whole of the matrix in an acute suppurative process. In exaggerated cases, the cellulitis may be diffused throughout the whole digital region. However, these cases are rare, as walking has become well-nigh impossible long before this takes place and the patient will have been under scientific treatment before the case has reached such proportions.

Treatment. From the standpoint of the podiatrist, there are two distinct methods of operative technic in ingrown nail cases, the radical and the palliative. They differ as to the exact technic of the removal of the ingrown portion, but agree on practically all other points.

In that but for the first part of the operation these two methods are similar, they will be discussed separately as to that alone, and the post-operative procedures and dressing of both will be combined into one general discussion. Under each heading the treatment of the surrounding tissues is mentioned, but the reader is referred to the heading "Prophylaxis" for a thorough and comprehensive discussion of the various procedures necessary to their proper care.

Asepsis. Proper aseptic precautions must be observed in all lesions and particularly so with ingrown nail cases. As has already been stated, conditions of this nature are prone to infection because the surfaces and recesses or the nail groove present excellent lodgment for bacteria, and this point should always be borne in mind.

The parts should first be thoroughly cleansed with ether. This removes all greasy or oily matter from the field of operation and allows the antiseptic solutions subsequently used to come in direct contact with the affected surfaces.

Some effective antiseptic should then be used as a spray to prevent the washing in of bacteria from the surrounding parts. There are a number of solutions which are useful for this purpose; liq. zinci et alumni compositus, N F., and liq zinci et ferri compositus, N F., are both highly recommended. Liq. cresolis compositus may also be used with excellent results, although it carries the somewhat disagreeable odor of the cresols. These solutions are all active in strengths ranging from two to five per cent

Iodine is unquestionably the best antiseptic that can be applied to the field of operation, but as its discoloration of the tissues prevents the operator from visually observing geographic points he may need for further diagnosis, and as this drug also acts as a corrosive to metal instruments, it is found advisable in many instances to refrain from its use.

As a substitute for iodine, alcohol is the next most efficient germicide. Sixty per cent. strength is recommended, as in that proportion it has greater penetrative and antiseptic value than the stronger solutions.

The alcohol, applied by means of a cotton wound applicator, is rubbed into the parts, or a pledget of sterile cotton or gauze, saturated in the solution, may be applied over the field and allowed to remain for two or three minutes prior to operation.

When the operator has followed the foregoing, or a similar line of procedure, the removal of the ingrown portion of nail may be begun. For simplicity's sake, the methods of treatment will be discussed, beginning with the uncomplicated case, and the various complications will be considered under separate headings.

UNCOMPLICATED CASES

Removal of the Ingrown Portion. Having obtained thorough asepsis of the affected and surrounding areas, the operator by means of a small, blunt sterile probe, should endeavor to locate the exact position and size of the ingrown portion of nail, which should then be removed by means of a sterile nail chisel.

The Nail Chisel. This instrument is a narrow steel blade set in a long or short handle, as the operator desires, the operating end of which is slightly oblique so that, upon direct pressure, the blade cuts in a diagonal manner. This is for the purpose of minimizing the danger of penetration into the nail bed. In the radical operation a broader and heavier chisel is sometimes used so that the softer tissues may be included in the incision.

The Radical Method. Proper antiseptic precautions having been taken, the circulation is cut off at the base of the toe by the application of a tourniquet. Under local anesthesia, induced preferably by the hypodermatic injection of novocaine, 1%, the nail is split longitudinally to the root with an ingrown nail chisel, care being taken not to split the nail at or near its centre—a procedure practised by some surgeons. When the nail has been cut through the root, the free portion is grasped with an artery forceps and is lifted out of the nail groove. It is often necessary to dissect the nail from adhesions which have formed

The proud flesh, should any be present, is now snipped off with a pair of curved scissors and if necessary a portion of the enlarged nail flap is also included in the cut. The soft tissues should be cut so that the structure remaining appears normal in size.

The nail matrix is thoroughly curetted over its entire exposed area, as is the nail bed along its whole surface to the distal end. This procedure must be thorough to insure against recurrence. Bleeding is of a capillary type and is easily controlled by digital pressure.

The Palliative Method. With a sterile nail clipper, a small cut is made on the affected side in the free edge of the nail. The chisel is then placed in this notch and gentle yet firm pressure is exerted so that the instrument cuts through and splits the nail.

The cut made is in the shape of an arc, following as nearly as possible the normal line of the lateral edge of the nail. The broadest part of the arc is at the anterior or free edge of the nail, gradually reducing the width of the piece to be removed until the lateral edge is reached. In this way a clean sweeping cut is made which does not invade and consequently does not irritate the tissues about the nail root.

The palliative method of operative technic in ingrown

nail cases is based on the theory that the condition is not one of a misdirected growth of the nail, but rather a case of the soft tissues adjacent to the nail crowding up, around and over the nail proper; and that the nail body as it pushes continually forward, cannot force this mass back into its normal position and, of necessity, must grow into it.

There is no lateral hypertrophy of the nail nor does it present any misdirected growth.

Keeping this theory in mind, it would seem unnecessary and poor surgery to remove the portions of the matrix of the nail from which the affected side develops when in reality it is not the nail that is at fault but rather the soft tissues adjacent to it; and the ingrowing of the nail body is purely secondary to the displacement of these soft tissues. As ever in surgery, however, it remains a matter of judgment as to which operation should be done so as to obtain the best results. When the palliative methods fail to be effective, the radical operation is permissible— never the reverse.

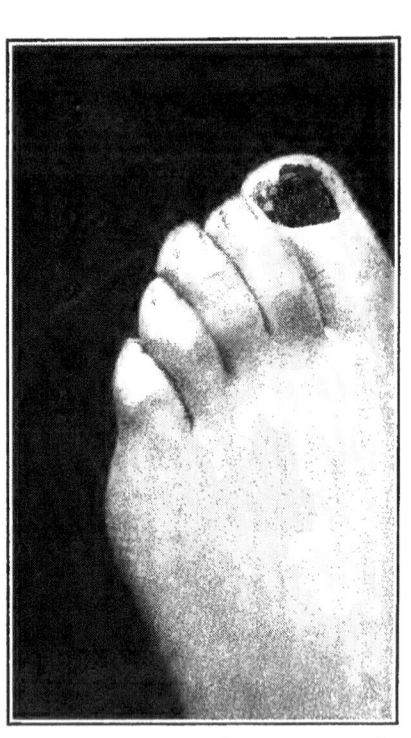

ONYCHOCRYPTOSIS (SUPPURATING)

The palliative method has for its object the removal of the portion of nail whose irritant free border is embedded in the tissues and, this accomplished, to treat these softer tissues in such a manner that they will become normal as to position and all else By such a manner and method of treatment, sufficient space is obtained at its lateral edge for the nail to grow to its full width and in time to become perfectly normal as to appearance, function and feeling.

The straight nail chisel, in most instances, can be used, but where the ingrown portion of nail is deeply embedded, a right or left curved chisel can be substituted with greater success. The curve in this variety of chisel aids the operator in lifting the nail out of its bed, while at the same time the cutting process is not hindered.

Dressing. Following the removal of the offending portion of nail, the operator should make sure that no nail slivers, previously existing or of his own making, remain in the nail fold Assured of this, the parts should then be thoroughly irrigated either with alcohol, 60%, or mercuric chloride, 1/4000 Hydrogen peroxide may be used as an irrigant where pus is present, but it should not be depended upon as a germicide as its action is very transient and superficial. A final dressing is then put in place.

There seems to be a wide diversity of opinion as to what constitutes a proper dressing after the nail has been removed. Whatever else individual experience may show to be useful, the dressing should be one embodying antiseptic, astringent and healing properties. The antiseptic, surely regardless of what other action is to be desired; the astringent, so that inflammatory symptoms may be speedily combated and the ulcerated areas contracted; and the healing so that granulation may be the more speedily promoted.

Three forms of dressings may be classified: the wet; the dry; the ointment.

The Wet Dressing. The nail groove is packed with a small piece of sterile gauze. Care should be exercised that a thin fold of the gauze be placed under the edge of the nail between it and the tissues into which the ingrown portion of nail was embedded. A piece of sterile gauze, of about three or four thicknesses and about two inches square, is then placed over the affected fold of the nail, covering the inflamed area and extending over the nail itself. This pledget is then saturated with a solution of the operator's choosing to meet the needs of the case under treatment. Two solutions seem to be favored above all others in this connection: mercuric chloride, 1/5000, or weaker, and liq. aluminum acetate. The latter solution is at most times preferable, as it possesses antiseptic qualities (nearly, if not equal to corrosive sublimate without exhibiting the toxic properties of the latter) and produces an astringent and antiphlogistic action on the tissues. Strong germicidal solutions such as the mercuric chloride are at times found to be decidedly detrimental, in that they not alone cause maceration and desquamation of the skin, but in some instances, if too strong, they destroy the newly formed connective tissue granules

The gauze square which covers the whole end of the toe, and which is saturated with either solution just described, is held in place by a roller bandage or by adhesive strips.

The usual method of applying these strips is to place one on each side of the gauze square, adhering them over the end of the toe and to and on the skin, and one over the centre of the dressing, carrying it over the end and down to and on the plantar surface of the toe. A circular strip is then carried around the toe, over the posterior end of the dressing, thus binding down the ends of the three strips previously applied

No impervious covering such as gutta percha, oiled silk, etc., should be used in this instance, or, in fact, in any condition where the skin is broken. The warmth and moisture produced by such a covering is congenial to the growth and development of hostile bacteria.

The wet dressing, then, should be left uncovered so that evaporation may take place and a quantity of the solution used should be prescribed for the patient, so that the dressing may be moistened with it from time to time. The dressing without impervious covering is antiseptic and heat reducing because of the evaporation and frequent replenishment of the solution

The Dry Dressing. Dry dressings in this sense consist in the application either of plain, dry, sterile gauze packed in the nail groove and unmoistened, or dusting the affected parts with some antiseptic powder to maintain asepsis in the wound and to bring about normal granulation.

Of these two forms of dry dressing, that constituted by the plain dry gauze is productive of better results than are obtained by the dusting powders. A lesion caused by the nail penetrating the soft tissues of the nail fold, in the process of healing, necessarily discharges a certain amount of waste material produced in the tissue repair In consequence, where a dusting powder is used, the serous discharge at times combines with the particles of the powder to form a crust which, in the confined areas of the nail groove, often becomes equally as irritating as was the ingrown nail itself.

However, in some instances dusting powders may be used with impunity and many practitioners favor and report success in their use.

Aristol (thymol iodide), dermatol (bismuth subgallate), bismuth subnitrate and boric acid (powder), preferably the first two named, may all be safely used in the treatment of ingrown nail cases. Aristol depends upon the liberation of iodine for its antiseptic action while the two bismuth salts, the subgallate and the subnitrate, combine marked astringent properties with their antiseptic qualities.

After the powder is dusted into the affected groove, a thin layer of sterile gauze is packed lightly under the lateral edge of the nail and a cocoon dressing is placed over the whole.

This form of dressing is applied until resolution of the inflammatory process and granulation of the wound has taken place.

The Ointment Dressing. All ointments are necessarily of fatty or oily consistency and, in consequence, when applied over a surface excreting a serous discharge, are liable to confine this discharge to the affected areas rather than allow it to be absorbed by the gauze dressing, and so drain the wound. For this reason the use of ointments on discharging surfaces is not particularly recommended. Many practitioners use them, however, and presumably with beneficial results.

Two classes of ointments may be used in this connection antiseptic and stimulating. Under these headings the following are suggested: sulphur, 10% (vaseline or lanolin base); ammoniated mercury (white precipitate), 5%; balsam of Peru, 10%, and scarlet red (medicinal Biebrich), 4%.

The ointment is placed in the nail groove by means of a spatula, and sterile gauze is packed lightly under the nail, holding the ointment in place. This is covered with a cocoon dressing and is renewed until the parts regain their normal condition.

COMPLICATED CASES

Proud Flesh. The development of unhealthy, exuberant granulations is a common occurrence in connection with ingrown nail cases, especially when they have been allowed to progress before proper treatment has been inaugurated.

In all cases the primary steps in the treatment are essentially similar to those described under "uncomplicated cases." Proper asepsis and antisepsis are at all times to be strictly observed, and any ingrown portion of nail should in all cases be first removed before additional treatment is administered.

The speedy and complete removal of the unhealthy granulations is at all times essential. This may be accomplished either by excision, by the actual cautery or by the use of escharotics. The operator must always remember that the presence of proud flesh in a wound not alone retards the normal healing process, but also prevents the wound from healing without the formation of an abnormal amount of new tissue. If, for instance, a mass of proud flesh the size of a pea were present in connection with an ingrown nail and allowed to remain without further treatment, the tissue would in time present a perfectly normal appearance. That is, the exuberant granules would sooner or later develop an epithelial covering which would be of like appearance to the normal surface of the skin. But in doing so, the tissues would still retain the shape and size of the original mass of exuberant granules and we would find a teat of tissue, the size of a pea, jutting out of the normal surface of the nail groove.

Keeping in mind, then, that to obtain a speedy and normal healing action in a wound the proud flesh present must be eradicated, it should appeal to the operator that the quickest means for its removal must be the best. Two quick and complete methods for obtaining this desired result are found in (1), excision (by the use of the scalpel or curved scissors), and in (2), the actual cautery.

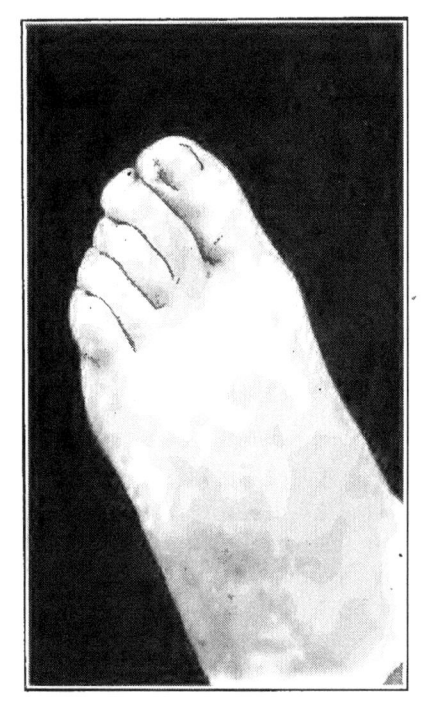

BEGINNING INGROWN TOE NAIL

Excision. Excision of the proud flesh cannot be resorted to in all cases, but in most cases at least the larger portion of the exuberant granulations can be removed in this manner.

The condition in which the use of the curved scissors is particularly advocated as most efficient is that in which the mass of proud flesh is found in pendulous form, where its base is narrow and covers but a small area and where the mass expands into an enlarged extremity. In cases where the proud flesh is found generally throughout the nail groove, and in some instances under the lateral edge of the nail itself, the scissors or scalpel cannot be used with good effect, if at all Then of course other means must be employed.

Method of Procedure. After the field of operation has been thoroughly sterilized and the ingrown portion of the nail has been located and removed, the exact situation and amount of proud flesh is ascertained. If at all practical, a sterile scissors (preferably of the curved variety) is inserted under the granulating mass and the whole is quickly snipped off at its junction with the normal integument. Where the mass is considerable, it will be found advisable to ligate the toe at its base by means of a few tight turns of adhesive tape or by the use of a rubber ligature. This precaution will lessen the resulting hemorrhage and it can be more readily controlled.

Where the amount of proud flesh to be excised is small, the blood flow is easily arrested by digital pressure

It will generally be found conducive to the best results to anesthetize the parts by hypodermatic injections of novocaine or by means of the ethyl chloride spray. This is not necessary in every instance, however, as the advisability of producing anesthesia depends upon the amount of tissue involved and the nervous condition of the patient.

After the exuberant granulations have been cut off, Monsel's solution, adrenalin chloride or some other styptic is applied to the bleeding capillaries.

It may be found advisable to apply silver nitrate, 50%, or even nitric acid, c.p., to the bleeding parts This serves not alone to check the hemorrhage, but the escharotic action tends to destroy whatever remaining shreds of the proud flesh may still be present.

The oozing arrested, the ligature is removed. The nail groove is packed firmly with sterile gauze (firmly, so as to further check the vascular supply to the parts) and a wet dressing of liq aluminum acetate is applied. In the event of no further recurrence of the proud flesh, the case is treated in any of the ways described under "uncomplicated cases."

The Actual Cautery. The electric cautery presents a quick and sure means by which proud flesh may be destroyed. Local anesthesia should first be induced by means of a hypodermatic injection of novocaine, 1%, or by use of a freezing spray, such as ethyl chloride. In most instances the use of the ethyl chloride will be found sufficient for the needs of the case although its anesthetic effect is quite superficial and transient. Novocaine, on the contrary, is both lasting and complete in its effect.

The argument against the use of the actual cautery is one of humaneness rather than one of science. Regardless of the lack of sensation produced by the anesthetic, patients will rebel at the sight of a white hot cautery. The mental shock of seeing one's flesh seared by a hot iron is pronounced, and at the present time no podiatrist can take liberties with the patient's feelings as does the surgeon, without jeopardizing his reputation and diminishing his clientele. On the other hand, while the mental anguish of the patient may be greater during the use of the actual cautery, the subsequent suffering is much less than that following the application of an escharotic.

After the use of the cautery, a wet dressing of liq. aluminum acetate or a solution of boric acid and alcohol, equal parts, may be applied and renewed until all acute inflammatory symptoms have subsided when a dressing may be employed to hasten granulation.

Escharotics. The use of caustics for the destruction of proud flesh is probably the most generally used method in vogue today. Nitric acid, caustic potash and silver nitrate, either in fused or in solution form, may all be used in most every instance.

Inability for any reason to resort to the use of a curved scissors, the scalpel, or the cautery compels us to look among the caustics for an agent to accomplish the desired results. Keeping in mind the aforementioned fact, that the quickest means for proud flesh removal or destruction is the best, we naturally lean toward the strong corrosives as a means to bring about this end

Nitric Acid. Nitric acid (aqua fortis), in all probability, is the most efficient member of this class of drugs, as its action is both energetic and penetrating In cases where the exuberant granulations are found involving the entire nail fold and in no particular localized area, aqua fortis is found very useful. Usually one application is sufficient to destroy all vestige of the unhealthy tissue, but in extreme cases added treatment may be necessary.

Care is taken to cover the surrounding healthy integument with some greasy substance (vaseline is generally preferred) to prevent the acid from coming in contact with it and avoiding the consequent bad effects. The acid is then applied by means of a cotton wound applicator (wooden applicators are preferred, as they are inexpensive and may be thrown away after being used) or a glass rod. The nail groove should be firmly packed with sterile gauze and a wet dressing of liq. aluminum acetate or of bichloride of mercury, 1/5000, or a boric acid and alcohol solution, equal parts, should be applied over the affected parts. At the next examination, any remaining shreds of the unhealthy granulation are to be looked for and, if found, another but lighter application of the acid should be applied It is wise to remove the eschar caused by the previous application so that deeper penetration and more efficient action from the drug may be obtained.

This is continued until all remnants of the proud flesh are destroyed, when the toe should be dressed to induce speedy and healthy granulation.

Caustic Potash. Potassium hydroxide (caustic potash) may be used in place of nitric acid for the destruction of proud flesh. The preference for the latter seems to be due to the fact that wounds caused by the action of nitric acid are prone to heal more rapidly than those due to the use of caustic potash; also because the action of aqua fortis can be more readily counteracted should the need for such action arise.

Caustic potash should be used with care, the same precautions to protect the healthy tissue being taken as in the use of nitric acid Apply caustic potash on a small cotton wound applicator, packing the nail fold with sterile gauze to be followed by a moist dressing of liq. aluminum acetate.

Silver Nitrate. The use of the silver stick or a strong solution of the salt to destroy any great amount of proud flesh is not advocated. In the first place the caustic action of silver nitrate is due solely to the nitric acid generated by its use, and so the aqua fortis should be used to obtain a speedier and more energetic removal of the unhealthy tissue. Secondly, silver nitrate coming in contact with the albuminous tissue, decomposes, oxidizing it and forming a metallic deposit on the surface which becomes an impermeable eschar. This hard crust not alone prevents the silver salt from penetrating into the tissues—the action of silver nitrate is thus called "self-limiting"—but also being unyielding, acts as a direct irritant to the denuded tissues.

Silver nitrate is, however, particularly efficacious after the great amount of the proud flesh has been removed by means of excision; in this situation it acts as a styptic to arrest the capillary flow of the bleeding stump, and as a mild caustic to destroy the remaining shreds of the unhealthy granulation It is also a beneficial application for hardening the tissues of the nail fold to prevent further recurrence of the ingrowing nail. This subject will be fully discussed under "Prophylaxis " After excision of the proud flesh, silver nitrate should be used in solution of fifty per cent. and the toe dressed as has been previously described.

Burnt Alum. Burnt alum is still another remedy used

in podiatry for the destruction of proud flesh. Its use is not now favored for that direct purpose, but there are some situations in connection with the treatment of the condition in which it may be used with good results. It is the least energetic of all the escharotics herein mentioned, and many prefer to class it rather as an astringent. The burnt alum is dusted in the nail groove directly on the mass of proud flesh and the groove is then packed with sterile gauze. Because of its extremely mild action, comparatively speaking, burnt alum will not accomplish its work of destruction with the rapidity nor the completeness of the other mentioned drugs; moreover it causes considerable irritation and pain to the patient. The modern practitioner is inclined to relegate this drug, as a caustic, to the shelf, to be used only in cases where a strong astringent action is desired.

Liquor Ferri Subsulphate. Monsel's solution has been used to dry up unhealthy granulations because of its astringent action rather than on account of its caustic properties.

Treatment of Acute Infective Inflammations. Infection is in all probability more generally met with in connection with ingrown nail cases than in any other ailment primarily occurring on the foot. The state in which the toe may be found is dependent upon the length of time the case has progressed without proper treatment. Cellulitis may be circumscribed or diffused, and lymphangitis, both of the reticular or tubular variety, may be present

Following the usual antiseptic and aseptic precautions relative to the field of operation, the operator's hands and the instruments, drainage of the suppurated areas must first be obtained.

In the average case, an abscess cavity is usually found in or adjacent to the lateral nail fold, and in many instances the pus sac will be punctured during the removal of the ingrown portion of the nail It is sometimes found necessary to remove an overlying portion of nail, other than the ingrown portion, to give free access to the suppurating process and to afford drainage for its purulent discharge.

A sterile chisel of the straight variety is generally used to accomplish the removal of the ingrown portion of nail, care being taken that the cutting edge is inserted deep enough to penetrate only the nail and not to pierce the underlying soft parts.

Some practitioners do not advocate the removal of portions of the nail and prefer rather merely to drill a hole through the nail body and excavate the pus through this channel. No doubt circumstances alter cases, but the writer would prefer having the septic tract wholly exposed so that thorough irrigation and proper treatment may be accomplished.

Having given free drainage to the pus cavities, the parts should again be sprayed with alcohol, 60%. Hydrogen peroxide, which manifests its greatest efficacy in pus cases, should then be freely applied until ebullition ceases.

In cases where the sinus is small and deep and an ordinary cotton wound applicator is too large for insertion into its recesses, a wooden applicator tipped with iodine (these applicators already prepared are now on the market) will be found fine enough for this accomplishment.

There is also on the market a fine, hollow, flexible needle, with a bulbous extremity in which there is an opening, that fits any hypodermic syringe. Two or three drops of iodine are drawn into the barrel, the needle is inserted into the sinus, and its contents are evacuated by piston pressure. This enables the operator to get the drug down into the sinus so that it comes into direct contact with its deepest surfaces. This needle is made of a non-corrosive metal.

The next point to be considered is the form of dressing to be used. If the case has progressed to a point where the operator feels the necessity of a surgeon's advice, the latter should by all means be called in as a consultant. The writer feels, however, that in most instances the modern practitioner of podiatry is well equipped to successfully treat even severe cases of this nature.

The affected nail groove is packed with sterile gauze and a large piece of the fabric, of several thicknesses, is placed over the whole inflamed area. This is saturated with a solution of mercuric chloride, 1/5000, and is remoistened at intervals by the patient so that it is constantly wet In some cases it may be wise to have the patient remain in the office several hours to make sure that the infected parts are kept constantly immersed in a solution of mercuric chloride, 1/5000. This treatment has been found to be extremely beneficial in reducing the inflammation so that a moist evaporating dressing, as described above, may be safely applied Rest is another feature to be employed in the treatment of these cases. The patient should be instructed to refrain absolutely from the use of the affected parts until such time when the inflammatory conditions have subsided or are under control. The podiatry patient as a rule is loathe to have his or her energies in any way curtailed, but the mention of "blood poisoning" is usually sufficient stimulus to send the patient to bed when so ordered.

Prognosis. The prognosis in all cases of ingrown nail under proper treatment is favorable. The length of time elapsing before a cure is affected is of course dependent upon the condition of the toe and the general condition of the patient

In cases where the nail penetration is slight, and the inflammatory conditions are in their incipiency, one or at most two treatments will be sufficient to heal the ulceration and to restore the toe to its normal condition. Complicated cases necessarily take longer to relieve and longer to cure

The surgeon is still rather reluctant to believe that an ingrown nail can be cured without removal of the affected half of the nail, the lateral nail fold, and a portion of the matrix. This method of procedure in nearly every instance incapacitates the patient for fully two weeks and it is doubtful whether anything is gained (taking all matters into consideration) over the methods of ingrown nail treatment as here outlined.

The surgical argument is based on the contention that unless the matrix underlying the affected nail be removed, the nail will again grow into the tissues. This is unquestionably so, but in a majority of cases, as explained previously, the trouble is not due to a misdirected growth of the nail, but rather to the tissues surrounding the free edge and lateral nail border crowding up, around and over the nail

It may then be safely stated that an ingrown nail properly treated and which has been subjected subsequently to proper prophylactic measures, is curable; not temporarily, but permanently.

PROPHYLAXIS

In considering the measures employed by which the general condition of the nail may be improved so as to prevent a further recurrence of the ingrowing tendencies, we will make, for simplicity's sake, six divisions. Five of these relate to the nail itself and to the subjacent tissues, and one to the footgear and hosiery of the patient.

1. Thinning the Nail Through Its Long Axis. When the acute inflammatory symptoms have subsided and the ulcerated areas healed, in other words when the toe and the nail have returned to normal, measures should be taken to prevent the latter from becoming again ingrown. With a rotary file, the centre of the nail should be ground to a paper thinness through its long axis. What is accomplished by this procedure?

The nail is normally convex on its outer surface and the apex of its dome is the centre of the nail body This portion, being the greatest point of elevation, naturally receives the brunt of the pressure from the shoe. If the nail, then, is allowed to remain thick in the centre of its body, the shoe pressing upon it will find the nail unyielding and in consequence will cause its lateral borders to be forced down into the nail grooves By thinning the body of the nail to such an extent that it becomes thin and flexible, the shoe presses upon a yielding surface, in consequence of which the nail "gives" or spatulates at its centre and the pressure upon its lateral borders is decreased if not prevented entirely.

Having done away with any untoward pressure which might be brought to bear on the nail, we next turn to:

2. Hardening the Nail Groove, and Shrinking the Flap. In many cases, after all acute symptoms of the disturbances have subsided, we find that the flap of tissue adjacent to the once affected nail and forming the outer side of the groove, is greatly thickened and enlarged.

This must be reduced in order that the new-forming nail will have sufficient room to develop to its normal width and we must also harden and toughen the nail groove so that it will present a surface that the nail, as it grows out, will not be able to penetrate, should it be so inclined.

Silver nitrate is the most generally used and most efficient agent to carry out a treatment of this kind. Solutions varying in strength from 5% to 50% are recommended, and the selection depends on what is to be accomplished and the length of time which may be given to the treatment.

By persistent use of silver nitrate solution, 50%, an enlarged and thickened nail flap may in time be reduced to normal. Applications about one week apart—in some cases ten days or two weeks to intervene—will usually work wonders in conditions of this kind. The groove should be thoroughly cleansed and dried and the silver solution should be applied on a small cotton wound applicator and painted well down under the nail and over the tissue in the enlargement. A dressing, usually cotton and collodion, is then applied and allowed to remain undisturbed until the patient's return. The action of this solution is astringent and sedative. It is bound to reduce the chronic inflammatory symptoms that may be present and, acting as an astringent, it gradually shrinks the enlarged flap until the normal line of the lateral nail fold is reached.

During the treatment, there is absolutely no pain nor inconvenience to the patient. Care should always be exercised that the silver solution be not applied if any hemorrhage has been caused in the removal of a previous eschar, as it is sufficiently caustic to cause ulceration should it come in contact with such a denuded surface. Packing of the nail groove will be discussed under the sub-heading "Packing."

Subsulphate of iron (Monsel's solution) may be used in the treatment of cases of this nature, but its action as an astringent in this connection is so mild that it is of necessity a slow process to effect a complete cure.

The solution, usually applied to the groove on gauze, is allowed to remain. In fact, the patient is often advised to procure a quantity of the drug and keep the gauze moistened.

The patient should be seen at periods of about a week or ten days, when both the dressing and the eschar caused by the action of the iron salt are removed. Fresh gauze is packed under the nail and the treatment continued.

Ferric chloride has much the same action in this connection as the subsulphate, but this drug has never been so popular, for the reason of its greater irritant qualities few of which are to any degree manifest in Monsel's solution.

Ointments or collodion containing large percentages of salicylic acid—as high as sixty to seventy-five per cent.—are sometimes used to destroy an enlarged nail flap by strong disintegrative action. The ointment is usually prepared on a cerate base and sufficient wax is added to thicken the paste so that the tendency to melt and run over portions of the integument, where its action would be detrimental, is minimized.

The oinment is applied in the groove and over the top surface of the mass to be destroyed and is allowed to remain for a few days when the disintegrated portion is removed and another application made. This action of salicylic acid, used in considerable strength, is at times painful and cannot be borne by every patient. The treatment is a good one, however, and is rapidly coming into the prominence and popularity it deserves. Salicylated collodion is similar in action to the ointments containing salicylic acid, and the same general procedure holds good for both applications. The collodion is applied on all surfaces of the mass, is covered with a cotton and collodion dressing and a second application is made upon the removal of the disintegrated portion.

It is sometimes advantageous to alternate the silver nitrate treatment with that of salicylic acid. An application of the ointment or the collodion is made and upon removal of the disintegrated portion, the silver solution is applied. After the lapse of about two weeks, the salicylic acid is again applied and the treatment continued alternately in this manner until the desired result is obtained.

3. Packing. We here come to one of the most important procedures necessary to a successful prophylactic treatment of an ingrown nail. Whether the nail groove is to be packed loosely or tightly is a question of great import and should be given careful consideration by the operator. Often the comfort of the patient and always the ultimate outcome of the case is dependent on the proper packing of the nail groove as an after-treatment.

There appears to be a great tendency to pack the groove full to overflowing with gauze, cotton, or what not, and, although there are some instances where a procedure of this kind is necessary, it is usually conducive to a great amount of pain to the patient and has a decidedly deleterious effect on the tissues under treatment.

In general, it is wise to pack the groove as lightly as possible, using only a small pledget of gauze or cotton and taking care that the fabric is well under the nail and interposed between it and the tender areas underneath. It must be remembered that no matter what fabric be used for packing, it rapidly hardens and becomes more or less irritant to the tissues. Should the nail groove be packed to such a degree that at the time of dressing it is unyielding and hard, it is easily realized what the condition of this dressing will be in the course of a few days.

The only time a nail groove might be tightly packed is in connection with the treatment of proud flesh when the tight packing tends to interrupt the circulation to the part and thus aids in retarding the growth of the superfluous granulations Another instance when a groove may be packed tightly is in a case where no inflammation is present and when it is the desire of the operator to hold the softer tissues down and away from the edge of the nail so that sufficient room may be allowed for the nail to grow out and attain its normal width. A word in connection with this theory. Silver nitrate solutions, twenty-five to fifty per cent., applied to the groove hardens the tissue by means of the eschar developed on its surface and a tight packing to hold these tissues in place is an ideal combination for the prophylactic treatment of a previously acute ingrown nail case, when by such tight packing no noticeable inconvenience is caused to the patient. If cotton is used as a packing it should be rolled into a loose thin pledget, the finer "point" of which is inserted under the edge of the nail near its posterior fold, and the thicker end is packed under the nail at its distal portion. One thickness of gauze is generally sufficient and, at most, two thicknesses may be used, unless, of course, tight packing is required.

In connection with this prophylactic treatment it may sometimes be wise to place a shield of felt or buckskin between the tender part and the adjacent toe to hold that member away from the affected areas and so that the medications applied may be allowed a chance to complete their therapeutic action undisturbed This shield is not strapped but is merely placed between the toes, resting on the interdigital web, and is just high enough to reach the base of the nail and so does not come in direct contact with the area under treatment.

4. Allowing the Nail to Grow Long. The nail should be allowed to attain as great a length as possible, particularly at its lateral points, without interference with the continuity of the patient's hosiery, and yet not long enough to cause pressure from the toe of the boot.

This can be best accomplished by cutting the free edge of the nail in a concave manner. The lateral points are kept, if possible, long enough so as to extend to a point slightly beyond the distal end of the nail fold and the rest of the free edge is cut in a circular manner so that at its centre it is no longer than just sufficient to cover the anterior edge of the nail bed. This manner of cutting, combined with thinning the nail body through its central longitudinal axis, prevents any great amount of pressure from being exerted by the shoe upon the apex of the nail's convexity. It will also, to a great extent, prevent the nail from cutting through the patient's hosiery. If the whole nail is allowed to grow long, and its free edge to extend over the end of the toe, some leverage is bound to be brought upon this extended portion and in consequence there is a tendency to press the lateral edges of the nail into the grooves, which, of course, is to be avoided at all costs.

5. No Lateral Cutting. In connection with the length which the nail is allowed to retain, it is absolutely imperative that no lateral cutting be done. Some cases of ingrown nail have been observed in even very young children (in one instance a baby of fourteen months). The primary cause in every case was found to be the overzealous care on the part of the parents to prevent just the condition they had caused by injudiciously removing from time to time the lateral edges of the sufferer's toe nails.

6. Proper Boots and Hosiery. In addition to the various means for preventing the recurrence of an ingrowing nail, great care should be exercised in the selection of the patient's footgear.

Shoes of sufficient width and length should of course be advocated so that at no time will the toes be cramped by any degree of pressure.

The wearing of a pointed boot or slipper in which there

is not sufficient width at the ends of the toes to allow those members proper latitude, should be discouraged. When footgear is worn in which this cramped condition of the digits is brought about, it will be generally found that the soft tissues lying adjacent to the lateral edges of the nail are crowded up alongside the latter and an enlarged and thickened flap, which is the cause of so much trouble, is formed. Lace boots are probably the most practical of any in that they may be firmly fastened about the ankles and over the instep, and thus prevent the foot from sliding forward and coming in contact with the toe of the boot. Pumps of all varieties are without a doubt the most detrimental footgear worn today—for they have absolutely no support or anchorage at the ankle and, in some cases, patients find themselves flexing the toes in the endeavor to retain the slipper on the foot.

Hosiery, too, should be neither tight nor short, as a short stocking or sock may cause pressure upon the toe nails and so be the forerunner of trouble

CHAPTER XV

DISEASES OF THE NAILS

The nails of the hands and feet are subject to various diseases. The chief of these are

>Onychocryptosis, or ingrown nail.
>Onychophosis, or calloused nail groove.
>Onychia, or inflammation of the matrix.
>Paronychia, or inflammation around the nail.
>Onychauxis, or club nail.
>Onychatrophia, or atrophy of the nail.
>Onychoptosis, or falling off of the nail
>Onychorrhexis, or brittle nail

Some of these diseases of the nails are the result of a general systemic disturbance, but only the local treatment of such conditions becomes the province of the podiatrist. It is often necessary to distinguish between a local chiropodical condition and a local manifestation of some serious systemic disease; it is then necessary for the medical practitioner and the podiatrist to join hands in making a diagnosis for the proper guidance of both practitioners.

Onychocryptosis, or ingrown toe nail, is a common affliction of the nail, and is thoroughly described in a separate chapter.

Derivation. From the Greek, onyx-nail, and krypto, I hide or conceal.

Onychophosis, or calloused nail groove, is also one of the common types of nail lesions, and is discussed separately. This lesion is often mistaken for ingrown toe nail, and treatment, improperly directed, often causes bad results.

Onychia or Onychitis is an inflammation of the matrix with suppuration and final shedding of the nail.

Derivation. From the Greek, onyx-nail, and itis-inflammation.

Etiology. Onychia may be due to trauma, causing malformation of the nail, and subsequent inflammation, but is most usually due to bacterial infection Removal of ingrown toe nails under septic conditions, or the entrance of bacteria through self-inflicted or other wounds offer opportunities for infective processes on a part of the body none too clean at best. Syphilis, tuberculosis and eczema are also often etiologic factors.

Pathology. Bacterial infection or trauma causes the nail matrix to become inflamed, with the accompanying pathologic changes that occur in all inflammatory processes. There is a gradual solution of the continuity between the nail proper and the matrix, and as the degenerative processes continue, namely the formation of pus and the solution of the tissues which comprise the matrix, the grooves in the nail matrix, which hold the corresponding ridges of the nail, are lost and the mechanical union of the two parts cease. The nail subsequently falls off. If the entire matrix has been destroyed, no new nail will grow, but this does not usually occur. Malformation of the new nail is quite common, due to partial destruction of the matrix

Diagnosis. The matrix of the nail is inflamed and severe pain is felt when pressure is brought to bear on the nail plate. The nail bed and the nail grooves are often involved and the inflammation may continue to such an extent as to involve lymphatics and cause destruction of a large area of tissue.

Pus forms at the root of the nail, and the nail itself gradually becomes loosened from its bed In cases due to injury or local infection, one or two toes may be involved, but when the cause is of systemic origin, all of the nails, including those of the hand, may become infected.

Treatment. The treatment of simple onychia consists

in protecting the part from further injury and irritation and it often becomes necessary to cut the shoe to accomplish this. In severer cases, shoes should not be worn until resolution commences.

Wet dressings are valuable, Burow's solution or boric acid solution being all that is necessary in mild cases.

When pus manifests itself, it is necessary to remove the nail over the abscess and to establish free drainage. Wet dressings of bichloride of mercury (1/5000) for 48 hours may be used, and when drainage is complete, the cavity may be swabbed with silver nitrate, 5 to 10%. Dry dressings of thymol iodide or boric acid powder will usually suffice to complete a cure.

The parts should be packed with sterile gauze so as to keep the soft tissues separated from the nail and to prevent irritation and pressure. This packing should not be too tight otherwise pus absorption with subsequent infection, is likely to occur.

In extreme cases, in which the surrounding tissues are involved and destruction has gone on to a greater extent, the entire nail must be removed, and the matrix destroyed by caustics or by curettage

Paronychia, or Paronychitis, is an inflammation of the tissues around the nail, and may involve all the tissues of the distal phalanx, including the bone

Synonyms. Felon, panaris, whitlow.

Derivation. From the Greek, para, beside, and onyx, nail.

Etiology. Paronychia is usually caused by local bacterial infection, due to treating the nail grooves with unclean instruments, or it may be of systemic origin It is often associated with onychia and in these cases is due to a spreading of the inflammation of the matrix to the surrounding tissues. Pressure of an ill-fitting shoe or stocking or of a foreign body may be a cause, and ingrowing toe nail may later develop into a paronychia. Syphilis often causes this lesion.

Pathology. The pathology of paronychia is much the same as that of onychia. The tissues surrounding the nail become inflamed, either by bacterial infection or by trauma, and all the signs and symptoms of inflammation manifest themselves. Swelling is marked and pus may or may not be present. Tissue destruction continues unless proper treatment is given, and the bone is often involved, causing periostitis or ostitis.

Diagnosis. Simple paronychia may exist without any hypertrophy of the nail itself, and may be due to pressure of a shoe or to a chronic ingrowing toe nail. The great toe is most commonly affected. The inflammation may be only slight and superficial, or it may be quite severe with great pain and swelling, terminating in a general intercellular infection with suppuration. Nourishment is interfered with and the nail may be shed much the same as in onychia. Pain is of a throbbing type which is immediately relieved when the abscess cavity is opened and the pus drained.

Treatment. Like onychia, paronychia should be treated with wet dressings and stimulating medications. In cases in which there is no suppuration, the following ointment will give good results·

    R Acidi salicylici   grs X
    Ung hydrarg. amm   ...   Oz I
  M ft ung. Sig. Keep on affected part constantly.

The corners and lateral edges of the nail should be separated from the soft tissues by means of sterile gauze, or they may be removed. Pus should be drained, with the assistance of antiseptic wet dressings such as bichloride of mercury, 1/5000, and if excessive granulations are present, they should be snipped off or destroyed with silver nitrate. If necessary, free incisions should be made, which will relieve the pain as well as assist in draining the pus.

In chronic paronychia it often becomes necessary to remove the entire nail, including the root, and under local anesthesia, this is easily accomplished. Rest is essential in these cases, and after suppuration has ceased, stimulants such as balsam of Peru or ichthyol may be used to good advantage.

In cases of paronychia, due to syphilis, it must be remembered that the treatment must be constitutional as well as local and the family physician of the patient should attend to the former feature of the treatment. Mercurial ointments, applied twice daily, are usually employed locally.

Onychauxis, or hypertrophy of the nail, is an overgrowth or enlargement of the nails of the fingers and toes. When the hypertrophy is accompanied by deformity, the condition is called onychogryphosis.

Derivation. From the Greek, onyx-nail, and auxe-increase.

Etiology. Enlargement of the nail is a result of hyperplasia of the papillae of the matrix, the thickening occurring at the base, front, lateral edges or over the entire area of the nail depending on the part diseased.

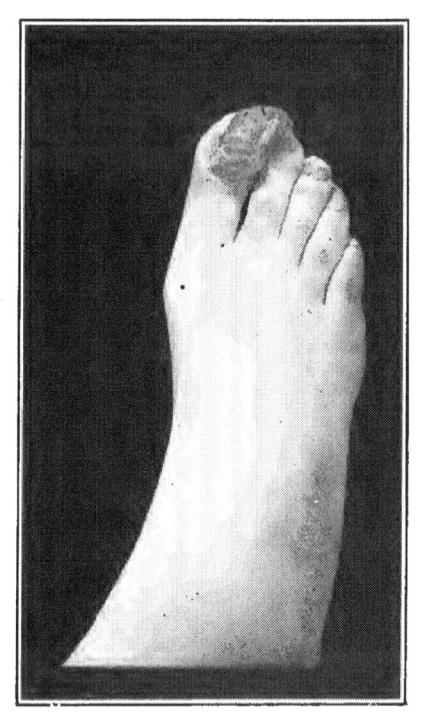

ONYCHOGRYPHOSIS

Pressure is no doubt a causative factor, and lack of care of the nails will also cause a thickening. Injury to the matrix will cause the nail to become hypertrophied, producing in most cases a true club nail (onychogryphosis).

Chronic cutaneous lesions, such as eczema or psoriasis

and other diseases such as syphilis, gout and rheumatism, and nervous diseases or injury to the nerves supplying the nails, may act as causes for onychauxis.

Pathology. Pressure or injury causes a widening of the nail fold which allows the formation of a thicker nail. The nail bed is irritated at the same time and a horny mass forms on it below the nail, which acts as a barrier to the forward movement of the nail cells, and by raising them up, determines more or less, the degree of deformity. The papillae of the matrix become enlarged, and may be seen protruding above the normal structure, when the nail is removed.

The thickened and deformed nail thus produced, is often the cause of other nail lesions, due to its pressure on the soft tissues. Bacterial infection is also common at this point, due to the fact that the mass of epithelial cells is a good breeding place for microorganisms.

Diagnosis. Onychauxis may be congenital or acquired, usually the latter. Simple hypertrophy of the nail is rarely found, but overgrowth with deformity is quite common. The nail becomes hardened, due to a closer cohesion of its component cells; its transparency is lost, and it assumes a dirty brown or even black color. The surface becomes rough, due to the presence of longitudinal and wavy tranverse ridges.

One or all of the nails may be affected; there may be a simple thickening or there may be a lateral overgrowth, which may result in paronychia. The inflammation may be slight or it may be severe and purulent. The nail, as it continues to become thickened, may assume various shapes resembling claws, talons, horns, etc. The big toe nail is the one most usually affected and often only the one foot is involved. This is indicative of a traumatic etiology.

Tuberculosis patients have a moderate onychauxis in most cases, particularly on the nails of the fingers, while hypertrophy is often seen in the inflammatory lesions such as eczema, psoriasis, etc.

Older persons are more liable to be affected with hypertrophy of the nail than younger persons, as there is a natural tendency to epithelial overgrowth in the aged.

Treatment. To affect a cure in case of hypertrophy of the nails it is necessary to recognize the cause. Thus, in cases of onychauxis, in which the general systemic condi-

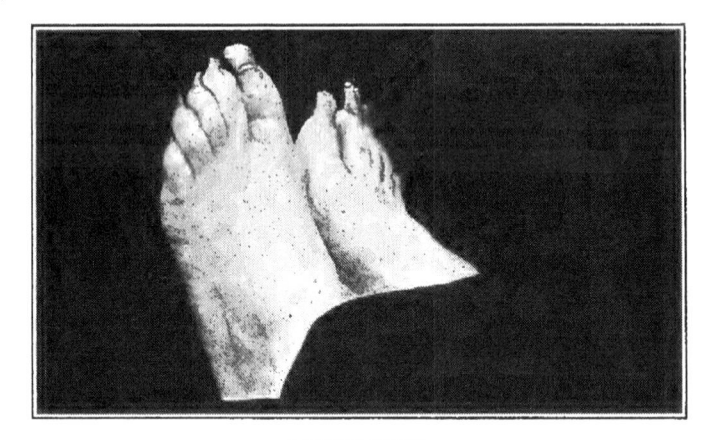

ONYCHAUXIS

tion is at fault, treatment must be directed by the family physician along constitutional lines and includes the taking of tonics, arsenic, mercury, etc. If a cutaneous lesion is the etiologic factor, it becomes necessary to treat the case both generally and locally. If the cause be an external one alone, local treatment is sufficient. For these latter conditions, the treatment is divided into palliative and radical procedures.

The *palliative* treatment consists in keeping the nail properly cut. For this purpose, the rotary file, or surgical drill, as it is called, is very efficient. Suitable burrs are used, and care is taken that the skin of the nail grooves is not injured. Infections are easily caused through the careless use of this instrument. After the nail has been thinned and is as nearly like a normal nail as is possible, the part should be cleansed with alcohol, and tincture of iodine (4%) should be applied. The grooves may be packed with sterile cotton and covered with collodion (cocoon dressing) which will avoid any tenderness that may be felt after the nail has been cut down The hard nails may also be softened by the application of sodium sulphide or liquor potassae and when softened, may be scraped away.

If thickened or club nails become very painful, it is often necessary to resort to *radical* measures, as this is the only permanent cure for this trouble. The entire nail must be completely removed under local anesthesia, and subsequently the entire nail matrix should be thoroughly scraped away by means of a sharp curette. The wound thus produced is kept in sterile dressings and is allowed to heal by granulation. It is quite common to find only a small area of the matrix that is vital, particularly in chronic cases of club nail, so that curettage is really a simple procedure A complete cure should be effected in from two to three weeks, the patient being able to walk with a cut-out shoe two or three days after the operation.

Onychatrophia, or atrophy of the nails, is a condition in which the nails of the toes and fingers become smaller and often are shed from the grooves in which they are contained.

Derivation. From the Greek, onyx-nail, and atrophia-atrophy.

Etiology. Atrophy of the nails may be caused by any one of many factors, among which are the inflammatory skin diseases, nervous diseases, constitutional disorders and injuries

Injury to the nail matrix causes complete or partial cutting off of nourishment If the nourishment is completely cut off, the nail matrix will disintegrate and cause the nail to be shed. New nails usually grow in these cases If the injury is less severe, there is only a temporary arrest in the nail growth, and the nail becomes thin and small discolorations are seen in the nail substance.

Inflammation of the soft tissues around the nail which is accompanied by suppuration, may cause atrophy and shedding of the nail. The nail will grow again as a rule, but often when the etiology is systemic, the new nails shed as soon as they are formed (onychia maligna).

In nervous diseases, such as cerebral paralysis, tabes dorsalis, syringomyelia, leprosy, division of the nerves, etc., from the vaso-motor disturbances due to the nerve lesion, a bleeding may occur about the posterior nail fold, and atrophy of the nail may result. The nails, as a rule, usually grow again.

In stasis of the blood stream in the extremities due to heart lesions, in venous congestion from emphysema, or in any lesion in which the circulation is impaired, the nails may undergo atrophy, particularly the nails of the fingers.

Diseases causing scarring of the nail matrix, such as pustular syphilides, gummata and variola, give rise to a partial destruction of the matrix and a shedding of the nail. Subsequent scarring may completely destroy the matrix, so that no new nail can grow.

In systemic diseases that cause wasting of the tissues, such as chronic tuberculosis, nephritis and diabetes mellitus, the matrix is usually under-nourished and the nails become discolored, soft and brittle, and often crumble.

Chemical poisons, such as arsenic, silver and lead, may cause atrophy of the nails. Those who work with chemicals and are compelled to put their fingers in acids and in alkalies often develop brittle, opaque nails. In general toxemias, the affliction of the nail is caused by interference with the nail nourishment at the matrix.

Pathology. When the nourishment of the matrix has been interfered with, the cells do not develop as rapidly as they should, and the nail becomes thin and streaked. The lustre is lost and the nails become gray or yellow, and often also become brittle. If the grooves in the nail bed are destroyed, the mechanical attachment between it and the nail is lost and the nail is cast off. Infective processes cause complete or partial destruction of the matrix by solution, and this in turn causes complete or partial loss of nail. White spots (leuconychia), said to be due to the entrance of air under the nails, are often seen, and gradually move toward the distal end of the nail

Diagnosis. Atrophy of the nails may be congenital or acquired, the former being rare and usually accompanied by imperfect development of the phalanges and scantiness of the hair throughout the body (alopecia universalis). Acquired atrophy in some form is the usual condition.

The nails present various appearances. They may be thin, soft, brittle, lustreless or opaque, split very easily, may be streaked or even worm-eaten in appearance. One or all of these conditions may be present. Thinning and splitting of the free ends may accompany systemic diseases, and some chronic inflammatory (especially scaly) skin lesions. Some nails are thinned at the ends with a central fissure extending toward the root. Transverse thinning or furrows are met with in fevers. The nails are always affected when nutrition has been lowered, due to depression of the general health.

In wasting diseases, such as chronic tuberculosis, diabetes, etc, the spoon nail is observed. This is a condition in which the lateral and free margins are raised, leaving a spoon-like depression in the centre.

Trauma, parasites, lowered nutrition and nervous diseases cause a crumbly, brittle nail. This is fairly common, and may be limited to one or more nails of the toes and fingers or it may be general. The atrophy may begin at either end, and extend forward or backward.

Treatment. Treatment of a local nature is worthless if the cause be systemic. Much like hypertrophy, the cure of atrophy depends on an exact determination of the etiology. Systemic treatment along proper lines will usually effect a cure. Local treatment consists in protecting the nails from irritation and sometimes even from water. The nails should be cut even and smooth and mollifying ointments and lotions are advisable. Cocoon dressings are very efficient for affording protection In atrophy, due to local circulatory interference, balsam of Peru (50%), in castor oil, or even pure, will stimulate nail growth. This should be applied once a day and can be retained by cocoon dressing. As a soothing agent the following may be employed.

R Acid boric.
Bismuth. subnitratis. . . .. aa. . . 0 60
Ung. aquae rosae
Unc. zinci oxidi. . .aa .. 16.0
M. Ft. ung. Sig. Apply to the nails morning and night.

Onychoptosis, falling off of the nail, and **Onychorrhexis,** brittle nail, are atrophies and have been discussed as such in the preceding sub-head.

CHAPTER XVI

FISSURES, BLISTERS, AND BURNS

FISSURES (*Fissura*)

Definition. Fissura or fissures, as used in this sense, are cracks or clefts in the surface of the skin, some involving only the epidermic layers, some penetrating deep into the corium.

Etiology. Fissures occurring on the foot, due to trauma, are far in the minority as compared with those occurring as secondary lesions in hyperidrosis, uric acid diatheses and other systemic conditions. They are usually due to a too strenuous drying of the interdigital surfaces with a rough towel. They may also be caused in like locations by excessive walking, but the condition of the skin of the patient has much to do with their formation. If the skin be dry and a great amount of its elasticity is gone, these lesions are much more prone to develop than where the skin tension is practically normal. The interdigital toe webs are often cracked or fissured in spreading the toes too far apart, and this has been caused, at times, by the podiatrist working between the toes and stretching them to obtain room for his instruments or dressings.

Treatment. The natural treatment for a condition of this kind would be to obtain astringent action. This may be accomplished by a number of drugs, principal among which is silver nitrate. Tannic acid preparations are also frequently used, but they cannot compare in efficiency with the silver salt. A number of mild vegetable astringents of the same group are similarly employed by podiatry practitioners.

FISSURES, BLISTERS AND BURNS

If the fissure is superficial, involving only the epidermic layers, compound tincture of benzoin, painted freely over the parts, after they have been thoroughly cleansed and dried, will be found advantageous in inducing rapid healing. Dusting powders such as tannoform, bismuth subgallate, bismuth subnitrate and thymol iodide, may also be successfully employed in these cases, but where the fissure is deep, the edges angry and red, and the whole area is involved in the inflammatory process, none of these are, as a rule, of avail, and more radical methods must be employed.

Nitrate of silver presents the most efficient means whereby astringent action may be obtained in the parts. Weak solutions, from 1% to 10%, are most generally employed, but it is often found necessary to use stronger solutions, even as high as 50%.

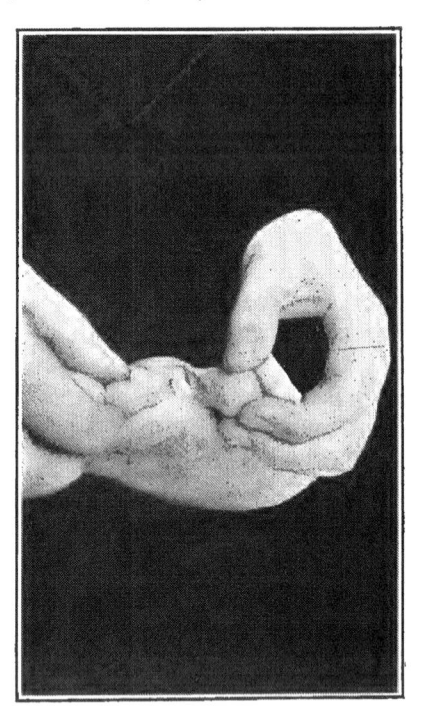

FISSURED TOE WEB

Technic. The parts are first thoroughly cleansed and any callous around the edges of the fissure is carefully and completely removed. This is an essential procedure, for no lateral granulation will take place, nor can direct apposition be obtained if this callous be allowed to remain.

Small particles of material from the hosiery or other foreign bodies should also be thoroughly removed. The recesses of a deep fissure present excellent places of lodgment for minute particles which are always to be found in footgear, and it is these bodies which produce infective processes. The above precautions having been observed, alcohol, 60%, should be freely applied and the parts thoroughly dried. Silver nitrate may then be painted deep down into the floor of the fissure, by means of a cotton-wound applicator. This will produce some smarting, but it is transsient and there will be no great amount of irritation. The silver solution should also be applied to the surfaces adjacent to the edges of the fissure, for it must be remembered that silver nitrate is sedative and this action is desirable in reducing the local inflammation.

Where the fissure is deep and of long standing, it may be found necessary to resort to a 25% or 50% solution or even to the fused stick. When cases are observed where proud flesh has developed in the fissure, due to continued irritation, it is necessary to use the stronger solutions or the stick at once. The proud flesh may be in such form as to permit of surgical removal. Where this can be accomplished, the bleeding stump is usually cauterized with silver solution, 50%. If a surgical procedure is impractical, the fused stick may be used to cauterize the neoplasm and thus eradicate it.

A dressing should be applied over the parts after the fissure has been treated. This may consist of several thicknesses of gauze, fashioned to fit between the toes, if the fissure be in that location; if the lesion be upon a plane surface, a square of gauze should be applied and held in place by adhesive strips.

A cocoon dressing may be substituted for that of gauze, and in many instances will be found more practical. It has been found necessary at times to apply some ointment or grease over the fissured area to aid in softening the parts and rendering them more flexible. Massage, at intervals, with olive oil or mutton tallow, will also be found advantageous in bringing about this result.

No dressing is applied over the parts after the use of compound tincture of benzoin, for this drug forms its own coating, which is practically impermeable. If a dusting powder be used alone, the parts are first thoroughly dried, whereupon the powder is dusted lightly into the fissure, and a wisp of cotton is placed over the part and held in place with collodion.

Pure ichthyol has also been found efficient in these instances; a drop is placed in the fissure and is retained there by means of cotton or gauze.

Astringent treatment, as described, should be continued until the fissure has entirely healed, and in the use of silver nitrate it will be found advisable to remove all remnants of the previous application before the drug is again used. The eschar is easily removed, but it must also be remembered that in some instances it may be advisable to allow the eschar to remain, and the wound to granulate under its protective covering.

This article has been confined almost entirely to fissures occurring in the interdigital webs for the reason that these parts are their usual sites of occurrence. At times, however, they do form in other parts of the foot—on the heels along the sides of the foot, and on the ends of the toes. The treatment in any locality is similar. When infection is present it should be arrested, if proud flesh has developed, that must be eradicated, in all cases astringent treatment is necessary to a successful outcome.

BLISTERS (*Bullae*)

Definition. A blister is a collection of fluid in the skin beneath the outer epidermic layers, which latter are raised to form the upper wall of the sac, the base of the blister being formed by the mucous layers of the epidermis or by the corium.

Etiology. The cause of practically all blisters met with in podiatry is traumatism Those occasioned by the friction brought to bear on the surfaces of the foot by a new or unyielding shoe predominate, but occasionally the podiatrist is called upon to treat these lesions arising from a burn. In discussing the subject of blisters under this heading, those of traumatic origin only will be considered. Those occasioned through burns, or superficial vesicular developments of specific origin will be discussed in chapters dealing with the disease or diathesis in connection with which they may develop

Pathology. The pathologic process causing the formation of a traumatic blister is a simple one. Due to the constant rubbing of a shoe, the superficial epidermic layers are loosened up, one layer from the other, and, owing also to this external irritation, the serous elements of the blood are caused to leave the vessels and thence find their way into the intercellular spaces caused by this loosening. Collections of fluid of this nature are known as bullae or blisters. The so-called "blood blister" is of a similar origin except that the injury (in this case usually a severe trapping or pinching of the tissue) is sufficient to cause the rupture of one or more capillaries whose blood contents extravasate into the overlying epidermic layers.

Usual Points of Location. Blisters developing upon the pedal extremities are most common in the spring of the year when people begin to wear Oxford ties or other styles of low shoes. They occur principally upon the posterior surfaces of the heel at the upper extremity of the os calcis, or upon the tendo Achillis, just above this point, and are caused by the rubbing of the stiff heel of the shoe upon these parts.

Bullae are also often found to develop over or immediately adjacent to the prominent extensor tendon on the dorsum of the hallux. In these locations the stiffness of the shoe in "breaking" over this point is found to be the irritant agent.

Whilst the two foregoing locations are the most general sites of occurrence, they are, at times, also found to develop upon the plantar surfaces, and in some instances upon the ends or between the toes.

Treatment. The method of treatment to be accorded these cases depends upon the condition that the affected part may be in at the time of observation.

Ordinary Conditions. When the blister is found to be unbroken and no great degree of inflammation is present, the sac should be opened and its contents evacuated. This is best accomplished by means of a fine pointed, sterile scalpel or bistoury. The blister is punctured through the unaffected epidermis immediately adjacent to its base, and thereupon gentle yet firm pressure is exerted until all the fluid contents are evacuated.

Once the contents have been removed, thorough asepsis should be inaugurated. The parts should be swabbed with alcohol, 60%, and allowed to dry by evaporation, or be dried with a sterile wipe. In dressing these conditions it must be remembered that protection must be obtained as well as granulation induced. Recognizing these to be important factors in treatment, the choice of a proper dressing should be carefully made.

The cocoon dressing (see *"Dressings and Bandaging"*) is practical in these cases, as the cotton serves to afford great protection to the parts and also to confine whatever medication is to be applied as a curative agent.

Dressings of sterile gauze or surgeon's lint may also be used, and consist of a square of gauze or lint applied over the part and held in place by means of adhesive strips

The cocoon dressing may or may not be reinforced by adhesive strapping, as the judgment of the operator determines. If strapping becomes necessary in this connection, half inch or one inch width plaster is generally used. The strips (each about three or three and a half inches in length) are applied in the form of a triangle, binding down the edges of the dressing. It is also found advisable to avoid using too much collodion on the cotton. These dressings should never be hard; it is, therefore, preferable to bind down the edges and then merely paint the collodion in one narrow strip across and with the fibre of the cotton If adhesive strapping is to be used for the adherence of gauze or lint, the one-half inch plaster is the most practical in almost every instance.

The strips are each cut about three inches in length, unless the size of the gauze or lint squares makes it desirable to have them longer, and they are placed in rectangular fashion over each of the four sides of the dressing. It should always be the endeavor, when possible, to bind down the edges of the fabric to the skin, and to accomplish this the adhesive strips are made adherent, half on the dressing and half on the underlying skin. This serves to hold the dressing more firmly in place and also to prevent foreign matter from getting under its edges.

Ointments are generally found to be the most advantageous applications in cases of ordinary bullae. There are several of these from which we may choose. Ammoniated mercury, 10%, and ichthyol, 10%, are probably the most generally used and are efficient.

Broken Conditions. In many instances the blister, through neglect and improper puncturing, has become broken and the affected epidermic layers are stripped off, being attached at one point only, or are entirely gone.

The parts should be thoroughly cleansed with alcohol, 60%, and all loosened epidermis removed. Never leave any flaps of skin about the edges of the denuded area, for they not alone serve as excellent places for the lodgment of hostile bacteria, but are also apt to curl up and, becoming thickened, may irritate the denuded surfaces by pressure.

The lesion being thoroughly aseptic, a dressing should be applied. If infection be already present in the part, the treatment should consist of the application of wet dressings of mercury bichloride, 1/2000, or weaker, until all inflammation has subsided. If no infection be present, a dressing which will be protective, healing and sedative should be placed over the parts. A shield is usually a necessary adjunct to every successful treatment in cases of this nature.

It will always be found advisable to have the aperture of the shield sufficiently large, not alone to protect the denuded area, but also to include some of the surrounding integument.

In locations about the os calcis region and along the surfaces of the tendo Achillis, an oval pad of a soft grade of felt is found to afford the best protection. In cases where the blister has developed over the extensor tendon on the dorsum of the great toe, a strip of white felt, about one inch long and one-half inch wide, placed parallel to the tendon, and of sufficient thickness to be higher than its elevation, is found to be the most practical means of shielding the affected area. An oval shield, if used in this latter instance, should have a groove fashioned on its under surface in which no adhesive is placed and which allows for the free play of the tendon in movements of the foot.

The choice of an ointment, if one is to be used, should be carefully made, for asepsis is to be at all times maintained and granulation must be induced.

Ammoniated mercury, 10%, and sulphur, 10%, are to be highly recommended as antiseptic ointments, and the latter, in particular, has tissue stimulating properties. Ichthyol, 10%, balsam of Peru, 5%, or scarlet red, 3%, may also be used, the latter two where the lesion shows signs of indolence and needs stimulation.

At times a dry dressing, either of plain sterile gauze, or gauze, combined with a dusting powder, secures good results in these cases. Thymol iodide and bismuth subgallate probably lead the list in popularity but a very efficient substitute is found in a combination of equal parts of bismuth subnitrate and powdered calomel.

The areas should be thoroughly dried before any dusting powder is applied. This is best accomplished by applying alcohol and allowing it to dry by evaporation, which may be hastened by blowing air upon the area. A practical means of applying dusting powder is afforded by compressed air. Under low pressure any powder may be blown from the nebulizer upon the parts in a thin and even coating.

Both the ointment and the dry dressing should be changed in from twenty-four to thirty-six hours until complete granulation is observed and the structures of the denuded corium are entirely covered. Dressings which are allowed to become stale and which harden, are apt to act as irritant agents to the tender granulating surfaces and not only retard normal healing but further break down the tissues.

Cocoon dressings may also be employed to apply either ointments or dusting powders, as just described for gauze. They will remain in place for much longer periods of time than will gauze or lint, but in these cases, as the dressing must be changed daily, this is not an important consideration.

Prognosis. The tissue lost in blister cases properly dressed and protected should be replaced rapidly and stimulation is seldom found necessary. The course is active but short. It is advisable to have the patient refrain from wearing the shoe which originally caused the disturbance so that no untoward irritation is brought upon the part during treatment. After the epidermis covering is complete, it will be found advantageous to paint the parts with silver nitrate, 50%. The eschar so formed will act as a protective agent to the parts until the skin regains its normal strength.

BURNS

The podiatrist is not called upon to treat many burns on the foot, and when these conditions are present they are, as a rule, not extensive. The subject is so important, however, and so much progress has been made in recent years along the lines of burn treatments, that a thorough knowledge of this subject is of great interest to the modern practitioner.

Definition. A burn is a lesion caused by heat or by

caustics. The lesion may be superficial in the tissue involvement or it may have penetrated to the deeper tissues and, if extensive, may cause permanent injury or death.

Pathology. Intense heat being applied to the surface of the body destroys the vascular supply, and so shocks the nervous sensibility of the part that the nerves are temporarily, sometimes permanently, paralyzed. This causes the tissue to slough and a more or less deep ulceration is formed. The edges are found to be a dark, angry red in color and the floor of the ulceration is usually a pale, unhealthy yellow or white. In small areas the pain is intense, while if large areas be involved to such an extent as to include the main trunks, the parts rapidly become anesthetized and gangrene ensues. Discharge from the ulceration is generally profuse.

As the podiatrist will only come in contact with the smaller burns the discussion in this chapter is confined to their consideration.

Treatment. The burn, whether caused by direct heat or by chemical reaction, is at first aseptic and this asepsis must be maintained throughout the entire treatment If the burn is very recent, an immediate application of carron oil (equal parts of linseed oil and limewater) will be found to relieve much of the pain, and to keep the tissues in fairly healthy condition. If this medication is not obtainable, a paste of sodium bicarbonate will also prove efficient. All air should be excluded as soon as possible, and many advocate the application of a simple grease smeared freely on the abraded surfaces. These are purely first aid procedures, however, and have no part in scientific treatment.

After the acute pain has been reduced or entirely relieved, treatment should be instituted which will at once induce granulation and maintain asepsis. Strong germicides, particularly those with toxic properties, should be studiously avoided, for it must be remembered that the vitality of the part has been severely shocked, even in a superficial burn. Nothing must be done to retard the healing process.

Ointment or dusting powder dressings are advocated in these cases, but the most efficient treatment lies in the use of one of the newer paraffin preparations (see *Dressings and Bandaging*). The method of application of these paraffins is as follows and is the original technic as formulated by Dr. de Sandfort, who is the originator of this method of treatment:

Method of Use. Paraffins are used warm, consequently in a liquid state (158°-176° F.).

Heating. Place a piece of the material in a bowl, tin cup, or other convenient receptacle, set in any vessel containing a little water, which should be kept on the point of boiling for ten minutes.

Precautions to Be Taken.

1. Care should be taken to prevent the splashing of the boiling water into the container holding the paraffin. When the water begins to boil, reduce the temperature to avoid drops of water being thrown into the wax. It must be remembered that these compounds, completely devoid of water (anhydrous), do not burn the tissues at 176° F., while even the smallest quantity of water added would have the contrary effect.

2. While the mixture is being heated, cut a piece of absorbent cotton of sufficient size to amply cover the burned area, and divide it into layers as thin as possible. At the same time, have ready the gauze and band, needed to bind and keep the waxen shell in place.

The Dressing. When the paraffin is in a liquid state, and is at a temperature of from 140° to 150° F., take a soft camel's hair brush, dip it into the mass and spread it on the wound, without pressing; that is, as much as possible dabbing it on and not brushing it on. This operation is repeated until the glazing is complete, taking care to leave no spot uncovered. Immediately afterwards, place quickly on the first wax glaze one of the thin layers of absorbent cotton already prepared, as explained above, so that it becomes easily impregnated with the wax, and then, with the same dabbing movement, brush on several more applications of the paraffin.

If the wound is extensive, the operation is done on small square surfaces, successively and close together (about 4 by 4 inches). These little surfaces become, by the application, part of one another. This proceeding is to avoid the first coat of glaze, because it is essential to form (on the whole surface of the wound) a shell uniformly warm which keeps its warmth a long time, thanks to the close attention of the wax with absorbent cotton. Two layers of cotton can be applied successively, saturated with the mixture, although this is not indispensable.

When the application is complete, the dressing is finished by binding with ordinary gauze or cotton, kept in place by bands. If desired, gauze can be replaced in part by oiled silk, or even paper.

Note. In not following the precise instructions already given, grave errors can be committed. Thus, should the layer of absorbent cotton be applied directly to the wound and afterwards covered with the first layer of the paraffin it causes:

1. A very painful burning sensation. These applications on a wound are very soothing, while cotton impregnated with the paraffin applied direct to the wound causes a distressing, burning sensation.

2. At the moment of removing the dressing, a pulling and even tearing of the tissues is caused. If the wound has not been previously glazed by an application of a first layer of paraffin, as explained above, the cotton will adhere

Removing the Dressing. For the first few days the waxen shell must not be left in place for more than twenty-four hours, on account of an abundant secretion of lymph, which takes place beneath it. The sero-purulent liquid flows under the wax covering (which proves that the waxen layer does not adhere to the tissues like collodion, with which paraffin has been wrongly compared) and exudes from under the edges of the dressing. After a few days, this exudation diminishes and the dressing can be left in place for forty-eight hours at a time and even longer.

To remove the dressing, untie the bands and take off the ordinary gauze or oiled silk, thus exposing the "shell." An incision is made in the "shell" by means of a blunt knife or scissors and it is easily peeled off. The dressing is removed more easily than a glove. The wound is afterwards bathed with boiled water and the cleansing is further perfected by washing with absorbent cotton soaked in boiled water. Then it is dried, either by a current of warm air or by a piece of cotton wool, care being taken not to rub, or cause the granulations to bleed. The new dressing is not applied until the surfaces are thoroughly dry.

Important Recommendations.

1. In washing the wounds, antiseptic solutions must not be used, unless extremely weak.

2. Anxiety need not be occasioned by the grey aspect and fetid odor which emanates from the wound when the waxen shell is removed. In fact, after this washing, it is seen that beneath this purulent liquid, the tissues present an intense vitality and an excellent appearance. In order to properly proliferate the elements of healing, it even seems as if they have need to bathe in this purulent liquid, which might be termed auto-serotherapia.

3. In application, the wax should be brushed on with strokes or daubs all directed the same way, and these should commence at the top of the part and be carried downward, never starting at the bottom and going upward.

After several days of treatment, skin granulation will be observed, white spots appearing more especially at those points, where the sero-purulent liquid has remained in the greatest abundance.

Care should be taken not to apply paraffin at a temperature of more than 105° F.

Contrary to the usual practice, the abundant granulations must never be cauterized with nitrate of silver or any other caustic. In spite of their development, at times considerable, little by little they begin to be strangled by the regenerating elements of the skin, which finally replace them.

In case of persistent atony of the wound or of excessive growth of granulations, the paraffin treatment can be interrupted every three or four days by a wet dressing (water slightly alcoholized) for a period of twenty-four hours. Paraffin treatment is afterwards resumed, which the patient often requests himself, on account of the comfort derived from the waxen shell.

After some days of treatment, there appears sometimes on the healthy skin surrounding the wound an eruption of sudamina, caused by the perspiration confined under the waxen shell. To make it disappear, cover it with an ointment of oxide of zinc, then powder with talc, always continuing the paraffin application over the wound.

Conclusions.

1. Paraffin preparations instantly alleviate the pain.

2. They constitute a warm shell, a heat retainer, under which the tissues, protected against outside contamination and maintained at a temperature always constant, rapidly heal.

3. They become non-adhesive after a short period, thus rendering removal instantaneous, without pain, without hemorrhage and without tearing the tissues of neo-formation, thus permitting the integral healing of the tissues, without apparent scars, without contraction of the skin or of the tendons.

4. Without causing persistent and incurable functional weakness.

Important. Heating these preparations in a bath of boiling water raises the temperature to nearly 212° F., therefore, before applying to the wound, they should be removed from the water bath and allowed to stand for a minute or two so as to reduce the temperature below 105° F.

If an ointment be used, a bland healing type should be

chosen. Among these ichthyol ointment, 5% to 10%, is probably found to be as efficient as any, although zinc oxide, 10%, balsam of Peru, 5%, and various sulphur ointments, 3% to 10%, may be substituted with equal results

On a freely discharging surface, of course, an ointment is contraindicated and a dusting powder must be resorted to or merely a dry aseptic gauze dressing applied. The dusting powders to be used are the two bismuth salts, subgallate and subnitrate, although the latter is found to be irritant at times; thymol iodide may also be used and its antiseptic and healing action makes for its general popularity in these cases.

The ointment or dusting powder is covered with a cocoon, gauze, or lint dressing which is held in place by collodion or adhesive strips, respectively.

The dressing should be changed daily until granulation is complete. Burns are stubborn lesions to heal and the podiatrist should not slight them in any way. They are prone to infective processes, and the least neglect is apt to cause the undoing of all that previous treatment has accomplished.

CHAPTER XVII

BURSITIS

Bursae are closed sacs or pouches containing fluid, found in all parts of the body, covering and protecting exposed or prominent bony surfaces, and interposed between tendons and parts over which they play. They serve as protective cushions to prevent physiologic wear and tear.

There are two varieties of bursae found in the human body: the bursae mucosae, those secreting a mucous or a gelatinous substance, and the bursae synovia, those secreting a thin, viscid substance, and which are similar in structure to synovial membranes.

The principal form of bursae found in the foot is of the synovial type and for this reason the treatment of this variety is that discussed in this chapter. Bursae may be either deep seated or subcutaneous and the latter variety are those which, through trauma, usually become inflamed and troublesome in the regions of the foot. The deeper seated bursae, however, often become involved in a pathologic process, and the podiatrist is called upon to treat these cases as well as those involving subcutaneous variety.

Definition. Bursitis is an inflammation of the bursa sac. The inflammation may be acute, subacute or chronic. Acute bursitis is a condition in which the general inflammatory symptoms are active, the course short, and in which the overproduction of synovial fluid has found an outlet and is discharging on the surface of the skin. Subacute bursitis is a condition in which the inflammation has not reached a true acute stage, but in which it is more in evidence and more active than in the chronic form. Chronic bursitis is a condition in which the inflammation is long standing and of an inactive nature and where no great amount of overproduction of synovia is in evidence. In chronic cases the walls of the sac itself are generally found thickened and leathery; where this condition occurs in the bursa over the first metatarsophalangeal joints it is often inadvertently called a "bunion".

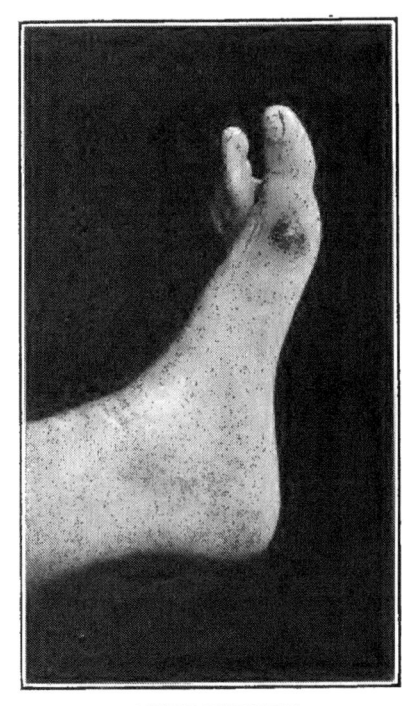

Etiology. Bursitis occurring in the foot is in nearly every instance due to trauma. A blow, a knock, a part being stepped on, or the continued pressure of an illfitting shoe, may be the exciting causes of t h i s d i s t u r b a n c e. Malalignment of a joint may be a secondary c a u s e, such as would occur in hallux valgus. In this instance the deep seated b u r s a would be affected. Bursitis would hardly develop from this alone, however, and the exciting cause is found in the pressure of footgear or some other injury to the part.

ACUTE BURSITIS

Location. As bursa sacs are only found covering a bony prominence, or interposed between the sheaths of tendons and muscles, or between these structures and the skin, serving in each capacity to prevent physiologic wear and tear, bursitis occurring in the foot will be found in these locations.

The first and fifth metatarsophalangeal joints (metatarsophalangeal bursitis); the interphalangeal joints of the toes (interphalangeal bursitis); the posterior and outer surfaces of the os calcis (retrocalcaneal bursitis); and the tarsometatarsal region on the dorsum of the foot (dorsal bursitis) are the principal sites of occurrence. The base of the fifth metatarsal is also a spot over which bursal inflammation will occasionally develop.

Pathology. The pathology of bursitis is primarily that of any inflammation. Due to trauma, the parts are subjected to a severe irritation which causes an engorgement of blood in that location. Serous infiltration of the tissues takes place and the functional activity of the sac is increased. Materials from the blood for the production of synovia, are secreted in abnormal amounts, and in consequence the sac becomes distended from the superabundance of fluid. In time this fluid must find some outlet, for synovia is secreted so rapidly that the lymphatic system cannot absorb the excess This outlet must naturally develop toward the point of least resistance, which, in these cases, is outward toward the periphery. The tissue is broken down to a small extent and a minute sinus is formed which permeates the tissues and opens upon the surface of the skin. From the peripheral opening the excess of fluid is thrown off, and when this stage is reached the distension in the part is naturally lessened and the patient is fairly comfortable.

Symptoms. *Objective Symptoms.* The parts will be found considerably swollen, red and hot Loss of function is noted and fluctuation is present.

Subjective Symptoms Pain on slightest pressure and at times upon forced movements; impaired function; heat, and a feeling of fullness or distension in the part.

Characteristics. The characteristics of bursitis, whether acute or chronic, are so plain that no error in diagnosis should ever be made However, many of these cases are mistaken for suppurated helomata, probably through the fact that both are conditions in which a discharge is present. Why this error should be made is a mystery, for while it is true that there is an exudation in both instances, the characteristics of the discharges are so different that only a careless or inexperienced person could mistake one for the other. The important characteristics are:

(1) The distension in the bursa sac proper causes a swelling of the parts adjacent and superjacent so that the whole area over and around the affected part will be found enlarged and puffy. Fluctuation is present and often the sac itself may be grasped in the fingers, so distended are its walls.

(2) Removal of the overlying calloused area, should one be present, brings to view the sinus opening, in the acute stage. The tissues are blanched in appearance and are leathery and hard to digital or instrument touch. The opening of the sinus is usually very small and its edges are circumscribed and even. The sinus itself has the appearance of a healthy granulating surface and at no time is there apparently any membranous lining. Probing will determine that the sinus follows an almost vertical course with no sub-borrowings or offshoots in any direction. There is no loss of tissue upon the surface of the skin, such as would be found in connection with an heloma involved in a suppurative process, except at the opening of a canal.

(3) Digital pressure exerted laterally and anterio-posteriorly usually is rewarded by the oozing of a thickish, viscid, almost colorless fluid from the sinus opening. There is nothing in the appearance of this fluid that should lead one to mistake it for pus. Very often this fluid oozes from the part of its own volition, due probably to the pressure of the excess fluid in the sac beneath. The fluid causes no active decomposition of hydrogen dioxide and the ebulition caused by the contact is almost negative. This constitutes one more point of differentiation between the changed synovial fluid discharged from an acute bursitis and a pyogenic exudation.

Treatment. The treatment of bursitis varies according to the degree of inflammation, and the general conditions present. We may divide the treatment into three classes: the radical operative, the non-radical operative, and the palliative The first mentioned is a purely surgical procedure, complete in itself, and consists in the removal or curettage of the inflamed sac. The last two are usually combined and are procedures which are generally practised by the podiatrist.

The Radical Operative Treatment. Under proper aseptic conditions an incision is made in the overlying tissues and the sac is removed in its entirety; the parts are then sutured, and a few days rest and elevation of the foot brings complete union. This method may be varied in that the sac is not removed, but a free incision is made into it and the parts thoroughly curetted. One other of the purely surgical procedures is to make a free incision into the sac to accomplish thorough drainage. This latter procedure is generally practised in cases of infected bursitis.

Inasmuch as the non-radical operative and the palliative methods of treatment are purely podiatry procedures and are usually combined, they will be discussed as one subject.

The Non-Radical Treatment. There are several methods by which bursitis in its various stages may be successfully treated. They vary in some details but all agree on two most important points: rest and the absence of pressure.

A bursitis developing over a bony prominence upon the foot, usually occurs in connection with some form of superficial callosity or an heloma. The inflammation of the sac may be due to the neglect of a growth of this nature, or, as previously explained, to some distinct injury to this part.

To successfully treat a condition of this nature it is found necessary at all times to accomplish the removal of the excrescence. This is done in the usual manner by either the shaving or dissection method These growths must be removed for several reasons:

(1) To remove all hardened and thickened epidermis so that no further irritation from that source will be present.

(2) To allow the operator a chance to effect drainage for the overproduction of bursal fluid.

(3) To allow the medications used to come in direct contact with the underlying tissues without the necessity of penetrating several layers of epidermis and expending their action upon and through them.

Under proper aseptic conditions, the superficial thickened epidermic layers are removed and the excess fluid is allowed to drain off. It will often be found that the callous forms a "plug" which extends down into the surface opening and prevents this excess fluid from being thrown off. Once this drainage is accomplished, other procedures, dependent upon conditions present, should be utilized for the alleviation and cure of the bursitis.

Rest. By far the most effective means of bringing about a speedy cessation of the inflammation occurring in the bursa sac is to procure absolute rest for the part involved. It has been noted that in a number of cases when no medical or surgical treatment has been afforded, inflammations of this nature resolve themselves speedily upon complete rest. There is nothing remarkable or supernatural about this for inasmuch as the bursa is only used during the movements of a part, it is easily understood why a trouble of this nature will clear up rapidly if the part is kept immobile.

Removal of Pressure. There are many cases of bursal inflammation which occur in people who are not able to lay up and give complete rest to the affected part. The next most effective measure in these cases is the judicious and proper use of shielding. In applying a shield to a case of this nature it should always be remembered that the parts affected are usually swollen to a considerable extent around the tissues immediately overlying the sac itself. For this reason a shield such as would be employed for the protection of an heloma in a like situation, is not practical. This is more particularly the case where the bursitis is located on one of the interphalangeal joints of the toes. In this location an individual shield which is to rest on the affected toe alone cannot be applied, for the whole area overlying the inflamed sac will be found swollen and leathery and the tissues anterior and posterior, as well as those covering the interdigital surfaces of the toe, are ordinarily more or less involved in the general inflammation. In this instance, then, we must resort to some sort of shielding which will take the shoe pressure from the part, and yet which will be distributed over the whole digital surface and not on the diseased toe alone. A dorso-digital oval or crescent shield (see chapter "Shields and Shielding") answers the purpose and is entirely effective in most instances.

Probably the most practical method of removing all pressure from the inflamed areas is to have a circular portion of leather immediately overlying the part removed from the shoe and another softer piece adhered over the opening. The appearance of this will be inconspicuous and the small pouch thus formed allows the patient to wear a shoe, affording comfort, which, however, exerts no pressure upon the lesion. It is wise to remove a piece of leather considerably larger than the circumference of the affected part, otherwise the edges of the aperture cut in the shoe may become depressed and press upon and irritate the already inflamed areas.

Strapping. Enlarging upon the theory of rest, inasmuch as complete absence of movement aids materially in reducing the local irritation, strapping is a practical means of immobilization.

This procedure, altho used in these situations, is not so practical in bursitis occurring over the first and fifth metatarsophalangeal joints, or over the interphalangeal joints, as it is in other locations upon the foot.

Adhesive strapping is applied in such manner and at such tension as to accomplish almost complete immobilization, and for this reason it will be readily seen that this method cannot be used in cases where the added pressure will produce additional irritation. Several lengths of adhesive plaster are placed over the part and adhered tightly to the surrounding integument so that very little or no movement is allowed in the affected part.

Strapping, to prevent movement, is particularly effective when the bursitis has occurred in the os calcis region between that bone and the tendo Achillis (retrocalcaneal bursitis). The foot is placed in plantar flexion and a long strip of 1½ or 2 inch plaster is anchored at the centre of the upper part of the calf and is then carried down over the heel on the plantar surface of the foot. This strip is then reinforced by transverse straps applied over the heel at the insertion of the tendon.

Aside from these general methods of procedure thus discussed, the podiatrist must resort, in a majority of cases, to local treatment which will hasten the ultimate resolution of the inflammatory process. These local methods of treatment are conveniently divided into six groups:

1. Hydrotherapeutic measures.
2. Moist and wet dressings.
3. Unguent dressings.
4. Counter irritation.
5. Massage.
6. Electricity.

Hydrotherapy. Hydrotherapeutic measures may be resorted to in the treatment of bursal inflammations and either thermal extreme may be used with equal results. As one person will react to one extreme more readily than to the other, the choice of heat or cold usually depends upon the individual case.

Hot Applications are probably most practical in these instances in the form of compresses. Several thicknesses of gauze, saturated in water, as hot as can be borne, are applied over the affected areas, the hot water being replenished as soon as the compress commences to cool. Hot applications act as mild poultices and their action is similar to them in a limited and modified form. They tend to hasten resolution of the inflammatory process by accelerating absorption. It is unwise, however, to continue hot applications for too long a period; it is found preferable to have the patient apply hot compresses for periods of one hour duration two or three times a day, allowing the part complete rest in the intervals.

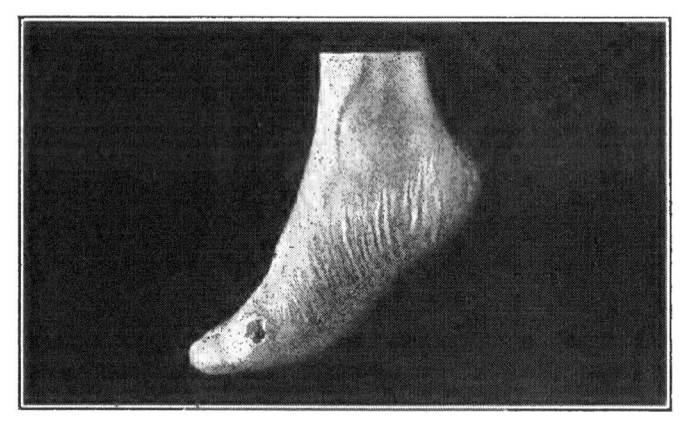

INFECTED BURSITIS

Hot compresses, applied continuously for some hours, are apt to bring about an over-stimulation in the parts to such an extent as to produce a slough. To be effective, it must be remembered that the compress must be kept hot for the entire period of application. This may be accomplished by immersion in hot water, by moistening intermittently, or by keeping the compress covered with some heat-confining covering. In the latter instance, oiled silk is in all probability the most practical agent, but even the use of an impervious covering does not relieve the patient of the necessity of remoistening the compress with hot water, at frequent intervals.

Cold Compresses, as here advised, are either applications of cold water on a compress of gauze or some similar material, kept constantly wet, the use of ice bags or packs, or a cold water drip. The surfaces of the foot, particularly if the bursitis be on the toes, are so small, however, that as a general rule, ice bags or packs are not practical. The cold produces anemia of the parts by contracting the calibre of the blood vessels, and forcing the blood from the capillaries. They also tend to anesthetize the nervous sensibility and are in that way also pain reducing. There is one bad feature, however, in the use of cold as a hydrotherapeutic agent. The resulting reaction, which is generally bound to occur, gives the patient considerable annoyance and is apt in time to increase the infiltration and distension in the part. Again, should the patient have any tendency toward chilblains, the moist cold is almost always sure to develop the tendency into a reality.

The Poultice is the older and now obsolete method of applying moist heat to a part. The stimulative action of this form of application is at times so severe as to cause deleterious effects upon the diseased tissues. A cataplasma should never be used where a distinct loss of tissue is in evidence, in the presence of pus, or where the vitality of the parts is considered to be subnormal, either from the age or condition of the patient, or because of the diseased condition of the part.

The most generally used materials in this connection are flaxseed, and slippery elm, and the most practical manner for preparing a poultice for use in podiatry is to make several small bags (about two or three inches square) from cheesecloth or some like material. These are filled half full with the meal and are dropped into a vessel containing boiling water. The bags and their contents are allowed to boil for eight or ten minutes and are then applied to the part as hot as can be borne. This method does away with the rather "messy" procedure of laying a cloth on the part and then applying the warm mass by means of a spatula, spoon or like implement; also the poultice, so made, may be used again and again. The usual method of procedure in using poultices, when recommended, is to have the patient apply them continuously for about an hour during some part of the day. It is found much more effective to have moist heat applied for a longer period at one time than to apply three poultices a day, one in the morning, one at noon, and the last at night. The patient removes one bag as soon as it starts to cool and replaces it with another taken hot from the boiling water. This form of treatment, of course, tends at first to increase the overproduction of synovial fluid, and proper drainage must at all times be preserved so that this excess may be carried off.

Baking. With the development of the modern baking apparatus, this method of applying heat to a part has come into use in cases of subacute or chronic bursal inflammations. The heat applied by this means is dry, in contradistinction to that obtained from hot applications of water and from poultices. As the synovial bursae are of similar structure to the true synovial membranes of the joint cavities and capsules, they are subjected to similar ailments. It stands to reason, therefore, that if baking is beneficial in several forms of arthritis, it is also beneficial in some forms of synovial bursitis. Some podiatrists have baking apparatuses installed in their offices; where this is not the case it is recommended that, when such treatment is thought advisable, the patient be sent to some hospital or institute where this treatment can be administered. Baking serves as a hyperemic agent (to bring an abnormal supply of blood to the part) and in this way to aid in the more rapid absorption of the exudates in the affected region.

Moist and Wet Dressings. In conditions of acute bursitis, an efficient means of reducing the inflammatory symptoms is found in the use of wet dressings. Moist dressings (those with mackintosh protection) should not be used in these cases when the skin is broken, when there is any suspicion of a discharge, or where infection is present.

The agents which may be used with such wet dressings are mercury bichloride, liq. aluminum acetate, saturated solution of boric acid and alcohol, equal parts, and lead and opium wash.

Mercury Bichloride may be used as a wet dressing in all cases of acute bursitis, but more particularly where infection is present. It should never be used with mackintosh covering, for even without the confinement thus afforded, its action serves to macerate the skin to a great extent The solution may be used either hot or cold and in no instance stronger than 1/4000. This strength solution should only be resorted to in cases where the infection is acute and has progressed to some extent, weaker solutions, 1/5000 or 1/10000, being found efficient in a majority of cases. Mercury bichloride, on account of its toxic properties, should not be used after the infective process has been reduced, and there are many arguments in favor of an efficient substitute for it even in the initial instance. However, no solution which is practical for use in these cases can be depended upon for beneficent results as surely as corrosive sublimate. In chronic bursal inflammations, corrosive sublimate is contra-indicated.

Liq. Aluminum Acetate can be used in place of bichloride of mercury in many cases of acute bursitis. The solution is decidedly astringent, and while this action is to be desired at times, nevertheless it has been found detrimental in the treatment of some cases of acute bursitis, because when it penetrates through the sinus into the bursal sac it has been found to create a decided irritation upon these deeper tissues. Liq. aluminum acetate, therefore, is shunned by many in the treatment of these cases, but aside from this one detrimental feature, the action of the acetate is efficient and is productive of good results. The drug may be used plain, or diluted with sterile water to reduce its irritant, astringent qualities. A dressing of liq. aluminum acetate, like bichloride, should never be confined in a mackintosh covering, as it will macerate the skin, quickly and thoroughly. This solution is particularly effective in subacute cases where no infection is present when its astringent action goes far to reduce the infiltration in the parts. It should be applied cold.

Boric Acid-Alcohol Solution may be used in all cases of acute or subacute bursal inflammations. It is efficient in septic cases and its quality of rapid evaporation aids materially in reducing the inflammatory symptoms, independent of the therapeutic action of the component drugs. This solution, on account of its rapid evaporation, must be renewed more often than either of the foregoing, but while this demands more attention on the part of the patient, it is immeasurably better for the general condition of the disease. The one disadvantage in having the patients attend to the moistening of the dressing is that often they will fail to carry out instructions properly; but a condition of this nature, properly attended, will respond as quickly to the boric-alcohol application as to aluminum acetate or to mercury bichloride, and with none of the irritant or toxic tendencies of both of these. This solution is applied cold.

Lead and Opium Wash may be used in the treatment of bursal inflammations, usually in the subacute or chronic stages. In cases where the integument is broken, avoid the use of this medication on account of the irritant qualities of the lead it contains. Prolonged applications are apt to develop a dermatitis, and if the skin is broken, local lead poisoning will not only be more pronounced, but will be manifest in a shorter space of time. Lead and opium wash, hot, is an advantageous application in the treatment of chronic bursal inflammations, the heated applications being continued for about thirty minutes at a time, at intervals of two or three hours. It should always be remembered in using this wash that it exhibits marked irritant qualities upon prolonged application.

The choice of a moist dressing to be used in subacute or chronic cases, especially the latter, should be carefully made. Boric acid, saturated solution, is an efficient and safe drug to use under rubber, fish skin, or oiled silk covering but, as before mentioned, mercury bichloride and liq. aluminum acetate are contra-indicated in this connection.

Unguent Dressings. Ointment dressings are used in

this instance under the same rules and considerations which govern their application in all other conditions. No ointment should be applied on any inflamed bursa where there is a discharge of any nature. The operator must never forget that the base of all ointments is either oily or fatty and a serous discharge, coming from any surface, cannot be absorbed by the fabric used as a dressing if even a thin unguent film is interposed.

Certain classes of drugs, however, which are known to be beneficial in certain stages in the treatment of bursitis, can be readily applied in unguent form and for this reason the question of using them may be profitably discussed here. The action demanded of drugs to be used in the treatment of bursal inflammations are antiphlogistic, analgesic and antiseptic. The latter action is particularly demanded in cases where surfaces denuded of epidermis are found Some stimulant action is at times desired and drugs which have properties of this nature may also be included in this armamentarium. The following named ointments may be used, therefore, with beneficial results in certain stages of bursal inflammations: ichthyol, sulphur, menthol, balsam of Peru, scarlet red and salicylic acid.

Unguentum Ichthyoli, 3% to 10%, is used in all cases where an emolient action is desired. The stimulating action of the drug in this form is negative, but it can be relied upon to reduce acute inflammatory symptoms. Ichthyol may be combined best with either lanolin or vaseline as a base; the former is preferred inasmuch as it does not become rancid when exposed to a variety of conditions as does the latter. Lanolin being a wool fat product is supposed to have a beneficent action upon certain pathologic conditions of the skin, and so it is used as the base of many ointments.

Unguentum Sulphuris, 10%, may be used in many conditions of subacute or chronic bursitis. Its antiseptic action makes it a desirable choice for use when the integument is broken or when a distinct antiseptic action, in addition to the general action of sulphur as an antiphlogistic, is sought.

Unguentum Balsamum Peruvianum is used in these instances, principally when some loss of tissue in the part is noticeable and where stimulation is required to accelerate granulation. Peruvian balsam is sometimes combined with ichthyol (5% of each) in ointment form. In this combination the ointment has marked stimulative and antiphlogistic qualities. Balsam of Peru is used in strengths of from 3% to 10% in a vaseline base.

Scarlet Red is a highly efficient stimulative ointment. It is used alone, with zinc oxide or with borated vaseline, and should never be applied in too thick a coating. The parts should first be made thoroughly aseptic and dried, and then scarlet red applied on gauze in a thin even coat. Care should be taken that the application of scarlet red does not cause overstimulation to the parts, and thus prove detrimental to the general condition of the lesion.

Unguentum Acidi Salicylici, 2% to 5%, may be used to good advantage where the parts overlying the thickened sac are found to be somewhat calloused. One application of an ointment of this strength will serve to disintegrate this overlying thickening, thus making the parts flexible and soft. A stronger ointment than this should never be used in these cases, as salicylic acid is a strong epidermic disintegrant and will cause decided irritation if used in greater than 5% strength. In such cases salicylic acid may also be combined with collodion in the same percentage, 5 grains of ext cannibis indica being added as an anodyne. Unguentum salicylic should never be used when the skin is broken or the tissues show any tendency to thinness. All ointments used in the treatment of bursitis are applied and kept in place by the use of a cocoon dressing. If a shield is to be used, it is first applied; the ointment is then placed in the shield aperture and the cotton and collodion dressing is made to cover the whole. The ointment should be renewed at frequent intervals in order that the dressing may not become hardened, and thus become an irritant.

Counter-Irritation. Counter-irritation means literally an irritation which is developed to act against a previous irritation. It would seem, theoretically, that in cases of bursitis, this form of treatment is particularly advantageous. A bursal inflammation is a fairly deep-seated condition which should readily respond to a counter-irritation developed on the surface overlying the trouble Counter-irritant agents should be used only in subacute and chronic cases, more particularly in the latter; for it is found that this form of treatment applied to an acute bursal inflammation tends to intensify rather than reduce the symptoms.

In treating such cases we have a number of counter-irritants which may be used with consistently good results iodine, capsicum, turpentine and mustard, are the most important and most commonly used.

Iodine is today, in all probability, the most generally used agent to induce counter-irritation in podiatry. Its present popularity as a germicide, however, has over-shadowed its action as a counter-irritant.

To obtain the maximum counter-irritant action from tincture iodine (U. S. P. 7%) it should be applied in a heavy coat at frequent intervals until such time as the inflammatory symptoms have entirely subsided The continued use of iodine after this has been accomplished should be avoided as the tincture is irritant and mildly corrosive, and numbers of patients will be found whose skin will not stand its activities. Churchill's tincture of iodine (about 16%) has been advocated for general use as a counter-irritant, but its action in many cases will be found too irritant for ordinary use.

The theory of counter-irritation, simplified, is that a drug applied at a spot more or less distant from an inflamed area will cause an irritation in this new locality and thus aid the original condition, inasmuch as it will draw away the excess blood in the original part and allow the vessels to contract to normal calibre and the circulation there to become normal. Realizing this, it is readily understood why tincture of iodine should not be used as a counter-irritant in acute cases. With a discharging sinus to contend with, applying iodine over its opening at the periphery might be the cause of a severe irritation in that location which would further increase the tissue loss and thus prove a detriment to the general condition.

Capsicum is generally applied in these conditions in the form of a plaster. It should never be used in acute cases as its greatest efficacy is apparent in those cases with chronic characteristics. Capsicum plaster is applied and renewed as necessary, until the symptoms of the deep inflammation have subsided. Shields are usually employed to remove the pressure while a chronic case is under treatment, and this removal of all irritation which the shoe might produce aids materially in the relief and cure of these conditions.

Turpentine may be massaged into the parts for the purpose of counter-irritation although its action is at times severe; it should never be used where the skin is broken or where a discharge is present. It is not so desirable an application as either of the foregoing for it is found impractical to give proper massage to the comparatively small areas which are affected in bursal inflammations.

Mustard has been recommended for use in cases of chronic bursitis, either in the form of a moderate local application or in a general foot bath. It is decidely energetic in action, and should be used with great discretion and care. Every skin will not stand the action of mustard and for this reason it is not advocated as a general counter-irritant agent. Upon the failure of any of the other drugs mentioned under this heading, however, it may be tried, and if properly used, may prove conducive to good results.

Massage. Massage is at times a potent factor in aiding absorption in chronic cases. There is no question but that the stimulation afforded by this procedure is efficient and will aid materially in returning the tissues to normal.

Some cases of bursitis which occur upon the foot, however, are confined to such limited areas that massage is impractical.

Several drugs which are reputed to have great powers of penetration are recommended as agents which can be safely massaged into the parts and even if the action claimed for them is overestimated, their use at least serves to reduce the friction upon the surface tissues.

Many of the so called "petrogen compounds"—drugs in combination with petroleum (mineral oil)—are recommended for use in these cases, and are undoubtedly of some benefit Petrogen iodine, 10%, and petrogen camphor, 5%, (Wyeth) are the two most generally used, and have been found to be productive of good results.

The compound is applied to the parts and then rubbed, first lightly, then gradually increasing the pressure, by the fingers and palm of the hand. It is found advantageous to massage the parts at first with a circular movement, confining the energy to the areas immediately overlying the enlarged sac. After about five minutes, the pressure is increased and considerable of the surrounding integument is included in the massage. The direction of the finger movements is then changed from a rotary one to a series of long strokes under considerable pressure, first toward the diseased sac, following as nearly as possible the blood supply to the part, and then away from the sac, following the outgoing vessels. This serves first, to increase the vascular supply, and then to aid in its quick removal, and reduce the congestion in the part. With this, the lymph activity is also increased so that it helps to absorb the waste products more rapidly.

Massage should be recommended as a daily treatment and should be continued until all signs of infiltration have disappeared. Perseverance is necessary, for in chronic bursal inflammation, the changes are not noticeable nor should they be expected to be rapid.

Electricity. Many forms of electrical application are

recommended in the treatment of chronic bursal inflammations. Among those most commonly employed are the high frequency, and the faradic currents. Vibration, induced by electric impulses, is also recommended and is employed generally by the podiatrist.

High Frequency Current, more popularly known or rather misnamed "violet ray," is generally found efficient and is more generally used than any other form of electric application This current serves to produce active stimulation in the parts and by this means tends to accelerate all functional activities and to hasten absorption. Whether the more popular priced and small sized high frequency machines on the market to-day really do create any but a very superficial stimulation, is a question, and for this reason a machine of greater power is recommended. The parts are treated daily, the glass electrode being applied for about eight or ten minutes at a time.

Faradic Current is also recommended for daily use being applied by means of a moistened sponge electrode The treatment is from five to ten minutes duration. Stimulation is obtained by this treatment which, as in the case of the high frequency current, aids the general absorption in the affected areas.

Vibration used in these cases may be produced by electricity direct, or through a modern air compressor, controlled by electricity. Vibration is only recommended in chronic cases; it increases the functional activities of the part. It should be applied daily.

Bursitis is a stubborn condition in any form, and can only be relieved and finally cured by scientific and rational treatment. The operator should bear in mind that rest and the absence of shoe irritation will do as much or even more for the general improvement of the condition than can be accomplished by drugs Surgical procedure is certainly to be recommended in cases where no improvement is shown under palliative methods, even though this requires a cessation of activity on the part of the patient, and means the transfer of the patient to the care of a practitioner of surgery.

CHAPTER XVIII

CHIMATLON

Chimatlon, or pernio, is an inflammation of the skin and of the deeper structures which is the result of exposure to reduced temperatures The severity of the condition depends upon the length of the exposure as well as upon the degree of temperature. If the skin alone is involved and there is no loss of tissue, chimatlon mild, or chilblains, is the term applied to the lesion; where there is an involvement of the deeper structures the condition is called chimatlon severe, or frost bite. In many instances it becomes difficult to distinguish between a severe chilblain and a mild frost bite. However, for the sake of scientific study, in all cases in which the deeper tissues are involved and suppurative processes affecting these structures manifest themselves, the condition should be considered as chimatlon severe, for these cases are usually due to prolonged exposure to low temperatures.

CHIMATLON MILD

Derivation. Chimatlon, from the Greek, meaning the severity of winter.

Synonyms. Chilblains, Dermatitis Congelationes, Erythema Pernio.

Definition. Chimatlon mild, or chilblains, is a local inflammation of the skin due to exposure to cold and dampness

Etiology. Chilblains are primarily due to exposure to cold in varying degrees. When the part is exposed to a decreased temperature, the vaso-motor nerves become affected and the cutaneous circulation is impaired. This interference with the blood flow produces congestion, leading to inflammation, which latter is followed by a serous discharge or even by the production of pus. Dampness hastens the affection of the vaso-motor nervous system of the skin, and where this organ is very sensitive, in the presence of moisture, only a moderate decrease in the temperature is necessary to produce all the symptoms of severe chilblains.

The parts of the body most usually affected are the hands and feet; the distance of the extremities from the heart is probably the reason for this impairment under the other abnormal conditions. Where the horny layer of the skin is thin, it receives its nourishment normally, regardless of the distance from the heart; but on the hands and feet the skin is thicker and is imperfectly nourished and a decrease in temperature, in the presence of moisture, results in local inflammation.

Females are more disposed to chimatlon mild than males, and young people more than old. Aside from cold as an etiologic factor, there is also the predisposition which is equally as important in the production of chimatlon mild and should be considered in every case. Imperfect circulation in the limbs, due to varicose veins and arterial disturbances, caused by a deranged nervous system, are often causes of chilblains and must be given consideration.

Any part of the body exposed to the air may become affected, particularly the ears and nose. Several cases of chimatlon mild of the skin over the throat have been recently reported, due to walking against a strong wind, with the throat bared to the weather.

Symptoms. The symptoms in the mild form of chimatlon vary with the severity of the exposure In very mild cases the only perceptible symptoms are a tingling or slight itch, and the part feels cold and clammy to the touch. The most common cases show the parts colored dark blue or purple, immediately after exposure and during the reaction.

The parts are inflamed and there is severe itching coupled with pain. After reaction has set in, the color of the lesions varies from a scarlet to a purple. There is no sharp line of demarcation between the affected and the surrounding area, but there is a gradual blending between the discolored and the normal tissues. There is considerable congestion, the parts are swollen and after a complete reaction, heat manifests itself. These symptoms may soon subside or they may persist for many months. In general, they are of a transient nature, but the parts remain permanently weakened and congested, and are easily affected from the slightest cause.

In the more severe types of chilblains, blebs are formed which, when opened, exude serum or even pus. The blebs are commonly found at the ends of the toes, and sometimes the entire distal end of the digit is covered by one lesion.

No pain is felt immediately after exposure, but as reaction commences, shooting pains develop, and if the reaction is severe, these pains become almost unbearable. Itching is present to a marked degree, and after reaction is complete, dull pains and burning are noticed until the affected parts become normal.

Pathology. The immediate effect of cold upon the skin is to constrict the small blood vessels and to retard the stream within them. Under quite severe or prolonged exposure there may ensue a destruction of the minute vasomotor nerve terminals in the arterioles, which control their constriction and dilation. This nerve function is thereafter permanently affected and the muscular coat of the vessels in the parts impaired, atrophies from disuse. It is this degree of chimatlon which is classified as chimatlon mild, or chilblains. (Destruction of tissue beyond this, is classified as chimatlon severe or frost bite).

In winter there is a natural conservation of heat, by the constriction of the superficial capillaries; the blood supply to the skin is diminished and heat radiation is thus controlled. This reduction in the peripheral blood pressure especially affects the feet and other parts remote from the heart.

Later on besides this natural deficiency in the blood supply, there is in chimatlon mild a deficiency of freely circulating blood, due to the blood vessels relaxing. The reverse condition may seem to be proven by the heightened color but in reality this redness is due to too much blood in the tissues. There is however, congestion; the blood entering the tissues has but little motion, the pulse wave is lost in the relaxed vessels and the stream is in consequence a sluggish one. The reduction in the supply of fresh blood is probably the direct cause of the pain; the lack of oxygen brought to the parts and the retention of excrementitious chemical substances, act as irritants to the sensory nerve terminals. Persons suffering with chilblains have feet which are generally cold to the touch in spite of their being surcharged with blood The blood in them is rendered sluggish and the heat is not retained long, nor is there a sufficiently rapid supply of fresh blood to replace it.

In summer time, when the general peripheral circulation is at its maximum, vascular conditions are equalized throughout the entire body surface and are congenial to conditions in affected areas.

All the peripheral vessels are dilated and the blood pressure within them is increased to facilitate heat radiation and the maintenance of a cool body. "The season is congenial to persons who suffer with chilblains in winter because the pathologic condition is compensated by the physiologic vaso-dilatation and heightened blood pressure." (Maximillian Stern, M.D.)

Diagnosis. Chimatlon mild is a true inflammation of the skin with or without bullous formation and serous or purulent exudation. The color varies from a light scarlet to a deep purple and the lesions blend gradually with the surrounding normal tissue. The part feels cold and clammy to the touch, this being a characteristic symptom in spite of the heightened red color. The blood present in the parts is sluggish so that its temperature is below normal.

Chilblains of the metatarsophalangeal joint of the great and fifth toes may be mistaken for bursitis. The chief difference between the two conditions is found in the history of the case, which in chilblains shows exposure, while in bursitis the lesion is usually accompanied by hallux valgus. The usual sites of chimatlon mild of the foot are the heel, the tips of the toes, the great and little toe joints and the webs between the toes. The pains of chilblains are transient and of a shooting variety, and are present with the shoe on or off, while those of bursitis are constant and dull, and are present only when the shoe is worn. Where inflammatory processes have con-

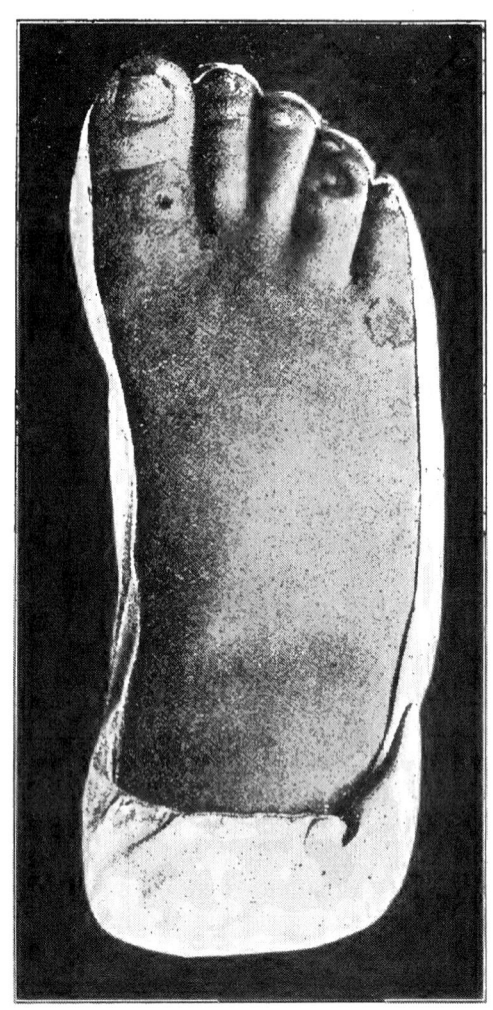

CHIMATLON MILD FROM THE JACOBI ATLAS

tinued so that the deep tissue are involved, the pains are of a throbbing nature in both lesions, so that other symptoms must be observed to determine upon a proper diagnosis.

Chimatlon Mild	Bursitis
History of exposure	No history of exposure
Hallux valgus not usually present	Hallux valgus usually present
Pains of shooting variety	Pains dull and steady
Pains present at all times	Pains absent with shoes off
Intense itching	No itching

The lesions of chimatlon are irregular in shape and may involve the entire fore foot, including both the dorsal and the plantar surfaces. The heel over the tendo Achillis, as well as the skin on the sole and lateral surfaces over the os calcis, are common sites of chilblains. These lesions are usually deeply colored, the redness gradually diminishing as the periphery is reached.

The blebs which have formed, may exude serum or even pus, and these lesions may be easily differentiated from the blebs of pompholyx and eczema by carefully noting the history of the case, the age of the patient and the general appearance of the foot and leg.

Prognosis. The ultimate cure of chilblains is uncertain Cases of a mild type often respond immediately, while others persist indefinitely. The painful symptoms are readily relieved, but the lesion itself often continues until the change of season, when the warmer weather brings about a cure. This is due to the changes that occur in the cutaneous circulation during warmer weather. Recurrence is the rule in those who have poor circulation from anemia or other causes.

Treatment. The treatment for chimatlon mild consists in bringing about a gradual reaction This should be commenced immediately after exposure, and is accomplished by rubbing the parts with snow or cold water. It must be remembered that the reaction must be gradual. If the parts exposed are rapidly warmed, the reaction will be equally rapid, and serious results may follow. After reaction has been established, the treatment varies with the severity of the resulting inflammation.

When the skin has been broken and blebs or bullae are present, the lesions must be healed first. For this purpose ointments are most desirable. The parts should be thoroughly cleansed with an antiseptic such as phenol (1-40) or bichloride of mercury (1-2000), and by removing serum or pus present, with hydrogen peroxide. The surface of the lesion may then be dressed with any of the following:

℞ Ichthyol .... 8.
    Petrolatum q. s ad . .. ... 32.
M. ft. ung Sig. Apply over affected parts twice daily.

℞ Acid. carbol...... .. .. 0.60
    Acid. boric ... . 2.
    Petrolatum q. s. ad .   . 32.
M. ft. ung. Sig. Apply on chilblain once daily

℞ Spirit. terebinthinae... .... 2.
    Acid. boric. . ... 2.
    Petrolatum q. s. ad . .. 32.
M. ft. ung. Sig. Apply on chilblain once daily

Wet dressing of Burow's Solution, diluted with equal parts of distilled water, applied for a few days, produces satisfactory results in lesions where there is marked inflammation and swelling.

In severe ulcerative processes that do not granulate readily, a strong stimulant, such as balsam of Peru or some iodine preparation, should be used until the entire area is healed

After the skin has been healed, or in cases where the skin has not been broken, the treatment varies with the severity of the lesion. In very mild cases, massage followed by an application of the compound tincture of benzoin, which, because it furnishes an occlusive coating and acts as a support for the skin, is often sufficient. The liquor alumini acetatis (Burow's Solution) may be used as an astringent wet dressing to reduce the swelling and inflammation. The part may also be painted with a four per cent. solution of silver nitrate at frequent intervals, to be then covered with raw cotton; or nitric acid, diluted with aqua cinnamoni, 15 minims to the ounce, may be painted over the unbroken skin.

A very satisfactory liniment which has been used extensively to relieve the pain and reduce the inflammation in this condition consists of the following:

```
R  Guaiacol . . . . . . . . . . . . . . . . . . . . . . 8.
   Spts. terebinth . . . . . . . . . . . . . . . . . 28.
   Ol. olivae q. s. ad   . . . . . . . . . . . 64.
```
M. ft. lin. Sig. Rub on affected parts at bedtime.

The itching, which is a marked symptom of chimatlon mild, can readily be controlled by the application of camphorated soap liniment. Its action is almost instantaneous

Ichthyol has proven to be a valuable agent in the treatment of chilblains; it may be used with collodion, or as an ointment, the following being found satisfactory:

```
R  Ichthyol   . . .    .    . . . . . . . . 8.
   Lanolin q. s. ad. . . . . . .  . . . . . . . . . . 32.
```
M. ft. ung Sig. Spread on gauze or lint and apply.

It must be borne in mind that the apparent cure of an acute lesion of chimatlon mild, is not in reality an absolute cure, and thorough precautions must be taken to prevent recurrence. Stimulation of the cutaneous blood supply and the vasomotor nervous system is essential, and for this purpose, massage and the alternate hot and cold foot baths are advisable. The latter treatment should be used at least once daily and if possible, twice a day. The feet should be kept in hot water for thirty seconds and then plunged into cold water and kept there for fifteen seconds. This is repeated for an entire ten minute period.

Electricity, in the form of the faradic or the high frequency currents, may be used to assist in the stimulation of the action of the skin. These treatments should be given for ten minutes, three times a day.

The hygiene of the foot is all important, and this should be explained at length to the patient. The feet should be protected by wearing woolen or cashmere stockings, the latter being preferred, and should be used from early in the fall until late in the spring. Hose of this kind prevent heat radiation, so necessary for those who suffer from chilblains; they also absorb excretory moisture, all of which prevents recurrence of the lesions. It is necessary to conserve the body heat as much as possible, and warm underclothing, covering the entire body, should be worn; the patient should be instructed to take some form of general exercise. Foot gear should be wide enough to allow freedom of the toes and the shoes should be made of either calf skin or vici kid. The wearing of silk stockings and patent leather shoes must be discouraged if good results are to be expected.

Where the skin is not broken, Dr. Charles T. St. Clair of Bluefield, West Virginia, advises as follows: "coal oil (kerosene) applied night and morning to old itching frostbites of the feet gives almost immediate relief. It should be applied with a cloth and cotton soaked in the kerosene and allowed to evaporate, which it will do in a few minutes. If the sock is put on and the person goes to bed with the foot still wet with the oil, it may burn the skin."

CHIMATLON SEVERE

Derivation. Chimatlon, from the Greek, meaning the severity of winter; severe, with extremely bad effects on the tissues.

Synonyms. Frost bite, pernio, dermatitis calorica

Definition. Chimatlon severe is a local inflammation of the skin and deeper structures, produced by exposure to extreme cold, and is a result of complete or partial paralysis of the vaso-motor nerves.

Etiology. The one cause for the severe form of chimatlon is prolonged exposure to an extreme degree of cold The decrease in atmospheric temperature lowers the temperature of the parts exposed, thereby causing complete or partial paralysis of the vaso-motor nerves and producing congelation of the blood vessels. When the congelation is complete the parts are deprived of their nourishment, and finally become devitalized.

Symptoms. Immediately after exposure, numbness develops and all sensation is gradually lost. The parts are congealed and if there is complete freezing, they present a white, blanched appearance. The tissues affected may be so completely frozen, that upon thawing, they are either found to be absolutely dead, or their vitality so greatly impaired that there is very little reaction and gangrene may result in a very short time. If the area is not completely frozen, the reaction is rapid, the tissues become purple, swollen and very painful. The parts may become gangrenous, in which case the line of demarcation and separation between the gangrenous and the healthy tissues evidences itself. The affected tissue is at first white but gradually becomes blue and finally black. The fluids in the tissues rapidly evaporate and the odor of decaying flesh is very apparent.

If the parts do not become gangrenous, the symptoms that present themselves are those of inflammation. The tissues become swollen and assume a deep purple color, which, as the circulation is restored, becomes lighter and, after inflammation has subsided, gradually disappears. Blebs may form and there may be an exudation of serum or even of pus.

Pathology. The changes that occur in chimatlon severe are much the same of those of the milder type, the former however, causing complete destruction of tissue, or the development of gangrene. The cold causes a constriction of the blood vessels and the stream within them is retarded The minute nerve terminals in the smaller arteries, which control the dilation and constriction, are destroyed and their function is lost. The vessels now contract and in extreme cases remain so. Where the exposure has not been severe enough to cause complete death of the vessels, there is a dilation after the contraction, with a very slow movement or even complete stasis of the blood stream.

Gangrene or necrosis will manifest itself in extreme cases almost immediately, and often after reaction has commenced, the tissues may be cast off. At the line of demarcation between the normal and the dead tissues, the changes that accompany inflammation take place.

Diagnosis. The diagnosis of frost bite is not very liable to be confused with any other condition, in that the history shows exposure to an extremely low temperature. The disease known as "Trench Foot," when it first manifested itself, during the world war, was considered a form of chimatlon, but since research work has been done along the lines of the new disease, it has been found to be quite another condition. Trench Foot will be discussed following this chapter.

The color of the part is characteristic. Immediately after exposure, the tissues are blanched, and as reaction progresses, the color deepens from a light scarlet to a deep red purple or black, depending on the length of the exposure and the severity of the condition. As reaction advances, the gangrenous tissue is separated from the normal tissue by a distinct slough, which, as previously stated, is known as the line of demarcation.

The milder cases of frost bite and the severer cases of chilblains are often confused, particularly in cases of the former when the loss of tissue has been avoided. The confusion, although of no great moment (inasmuch as the treatment of both lesions is identical), may be avoided by remembering that frost bite develops quickly and that the parts have been exposed to a very low temperature, while chilblains develop more slowly, are less painful and do not require exposure to a very great decrease in temperature for their causation.

Prognosis. When the part has been completely frozen and the circulation to the parts has ceased, there is no possibility of saving the tissues. However, in cases seen immediately after exposure, in which proper treatment is commenced at once, it is often possible to save large areas that would otherwise be lost. Amputation is the only cure in cases where gangrene has developed. The ulcers which result after the dead tissue has been removed, respond very slowly, requiring from one to four months to heal.

Recurrence is the rule, due to the fact that the vasomotor nerves never regain their normal vitality, and persons who have had frost bite will develop symptoms from the least imaginable cause.

Treatment. In all cases of frost bite, even when the parts seem hopelessly frozen, the first treatment should consist of bringing the parts back to normal temperature by a gradual reaction. This should be carried out as thoroughly as possible, for it often is the means of saving large areas of tissue. A case in which the entire fore foot is involved may be thus saved so that only one or two toes are lost. Such a patient would be able to walk comfortably, whereas if no care were taken with the preliminary treatment, the patient might become a hopeless foot cripple.

A gradual reaction is brought about by rubbing the parts with snow or cold water. The affected parts may be placed in a vessel containing cold water, or they may be wrapped in cloths wrung out in cold water. The final result depends largely upon the length of time elapsing between the exposure and the inauguration of the first treatment.

If the parts are completely frozen, gangrene will soon manifest itself. If the affected part is only partly frozen, a gradual reaction can be brought about by the above described means and if the subsequent inflammatory reaction is gradual, gangrene may be averted or at least limited. Cold water dressings should be continued for some time after reaction has occurred, and should be maintained until the certainty of the avoidance of gangrene is fixed. The line of demarcation and separation will be indicative of this fact.

When all of the gangrenous tissue has separated, the remaining ulcer should be treated just as though it had arisen from any cause. In cases of gangrene of the toes and feet, complete or partial amputation should be practised as soon as the lines of demarcation and separation are well established When gangrene has been avoided in frost bite, the treatment consists in stimulating the affected area. Various medicaments are useful, among which may be mentioned oil of turpentine, balsam of Peru, tincture of iodine, ichthyol and strongly carbolized ointments.

If the frost bite is of the bullous, pustular, vesicular or escharotic type, soothing agents such as ichthyol, Burow's solution, etc., should be applied to the affected parts.

Wrapping the affected parts in dry salt has been suggested by a western chiropodist, who claims to have obtained excellent results by the use of this agent.

In cases where gangrene has been averted, the following have proved of great value:

    R Acid carbol. ... . 1.
        Acid. boric 2
        Petrolat, q. s. ad.... . .. .. 32.
    M. ft. ung. Sig. Apply every morning.

    R Ichthyol .... 8.
        Lanolin q. s. ad. .. .. .32.
    M. ft. ung Sig. Apply on lesions once daily.

    R Ichthyol .... 8.
        Aquae q. s. ad... .... 32.
    M. Sig. Paint over the affected area.

In frost bite, after the gangrenous tissue has been removed, the resulting ulcer may be treated with a stimulant. For this purpose balsam of Peru, iodine, ichthyol and other agents have proven successful. These ulcers do not respond readily, because of the decrease in vitality of the surrounding tissues, and patience is essential for a final cure. The patient must be told that the lesion will require a long time to heal.

Hernance (Therapeutic Gazette, 1895) draws the following conclusions from the study of thirty cases: "1. Ichthyol is the drug that gives most relief to pain and is as good a protector as any other application. 2. Acetanalid ointment is the best dressing when the parts are raw and ulcerated, preventing suppuration and promoting granulation. 3. In a certain number of cases one can do nothing but keep the parts clean and wait until nature throws off the diseased tissue."

Massage is a very good therapeutic agent for chimatlon severe, and should be applied twice a day, if possible. This will help stimulate the circulation and tone up the faulty nerve endings. Electricity should also be used wherever possible, the high frequency and the faradic currents being the best. Applications directly to the affected parts for ten minutes, once or twice a day, will aid materially in bringing about a rapid cure.

The prevention of the recurrent attacks may be accomplished by treatment commenced in the early fall, and including massage, proper shoes, cashmere stockings, and other prophylactic measures. This treatment is essential, particularly for those who are anemic and under-nourished

CHAPTER XIX

DISEASES OF THE SWEAT GLANDS

HYPERIDROSIS

Derivation. From the Greek *hyper,* in excess, and *hidros,* sweat.

Synonyms. Idrosis; ephidrosis; hydrosis; sudatoria; polyidrosis; excessive sweating, sudorrhea.

Definition. Hyperidrosis is a functional disorder of the sweat glands (usually of the hands and feet) characterized by the excessive excretion of sweat. The condition may be limited to certain areas or it may be distributed over the entire body.

Etiology. When hyperidrosis is general it is caused by faulty innervation. The cause in localized forms is doubtless varied from that of pure idiosyncrasy to grave systemic disturbances. In instances there seems to be an inherited tendency to this disturbance. Excessive drinking of water or tea will produce hyperidrosis pedum in some people. Localized sweating may follow some debilitating diseases for a period of time. Anything that causes a depression of the nervous tone, may be an etiologic factor. Neurasthenics often display this symptom. Physical or mental excitement will cause profuse sweating in many individuals.

Pathology. The normal sweat excretion is closely related to the nervous system, hence pathologic excretion must have some nervous cause It is most probable that any disease or injury that affects the function of the sympathetic nervous system, is the direct cause of excessive sweat excretion. Examination of sections of the glands fails to show any increase in size or in the epithelium of the gland.

Symptoms. Hyperidrosis may occur as a result of a general disease such as rheumatism, tuberculosis, malaria, etc., or it may be idiopathic and persist for a long period. The latter phase is of most interest to the podiatrist The disease is quite common. The sweating may be immediate or profuse, and is always more marked in regions where excessive sweating is normal, such as the hands, feet, axillae, etc. It is more pronounced in hot weather, but is excessive even in cold weather, and is increased by the least exertion. In hot weather it is frequently accompanied by miliaria, intertrigo, or acute eczema.

On the feet, hyperidrosis is often disgusting, and may become exceedingly troublesome. The excretion is excessive and the feet are constantly damp or wet and clammy. The stockings become moist and the shoe may become watersoaked. Sweating is most profuse on the soles and between the toes. The skin is soggy and macerated and, in severe cases, the sole and surrounding areas are reddened, puffy and irritated, with ill-defined vesicular or flattened bullous lesions. In ordinary hyperidrosis of the feet, the sweat is not offensive immediately after it is exuded, but rapidly becomes so, unless the footgear is changed frequently. Bromidrosis is often associated with hyperidrosis.

Prognosis. As a rule, localized cases are obstinate, but with continued treatment, good results will follow. It is often necessary to change the treatment from time to time. Relapses are not uncommon.

Treatment. The treatment of hyperidrosis is divided into two groups, local and general. Excessive general sweating following fevers and debilitated conditions of the system should receive general treatment at the hands of the physician. When nervous disorders produce sweating in limited areas, they also require specially directed general treatment. In localized sweating of indefinite cause, under the advice of the physician, it is often advisable to administer general tonics, and remedies such as ergot, belladonna, gallic acid, etc., may be locally applied. Precipitated sulphur, taken internally, one dram twice daily, is the resort of many physicians in such cases and the treatment has given satisfactory results.

While constitutional treatment should be used in every case of hyperidrosis pedum, the external treatment is more positive in result and therefore is more essential. This external treatment consists of the application of ointments and powders, with frequent washing and the use of lotions. Astringent lotions, used for the purpose of hardening the skin may be chosen from the following:

>   Alum powdered . . . . . 1 ounce.
>   Water . . . . 1 pint.
>
> or
>
>   Zinc sulphate . . . 2 drams.
>   Water . . . . 1 pint.
>
> or
>
>   Formalin . . . . 3 drams.
>   Alcohol . . . . 1 pint.

The feet should be thoroughly cleansed and dried Lotions applied two or three times daily, should be allowed to dry on the foot. This may then be followed by a dusting powder of the following:

>   Acid salicylic . . . . . .15 grains.
>   Boric acid . . . . 1 ounce.

The local application of belladonna in the form of the diluted tincture, the liniment or the ointment, has given excellent results in some cases, but great care should be exercised in their use, as belladonna may produce toxic effects, through absorption.

Many cases have responded readily to the alternate foot bath (See Chapter, *The Care of the Foot*). After the alternate foot bath, the feet are thoroughly dried, and in severe cases, the lotion of formalin and alcohol may be used, or in ordinary cases, grain alcohol is applied. When the lotion has dried, the feet are dusted with the following powder:

 ℞ Acid salicylic............ . .15 grains
  Alum powdered
  Lycopodium . .. .aa 1 ounce
  M Sig. Dust on feet morning and night.

Diachylon ointment, freshly prepared, is the best remedy among the unguents. It is prepared as follows

 ℞ Lead plaster.............. 1 ounce
  Oil of lavender flowers ....15 grains
  Olive oil, q.s. ad . ... 3 ounces
  M. Sig. Apply on gauze and bandage.

Another ointment which has astringent properties and which has been used with some success is ·

 ℞ Tannic acid........... ......2 drams
  Petrolatum . ...1 ounce
  M. Sig. Spread on gauze and bandage.

Before these ointments are applied, the parts should be thoroughly washed with soap and water, dried, and the ointment spread on gauze and held in place with a bandage. The application should be removed after twelve hours, the parts rubbed dry with a towel, and the ointment reapplied This should be continued for a week or two, when, if results have not followed, other forms of treatment should be used.

The X-rays have a drying influence upon the skin, but if this treatment is used, great caution should be exercised, as the rays are likely to have a very harmful influence upon the tissues generally.

At the suggestion of a prominent chemist and physician, a series of experiments were performed with oxygen gas and vanadium chloride solution for the treatment of hyperidrosis, which proved more or less successful. The solution of vanadium chloride (1-20,000) was applied to the foot, and the oxygen gas was slowly sprayed on the foot, from a large gas container. This treatment lasted for ten minutes and was applied twice a week. In one particular case, which had resisted the ordinary methods of treatment, the use of this remedy was of great benefit to the patient After several weeks, the case showed marked improvement, but the inability of the patient to continue treatment prevented further trials. In many other ordinary cases of hyperidrosis, the results were excellent, while in others there was no marked improvement*. The use of formalin and alcohol solution in conjunction with the oxygen treatment, has proven very effective. The lotion is used at night, immediately before retiring.

Stillians, in the Journal of the American Medical Association, states that a 25% solution of aluminum chloride in distilled water, dabbed gently on the part every second or third day and allowed to dry, will cause a rapid amelioration of the excessive sweating; three such applications are usually sufficient. If the condition recurs, the treatment may be repeated.

Potassium permanganate solution, 5 parts to 1,000, has been found efficient as a wash for the feet. More active, and therefore to be used with more care, are "chromic acid" solutions, as:

> Chromium trioxide 2.5
> Water .. ..50.
> Sig. Use as a paint once a week.

Less active, but more pleasant than the foregoing, is:

> Tannic acid .. .. 5.
> Alcohol ....100.
> Water, q. s. ad.... . ...200.
> Sig. Use as a wash twice a day.

The lotions and washes should be used in conjunction with drying powders, such as have been already mentioned.

The use of the various solutions of aluminum chloride, or of chromium trioxide, may, in some cases, cause a mild

---
*These experiments were carried on at The First Institute of Podiatry under the direction of Monroe Redell and W H A Fletcher, clinicians, and on the suggestion of Dr. F Oefele

dermatitis, perhaps with itching. This may be relieved by the application of protective dressings to prevent scratching, and the application of ointments, such as cold cream containing 12 per cent. boric acid, or a calomin lotion. Itching may be relieved by adding 0.5 per cent. phenol to the calomine lotion.

BROMIDROSIS.

Derivation. *"Bromos,"* a stench; and *"hidros,"* sweat.

Synonym. Osmidrosis.

Definition. Bromidrosis is a functional disorder of the sweat glands, characterized by a sweat excretion which has an offensive odor.

Etiology. The etiology of bromidrosis is much the same as that of hyperidrosis, occurring in those who are anemic, chlorotic and nervous and in those who are compelled to stand for long periods. Eating certain foods and drugs will give peculiar odors to the perspiration, among which are garlic, onions, assafetida, and sulphur. The cause of the odor of the sweat in bromidrosis pedum is the decomposition of the fatty acids of the sweat, as well as the presence of the bacterium fetidum, which is found on the feet, especially between the toes.

Pathology. Immediately after the sweat is excreted, it is not offensive, but soon becomes so, due to the presence of microorganisms and the decomposition of the fatty acids

Symptoms. The sweat has a disagreeable odor and is usually associated with hyperidrosis, but not necessarily so, as it may occur in persons having a normal sweat excretion. When the excretion is excessive, there are the usual symptoms of hyperidrosis, viz., puffiness, tenderness, sogginess and possibly blebs or vesicles. The odor is offensive, stale, penetrating and peculiar and often is sufficient to make the sufferer unfit for society.

Treatment. The treatment is essentially the same as for hyperidrosis, coupled with absolute cleanliness and frequent change of footgear. Shoes should be allowed to stand in the air for at least twenty-four hours after having been worn, so that several pairs are required. Constitutional treatment is the same as for hyperidrosis as is also the external treatment. The feet should be washed in boric acid solution, and the powder used freely in the socks and on the feet.

The feet may be painted once every three weeks with a 5 to 10 per cent. solution of chromic acid, or they may be washed every other day in one per cent. solution of potassium permanganate, and in the interval the following powder proves efficacious:

  ℞ Acid salicylic .. . .. 10 grains
    Tannoform . ... 2 drams
    Zinc oxide
    Talc . .. . aa 3 drams
    M. Sig. Dust on feet morning and night.

ANIDROSIS

Derivation. *a,* without; and *hidros,* sweat.

Synonym. Decrease or absence of sweating.

Definition. Anidrosis is a functional disorder of the sweat glands characterized by a diminution or suppression of sweat.

Etiology. Anidrosis is rare as an idiopathic condition, occurring generally in diabetes and fever, also in some skin diseases such as ichthyosis and pityriasis rubra pilaris; also in the parts affected by anesthetic leprosy, scleroderma and keloids. Localized sweat suppression follows injury to the nerves.

Symptoms. The skin seems to be abnormally dry, and this dry skin may be a form of ichthyosis or may predispose to eczema. When the sole of the foot is dry and the skin shows clefts, which contain helomata miliare, and has a yellowish color, diabetes may be suspected. There may be but slight diminution of sweat excretion, or total absence.

Treatment. In congenital cases, nothing is of much

avail. In the acquired cases, applications of hot water or vapor baths externally, and general tonics, the free drinking of water and the use of warm clothing, are indicated. Pilocarpin or jaborandi may be given internally, but this must be on the prescription of a physician. Massage with oil or the application of galvanic or faradic electricity have proven of benefit. Hot alkaline baths, preceding the massage with oil, are also at times beneficial.

In addition to the above there are a number of rare granular perversions which occasionally are seen by the podiatrist and of which but brief mention need here be made:

Chromidrosis. A condition in which the sweat is colored, usually black. When this condition arises from accident, the sweat may be colored green. Red sweat, which occasionally occurs in the axillae, is due to the action of bacterium prodigiosum.

Sudamen. A collection of sweat in the upper layers of the epidermis, due to obstruction of the sweat-ducts, which gives rise to an eruption of numerous pinhead, transparent vesicles. Occurs during the course of fevers and is usually of but short duration.

Uridrosis. Characterized by the excretion of urine constituents through the sweat glands. Usually the result of suppression of urine by reason of impaired kidney function, whereupon the sweat glands assist in the elimination of the urinary deposits. There is a urinous odor to the skin.

Hematidrosis. Characterized by hemorrhage from the sweat glands. A very rare condition.

Phosphoridrosis In this very unusual disease the sweat glands exude a phosphorescent sweat, said to be due to a species of photobacterium following the ingestion of phosphorus or of food stuffs containing phosphorus.

Miliaria. A mild inflammatory affection caused by obstruction of the sweat ducts, characterized by the occurrence of small papules and vesicles at their mouths

Hydrocystoma. A condition characterized by the

formation upon the face of firm, pin-head sized vesicles, due to sweat gland obstructions.

Hydradenitis Suppuration An inflammatory disease of the sweat glands followed by deep-seated, shot-like nodules, which suppurate and leave scars.

Seborrhea. A lesion of the fat-producing glands characterized by an increased and altered secretion of sebum resulting in an oily or scaly condition of the skin.

CHAPTER XX

ULCERS

Definition. An ulcer is a lesion of a cutaneous or mucous surface, caused by a molecular disintegration of the superficial parts, usually attended by more or less suppuration. A wound, or superficial loss of tissue due to traumatism, is not primarily an ulcer, but may become such if the healing process is arrested or the wound becomes infected with pyogenic microorganisms.

The following ulcers frequently come under the observation of the podiatrist:

Simple Ulcer, a local non-constitutional lesion attended with no marked pain or inflammation.

Indolent or Callous Ulcer, a chronic lesion, with hard, elevated edges and few or no granulations and showing no tendency to heal.

Varicose Ulcer, localized destruction of the skin over a varicose vein, usually of the leg, due to mechanical pressure, to nutritive disturbances, or to bacterial action.

Perforating Ulcer of the Foot, malum perforans pedis, a round, deep, trophic lesion of the sole of the foot, following disease or injury (in any part of its course from the centre to the periphery) of the nerve supplying the parts.

Syphilitic Ulcer, due to syphilis in late secondary or in tertiary stages.

Before describing the characteristics of the various forms of lesions just mentioned, together with their differential diagnosis, treatment, etc , it is deemed advantageous to briefly discuss the general etiology and pathology of all ulcers.

Etiology. One or several factors may be concerned in

the etiology of ulcers, which are grouped under. (a) predisposing causes; (b) exciting causes. The first group includes local as well as general causes.

Predisposing Causes. Age can hardly be considered as a very important factor, except that old age is accompanied by retrogressive tissue changes, hardening of the arteries, impaired circulation, etc., and one would therefore expect the statistics to show a greater proportion of ulcers during the later years of life.

As regards sex, ulcer is more common among men than women in the ratio of about three to one. Alcoholism, syphilis, and traumatism may in some measure explain why ulcers are more common in men than women. Occupation seems to have little to do with the etiology beyond the fact that it may predispose to various forms of infection, and it is due to this element that we have the most important factors in the causation of ulceration. Varicose ulcer is always associated with varicose veins in the lower extremity, and these may be described as veins whose valves are incompetent. The most obvious cause of the breaking down of the valves is hard work, that is the lifting or carrying of heavy loads, as in the case of laborers, freight handlers, and longshoremen. The great strain occasioned by work of this kind lays a heavy load upon the veins of the legs. Whether the valves become useless through stretching of the vein walls, or are directly broken, is immaterial. The occupations which involve standing for long periods without moving the legs are, in a lesser degree, a source of valvular incompetence, and this is not from excessive back pressure but from stasis due to lack of muscular movement. Among women, the venous engorgement of the legs, so often seen in pregnancy, may, after the birth of several children, result in varicosity.

Many of the constitutional diseases such as gout, anemia, diabetes, syphilis, and tuberculosis, which lower the vitality of the tissues, and other conditions, such as valvular disease of the heart, general obesity, and arterial hardening which prevent proper circulation, predispose to the formation of ulcers when there is in addition some exciting cause.

Embolism, which cuts off the nutrition of the part, may also act as a local cause. Certain vasomotor disturbances, such as occur in frost-bite and in Raynaud's disease, may produce small areas of localized gangrene which subsequently become the seat of an ulcer.

Interference with the return of venous blood from a part predisposes to ulceration. Where phlebitis and periphlebitis occur, especially in the smaller venous radicles, small abscesses often form, the adjacent skin becomes involved, and an ulcer results; or the rupture of the diseased wall of one of the small veins may become infected, and ulcer develops.

Perforating ulcer of the foot is a frequent complication of tabes dorsalis. Myelitis, and other pathologic conditions of the nervous system may also, either through trophic changes or by reason of impaired sensation, bear a distinct relationship to ulcerative processes.

Exciting Causes. Traumatism is one of the most frequent causes of ulcer formation. Its degree may, of course, vary greatly, and whether it will produce an ulcer depends upon one or more of the predisposing causes already mentioned. Infection by any of the staphylococcus or streptococcus group of organisms as well as by the tubercle bacillus will produce ulcers; malignant ulceration also occurs.

Pathology. The pathology will vary according to the conditions causing the ulcer, although in the non-specific forms of ulcer the phenomena of congestion, exudative and necrotic inflammation, together with reparative inflammation or granulation, will only be in evidence. In the development of an ulcer the degenerative process predominates; in the healing stage, the reparative. When the ulcer develops from without, as when infection enters the skin through an abrasion, congestion first occurs. This is rapidly followed by the emigration of leucocytes, by a diapedesis of red blood cells which rapidly disintegrate, and by an exudation of serum and fibrin. At the same time there is a proliferation of the epithelial cells and also a proliferation of the connective tissue cells of the corium. The tissue next becomes softened by the exudate between the cells. Then, as a result of the pressure of the exuded serum, of the crowding by the leucocytes, and of the cutting off of the blood-supply, and also in some measure through the effects of the toxins furnished by the bacteria, there occurs necrosis of the cells, which are thrown off from the surface with the products of exudation, until there is formed an ulcer with its base consisting of spheroidal and a few epithelioid cells developed from the connective-tissue cells by proliferation.

When an ulcer in its complete stage of development is examined, the surface is found to be covered with a layer formed by the overproduction of new round cells, together with the exudate of fibrin, serum, and the cellular elements of the blood. When the discharge from the ulcer is profuse, this may be constantly washed away. When the ulcer is sluggish, it may be in a condition of coagulation necrosis. In this latter condition a croupous material covers the base of the ulcer, and below this is a more or less distinct layer, largely composed of cellular elements, with very little cellular substance, the cells being spheroidal and epithelioid in character and mingled with polynuclear leucocytes. As we go deeper, the amount of intercellular substance increases, and a number of transparent fibres and fusiform cells are found. In this layer of granulation tissue are also the newly formed blood-vessels, the most superficial branches being vertical to the surface, and developing by a process of budding from the endothelial cells of the capillaries deeper down. This layer is paler in color than the layer made up of the cellular elements, but may contain pigment from the disintegration of the red blood cells. It gradually merges into a layer of cicatricial connective tissue which lies beneath the ulcer.

A section of a chronic ulcer would show an enlargement

and prolongation of the papillae, with a marked proliferation of the epithelial cells covering them. This is most pronounced in the condition known as callous ulcer, where the edges may, by proliferation, be considerably raised about the level of the surrounding skin, and often overhang the base of an ulcer. Under proper treatment the reparative process proceeds faster than the degeneration of the cells and the ulcer begins to heal by granulation. Small sprouts or buds of protoplasm protrude from the capillaries below or in the base of the ulcer, developing from the cells in their walls These are hollowed out by the blood-pressure and form new blood-vessels which anastomose with others. Nuclei form in the protoplasm and thus endothelial cells develop At the same time small spheroidal cells, developing from the connective tissue cells, become grouped around the blood-vessels. These are closely crowded together at first, being separated by only a small amount of fluid intercellular substance. Some of the round cells then become larger and fusiform or branched. The larger cells are known as epithelioid cells. Some of the fusiform and branched cells, called fibroblasts, develop the new delicate fibrillar intercellular substance, while others form the connective-tissue cells. Gradually the fibrous intercellular substance increases in amount, while the cells become fewer and flattened, and cicatricial tissue is formed. The contraction of this cicatricial tissue constitutes an important element in the healing of an ulcer.

During the process of granulation, more of the round cells are produced than are necessary. These die and are thrown off in the discharge. Healthy granulations should be small, even, and of a reddish pink color. Where the growth of the blood-vessels proceeds more rapidly than the development of the cells and the formation of connective tissue, there is produced a soft, pale, flabby condition known as exuberant granulations, or proud flesh. On the other hand, both the cells and the blood-vessels may develop very slowly, forming indolent or sluggish granulations. In order that the ulcer may heal it must eventually become covered with epithelium, and this can develop only from the epithelium at the edges of the ulcer Under favorable conditions, when the granulations reach the level of the surrounding skin, the epithelium begins to spread in a thin bluish white line from the edges out over the surface, until the latter is entirely covered, when the ulcer is healed.

Simple Ulcers. By far the greatest number of ulcers coming under the observation and within the province of the podiatrist are of the simple variety Heavy calloused areas which are neglected are apt to become so irritant as to cause the softer tissues underneath to break down and ulcerate, and a similar condition very often occurs in connection with helomata, particularly heloma molle

Constitutional diseases, either trophic or specific, may be predisposing causes of these conditions but the exciting cause is surely traumatism.

Simple ulcerations are most generally found upon the plantar surfaces of the feet, under the heads of the first or fifth metatarsal bones. As has been previously mentioned, however, the interdigital surfaces are also prone to these conditions. In this latter location the amount of perspiration excreted in the locality undoubtedly has much to do with the lowering of the vitality of the skin covering the part, and renders it susceptible to disintegrative processes.

Treatment. All the overlying callous must be immediately removed so that the parts may be properly cleansed and so that drainage may be maintained. This may be done with a sharp sterile scalpel, but sufficient care should be exercised so that no hemorrhage is caused. After the hardened tissue has been cut away, all necrosed tissue adhering to the floor and edges of the ulcer should be removed. A spray of alcohol, 60%, may then be employed to obtain thorough asepsis and after the parts are thoroughly dried, a dressing is applied in keeping with the conditions present.

Wet Dressing. If infection is present, or if the parts be considerably inflamed, due simply to the traumatic irritation, a wet dressing of mercury bichloride, 1/4000, liq aluminum acetate, or alcohol and boric acid, equal parts, should be employed for a sufficient time to reduce all infective or other inflammatory symptoms. Bichloride of mercury should not be used for a prolonged period of time in these cases, for its corrosive action will prevent new granulations and thus retard healing. The aluminum acetate and alcohol, boric acid combination may be used without fear of toxic irritation. If simple inflammation is present in the parts, Goulard's extract may be employed to reduce the acute symptoms, but care must be exercised and the parts watched so that no lead dermatitis shall develop from the drug

It is unwise under any condition to prolong the use of wet dressings beyond a time when they are thought to be necessary. The constant moisture is not conducive to prolific or to healthy granulation and for this reason these applications are best discontinued as soon as possible.

Boroglycerine, a combination of boric acid and glycerine, applied to a simple ulceration, particularly one of the indolent type, is found to stimulate granulation and thus aid materially in the healing process It is applied on sterile gauze and allowed to remain unchanged for from twenty-four to forty-eight hours.

Dry Dressings. Dry dressings, either of plain aseptic gauze or of dusting powders, are found effective in the treatment of simple ulcerations. The choice of the dusting agent is, of course, dependent upon the conditions present, but it should combine astringent and antiseptic properties.

Thymol Iodide, while not astringent, is a general favorite for most simple ulcerations. Contrary to the action of most powders, this combination of iodine and thymol induces a discharge rather than prevents it. This is due to the action of its constituent thymol and is desirable in dry ulcerations where more or less coagulation is present. This powder, known best by its trade name, aristol, has an energetic, antiseptic action due to the liberation of iodine and is used practically to the exclusion of all other iodine powders. It is principally used as an iodoform substitute, having none of the disagreeable odor of this drug.

Bismuth Subgallate, a combination of gallic acid and bismuth, is an efficient powder for use in these conditions. Its action is markedly astringent and it can be depended upon for antiseptic action as well.

Bismuth Subnitrate is also an astringent and antiseptic powder which may be substituted for the other bismuth salt in these conditions. The molecules of this powder are very fine and there is a tendency for it to cake so that when used, the dressing should be changed at regular and short intervals; the parts should be thoroughly cleansed of the dried powder from previous application before the new dressing is applied.

Zinc Powders, such as the oxide and the stearate, are also applicable in cases of simple ulcer. Zinc oxide may be combined with various other powders and numerous such combinations are now in the market. Zinc stearate is used alone and can be depended upon for a mild astringent action, although not comparable with either bismuth subgallate or subnitrate.

Ointment Dressings. The use of ointments is contraindicated in the presence of a discharging surface and for this reason drugs in fatty or oily bases are not generally used in all stages of ulcer regeneration. Several ointments may be used, however, either for antiseptic or stimulative action after the acute discharge, if present, has subsided or if no great amount or exudation is present.

Ung. Hydrargyri Ammoniati, white precipitate of mercury, will be found useful where antiseptic action is desired.

Ung. Acidi Borici, an antiseptic ointment, is also used in this connection.

Ung. Acidi Tannici, twenty parts of tannic acid, twenty parts glycerine, sixty parts cerate, is an astringent ointment efficient in these cases.

Ung. Eucalypti is used as an antiseptic and stimulant application for indolent ulcers.

Ung. Zinci Oxidi is a soothing and mildly astringent ointment which can be used advantageously.

Ung. Balsam of Peru, a 3% to 10% ointment of Peruvian balsam in vaseline or lanolin, is both antiseptic and stimulant.

Scarlet Red, an ointment prepared from medicinal scarlet red (Biebrich), may be used in strengths from 1% to 8% as a stimulant and healing application.

In the use of all ointments it is advisable to place only a thin film of the mass over the parts. Avoid the tendency to use a large quantity of any ointment

A shield may, at times, be used in connection with the application of the dry or of the ointment dressing. These appliances, however, particularly if made from a thick material, tend to arrest the circulation to the localized area, and, as free blood flow is to be desired at all times, the shield should be omitted in cases in which an ointment dressing is being used, unless it is sure that circulation is not being thereby impeded

Squares of sterile gauze held in place by adhesive strips or by a soft cocoon dressing, are practical means of retaining a powder or an ointment to the part. In choosing the latter form of dressing, never use a great amount of collodion in binding down the cotton fibre. If applied too freely, it is absorbed by the cotton and is apt to come in contact with the ulcerated surface itself. The dressing, if applied over a discharging area, should be absorbent, and this possibility is nullified when it is hardened by collodion.

INDOLENT OR CALLOUS ULCER.

This form of ulcer occurs principally on the leg, but occasionally is found on the foot and ankle. Callous ulcers vary in size from a five cent piece to the entire circumference of the part attacked

The surface is usually smooth and glistening and of a

dirty yellow color, with perhaps a few badly formed granulations. The edges are hard and sharply cut and elevated considerably above the surface, while the surrounding skin may be inflamed over the margin and is either covered with sodden cuticle or is congested. The skin surrounding the part is often deeply pigmented from chronic congestion, the pigmentation starting in separate papillae as maculae, which gradually coalesce. The discharge is purulent or serous and may be so abundant and irritating as to cause eczema of the skin. The base is adherent to the underlying tissues and this constitutes one of the main difficulties in healing, as contraction is thus prevented If the ulcer is situated above a bone, such as the tibia, chronic periostitis may result. Such ulcers are sometimes very painful from pressure on cutaneous nerves, or from a localized cellulitis associated perhaps with inflammation of veins and lymphatics. Thrombosis not infrequently occurs in both sets of vessels, leading to chronic edema of the feet.

Etiology. *General Causes.* (a) Various devitalizing fevers and diseases such as typhoid, scorbutus, diphtheria, chronic nephritis, etc. (b) Mineral poisoning, such as is produced by phosphorus (c) Anemia and debilitating conditions brought on by starvation, improper food, poor hygiene, overwork, lack of sleep, etc.

Local Causes. (a) Old scar tissue, the contraction of which has cut off the circulation. (b) Continuous pressure, from splints, lying in bed, etc. (c) Local destruction of the tissues such as is produced by extremes of heat and cold. (d) Local irritation or injury of tissues from violence (e) Various diseases of the skin, for example, pemphigus

Symptoms. These ulcers are most commonly found on the inner side of the lower third of the leg They show great variety in size, shape and appearance, of base, edges, and surrounding area, and in accordance with these differences, many different names are applied to them They may be round, very irregular, or funnel-shaped, as in perforating ulcer of the foot When the granulations are large, irregular, and bleed easily, they are spoken of as exuberant or fungating; when pale, soft and flabby, as weak or edematous; when small and growing slowly, as indolent. Sometimes the base is covered with a grayish or yellowish-white necrotic layer formed of fibrin and necrotic cellular elements. When this is removed, no granulations appear, but instead it presents a smooth, shining base resembling mucous membrane. This form is known as the croupous ulcer. The edges also vary greatly. They may be irregular or sharply cut, moderately thickened, or very much so, due to chronic congestion and edema, with enlargement of the papillae and proliferation of the epithelial cells When this is a prominent feature, the name callous ulcer is applied. The edges may be adherent to the deeper structures, thus preventing contraction and healing; they may be rounded, elevated, undermined, or overhanging.

The discharge from an ulcer is usually slight in amount, serous in character, and contains very few pus cells. The surrounding area may be swollen, red, congested, pigmented, edematous, eczematous, or the ulcer may be surrounded by smaller sores, by vesicles, or by masses of varicose veins. As a rule, there is an absence of severe pain accompanying leg ulcers, unless there is an exposure or involvement of some nerve filaments; but frequently, after the patient has been on his feet for a long time, there is a dull, aching pain in the part, due to chronic congestion which causes tension in and about the ulcer.

Differential Diagnosis. The diagnosis of a chronic indolent or callous ulcer can be easily made by the character of the granulations and by the location of the ulcer itself. The history points usually to an injury or infection and the situation of the sore is at the site of the previous injury or infection. The base is shallow, inflamed and often of a grayish-yellow color, with no thickening or elevation of its edges. The surrounding area is usually round and inflamed. A varicose ulcer is differentiated by the history of varicose veins or phlebitis, by its occurrence at the lower third of the leg and by the undermined thickened and irregular-shaped edges. A syphilitic ulcer is diagnosed by the history of lues; by its usual occurrence at the upper third of the leg; by a dirty sloughing and deep base; by punched-out, thin, dense, firm and undermined red edges; and by scars of a dusky red color. A tuberculous ulcer, by the history of previous glandular bone or lung disease; soft, pale, edematous granulations; thin undermined edges; involvement of glands and other signs of tubercular sinuses, bone disease, etc. A perforating ulcer, by the history of the case; the appearance of the ulcer upon the sole of the foot or in the vicinity of the heel; the presence of a sinus leading to necrosed bone; the pale, flabby granulations; all these signs should make the diagnosis easy.

Treatment. This naturally depends upon the stage at which the ulcer is seen and the conditions present. If there is considerable inflammation, accompanied by marked cellulitis and pain, wet dressings are indicated. Two distinct therapeutic actions may be derived from the wet compress, depending upon whether or not an impervious covering is employed. These actions are antiphlogistic and hyperemic, and these in turn may be either antiseptic or astringent. The wet dressing, without a covering, is cleansing and heat reducing, because of evaporation. There should be frequent replenishment of the solution where there is considerable discharge, or where it is desirable to reduce inflammation. A wet dressing with an impervious covering is contraindicated in the presence of pus, the warmth and moisture of such a dressing, being congenial to the growth and to the multiplication of bacteria. For the relief of pain and for the reduction of inflammation, wet dressings are the most effective form of treatment because (1) they are aseptic; (2) they permit free drainage; (3) no new granulations are disturbed in changing the dressing.

A great many different solutions are used and among these are: (1) sterile water; (2) ordinary saline solution (a teaspoonful of salt to a pint of water); (3) saturated solution of boric acid (prepared by dissolving a teaspoonful of boric acid in a pint of water); (4) Thiersch's solution (prepared by dissolving 15 grains of salicylic acid and 90 grains of boric acid in a pint of water); (5) Burow's solution (prepared by dissolving 675 grains of alum and 270 grains of lead acetate in a pint of water); (6) solution of

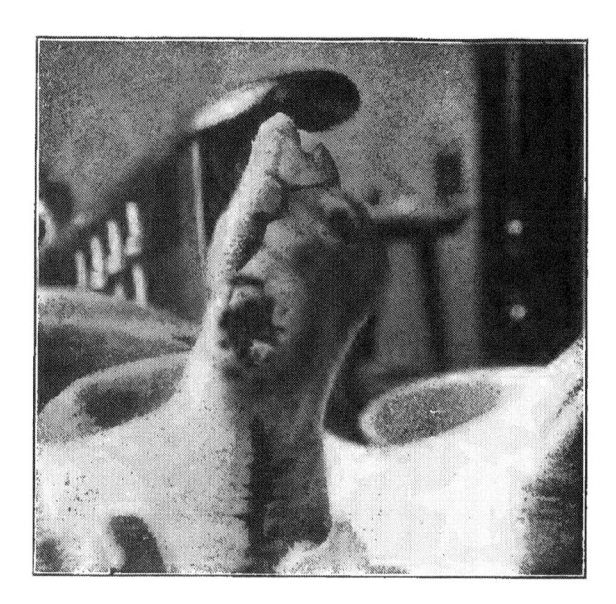

CHRONIC ULCER OF THE FOOT
(BEFORE OPERATION)

bichloride of mercury (varying in strength from 1 to 3,000 to 1 to 10,000); (7) lead and opium wash (U.S.P.); (8) Dakin's solution (hypochlorite of soda).

After the reduction of the inflammation, the next step is the cleansing and sterilization of the ulcer. Before healthy granulations can form, the removal of sloughs and the cleansing of the base must be accomplished as thoroughly as possible. Many means toward this end may be effective. A one-half to two per cent. creolin or lysol emulsion is very useful for those dirty ulcers from which a profuse, foul discharge escapes. A one per cent. solution of formalin is of great value for smaller ulcers, especially those due to tuberculous disease. The destruction and removal of sloughs may be hastened by cauterization with the solid stick of nitrate of silver. The use of certain ferments,

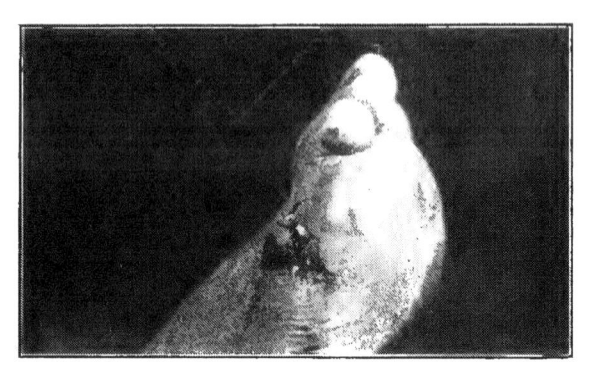

CHRONIC ULCER OF THE FOOT
(AFTER OPERATION)

such as brewer's yeast, papoid, or protonuclein, may help to clean up a chronic ulcer. The most frequent means employed for the cleansing and sterilization of the ulcer, previous to the application of some stimulating dressing, is washing the part with tincture of green soap and water. Peroxide of hydrogen can next be used, then sulphuric ether, and finally ninety-five per cent. alcohol. Where there is an accompanying eczematous condition, the scales can best be removed with benzine.

Having reduced the inflammation and succeeded in cleansing the ulcer, the next thing to consider is the means by which granulations may be stimulated. This may be accomplished by applications in the form of powders, solutions, ointments and grafts.

Dusting powders are employed either as antiseptics or as astringents or for both purposes. Their use in this instance is limited, and they are employed only where the secretion is scanty. Among the various powders used are: aristol, dermatol, boric acid, orthoform, calomel, protonuclein, alum, zinc oxide, etc. Thymol iodide, or aristol, is a superior antiseptic powder and enjoys the advantage over iodoform of being inodorous. Iodoform should be used only in tuberculous conditions; calomel only in syphilitic cases. Dermatol, or bismuth subgallate, combines the astringent and mildly antiseptic qualities of bismuth and gallic acid. Boric acid is mildly antiseptic. Zinc oxide and alum are both astringent. Scarlet red, five per cent., with boric acid, ninety-five per cent., is indicated when the granulations are sluggish

Among the various solutions used are silver nitrate in various strengths, zinc and copper sulphate, ichthyol, balsam of Peru, and calamine. Silver nitrate, zinc and copper sulphates are employed for their astringent action. Balsam of Peru, fifty per cent., with castor oil, fifty per cent., is used for its stimulating action.

Ointments are used in the treatment of ulcers either to stimulate the granulations or to soften thick epidermis Ointments should never be employed where there is a profuse discharge. Many different kinds of ointments are used, prominent among them being: balsam of Peru, in a ten per cent. strength for the stimulation of the granulations; boric acid and ichthyol, in the same strength; Lassar's paste (which consists of salicylic acid, one dram; starch and zinc oxide, each one ounce, and vaseline to make four ounces). This latter ointment is especially indicated when there is an eczema present. An ointment which has given good results is scarlet red, 1% to 5%. Scarlet red (Biebrich) was originally prepared as a dye for wool and silk, and is so named because of the fact that it was first manufactured in the town of Biebrich. Its application to granulating surfaces induces healing, not by the formation of scar tissue, but in every case by producing a high grade of normal skin which very soon becomes freely movable on the underlying tissue. The return of sensation in the healed area takes place from the periphery inward, instead of upward from the underlying tissue. Usually the dressing should be left undisturbed for from twenty-four to forty-eight hours, then reapplied, as indications warrant. In removing the dressing, if it be adherent to the granulations, peroxide of hydrogen should be used to loosen it. The skin about the granulating surface is best cleansed by benzine, as this removes all traces of scarlet red better than any other solution. The following formulas are recommended·

Scarlet red (medicinal Biebrich) fifteen grains, ungt. acidi borici, q. s. ad three ounces (one per cent.).

Scarlet red (medicinal Biebrich), forty-five grains; ungt. zinci oxidi, q. s. ad three ounces (three per cent).

Scarlet red (medicinal Biebrich), seventy-five grains; balsam of Peru, seventy-five minims; petrolati, q. s. ad three ounces (five per cent.)

The first is indicated where scarlet red is desired over a large area and for a long time; the second, where an astringent action is required because the granulations are profuse; the third, where the granulations are sluggish and require stimulation.

VARICOSE ULCER.

Etiology. To chronic ulcers of the leg, associated with varicose veins, especially of the smaller venous radicles, the name varicose ulcer has been given. The usual development of this variety of ulcer is as follows: persons who suffer from varices of the leg usually complain, for some time before the external manifestation of the disease, of a dull, aching pain in the limb, with a sense of weight, fullness and fatigue. In a more advanced state of the disease the ankles swell after a day's hard work, and the feet are constantly cold, an embarrassed state of circulation is denoted by these symptoms and the deep-seated veins begin to swell. After a time, which varies with the idiosyncrasy and occupation of the patient, small, soft, blue tumors are seen at different points of the leg, most of them disappearing on pressure, but returning when it is removed, or when the patient stands up. Each little tumor is caused by a vein, dilated at the point at which it is joined by an intramuscular branch. Around many of these tumors a number of minor vessels of a dark purple color are clustered; these are the small superficial veins which enter the dilating vein and in which the passage of the blood is retarded. An increasing area of veins gradually becomes involved and a number of irregular, knotty, consolidated tumors are developed, grouping themselves around the point at which the dilatation first began The external and internal saphenous veins are those primarily affected, but long tracts of tortuous veins may extend up the leg and thigh Dangerous and even fatal hemorrhage may ensue from the bursting of a varix through the skin. The vessels may become filled with clots and permanently obstructed, and ulceration with thrombosis or phlebitis may be the sequel The capillaries become engorged with blood, and hence the assimilation changes are retarded and sometimes altogether checked. Gradually the entire circulation of the part is arrested The vitality of the superficial structures becomes permanently impaired; consequently they are unable to resist the effects of slight injuries and repair fails to take place after a portion has been destroyed, and an open sore or ulcer is established.

Symptoms. The varicose ulcer is usually single, oval, round or irregular in outline, and is most often seen on the lower third of the leg near the internal or external malleolus. The edges are thick, everted, and swollen. The swelling is largely due to edema and is found to pit on pressure The floor is generally covered with rather large granulations which bleed freely when touched. In a varicose ulcer the destruction of tissue often begins at the margin of a congested area and advances toward the centre. The size varies from the small ulcers, less than one-half inch in diameter, formed by the breaking down of an area of periphlebitis around a small vein, to those several inches in diameter. Several ulcers may be present on one limb. The granulations, as a rule, are weak and flabby. The discharge is thin, serous, mixed with débris, and may be blood-stained. The skin surrounding a varicose ulcer is often of a brownish blue color, due to a deposit of pigment. The recognition of varicose ulcers is usually easy; but the mere presence of enlarged veins, it should be noted, is not pathognomonic, because they may exist along with ulcers of other origin—the luetic, trophic, etc. The most frequent complication is phlebitis; cellulitis is also seen. This latter may sometimes be so severe as to necessitate operation. Complications such as necrosis of bone, involvement and ankylosis of the ankle joint, together with atrophy and contracture of muscles and adhesions of tendons (perhaps giving rise to various deformities of the feet, such as flat-foot or even club-foot) are extreme and unusual complications.

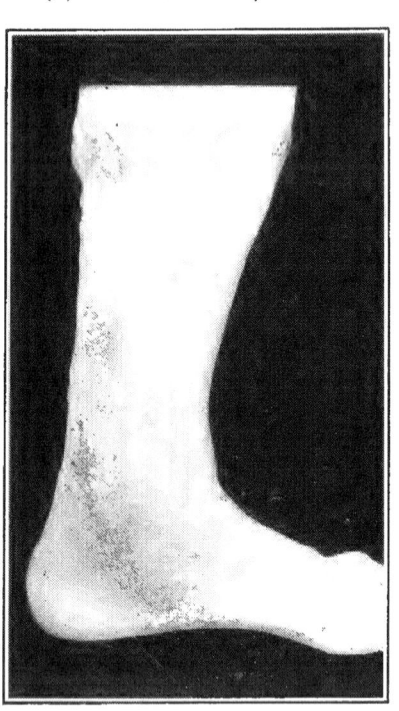

VARICOSE ULCER

Where the varicose ulcers have persisted for a long time and refuse to heal, it is always advisable to apply the Wassermann test in order to exclude the possibility of syphilis. In doubtful cases it is also advisable to test by the Noguchi luetin skin reaction.

Treatment. In these cases of varicose ulcers it is impossible to effect a cure until the chronic congestion of the limb is relieved and the blood supply of the part approaches normal. Often all that is necessary is a gauze, muslin, rubber or flannel bandage.

A bandage, when applied with moderate, even pressure, has for its purpose the relief of congestion. In a great many cases rubber has an irritating effect upon the skin, and that kind of a bandage should therefore be cautiously used. When the granulations are almost on a level with the skin, and also where there is considerable thickening of the edges of the ulcer, the best means of keeping up an even pressure and causing absorption of the thickened margins, as well as of hastening epithelial growth, is to apply zinc oxide adhesive plaster in strips, one-half to one inch in width. These strips should overlap to the extent of about one-third of their width, should extend about three-fourths of the way around the limb, and should be evenly and smoothly applied. They should be started about one inch below the ulcer and should run from two to three inches above it

In order to effect a permanent cure, varicose veins must be operated upon, and a number of operations have been devised, as follows: the ligation of the internal saphenous, as advised by Trendelenburg, the multiple percutaneous ligations of Schede; the total extirpation of the internal saphenous, as recommended by Mayo; the dissection after the method of Madelung; and the spiral of Rindfleisch.

Perforating Ulcer of the Foot. This type of ulcer usually occurs where pressure and irritation are greatest and is therefore commonly found on the plantar surface of the foot under the heads of the first and fifth metatarsal bones, and on the under surface of the great toe. Occasionally, however, they develop on the dorsal surfaces or ends of the toes, in cases such as hammer toe.

Etiology. There are various theories relative to the causation of lesions of this nature. One claims injury to be the sole cause; another attributes it to arteriosclerosis and capillary thrombosis; still another charges it to chronic peripheral neuritis and alteration in the nerve terminals. One writer states that traumatism is an important factor in their development, conceding, however, that various systemic conditions must necessarily enter into the etiology, among them, locomotor ataxia and injuries to the spinal cord, diabetes and injuries to the peripheral nerves. This latter, known as the "mixed theory," is the one most generally accredited and is in all probability most correct.

This type of ulcer is found more frequently in males than in females and it occurs almost exclusively in adult life (between 40 and 60 years). Occupation is a predisposing factor, and work demanding long periods of standing or walking unquestionably has much to do with the development of a perforating ulcer, all other conditions being equal.

Characteristics. The ulcer is usually found to be irregularly circular in shape, with a tendency to progressive development, involving the deeper soft tissues, finally attacking the periosteum and the bone itself, causing necrosis. The superficial edges of the ulceration are heavily calloused and the lesion shows little or no tendency to heal. One of the most marked characteristics is the entire loss of sensation. Many cases have been observed where the patient feels no pain, even when the lesion is deeply probed.

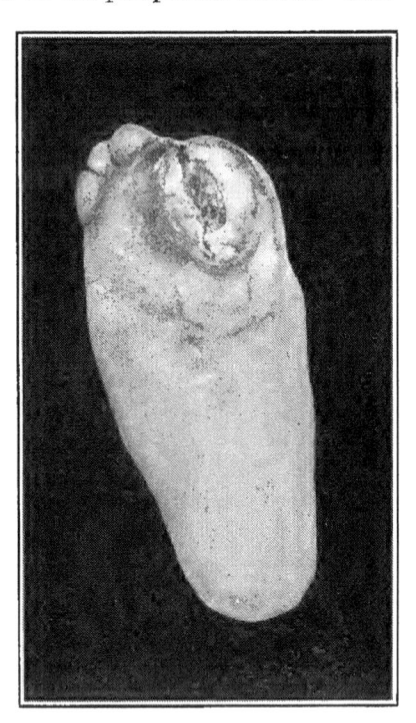

POST-OPERATIVE DIABETIC ULCER

Symptoms. At times, particularly in diabetic patients, a purulent blister is the initial lesion, but in most instances these lesions develop under a heavy callous, the centre of which breaks down into an indolent superficial ulceration, discharging a thin, discolored, odorous pus, but never in great quantities.

The fact that changes in the peripheral nerve supply usually take place in the development of perforating ulcer probably accounts for the absence of pain, as above mentioned, and also explains the progressive degeneration which takes place, allowing the ulcerative process to progress into the deeper tissues.

Treatment. The systemic disturbances which may be present are important factors to be considered in the treatment of perforating ulcer, but local applications may be made and local conditions must be considered. If the ulcer be upon the plantar surfaces of the foot, walking and standing, which would bring continued pressure, must be avoided. Shoes must be well fitted and must not irritate the parts, and cleanliness must be obtained and maintained. All callous must be removed from the edges of the ulcer and proper drainage is of great importance. All necrosed tissue must necessarily be removed and any burrowing sinuses should be thoroughly opened. Artificial hyperemia, massage and electricity are found to be of benefit in improving the general circulation in the foot and leg.

In the local treatment of the ulceration itself, prolonged application of strong germicidal solutions is to be avoided at all times. Cleansing with warm normal salt solution is recommended as a non-toxic and stimulant application.

Dressings may be of plain aseptic or iodoform gauze packed lightly into the ulcer. These lesions are discouraging to treat, inasmuch as even after complete healing, relapses usually occur which leave the parts as bad or worse than the original lesion.

Stimulant applications may be employed locally, with some success in connection with internal medications for the systemic disturbance present. Balsam of Peru or scarlet red (1% to 3%) are advocated in this connection.

The prognosis in cases of perforating ulcer is bad, inasmuch as the progress of the lesion sooner or later involves sufficient tissue in the degenerative process to necessitate surgical interference—perhaps amputation of the foot. As has been previously mentioned, even when fully healed, relapse almost always occurs.

The Syphilitic Ulcer. The syphilitic ulcers do not properly come within the province of the podiatrist for treatment, but he should be able to recognize them. They may develop from pustules or begin as original lesions in the tertiary stages of the disease. Developing in this latter instance from gummata, they are immediately deep ulcers.

The worst superficial ulcers of syphilis may develop early in the course of the general disease.

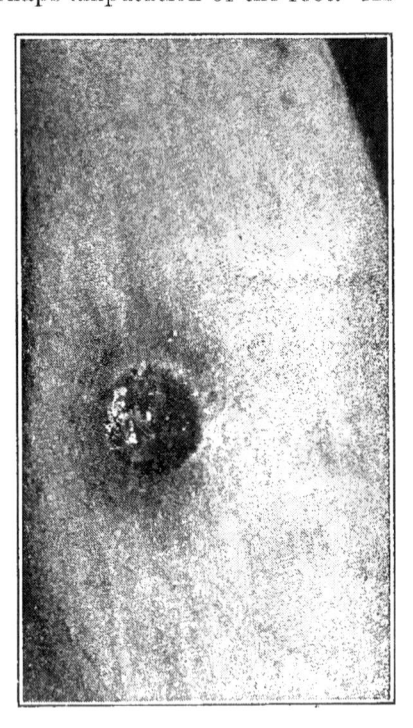

SYPHILITIC ULCER OF THE LEG

Symptoms. These ulcers vary in size from a quarter to a silver dollar and occur on the upper third of the leg, occasionally on the upper part of the middle third. During the early stages of the lesion it is surrounded by an inflamed area of skin at the ulcer and presents an even, "punched out" edge. Being a new growth, developed in the corium, the edges are usually more firm and dense than in other forms of ulcer. The floor of the lesion is of a dusky red or coppery color, and has a characteristic slough of a greenish color. The discharge is frequently bloody and is filled with broken down tissue.

If on account of the presence of enlarged veins, it is difficult to distinguish a syphilitic from a varicose or other type of ulcer, a positive Wasserman test will confirm the diagnosis.

Being merely a local manifestation of a general infection, the systemic disturbance must be treated by a licensed physician. It is generally found that a lesion of this type, once healed, remains so.

Treatment. Treatment for syphilitic ulcers comprehends the use of mercurials as local applications. Mercury bichloride 1/10000 may be employed with beneficent results in most cases where a profuse discharge is present. Where there is little or no discharge, calomel powder dusted into the ulcer will give good results.

As in most cases where a syphilitic lesion has developed locally on the leg, the patient is or has been under a physician's care, practically none of these cases come to the podiatrist for his treatment alone. Many times, however, he is called in by the physician to do local dressings under his direction, and it has even happened that the podiatrist has been the first to recognize the significance of the local lesion.

CHAPTER XXI

CUTANEOUS MANIFESTATIONS OF SUPER-ACIDITY

A surcharging of the blood with an abnormal amount of acidity leads generally to conditions which come under the domain of the physician. So-called rheumatism, gout and kindred ailments of all forms and varieties are everyday occurrences, and, being symptoms of systemic disturbances, should be treated by internal administration.

The podiatrist, however, in his daily treatment of foot troubles is called upon to treat locally certain forms of skin disturbances due to hyper-acidity which manifest themselves upon the surfaces of the foot

. Uric acid eczema is the general term employed to designate these annoying conditions and is synonymous with the older and now obsolete terms, lithemia and uric-acidema.

Definition. Uric acid eczema is a skin eruption due to a surcharge of uric acid in the blood and a precipitation of this acid in a certain part, so that the acid elements or urates are carried by the blood stream to the skin and there set up a dermatitis.

Characteristics. These manifestations may be found in all varieties and degrees from a mere dryness and hardness of the skin, in which the normal flexibility is gone, and in connection with which there is usually intense itching and burning, to the formation of deep fissures (usually found in the toe webs) and small ulcerative processes which may manifest themselves in any part of the foot and often present a stubborn resistance to all endeavors at healing. These symptoms may occur singly or, as in the most instances, in combination.

These conditions are usually met with in the spring of the year and no doubt are brought about by a series of changes in habits and diet which occur at this time.

Etiology. During the winter months the average person takes but little physical exercise as compared to his activities during the warmer weather. The foot, being at the base of a column of blood which must be forced back to the heart, against gravity, is coming constantly in contact with cold surfaces. This, together with a lack of exercise, tends to stagnate the blood circulation in the pedal extremities. Coupled with these two conditions, during the winter months, people are inclined to over-eat and over-drink, the waste materials from which excesses are but improperly eliminated, due also, to a great extent, to insufficient exercise. Here, then, we have a stagnation of the blood current in the pedal extremities, a surcharging of the blood in the feet with certain urates, and a precipitation of these solid constituents, due to the cold surfaces with which those members constantly come in contact.

This condition is present in the spring of the year when fresh vegetables and fruits begin to come into the market. A great many of these edibles, particularly strawberries and tomatoes, are markedly acid and when ingested tend to exaggerate the conditions in the blood already present. The result is generally a cutaneous eruption which may appear on any part of the body and which frequently occurs in the feet. (See chapter on Fissures and Burns.)

Fissures. Probably the most common condition met with from this cause is the cracking or fissuring of the toe web. This may be accompanied by itching and burning in varying degrees, but these latter complications are not always present. The skin between the digits is found to be blanched and macerated and often the superficial epidermic layers will become slightly thickened and exfoliated. The fissures occur in the web and are due to the skin losing its normal flexibility so that the tissues, as they expand in walking or in drying the parts with a heavy, rough towel, are not sufficiently extensible, and so they crack or fissure. These cracks may be merely superficial splits through the epidermic layers or they may become deep and ugly fissures which penetrate well into the corium. When they reach this latter stage, the parts are found to be exceedingly tender and the irritation to the tissues is severe These fissures are prone to infective processes as their deep recesses present an excellent lodgment for invading bacteria.

The fissured area is usually confined to the web, but may be found extending around under the toe on either side or upon the plantar surface of the foot When these conditions are of long standing, the edges of the fissure will be found to be thickened and calloused; it is found necessary to remove this growth before normal granulations may be expected.

Treatment. In cases where only pruritis is present and no distinct lesion manifests itself, tr. benzoes compositas will be found an efficient agent in reducing the itching and in aiding the general irritation to subside. In superficial fissures, tr benzoin compound may also be used in many cases with good results. The parts should first be thoroughly cleansed with alcohol, 60%, dried, any loosened or exfoliated epidermis to be removed before the benzoin is applied More or less smarting is to be expected from the application of the tincture, but as this is very transient, no great amount of pain is suffered by the patient. The tincture is applied by means of a sterile, cotton-wound applicator, and is painted well down into the fissure itself, and over considerable of the surrounding integument. This tincture is very sticky and should be allowed to dry thoroughly before the hosiery is replaced. As compound tincture of benzoin forms a thin film or coating upon thoroughly drying, no gauze or cotton need be placed over the painted areas This application may be renewed daily, the coating from the previous application being removed by alcohol and the parts cleansed and dried before the second application is made.

Mild vegetable astringents may also be employed in such cases. Principal among these are gallic and tannic acid. These drugs may be used in solution, ointment or dusting powder form and seem to be efficient in all. Dusting powders are usually preferred and the two most popular are bismuth subgallate (dermatol), a combination of bismuth and gallic acid, and tannoform, a powder containing 5 to 10% of tannic acid. These are applied after the parts have been made aseptic and thoroughly dried. Bismuth subnitrate may also be used with good results in this condition, as may thymol iodide (aristol). The latter has very little astringent action and, therefore, except for its antiseptic properties, cannot compare with the other powders mentioned. Pure ichthyol may also be used in the treatment of superficial fissures. The drug is dropped into the lesion and covered with gauze or cotton, as are the dusting powders. Another drug recommended in these cases is sodium bicarbonate. This agent is alkaline in its reaction and, coming in contact with the perspiration (acid) in these parts, serves to neutralize this excretion and so aids in returning the tissues to normal.

There are many other preparations, any of which may be used in the treatment of fissured toe webs. Among these are ichthyol ointments, 5 to 10%; balsam of Peru, scarlet red, and a 5% ointment of ammoniated mercury. Reports of cases treated by the above varying drugs show good results.

When the fissures are deep, and the discharge from their surfaces is considerable, slightly different measures must be adopted to hasten granulation. The edges of deep fissures are almost always found to be calloused and thickened and this condition, of course, must be eradicated before further treatment is administered. This is accomplished with a knife or shallow curette and the operation is usually painless to the patient and creates no hemorrhage. After the removal of this tissue, if the fissure be deep, silver nitrate, 5% solution, will be found efficient as an astringent to contract the parts and reduce exudation. After this application, a bland ointment is smeared over the area for the purpose of keeping the tissues soft, and this is covered by a sheet of gauze or cotton to hold it in place. Applications of the silver solution are made at frequent intervals until the desired result is obtained, when it may be discontinued and some dusting powder resorted to, to complete the healing process. Should proud flesh have developed in a lesion of this nature, through neglect, stronger solutions of silver nitrate or the fused stick must be resorted to for reduction of the superfluous granulations, followed by a wet dressing of liq. alum. acetate to aid in the reduction of the accompanying inflammatory symptoms. Lanolin and cocoanut oil have both been found efficient to massage into the parts in order to keep them soft and to prevent continued dryness and fissuring.

Blebs. Aside from the fissuring of the interdigital webs, super-acidity manifests itself upon the skin of the foot, and the whole body for that matter, in the formation of yellow or brownish blebs or vesicles. They are found to be a more or less circumscribed eruption and are met most frequently in the foot on the plantar surface in the hollow of the longitudinal arch. They range in size from a pinhead to a pea and, in most instances, are but slightly elevated above the surface of the surrounding epidermis. This is in all probability due to the involvement of the superficial parts of the true skin

These lesions are usually uniform with a tendency to coalesce, and cases have been noted where patches of these eruptions covered a considerable area, in one instance, from the under surface of the foot, over its inner side, to the internal malleolus Vesicular developments of this nature seldom occur singly but are often found in several groups on different parts of the integument, each group consisting of two, three or four distinct blebs.

Pruritis may or may not be present in connection with this dermatitis. When itching is present it is usully intense and the patient often breaks and tears the skin in an effort to relieve the irritation.

The areas of normal tissue adjacent to the eruptions may be found involved in a slight inflammatory process, although this is not common. These inflammatory symptoms usually subside rapidly under treatment.

Treatment. It is usually found advisable, if possible, to allow these blebs to remain intact, making no effort to puncture them but simply applying a dressing which will promote and hasten their absorption. Cases have been noticed where these lesions have been opened and have developed into angry, deep ulcerations which showed a marked tendency toward indolent granulation accompanied by profuse discharge.

However, when a bleb for any reason must be opened, it is best accomplished by use of a sharp pointed, sterile knife. The fluid contents are found to be a thin, syrupy, translucent, discolored serum, without any great odor, although resembling ichorous pus to some degree. There is a distinct loss of tissue as the ulcerations are often found to involve the upper parts of the derma. Upon evacuation of the fluid contents, the parts should be thoroughly sprayed with alcohol, 60%, and a moist, unguent or dusting powder dressing, as the operator desires, applied.

The solutions which may be used as moist applications are liq aluminum acetate, or boric acid (saturated solution). Powerful germicides, such as mercury bichloride, are not necessary unless an infective process be present, and when used needlessly, they simply prevent or break down new granulations.

The dusting powders found useful in this connection are aristol (thymol iodide) and dermatol (bismuth subgallate). The parts should first be thoroughly dried before the powder is dusted on. If the discharge is found negative and the pruritis still persists, an ointment of ichthyol and sulphur, such as follows will prove efficient in reducing the itching and in stimulating healthy granulations·

Ichthyol	1.
Sulphur	1.
Menthol	1.
Vaseline	32.

This unguent is best held in place by a cocoon dressing and should be renewed until granulation is complete. Other unguents which may be used in this connection are sulphur, 10% (lanolin or vaseline base), balsam of Peru, 5%, and unguentine (a proprietary but useful combination of ichthyol, balsam of Peru and zinc oxide). These, however, do not tend to relieve the intense pruritis which usually accompanies these lesions as efficiently as the first mentioned combination.

URIC ACID AND THE NAILS

The toe nails also manifest conditions of super-acidity. They may be affected as to color or texture, and sometimes in advanced or neglected cases, as to size and shape.

Discoloration. The nails, due to functional derangements in the matrix, become loosened and discolored from the presence of an abnormal amount of uric acid. They may be whitish, yellowish or brown, and in some cases are found almost entirely black, as if bruised. The nails in these instances are usually entirely loosened, or at least in part, from the bed, and sometimes fall off, practically of their own accord.

Treatment. Nothing much can be done locally for these conditions, and the main concern of the podiatrist is to see that the edges of the loosened nail are not allowed to irritate the softer tissues adjacent. This is best accomplished by packing cotton or gauze under these edges so that the nail, if movable, will rub upon this packing and not upon the skin. It may be found advisable to first clean out (from under and around the nail) any excrementitious matter which is always present to a greater or lesser degree. However, too much "digging" about these parts should never be indulged in, as the operator is liable not only to cause a lesion, but to loosen the nail to such a degree that its removal is imperative. If possible, this is to be generally avoided, for it has been found advantageous to allow the older nail to remain in place as long as possible in order to protect the new-forming nail beneath. Alcohol, 60%, sprayed over the part after removing the disintegrated material, will serve as a cleansing agent and will insure asepsis to the parts.

Texture Changes. Under the influence of uric acid precipitation in the pedal extremities, the texture of the nail is often found changed to a marked degree. The nail becomes exceedingly hard, dry and brittle so that it powders, chips off and breaks away under any sort of pressure. The nails are often found ridged, and in some instances these longitudinal ridges have become decided and permanent cracks in the nail body.

Treatment. In clipping nails of this nature, care should be taken that too much does not chip off or break away from the pressure of the clipper blades It will be found advisable to cut but a small portion of the nail at a time, and that very carefully. The waste material found around or under the nail body should be carefully removed and, if necessary, the nail itself should be thinned out by the use of a rotary file. The parts should be thoroughly cleansed, and the grooves and free edge should be packed with gauze or cotton to prevent the nail from moving during the movements of the toe and thereby developing trouble.

Changes in Size and Shape. The so-called "club" nail is found in many cases where the patient is a sufferer from a uric acid diathesis This does not occur as frequently in cases of acute dermatitis as in cases of chronic rheumatism and gout. These are cases where there is functional derangement of the matrix which causes the nail's longitudinal growth to be arrested, followed by an increased vertical development.

The nail is generally found to be about one-half its normal length and may be from one-sixteenth to one inch or more in thickness. Cases have occurred where the nail in appearance and structure closely resembled a cow's horn.

Club nails of this variety do not, as a rule, cause a great amount of discomfort and then only when they develop to such thickness as to receive and transmit direct pressure from the shoe.

Treatment. Club nails are not curable and the treatment is merely cosmetic. It consists in grinding and filing the nail down to what would be its normal thickness, or as nearly that as possible. This, of course, is best accomplished by means of a rotary file. As much of the nail is clipped away as is possible, when the rotary file with a coarse-grained "barrel" bur is used. Considerable pressure should be brought to bear unless the patient complains of heat due to the friction. When the greater portion of the nail is thus removed a "finishing" bur is substituted and the roughened surfaces are smoothed off. The clippers should then again be used to give the nail a fairly normal shape and the parts under the nail are to be then cleansed out as much as is advisable.

In using a rough cutting bur the operator must exercise great care that the skin covering the posterior or the lateral folds is not broken. If the handpiece of the file is grasped firmly in the palm of the hand and directed by the index finger while the thumb is rested on the toe and the bur is directed to it (the thumb), the operator will always have complete control of the instrument, and this danger is minimized. It will be found advisable, after cleaning under and around the nail, to spray the parts with some antiseptic solution or to paint the parts with tincture of iodine. This is done to insure complete asepsis. Should the skin be broken during the filing or cleaning, the parts should be first made thoroughly aseptic and a dressing to prevent contamination should be applied.

Prognosis. It must always be remembered that these lesions are merely local manifestations of a systemic derangement and although the painful or annoying characteristics may be alleviated or cured, the cause of the trouble must be reached, through internal channels.

Diet is the principal means of removing this surcharged acid condition of the blood and, although some medicines or waters may be and are ordered by the physician as eliminants, proper care as to dietetics is essential to the patient's well-being Systemic treatment by the physician, combined with local applications by the podiatrist, are usually conducive to beneficent and lasting results. In cases of manifestations of a uric acid diathesis in the nails, nothing much can be done except through the channels just described, and in cases of club nails due to a like etioligy, nothing can be done to cure them. Removal of the nail does not, as is sometimes supposed, effect a cure, and in many instances serves but to make the new nail even worse than its predecessor.

CHAPTER XXII

VOCATIONAL FOOT DISORDERS

Among the numerous diseases of the foot, there is a class of lesions produced by strain and misuse, in consequence of the occupation of the individual. Many occupations cause those who are engaged in them to stand or walk for long periods of time on hard and unelastic ground, and others subject the foot or a part of it to such unusual work that the entire foot, or a part of it, ceases to functionate normally.

Weakfoot. The general term "weakfoot" is used to indicate all types of disability caused by improper functioning of the foot. It is particularly applied to that condition of the foot in which the muscles and ligaments on its inner side have become weakened by overuse or by improper use, and it is, as a vocational foot disorder, common among barbers, waiters, letter-carriers, policemen and servants. It manifests itself by pain in the foot, particularly in the heel and on the inner side, and sometimes by pain in the calves of the legs, in the knees and lower part of the spine.

At rest, the foot has a normal appearance, but, under weightbearing, it assumes an attitude of deformity varying in degree with the extent of the overwork to which it has been subjected. The chief characteristics of weakfoot are abduction of the forefoot, an inward rotation of the upper part of the heelbone and a flattening, or obliteration, of the longitudinal arch under weightbearing, only. When seen in its incipiency, an anatomically correct shoe, together with suitable exercises, can be made to arrest the progress and effect a cure of weakfoot, but when found in the advanced stages it takes from several months to several years of conscientious work on the part of the practitioner and the patient to get results. In such cases, massage, adhesive plaster strapping, corrective braces and shoes, exercises and sometimes immobilization in an overcorrected attitude by means of plaster of Paris dressings, have to be employed in order again to get a normally functionating foot.

Flatfoot. This is a condition in which the longitudinal arch is depressed and does not regain its normal position when relieved from pressure. The forefoot is abducted, the head of the astragalus rotates downward and inward, and the os calcis rotates inward from above and outward from below. It is the successor to the weakfoot and differs from it only in that it exhibits also at rest, the abnormal attitude that a weakfoot assumes under weightbearing only. In flatfoot this attitude is static, in weakfoot it is only temporary. The person afflicted with it walks with a shuffling gait, due to the accommodative changes that have taken place in the muscles and ligaments of the foot.

The Subjective Symptoms are similar to those in weakfoot and quite often are not as pronounced as in weakfoot, due probably to the fact that in this condition a further stretching and strain of the ligaments is impossible as the limit has already been reached.

The Treatment is similar to weakfoot, but must be augmented by means to overcome the accommodative changes in the foot and leg. The same class of patients suffer from this condition as are sufferers from vocational weakfoot.

Chauffeur's Foot. As the term indicates, this condition is found in people who professionally, or otherwise, drive an automobile for many hours each day. It is an affection, usually of the right foot and leg, due to the excessive use of those members while "feeding the car"

The constant pressure of the "ball" of the foot on the accelerator causes pain in that part of the foot, followed by a numbness of the entire foot. The foot feels as if it were dead and when moved, later on, feels as if a thousand needles were penetrating it. Cramps in the calf muscles are usually associated with the symptoms in the foot.

Treatment. Massage of the foot and leg together with flexion exercises of the foot and toes.

Policeman's Heel. When a person is compelled to stand upon hard pavements for a long period of time, great strain is put upon the tissues over the os calcis or heel. The calcaneo bursa becomes inflamed and gives rise to pains in that region. This inflammation may affect the periosteum, causing periostitis and finally a spur may develop on the under surface of the heel bone, which will become a source of constant pain.

The Treatment consists of rest to the part, and of transferring the weight to a place other than the painful area, by means of a felt pad or a brace. If a spur has developed, surgical intervention will be necessary.

Dancer's Foot. This is a foot lesion first described by Miss Bryde Campbell, of New York City, who termed it the "Modern Dancer's Foot," because she found it to occur almost invariably in women who were in the habit of dancing excessively in a modern high-heeled slipper. It is a painful enlargement of the tissues under the head of the first metatarsal bone and is found, as a rule, in the left foot only. The under and inner side around the head of the first metatarsal bone becomes painful to the touch, and under weightbearing. It is best described as a periarthritis although it is often complicated by a bursitis.

Treatment. Measures to relieve the painful part from weightbearing. (Felt pads, braces, etc.) Rest and means to reduce the existing inflammation.

Golfer's Foot. The attitude assumed in playing golf, especially when driving the ball from the tee, often gives rise to a painful condition called "Golfer's foot." This pain is felt on the dorsum of the foot over the course of the extensor brevis digitorum muscle. The extreme extension of the foot, while striking at the ball, is the direct cause of the pain. Massage and rest have proven of benefit in Golfer's Foot.

(Full details of all orthopedic lesions have been but superficially treated in these pages by reason of the fact that "Podiatry Orthopedics," a volume now in the course of preparation and the next of this series (Otto F. Schuster and Alvah H. Stafford, authors), will provide exhaustive material bearing upon all phases of foot orthopedics).

CHAPTER XXIII

LOCOMOTION AS AN AID IN DIAGNOSIS

One need not be a very experienced physician to know that there is a group of diseases, mostly of the nervous system, which at a certain point of their evolution, stamp the sufferer with a characteristic mode of locomotion. To observe such a modification of the normal walk is often sufficient to make a correct diagnosis.

It is strange, however, how little attention this important subject has received from the medical profession. In fact, other than the work of the brothers Weber, who established the physiology and mechanism of human locomotion, of Neugebauer and of Gilles de la Tourette, who developed the ichnogram method of gait study, scarcely anything of importance has been done along these lines for the last quarter of a century. The study of the mode of locomotion in various diseases and ailments remains, therefore, a fertile field of research for the podiatrist.

Elements of Locomotion. The act of locomotion or the *power* of progression is not a simple one. Various co-related movements combine to form what we ordinarily term the *walk*. The three chief elements are: (1) *Posture,* (2) *Station,* and (3) *Gait.* These three factors may be influenced by local or general diseases, either separately or together.

Posture. Posture is the term applied to the position of the body in space and is not of much interest to the podiatrist except as corroborative of the two other elements of locomotion. It has, however, its value in diagnosis and the new practitioner of podiatry will do well to learn to observe the position of the body at various angles and in various diseases. One should learn early, for instance, that *immobility* is not always due to paralysis It may be due to *pain*, as in rheumatism or to a disinclination to move as in scurvy, rickets or any condition causing dyspnea. The *restlessness* in fevers and in large hemorrhages, as well as the *throwing about* in renal, gallstone or intestinal colics, is known to all Equally characteristic are the *agitation* and irregular movements in chorea and hysteria, the *gun-hammer posture* in cerebrospinal meningitis, and the *opisthotonos* in tetanus and strychnine poisoning

Station. Station is the *power* of standing more or less firmly on one's feet. It includes *attitude* which is the *manner* of standing, i e., the relation of the rest of the body to the erect position. The carriage of the head and shoulders should be noted; the shape of the entire body whether bending *forward*, as in "stooped shoulders" (faulty attitude habit) and in paralysis agitans, or bending *backward*, as in ascites and abdominal tumors, should be closely studied and differentiated from the actual lordosis which is seen in spinal diseases, in advanced pregnancy, in pseudo-hypertrophic paralysis and in cretinism. The strictest attention should be paid to the attitude of the lower limbs, their individual shapes and their relation to each other when the erect position is assumed. The degree of firmness with which the individual stands should always be taken into consideration before a final diagnosis is made *Swaying* is the term applied to any departure from the ideally rigid erect attitude and perpendicular station. The normal individual, with eyes open and heels close together, sways about one inch forward and three-quarters of an inch from side to side. In functional and static ataxias, the swaying may become so extreme as to produce absolute incapacity to stand

Gait. This term means the specific *manner* of walking It is a narrower term than locomotion which is the *power* of walking. It is, however, the chief factor in the act of progression and in the majority of cases it is characteristic enough to stamp itself indelibly on the normal as well as on the diseased individual. While in character reading, gait expression may not be as popular as face expression, it is often more reliable and in certain diseases it is simply invaluable as an aid in diagnosis.

METHODS OF DIAGNOSIS

A.—The Observation Method. This is the usual method of ascertaining the gait of an individual It is practised by the average physician and podiatrist and consists in observing the patient while he or she walks up and down the room, taking notice of the peculiarities of gait which may develop The patient may be allowed to roam freely about the room or should be directed to follow a carpet seam or a crack in the floor at right angles to a previous line of vision This may be varied by opening or closing the eyes, stretching out the arms, with legs wide apart, or keeping them close together. Brisk walking should alternate with a slower gait and the effect of stopping abruptly and turning sharply at command should be closely observed.

It is best to have the patient uncovered from the hips down In women, the nightgown or chemise can be pulled tightly between the thighs and fastened anteriorly with a safety pin.

Caution. Due allowance should be made for nervousness and a careful watch must be maintained against a serious fall.

B.—The Ichnogram Method consists in studying the impressions left by *both* soles (previously colored) when walking on paper for a distance of about twenty-five feet. Ichnograms (from the Greek—*ichnos*—trace, and *gramma* —to write) as a method of gait diagnosis are more exact than the method of observation and should supplement it Besides, they inform us, at the same time, of the state of the plantar arch as each *pelmatogram* (the impression of a single foot) shows more or less clearly a posterior oval which changes but little, and an anterior oval as well as toe marks which undergo characteristic contour changes, depending on the state of the ligaments, of the tarsal and metatarsal bones and phalanges, and the relation of these struc-

A FIG. 1 *B*

A. PELMATOGRAM OF A NORMAL FEMALE FOOT

B. MODIFIED PELMATOGRAM SHOWING WEIGHT BEARING POINTS

FIG. 2
ICHNOGRAM OF A NORMAL GAIT

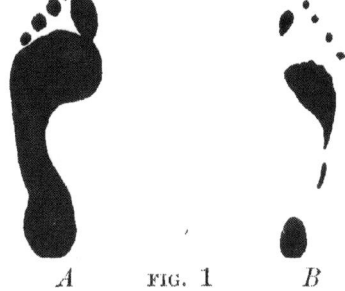

FIG. 3
PELMATOGRAM OF A MALE, SHOWING FLAT FOOT

tures to the musculature and innervation of the foot.

Comparatively little has been accomplished along this line of endeavor, although it offers a vast and fruitful field for podiatric research. In fact this branch of podiatry deserves a special treatise, and it will be discussed in fuller detail in our forthcoming book on Podiatry Orthopedics

Classification of Gaits. Strictly speaking there are only three types of gait: (1) the *paretic,* (2) the *ataxic* and (3) the *choreic.* In some diseases there may be a combination of the three, while in others one type of gait predominates during the early stage and another during the later developments. At times, one comes across a gait that combines characteristics of the three types and hence is difficult of classification.

I.—Paretic Gait. *Paresis* means a lessening of the normal motility of a muscle, while the term *paralysis* denotes entire absence of motor power. We may have, therefore, two or three distinct paretic gaits according to whether the muscle is slightly or severely weakened or entirely paralyzed.

    A.—The mild paretic gait.
    B —The moderate or flaccid paretic gait.
    C —The severe or spastic paretic gait.

A.—The Mild Paretic Gait is caused by muscular weakness due to a large number of etiologic factors. It results in slowing of locomotion, the steps being shortened on account of an exaggerated flexion at the knee joint The following are examples of mild paretic gaits·

(1) *The Pompous Gait.* The upper part of the body leans backward, the back is hollowed, the abdomen is protuberant, the feet are widely separated and appear to move with deliberation and dignity, giving the impression of conscious importance—hence the name. This gait may be seen in obesity, pregnancy, ascites, large abdominal tumors, cretinism and rickets

(2) *The Hobbling Gait* The pelvis tilts towards the

sound side, while the trunk leans over to the affected side, causing more or less pronounced *limping*. This gait is seen in people afflicted with corns, rheumatism, gout, sciatica, plantar neuralgia, Morton's neuralgia, metatarsalgia, hip or knee joint disease or injury (recent or old), sacroiliac disease, sprains, inflammatory diseases of the lower extremity, chimatlon, short leg, paralysis of one leg, abdominal aneurism, and subacute and chronic appendicitis.

(3) *Intermittent Limping* (disbasia angiosclerotica or intermittent claudication) may be classified here and is a curious limping gait which develops in arteriosclerosis of the lower extremities. There are pain and fatigue on walking, which disappear after a short rest, to reappear again soon after walking is resumed. The pulse is weak or absent below the knee

(4) *The Waddling or Goose Gait*. The pelvis and head of femur are jerked forward at each step, knee advanced and extended only after foot is flat upon the ground There is more lordosis and swinging of the body from side to side at each step, than in the pompous gait It resembles the gait of a goose The patient cannot stand on tiptoe It is seen in congenital dislocation of both hip joints and in pseudo-hypertrophic muscular paralysis, a hereditary disease seen mostly in boys under ten years of age, and characterized by inability to get up from the floor

(5) *The Wobbly Gait*. Resembles the above and is due to atrophy or paralysis of the three glutei muscles and prevents the patient from climbing. This inability to climb is also seen in those exhibiting the waddling gait

(6) *The Tottering Gait*. Seen in those who have taken large doses of bromides for long periods, also in hydrocephalus, in Korsakoff's disease (psychosis polyneuritica) and in idiopathic muscular atrophy.

(7) *The Shuffling Gait* is the gait seen in normal old age or senility and is associated with slowly progressive loss of strength and mentality. It is also seen in general paresis and is the "normal" gait of the long-term prison inmate.

The patient gives the impression of being too lazy to lift his feet and instead pushes them along with his legs.

(8) *The "Charlie Chaplin" Gait* has been erroneously described as an ataxic gait. It is rather a combination of the "funny part" of several gaits in which the waddling, shuffling, tottering paretic gaits predominate and to which some elements of the spastic-paretic, as well as the ataxic gaits, have been added. The inspiration must have come originally to the celebrated movie star from some waddling cripple whom he proceeded to imitate and later burlesqued.

B.—The Moderate or Flaccid Paretic Gait. In this form of the paretic gait there is commonly a paresis of a certain group of muscles, usually the extensors of the foot or the peronei, causing "toe drop" and apparent lengthening of the affected extremity. It corresponds to the "wrist drop" of the upper extremity. To compensate for the lengthening of the limb, overflexion at the hip or knee, or at both joints, takes place. The limb is flaccid or flabby.

The foot is lifted high up with each step in order to raise it clear off the ground and avoid tripping. As the foot is brought down, heel first, this gait may sometimes be confused with tabes and is therefore sometimes referred to as the pseudo-tabetic gait. It is, however, easily differentiated from the true tabetic gait by its characteristic "high action" or "high stepping" quality which made Charcot compare it to the gait of a horse and hence called it:

(1) *The Steppage Gait,* mostly seen in the chronic intoxications producing neuritis. It resembles the gait of a man walking through thick grass or brushwood and stepping over constantly recurring but non-existent obstacles. The typical steppage gait is seen in arsenical neuritis with ankle drop, also in alcoholic neuritis, polyneuritis potatorum (ataxia of drunkards) and in lead neuritis (lead palsy, plumbism, saturnism), in which first the peroneal muscles are affected, later the extensor communis digitorum and finally the extensor proprius hallucis. Phosphorus,

copper and grain (ergotism) poisoning may give rise to a neuritis in the lower extremities and produce the characteristic steppage gait. Tuberculosis, malaria, diabetes and diphtheria (motor form) may sometimes produce this gait. It may also develop as a sequel of sunstroke (thermic fever, insolation) and in fact following any disease which will cause peripheral neuritis of the anterior tibial nerve.

(2) *The Prancing Gait* is an exaggeration of the preceding gait. It is seen in epidemic anterior poliomyelitis (infantile paralysis) when the disease affects the anterior horn cells of the lumbar cord, causing atrophy of the extensor muscles of the foot, resulting in "foot drop." It is also seen in acute ascending paralysis (Landry's disease), which is probably a form of poliomyelitis, and in progressive hereditary muscular atrophy of the leg (Charcot-Marie-Tooth type) where the muscles of the leg, not the foot, are primarily affected, i e., first the peronei become atrophied, later the extensors of the toes and finally the calcaneal muscles. Finally the prancing may be seen in connection with certain tumors of the cord, unilateral hip disease, dislocation or injury and in multiple neuritis and beri-beri (epidemic multiple neuritis).

C.—The Spastic or Severe Paretic Gait. The spastic gait is due to the hypertonicity of the weakened muscles, the resulting stiffness causing a slowing of locomotion and diminished excursion of the affected limb. The hypertonicity is produced either by direct stimulation of the motor cells in the anterior horn of the spinal cord, as in traumatic myelitis, or by impulses coming down from the cerebral cortex. The limb is spastic or rigid, due to the tonic spasm. When the tonic spasm is of long standing, it is termed a *contracture*. The lower extremity moves as a whole, the toes clinging to the ground, scraping it and very often "catching." Contrary to the moderate paretic gait, this group presents difficulty in flexion which is partly overcome by the elevation of the pelvis on the side of the swinging leg.

(1) *The Mowing or Hemiplegic Gait.* This is the prototype of all spastic gaits and is encountered in its simplest form in all hemiplegias, i.e., in paralysis of one side of the body, which may be caused by cerebral hemorrhage, embolism, thrombosis, syphilis, brain tumor, multiple sclerosis of a cerebral hemisphere, meningeal hemorrhage or suppuration, Raynaud's disease, general paresis of the insane; sometimes it may be due to hysteria (functional hemiplegia) or to uremia (transient hemiplegia). No matter what the cause of the hemiplegia, there is always the typical mowing gait. This mowing movement is due to the fact that the spastic limb swings lateralward, describing an arc of a circle (outward), and strikes the ground in a flail-like manner. Technically speaking, circumduction takes place by tilting of the pelvis and the swinging of the foot outward and around to the front. The patient afflicted with hemiplegia makes the same movement with his limb as does the reaper with the hand in which he holds the scythe. *Exception* the only paralytic gait in which there is no mowing movement occurs in hysterical (functional) paraplegia, which is very rare In this condition the leg is dragged forward instead of outward.

Important shoe sign in paraplegia. The sole of the shoe is worn down on the inner side.

(2) *The Small-step Gait* (la marche à petits pas). This gait is seen in cerebral softening following an apoplectic stroke, especially in pseudo-bulbar paralysis; the steps are very short and the feet are lifted from the ground with difficulty, the patient seeming to count his steps.

(3) *The Cross-legged Gait.* This gait is due to a spasm of the adductors of the thigh causing the knees to rub against each other, resulting in cross-legged progression, the lower limbs having a tendency to cross during locomotion. It is seen in both Little's congenital and Erb's syphilitic form of lateral spinal sclerosis. In the syphilitic form, a dragging and shuffling gait is often associated with the cross-legged type.

(4) *The Ill-defined Spastic Gaits.* Ill-defined spastic gaits are seen in tetany (paroxysmal tonic spasm) from any cause, and in amyotrophic lateral sclerosis, which is the spastic form of progressive muscular atrophy (Charcot's disease). This involution disease, due probably to developmental defects of the lateral pyramidal tracts, has the combined symptoms of spastic spinal paralysis, anterior poliomyelitis and bulbar palsy, hence the difficulty in classifying it. Myelitis (inflammation of the spinal cord) may be due to trauma, alcoholism, syphilis, vertebral caries (compression myelitis), tumors, aneurism, hemorrhages into the cord, etc., and will exhibit various gaits according to the stage and severity of the disease It may begin with a mild paretic gait passing through several stages of the spastic gait or to complete paraplegia (paralysis of both lower extremities). In complete paraplegia there is of course no gait, as the patient cannot walk, there being a loss of the power of locomotion but not of progression (a patient so afflicted may still move from place to place on his hands)

(5) *The Dragging Gait.* In hemiplegia one foot only is dragged Dragging of both feet is seen in multiple neuritis, hereditary peroneal atrophy, spasmodic spinal paralysis and spinal and syphilitic spinal paralyses.

(6) *The Dromedary Gait,* so called on account of its resemblance to the gait of a camel, is seen in children suffering with progressive torsion spasm (Flatau-Sterling disease).

Finally, spastic paretic gaits are often observed in pellagra (maidism, Italian leprosy, Alpine scurvy) and in lathyrism (lupinosis), where the slow toxic spinal sclerosis finally leads to spastic paraplegia and loss of the power of locomotion; also in caisson disease (diver's paralysis)

II.—The Ataxic Gait. The ataxic gait may be either:

A—The Static ataxic gait, or

B—The Functional ataxic gait

and these are termed either (1) spinal or (2) cerebellar, according to the location of the lesion

A.—The Static Spinal Ataxic Gait is the most easily recognized gait, and once seen, is never forgotten. There is an exaggeration of all the movements of locomotion. The hips are overflexed and rotated laterally, the foot is raised suddenly and too high, the toes are lifted and the whole limb is thrown suddenly forward with unnecessary vehemence and is then brought down heel first or flat-footed, with a stamping sound. The feet are kept wide apart and while in the air they move in an undecided manner, as if the patient was doubtful where to put them. The eyes of the afflicted person are glued to the ground or fixed to the limbs so as to supplement the lack of muscular and articular sensation by the sense of sight.

In the cerebellar type of this gait the movement excursion is not as extensive as in the spinal type. A sudden turning movement or an abrupt sitting posture is difficult or impossible to assume in this type of locomotion.

In order to test static ataxia, the patient is made to stand heels and toes together, whereupon marked swaying takes place. The swaying is increased when the eyes are closed and the patient looks like a "chicken on a clothes line." If there is more than one inch forward swaying and more than three-quarters of an inch lateral swaying, the patient is considered ataxic.

In the disease known as tabes dorsalis, or locomotor ataxia of syphilis, the swaying may be so pronounced as to produce absolute incapability to stand or to walk.

B.—The Cerebellar (functional) Ataxic Gaits. These gaits are produced by a disturbance of the equilibrium accompanied by vertigo resulting in a very irregular swaying from side to side, resembling the gait of an intoxicated person.

The patient makes short steps, keeps his feet wide apart, staggers, rolls, sways to and fro and reaches a set point by zigzagging toward it. The swaying is relieved when support is given under the armpits.

(1) *The Titubating Gait* is a form of functional cere-

bellar ataxic gait seen in the following affections: Friedreich's (disease) ataxia; hereditary cerebellar ataxia; dementia paralytica; ataxic paraplegia; labyrinthine disease and to some extent in vertigo; syringomyelia; and in some cases of general paresis, and various chronic intoxications like lead or arsenic or alcohol poisoning affecting the cerebrospinal system.

(2) *The Reeling or Staggering Gait* is seen in acute alcoholic intoxication and Mésnière's disease (disease of the middle cerebellar lobe).

III.—The Choreic Gait. The choreic gait, sometimes called *tremor* gait, spasmodic or hysterical gait, is very variable in quality depending on the cause of the tremor. It consists of a series of quivering or trembling movements of varying intensity, but nearly all due to clonic spasm and disappearing during sleep or passive motion. This distinguishes it from the spastic or paraplegic gait in which the spasm is tonic in quality, lasting from one minute to one month. The clonic spasm, on the other hand, consists in rapidly alternating contractions and relaxations of the muscle.

(1) *The Stumbling Gait* is seen in chorea (St. Vitus' dance) and Huntington's (hereditary) chorea, in Friedreich's paramyoclonus multiplex (which is not to be confounded with Friedreich's ataxia), in Unverricht's progressive myoclonus, and in multiple sclerosis of the spinal cord. The gait resembles that of a schoolboy, who clownishly stumbles or trips over his heel to attract attention. Technically it consists of spasmodic adduction, extension and outward rotation of the legs which soon renders locomotion impossible. When these abrupt twitchings and jerking movements, which are involuntary and purposeless, affect only one-half of the body, we speak of the condition as hemichorea. The patient appears restless, unsettled and fidgety.

(2) *The Festination Gait* is typical of the disease known as paralysis agitans (Parkinson's disease, shaking palsy) and is an advanced choreic gait in which there may

be observed the curious phenomena of propulsion and retropulsion, i.e , the impossibility of stopping, once the patient is pushed either forward or backward. In some instances, when pulled suddenly backward, the patient will take a few backward steps with increasing rapidity, also the body remains in the characteristic posture of paralysis agitans; namely, in the forward-leaning attitude. In festination "the body tries to overtake its centre of gravity" (Trousseau).

(3) *The Saltatory Gait* ("The jumpers"), is a very rare condition occurring the instant the weight of the body is put upon the feet. It consists in strong and rapid contractions of the muscles of the thigh and leg causing the patient to jump up violently. It is probably a hysterical spasm.

(4) *The Myotonia Gait* occurs in Thomsen's disease and consists of tonic, *painless* spasms whenever a certain group of muscles begin to functionate The steps are first checked and delayed; but this gradually wears off. This curious condition returns again when the same group of muscles are called into action Owing to the tonic spasms, this gait might have been properly classified as a spastic-paretic gait, were it not for the fleeting and irregular character of the spasticity.

(5) *The Hysteria Gait,* known also as astasia-abasia, is notable by the ease with which it may simulate any and all of the gaits described above, the spastic as well as the flaccid types of paralyses,—even the cross-legged gait, ending in complete inability to stand or walk. It differs from all of them, however, in the ability of the patient to perform all the nervous functions of the limb when lying in bed. The hysterical gait may also end in:

Catalepsy which is a state of muscular rigidity enabling a limb to maintain a posture in opposition to gravity for one hour or more (waxy flexibility) This curious phenomenon of retaining the leg or any other part of the body in a fixed attitude (given to it by the operator) is sometimes seen in catatonia, general paresis, brain tumors and, (rarely) in meningitis.

(The above chapter was especially prepared for "Practical Podiatry" by Paul Luttinger, M D , Professor of Bacteriology in The First Institute of Podiatry It is the first compilation of its kind ever published and should prove a valuable aid to both practitioners of medicine and of podiatry—*Editor*)

CHAPTER XXIV

MISCELLANEOUS FOOT LESIONS

TRENCH FOOT

A foot lesion has arisen during the present war, which, because of the fact that it appears on the feet of those who have been subjected to long sieges of service in the trenches, has been called "Trench Foot."

The condition has been and is being investigated by many medical men of note, and although the literature available has been rather meagre, several facts have been established and some of the data has been classified.

This chapter has been compiled from various papers upon the subject written by those who are now serving their respective countries in France, and who have had experience in dealing with the lesion. Articles by the following writers have been used, and all of the statements contained therein have been verified B. Sherwood Dunn, M.D., of Paris, in *The Medical Record;* "Anonymous," in the same publication; H Oswald Smith, in *The Lennox,* a journal devoted to dentistry, and several articles in the *Journal of the American Medical Association*

Trench foot is a lesion found in the lower extremity and is a result of exposure to cold and dampness in the trenches It has been likened to frost bite, but cases reported during the summer months show that the parallel is not justified. There are several stages to the disease, and they are classified by Smith into four groups: (1) Neuritic—producing acute pain and preventing the patient from walking or sleeping. There is no swelling or discoloration of the foot (2) Edematous—without discoloration, but acute pain is

357

present, produced by the pressure on the nerve endings
(3) Edematous—with blisters and varying discoloration of
the skin, short of gangrene. (4) Gangrenous—partial or
circumscribed, with edema and blisters and reddening of the
skin involving the lower leg.

Etiology. The lesion is found chiefly among men of
from twenty to thirty years of age who have been in continuous service in the trenches for a minimum of three days.
That it is truly the result of trench life is proven by the fact
that men in the artillery, who do not see trench service, are
not thus afflicted.

The constriction of the foot in ill-fitting shoes and
stockings with lack of cleanliness are also etiologic factors.
Cold is not accepted as the cause of trench foot, as the
trouble occurs in weather above freezing and some cases
have developed in the summer time. Neuritis, produced by
humidity, is the cause of the lancinating pain.

Raymond and Parisot have stated that the disease is
caused by bacterial invasion. They have isolated the
microbe, from the mud of the trenches, and have reproduced
in animals the various symptoms manifested in trench foot.
The microbe was found in the purulent layer of the vesicles
and the injection of these germs into the epidermis of the
rabbit and guinea pig caused the same lesion as is found in
man. They have reached the conclusion that the disease is
similar to mycetoma, the fungus foot of Madura and misnamed by English surgeons "tuberculosis foot."

The disease is prevalent among those standing in the
soft, slushy mud or in the muddy water of the trench. The
skin of the feet becomes soft and macerated, and while in
such condition offers easy ingress for the microorganism,
especially along the nail grooves or through abrasions
caused by shoe friction.

A committee of United States army surgeons in France,
headed by Major R. P. Strong, are making extensive tests
in order to ascertain the cause of *trench fever*. Their unfinished report (they are still investigating) shows as fol-

lows· (a) the organism causing trench fever is present in the plasma of the blood, (b) the organism is not filtrable; (c) the disease is transmitted naturally by the body louse (pediculis corporis); (d) this method is apparently the important and common means of the transmission of the disease[*].

Symptomatology. The symptoms of trench foot are always the same The ball of the great and second toe are swollen and edematous, the skin is distended and glossy and there are occasional blisters or vesicles. The edema may extend to the remaining toes and to the ball of the foot, and, from being white, may become rose-colored or even red and violet. In grave cases the liquid in the vesicles changes from citron color to a hemorrhagic hue, the skin becomes blue-black, then livid and gangrenous. Some of these vesicles may dry and the scab fall off, leaving no scar; the base of the vesicle may change in color from brown to black, and this change may extend beyond the borders and cover the entire area affected by the edema. This change is the forerunner of gangrene; the vesicle becomes a crust; when it falls off it leaves a putrid base which may gradually eat into the tendons and articulations and periosteum It is not infrequent to have the first crust followed by a second and third, and when the disease has progressed to this stage, no medication seems to avail and the member has to be amputated at a healthy point beyond the parts affected.

There is little if any fever accompanying the lighter forms, but a temperature of 104 degrees F. may attend the graver forms, with general disturbances of the nerve trunks. Albuminuria is not infrequent

The patient complains of lancinating pains which interrupt sleep and cause difficult locomotion. Walking is accomplished on the heels, with the toes elevated. The pain is excited at several points, chiefly by pressure on the heads of the metatarsals In the lighter forms, the patient complains of numbness (but only in the affected members) which at

---
[*](Capt V N Sorapure, R A M C, who has lectured to the students of The First Institute of Podiatry, has contributed to the literature on this subject; see Journal of the A M A, July 6, 1918)

times extends to a condition of anesthesia. The mildest form is characterized simply by pain and paresthesia.

The trouble appears, as a rule, after the patient has spent his assigned period in the trenches and manifests itself when he has retired to the sector for repose and removes his shoes for the first time in several days.

In the very worst cases there is gangrene accompanied by all of the dangers of infection, by destruction of tissue and loss of limbs. There is a tendency to contracture of the foot, usually described as a turning under of the foot.

Prognosis. Trench foot has a duration of from two to three weeks, in the lighter forms, and from six weeks to three months in the severe cases. The simpler lesions respond well to treatment, and in the type in which vesicles have formed, these latter dry and fall off, leaving no scar. A cure is effected in about one month. In more advanced types, in which extensive ulceration is present, the toes alone are lost and the rest of the tissues are saved under proper treatment. When general septicemia develops, and according to statistics of two thousand cases treated from October, 1916, to January, 1917, there have been only two such cases, the patients have immediately succumbed.

Complications are frequent accompaniments of the malady—abscess, neuritis, lymphangitis, etc. Tetanus has been observed with sufficient frequency to cause all patients to be injected with antitetanic serum upon admission for treatment.

Treatment. The prophylactic measures that have been adopted since trench foot has been more thoroughly understood, have eliminated it to a great extent, and the disability that it caused at that time is gradually being controlled. The perfection of general sanitary methods and the construction of better trenches have helped to diminish the incidence of the condition as well as to reduce disease and disability in general. The smaller sectors and the greater reserve of men, allowing for more frequent change, have of themselves, without the actual preventive methods instituted, reduced both the severity and the occurrence of trench foot. Where previously the men had to stay in the trenches for long periods, at present there is a change every few days.

As a general preventive measure against the lesion, it was found that the wearing of looser boots, perhaps a size too large, was of great help. This measure prevents the restriction of the circulation, which is so large a factor in the causation of trench foot. The general circulation of the body can be maintained by warmth and by appropriate movements and exercises. Socks must be changed very frequently and must be kept dry. Torn socks are especially liable to constrict the blood vessels and to produce injury to the foot. Foot rags, well paraffined, have been tried, with more or less success, to obviate the difficulty of keeping socks whole. If these foot rags are well applied, they are found to be far more comfortable than socks. Puttees must be loosely applied. Boots must be thoroughly greased before being put on. Rubber boots have been extensively used and are looked upon with favor. Thorough greasing of the feet was tried at the beginning, but was found to be offensive to the men, and consequently was not conscientiously carried out.

The newest and apparently most successful method of preventing trench foot is by means of the so-called "trench-foot washhouses." Immediately before returning to the trenches the men go to these washhouses for treatment. Here they have their feet soaked in warm, not hot, water and washed with a special soap composed of soft potash soap 1000 parts, powdered camphor 25 parts and borate of soda 100 parts. The feet are then carefully dried and treated by the regimental surgeon or podiatrist, and are finally dusted with a mixture of powdered camphor, talc and borate of soda. In the trenches, the soldiers must be served with hot food in order to maintain warmth and keep up the general circulation. No amount of attention to the feet of the soldier can be too painstaking as regards cleanliness, shoeing and physical condition. To escape disability as the result of actual war violence and to acquire it as the result of preventable sanitary conditions, would be indefensible.

The treatment of the lesion itself, depends upon the severity and the extent of the condition.

1. **Simple Edematous Form.** In the beginning, the erroneous diagnosis, and the subsequent treatment directed along the lines of frost bite, and the taking of potassium iodide, salversan-methylene blue, and the application of tincture of iodine and copper sulphate, did more harm than good in some cases, and the results, at best, were irregular. The statistics of Raymond and Parisot, who have treated more than 2000 cases in a short time, are the best compiled, and as their results have been excellent they are here given

At the earliest moment possible the feet of the patient should be thoroughly soaked in warm water and washed with liberal quantities of the soap, previously mentioned, and composed of soft soap, camphor and sodium borate. The cleansing should be thorough, but with care not to break the skin or to open any existing vesicles The skin must be dried carefully with a soft towel and the following applied· cover a layer of absorbent cotton of the thickness of the hand with gauze; soak this in a solution of camphor, 1.1; borate of soda, 15, boiled water, 1000, and apply while still thoroughly wet (being careful to cover the ends of the toes) to all the edematous surface as far up the leg as it extends Cover the whole with oiled silk or rubber sheeting, and fit by adhesive strips. If a roller bandage is used, it must be applied loosely The dressing should be damp when changed the following day

Renew this dressing daily, until the edema disappears, which should be from the second to the sixth day, after this, continue the same dressing for two or three days without the impermeable covering: following this, camphorated oil is to be applied without rubbing.

When the disease proves obstinate and is accompanied by persistent pain, some relief is afforded by bathing the feet at the time of the daily dressing in warm water, using the same liquid soap as at first.

2. **Vesicular Form.** The small vesicles, not larger than a ten cent piece, should be left undisturbed and will dry up without scar with the above-described treatment. When they are extensive, and especially when the contents are hemorrhagic, they should be completely denuded and the gelatinous base should be carefully removed by aid of a sterile tampon, and then these denuded surfaces should be covered with compresses soaked in a solution of camphor, 30, ether, 1000. These compresses and the whole affected surface are covered by the fomentation previously described, and should be changed daily.

When the edema subsides, omit the fomentations and continue the application of camphorated ether solution, and as the denuded surfaces show improvement, dust them with camphor powder or with boric acid powder.

3. **The Formation of Crusts.** The foregoing treatment will ordinarily prevent the formation of crusts or scabs; when these do form, steps must be at once taken for their removal without undue force or surgical aid, as they cover the most virulent germ collections, which are liable to produce a general infection if permitted to contaminate freshly cut surfaces. On the other hand, if permitted to remain, the germs thus protected have a tendency to burrow profoundly, involving the tendons and articulations.

The crusts must be softened and carefully removed from their borders daily, little by little, by aid of the forceps, the operator being careful to cause no bleeding. To soften the crusts, the following are recommended: (1) liberal dressings soaked in camphorated ether and covered with oiled silk or rubber sheeting; (2) collodial silver dressings; (3) camphorated oil and borated vaseline. As the crusts are gradually removed each day, the uncovered surfaces should be treated with the camphorated ether.

Not infrequently the crusts will re-form, in which event it is well to treat them with pomade of Reclus, made as follows: vaseline, 200; boric acid, 3; iodoform, 1; antipyrine, 5; salol, 3, carbolic acid (crystals), 1; bichloride of mercury, 0.1.

4. Extensive Invasion. Where the processes have progressed and involve a considerable amount of tissue, evidenced by a congested, violet-red surface, but with little or no erosion or vesicles, we recognize the presence of the malady in its worst form, and prompt measures must be taken to save the member. In these cases the germs have penetrated beyond the surfaces, and in order that they can be subjected to contact treatment and destroyed, we must reach the hidden centres of their activity

After surgical preparation of the surfaces, they are incised by a sharp pointed bistoury in the long axis of the foot and down to the level of the infection, indicated by a purulent layer of fetid edema. If a collection of pus is found, a free and extensive incision is made and the tissues thus exposed are thoroughly washed out with an antiseptic solution, by aid of a syringe The thermocautery should not be applied, as the results of its use in such cases have been very bad.

When the infected parts are opened they are treated with the previously mentioned camphorated ether, or with collodial silver dressings or, in the presence of purulent infiltration, with collodial gold, which can be varied by the following: eucalyptol, balsam of Peru, guaiacol, gomenol, camphor, of each 10, in ether, 1,000. Under the influence of these dressings, the hardened infiltrated surfaces soften and can be removed little by little by the aid of the forceps, in measure as the sloughing continues, until the destroyed and contaminated tissues are eliminated.

In so far as possible, surgical intervention should be avoided; where the bone is attacked, it is better to permit it to be eliminated by the progressive destructive action of the disease. Tentative or conservative operations upon the bone have been followed by extensive destructive ostitis If an amputation becomes necessary, it should be made at a healthy point beyond the infected area.

5. **Reparation Stage.** When the necrosis has been arrested and the granulations show that the affected parts are disinfected, the usual emollient applications can be employed to aid the repair, but here, a treatment brought into use by Rathery and Bauzil is recommended This forms an impermeable covering easily applied and changed, and possesses self-evident advantages It is composed of naptholate of soda, 2; essence of thyme, essence of origanum, essence of geranium, of each 3; vaseline 1,000, paraffin (45°-50°), 5,000. Melt and thoroughly mix by aid of heat and put aside in pots holding 125 grams each; sterilize for twenty minutes at 120°.

At the time of the daily change of dressings, place the number of pots necessary in a bath of boiling water to melt the wax, cover the affected parts with a single layer of sterile gauze and paint thoroughly with the melted wax This dressing hardens as fast as it is applied. Apply a second and third layer in the same manner, to form a perfectly occlusive dressing. Cover with cotton and bandage. Dressing comes off easily and completely without pain, and gives remarkable results in healing and repair and renewal of the skin to the parts.

6 **General Treatment.** In the cases complicated by septicemia, subcutaneous injections of camphorated oil in doses of from 5 to 15 c.c. per day, or intramuscular injections of collodial camphor in doses of 2 c c per day, are advisable.

7. **Complications.** The most frequent is tetanus Every patient should at once be injected with anti-tetanic serum, and this should be repeated every eight days.during the period of ulceration and sloughing. It is even prudent to augment the second injection in those gravely afflicted (20 c.c. of the Pasteur Institute serum, or 3000 units of the American).

Gaseous gangrene is infrequent with the treatment here

indicated. If present, it can be treated in the usual way.

Smith has employed subcutaneous injections of oxygen in cases of this condition which have been neuritic, or edematous without discoloration, edematous with blisters, gangrenous, partial or circumscribed. The technic of the oxygen treatment is as follows. a Woulfe bottle is required, with two glass tubes bent at an angle and inserted into a tightly-fitting cork. To the end of one glass tube is fitted three yards of red rubber tubing connected with the usual oxygen cylinder; to the end of the other glass tube is fitted two yards of a finer rubber tube, and the distal end of the tube has fitted on it a salvarsan needle. The bottle contains a saturated solution of sodium carbonate. The needle should be sterilized in boiling oil for each individual case. The operator, having sterilized his hands, uses iodine on the proposed sites of the puncture. The needle is inserted into the subcutaneous tissue at a point midway between the heel and the external malleolus. The oxygen is allowed to enter slowly until the foot is filled up. The needle is then withdrawn and inserted midway between the internal malleolus and the heel. If the toes are black and cold the needle is inserted in the mid line at the base of the toes. It is important that the oxygen should be injected slowly. If the part is almost gangrenous, injection into the deeper tissues is of advantage.

The treatment is based on the conclusion that trench foot is akin to Raynaud's disease. The edema produces stasis in the veins of the foot, impeding or stopping circulation, and the venous blood, if oxygenated, will help to keep the tissues alive until the serum can be drained away, while the oxygen helps to drive out the serum, slowly but steadily, through the puncture holes. Mere puncturing has been found useless in relieving the edema. The oxygen balloons the subcutaneous tissue, thus relieving pressure on the blood vessels and lymphatics. When the oxygen is absorbed and the serum drained away, circulation is quickly restored to the limb.

There is marked relief to pain at once, and under the eye of the observer certain changes can be seen taking place. The reddish blue appearance changes to pink; the redness which often extends up the leg disappears, and where blackened areas exist, a white line makes its appearance and any living tissue is noticeable by its pink color. The white line indicates what would ultimately be the line of demarcation of gangrene, and it is noted that healthy granulations start from this white line after injections of oxygen The destruction of parts is greatly lessened, and is often confined to the tips of the toes Areas of black blood on the dorsum of the foot rapidly undergo change, becoming grayish white and pink, and more nearly resembling healthy tissue In many of the severe cases, recovery of the whole foot has taken place, and in some the loss of but a single digit has had to be recorded.

A minor but important point is the treatment of all blisters. They should be drained by sterilized thread passed through by means of a straight surgical needle and the ends cut short. The dead skin should be left in situ as a protective, unless pus is present.

The oxygen causes an increase in the pulse of the posterior tibial artery. There is no rise in temperature, pain is relieved, and sleep promoted. Lint, wrung out in 1 per cent. solution of picric acid, is applied to the parts and renewed every day. No cotton-wool should be employed or disastrous results will ensue. The lint and bedclothes next day will be found saturated with serum, sometimes clear, and sometimes bloodstained. The skin will have a peculiar wrinkled appearance, pointing to the previous state of edema. The foot is warm even at the toes, and movement will have returned. At the end of the second day tingling sensations arise. In cases which are semi-gangrenous and where the edema still persists, a second injection may be given. One injection is usually found to be sufficient, but picric acid should be used once or twice a day to keep the part dry and sweet. The effect of the oxygen on the deep layers of the true skin is notable, a rich red velvet color persists for several days.

Smith advocates conservative treatment in all cases of trench foot unless gas gangrene or grave toxemia be present. Repair is slow but sure and many hopeless looking cases have recovered with useful limbs and minor loss of structure. The cost of the oxygen treatment is small, and oxygen is usually available. There is no risk to the patient if this treatment be intelligently used, but healthy tissue, as far as possible, should be utilized for injection purposes. The length of time for repair and recovery of the part is long in the semi-gangrenous and in the gangrenous cases. The granulation tissue is often indolent with the epithelial margin heaped up, and here, again, oxygen has been found to stimulate epithelial growth, a hypodermic needle being utilized in place of the salvarsan needle.

The conclusion drawn is, that if the edema can be relieved by withdrawing the serum, the circulation can be re-established, and during this withdrawal the tissues are supplied with oxygen to keep them nourished

GROUND ITCH OR UNCINARIAL DERMATITIS

Prof. Paul Luttinger in addressing the students of his class at The First Institute of Podiatry gave the following outline of this disease· "this condition is known as water itch, water pox, water sores, sore feet of coolies, panighao, mazamorro (Porto Rico), tunnel-digger's sore foot It is an erythematous or papulo-vesicular irritation of the feet, due to infection with the larvae of the hookworm. These latter gain entrance through the skin of the lower extremities and cause the very grave tropical disease known as uncinariasis (hookworm), or tropical chlorosis ,

"The eruption, which is very itchy, appears first as reddish spots between the toes and on the dorsum of the foot. These spots become macules and later vesiculate In some cases blebs may be formed which, upon rupturing, become raw, oozing surfaces accompanied by considerable local swelling Pustulation and ulceration may result if these surfaces become infected with pus producing micro-organisms.

Treatment. Under proper treatment, this condition will subside within a few weeks; otherwise it may take months or until the systemic disease develops Sometimes gangrene of the part may result. Cleanliness, combined with mild antiseptic lotions, is all that is necessary to cure the disease in its early phase. A three per cent. alcoholic solution of salicylic acid has been highly recommended by Barlow, who opens the blebs and applies pledgets of cotton dipped in this solution twice daily for five minutes.

The proper disposal of excreta in rural communities and the avoidance of going barefoot in the warm and rainy season, are the best methods of prevention.''

GAS INFECTION AND GAS GANGRENE

Gas infection is a very common condition found in the wounded in the present war It is controlled successfully if it is seen and treated early in its course, but when it has progressively developed it causes a most dangerous condition called gas gangrene.

Etiology. The infecting agent is called the bacillus of Welch, the bacillus aerogenes capsulatus or the bacillus perfringens. The bacillus is of the anerobic type, and being lodged in deep wounds with ragged tissues, recesses and pockets, and completely obstructed by fragments of broken-down tissues, all of which prevents the air from reaching them, they multiply rapidly with the formation of gas followed by a great destruction of tissue

The bacillus of Welch grows rapidly and it is on that account that immediate and radical action is essential if loss of life is to be prevented Kenneth Taylor has obtained a pure culture in a very short time as follows: a series of six or more culture tubes are inoculated, each tube from its predecessor, at intervals of only half an hour. Even in this short period bubbles of gas became evident in the successive tubes. By the time the sixth or the seventh tube is reached, one may obtain a pure culture, so far has the gas bacillus outgrown the other germs.

Symptoms. The rapidity of the development of the bacteria is responsible for early symptoms of the infection, and Bowlby has observed well-marked infection with the formation of gas within five hours, and death of an entire limb has occurred from gas gangrene in sixteen hours.

The course of the disease varies somewhat, being at first, a *local* condition; bubbles of gas appear in the discharges from the wound, and crackling from gas may be felt in the tissues immediately surrounding. Prompt and radical treatment will prevent further development and will restrict the lesion to a limited area. Certain muscles will be lost and with them the corresponding motions, leaving the patient crippled to that extent, but beyond this, recovery will follow.

A more serious and fatal form, is the *diffuse* or rapidly spreading process. The skin is discolored, the limb is extremely swollen and edematous, gas penetrates the cellular tissues and advances rapidly, so pressing upon the muscles as to render them useless, and obstructing vessels and nerves; the pulse is small and rapid, the extremities are cold; vomiting and hiccough may occur. The patient is profoundly toxic but he may not feel very ill. If improvement cannot be secured by thorough exposure of all pockets and excision, death ensues, the gas spreading rapidly upward to the abdomen, chest, and then to the neck, causing distressing pressure and finally loss of life.

In other cases the whole limb is involved suddenly, beginning within a few days of the initial injury. A wound which is doing fairly well at night may reveal a condition of gangrene—swollen, tense, and discolored in the morning; the patient, already in collapse, succumbs before the gas itself has apparently spread far enough to cause death.

Treatment. The paramount importance of the earliest

possible treatment during the first stage of rapidly spreading infection, before the production of gas in any serious quantity has occurred, is self-evident. Every hour counts against the patient.

Taylor points out clearly what is to be done:

1. Destruction of the bacillus.

2 Removal of the tissues especially favoring its growth, which are the necrotic muscles.

3. Measures to prevent the destruction of the muscles as a result of mechanical pressure.

For the destruction of the bacilli, Taylor recommends a one per cent. solution of chlorhydrate of quinin. Others have found Dakin's fluid effective.

All foreign bodies (clothing, etc.) in the wound, must be removed as they will keep up the anerobic infection; *all* dead tissue must be removed, the wounds kept open, and frequent antiseptic dressings used. Dakin's fluid or Taylor's quinin chlorhydrate, when properly used in connection with the above absolutely necessary means, will enable the surgeon to conquer the infection at the start if he sees the patient as early as possible—certainly within the first twenty-four hours

The muscles should be opened by numerous longitudinal incisions, incisions of the muscular sheaths, and the excision of all necrosed tissue. Sometimes single muscles or a group of muscles may need to be excised. The dead muscle can be distinguished from the living by its dirty brick-red color, in contrast to the normal purple-brown The dead muscles also lose their contractility. The focus of infection, if known, should be excised. The wound should be dressed with the chosen antiseptic solution. The incisions should be kept open by light gauze compresses, wet with this solution. No circular bandages which can exert the least compression, and so hinder the escape of the gas, are allowable. Nothing should obstruct the free escape of the gas. Everything should be done to promote it.

If gas gangrene occurs or has already set in, the same

free incision should be made, unless this has already been done.

Bacteriologic diagnosis in the early stage is most important. Soon the discoloration of the skin, blebs, and crepitation make the diagnosis positive, but crepitation often appears late rather than early. The X-rays may disclose the bubbles of gas in the tissues. On incision, if the muscular tissue is bloodless, pale, dry, of a brick-red color, gangrene already exists. The best judgment then will be required to decide whether free excision of this gangrenous tissue, with suitable subsequent dressing, or immediate amputation should be done. If the limb is amputated, it should be by the so-called "guillotine" method, i.e., without flaps. The wound should be dressed with the end of the stump entirely uncovered until the infection has been conquered. Then the skin may be drawn down by lacing or by weights, and sutured as soon as feasible. The bone may have to be shortened.

Antitoxin Treatment. One of the most important contributions to surgery as a result of the war has recently appeared in the form of a paper by Carrol G. Bull and Miss Ida Pritchett, of the Rockefeller Institute. This paper describes a lengthy series of experiments with the bacilli Welchii, which were cultured from wounds caused by the war. A very powerful, soluble toxin, produced by the bacilli has been found, which has killed animals almost instantly. The most important result of the experiments is that they give promise of an antitoxin which may be as potent in the prevention of gas gangrene and gas infection as other antitoxins have been effective in their respective spheres. Among these are antitetanic, antityphoid and other antitoxins.

(The above material has largely been taken from "The Treatment of War Wounds," by Dr W. W. Keen, and from "Surgical Nursing in War," by Dr Elizabeth R Bundy)

SYPHILIS

Although syphilis is a disease that is usually considered as of a systemic nature and manifests itself in every part of the body, the skin is a very common place for its appearance (syphiloderma), and the foot is often involved. It then becomes the function of the podiatrist to diagnose the lesion, and as this necessitates a knowledge of the general characteristics of the disease, the following should prove of interest

Derivation. From the Greek *sus* and *philos,* "a companion of swine."

Synonymns. Syphilis cutanea, lues, syphilis of the skin

Definition. Syphilis is a chronic, specific, contagious, sometimes hereditary disease, caused by a germ, the spirochaeta pallida, involving the skin and nervous system, but capable of affecting any organ or tissue. Inoculation occurs usually at some part of the genitilia, the first evidence of the disease being the initial lesion or "chancre," but inoculation may occur at any other part of the body forming the so-called "extra-genital chancre."

Etiology. Syphilis may be hereditary, i.e., transmitted by the parent. In the majority of adults it is acquired directly from an existing chancre or other lesion, the spirochaeta pallida being conveyed directly from one to another Extra-genital chancres are caused by kissing, by towels, by drinking cups, or by infected instruments, bites, etc. The extra-genital chancre may occur on the mucous membrane or at the site of any skin abrasion. It is essential that infected persons be informed of the danger of transmitting it to others. The contagious period exists to the end of the second year and any secretion, from the possible presence of mucous patches, may be infective

Pathology. Syphilitic deposits are new growths and consist of round cell infiltration, especially about the vessels, generally endothelial proliferation, and in the tubercular and some other lesions, a variable number of giant cells. The initial changes are noted in the upper part of the corium. The rete, the corium, and, in the deeper lesions, the subcutaneous tissues, are involved, the retrogressive steps being by involution, through fatty degeneration and absorption, or by necrosis and ulceration

All the various syphilitic lesions are structurally the same amounting to an endarteritis of a special kind, slowly obliterating and tending to the production of hypertrophy of the tissues about it. The coppery ham color in syphilitic lesions is due to blood coloring matter from the extravasated red blood corpuscles and to the sluggish nature of the inflammation. These exudation processes are found for months after the process has healed clinically.

Diagnosis. Syphilis usually runs a mild course, but occasionally it is malignant. In some instances its cutaneous symptoms resemble other skin lesions, and it is on that account that diagnosis is often difficult The general points to be observed are the distribution, color, form, course and duration.

Distribution. The secondary lesions are more or less general and symmetric in distribution The lesions vary in duration and may show a preference for certain locations, such as the upper part of the forehead, anus, palms and soles. The late secondary lesions, and particularly those of the tertiary period, are usually confined to one region, are grouped, and are not bilateral in distribution.

Color. Syphilodermata are dull coppery-red or ham-color. Exposure to cold air often makes the eruptions on the body more distinct. Color alone cannot be depended upon to make certain a diagnosis.

Form. The earliest lesions are round or oval, showing no tendency to grouping. In the late secondary, and in the tertiary stages, grouping occurs and the lesions may be serpiginous and circinate. This is an important point in diagnosis.

Early ulcers are superficial and the scars are insignificant. Later ulcers are deeper, and the scars, often pigmented, are sometimes diagnostic.

There are many and various forms of syphilis, all of which have characteristic symptoms, but for the podiatrist, who usually sees the later lesions, and who cannot make an examination of the entire body, it will be necessary to recognize those that appear on the foot only.

The nails are occasionally involved in syphilis. Onychia and paronychia are found in the active secondary stage of the disease. The inflammation starts in the matrix or in the nail folds, followed by nutritive disturbances, and subsequent thickening, friability and opacity, furrows and depressions. The nail is lifted up, as a rule, and if there is much ulceration, the nail falls off. Such lost nails are generally replaced by new nails which are ill-formed at first, or they may remain deformed permanently. The skin surrounding the nail is swollen and infiltrated. In infants, the ends of the toes become club-like (syphilitic dactylitis). This condition is rarely seen in adults. The pain is not severe unless accompanied by further pyogenic infection or by mechanical disturbance.

PLANTAR SYPHILID

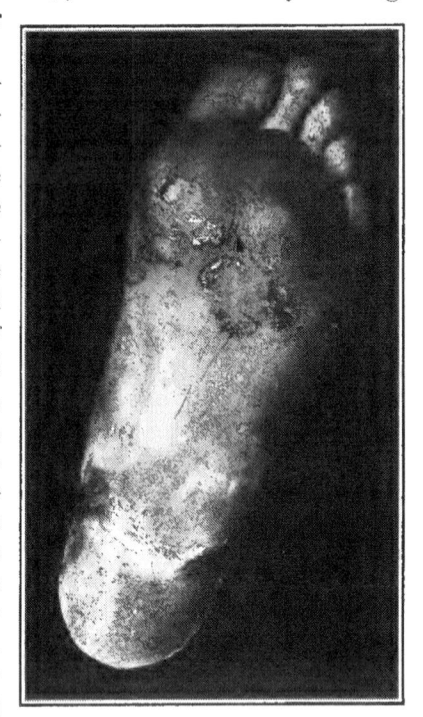

Plantar Syphilid. The plantar surface of the foot is a common site for dry syphilids. The palm of the hand, and the sole of the foot are the most common locations for the papulosquamous lesions of the late secondary stages of the disease. The lesions are not so elevated and their edges are not so well defined, papules looking more like macules; infiltration, however, is distinct. The shape may be irregular and the usual ham-color does not appear on the surface on account of the scaliness or dry heaped-up epidermis. There is usually a central brownish, gray, callous-like thickening, surrounded by a partly visible band of brownish-red, underlying, papular infiltration The color is disclosed by removal of the scale. Surrounding the lesion is an encircling edge of partially detached epidermis with its loose, ragged edge directed toward the centre. This semi-detached edge is of extreme value in the diagnosis of plantar syphilids.

The plantar lesions come on slowly and spread gradually. They are usually limited to one sole, but may be found on both feet There is no itching, but they may be painful if fissures are present. If the plantar lesions are a part of a generalized eruption of the second stage of the disease, they yield readily to treatment, but if they are a recurrence of a generalized eruption, they are more obstinate. Occurring as a late manifestation, they may be extremely rebellious.

Papulosquamous syphilis is the most common lesion of syphilis found on the foot, and is most apt to be confused with eczema The latter often occurs on the soles of the feet; the following table will show the differential diagnostic points:

PAPULOSQUAMOUS SYPHILODERM	ECZEMA
1. History of syphilis	1. History of previous outbreaks.
2. Concomitant signs present.	2. No associated signs.
3. Favorite seats, palms and soles.	3. Favorite seats, flexor surfaces.
4. Itching usually absent.	4. Itching present.
5. Edge of lesion surrounded by detached scales.	5. Scales completely detached.
6. Scales scanty and dirty-grayish.	6. Scales abundant, and granular
7. Infiltrated, dull red papules beneath the scales.	7. Flat, reddish patches beneath the scales.

Eczema can also be differentiated by the more inflammatory aspect, the involvement of the toes and toe-ends, by its appearance on the dorsum of the foot as well as on the plantar surface, by the itching, and by the presence of inflammatory exudation. There is no attempt at configuration in eczema, while this is characteristic of syphilis. In addition, some of the elemental lesions of eczema will usually be found around one of a doubtful nature

Blood Tests. Testing the blood is practised to a great extent for determining the presence of syphilis, but this method of diagnosis is not absolute. The Wasserman complement fixation test and the later modification by Noguchi are of value when they are positive. A negative reaction is no absolute proof of the absence of the disease. They are positive during the active secondary stages, but in the first week or two they are usually negative In the late stages, when the bacteria may be encapsulated in a lesion, the reaction may be negative. This may be made positive by the administration of potassium iodide, which causes the germs to enter the blood or lymph stream. One should be able to make a diagnosis without the aid of the blood tests in cases of syphilis in which there are skin lesions.

The luetin test, a vaccine test, is of most value in the late stage of the disease.

Course and Duration. Secondary lesions appear rapidly and are fully developed at the end of two weeks, and in time disappear spontaneously. Palmar and plantar lesions are apt to be more persistent. There is little tendency to spontaneous disappearance of the tertiary eruption.

Treatment. The treatment of syphilis is entirely out of the domain of the podiatrist, and when such a case is discovered, it should be turned over to the dermatologist or to the general medical practitioner at once. Plantar syphilids should be treated with soap and warm water so as to remove the scales and thickened epidermis, and this may be followed by an application of salicylic acid ointment, 5 to 10%. Thereafter ointment containing mercury, the white precipitate (ammoniated mercury) preferred, should be used twice a day.

Constitutional treatment is absolutely essential if the disease is to be cured, and this should be vigorous during the first few months after inoculation. The general health must be maintained and nutritious, plain diet, rest, moderate exercise and abstinence from alcohol and tobacco must be urged upon the patient. With all of the above precautions, accompanied by the proper use of remedies, recovery is usually prompt and the symptoms are limited

Mercury is the one drug that is used almost exclusively. It is very dependable, and should be employed freely, up to the limit of tolerance, during the active stages of the disease. In the tertiary stage, potassium or sodium iodide, in addition to the mercury, is administered. These drugs are used in various forms and in various doses, all of which are of no interest to the practitioner of podiatry.

Recently many practitioners of medicine have been using a complex compound of arsenic, viz., arsphenamin, (salvarsan). This drug is injected into the muscles or the veins. Although many have taken up the use of salvarsan and like chemicals, most practitioners still rely upon mercury. The newer preparations are used more as adjuvants than as specifics Lesions of the mucous membranes disappear rapidly under treatments with these drugs

Formerly it was difficult to tell when a case of syphilis had been cured, however, with the advent of the various blood tests this has become a less doubtful matter. When the various reactions of these tests are negative in uncomplicated cases, toward the end of the second year, it is safe to say that the disease is cured.

(The above is largely compiled from the lectures of Dr. Andrew H Montgomery, Prof. of Dermatology at The First Institute of Podiatry)

FOCAL INFECTION

Focal infection is the name given to a pathologic condition in the human body, which manifests itself in a part remote from the original focus of infection, or from the original lesion.

Up to a few years ago, focal infections were not recognized by even the most advanced members of the medical profession, and many thousands of people have suffered and died, due to the fact that lesions of this type remained undiagnosed.

Thanks to the efforts of Dr. M. L Rhein, of New York City, and Prof. Gies, of Columbia University, who drew the attention of the scientific world to the intimate relationship between tooth infections and indefinite ailments in the body, including those of the feet, a large quantity of material has been accumulated on this subject, which throws an interesting light upon it.

It has now been firmly established that the teeth, the tonsils, the adenoids, the male and female urethra, the uterus and the gall bladder, in fact, any part of the body which serves as a portal of entrance to any infection, may become the reservoir of a chronic pathologic condition, and cause disease in any other part of the body. So the teeth, harboring certain microorganisms, have been shown to be directly responsible for heart, stomach and kidney lesions, as well as arthritis and other joint and bone diseases

Mode of Infection. The bacteria responsible for focal infections thrive best upon dead or necrotic tissue. These bacteria, when they locate in a place where such necrotic tissue is available, such as a tooth in which some of the dead pulp remains, or in a diseased tonsil or urethra, develop so that they throw off toxins or poisons without causing any visible signs of inflammation. These toxins circulate in the blood stream, and locate in various parts of the body, especially in those which offer the least resistance to the invasion.

Relationship Between the Foot and Focal Infection. The most common lesion of the foot due to focal infection, is arthritis or inflammation of the joints. This is due to infection of the teeth, tonsils, nose or adenoids with the common microorganisms such as the staphylococci, streptococci, influenza bacilli, etc., that infest the cavity of the mouth. It may also be due to an infection of the valves of the heart with the streptococcus viridans, or of the gall bladder with typhoid bacilli, or of the genital organs with the gonococcus. In some instances, arthritis of the foot may be traced to an auto-intoxication of the intestinal tract or of the bladder by the colon bacillus.

Osteomyelitis, or inflammation of the bone marrow, periostitis or inflammation of the bone covering, and less often, osteitis or inflammation of the bone proper, may be caused by the typhoid bacillus or its toxin, which originally manifests itself in the intestinal tract. These diseases may develop during an acute attack of typhoid, but usually appear after the acute symptoms have subsided.

Gonorrheal Heel is a well defined type of focal infection due to original invasion of the urethral tract by the gonococcus. The microorganism, or its toxin, reaches the inferior surface of the os calcis, at the point where the flexor brevis digitorum muscle arises, lodges there and causes a chronic inflammation of the periosteum and the bursa. The process is a mild and slow one, and gradually the periosteum is absorbed. With their covering removed, the bone cells increase in number, causing the formation of a spur or exostosis. Walking upon this growth causes the characteristic pain referred to as "painful heel."

Painful Feet in Women. Dr. Henry Frauenthal, of New York City, has recorded a large number of cases of painful heel in women, in which the foot manifests no signs that would warrant such pains. Investigation has shown that these women were suffering with leucorrhea Such cases often come to the podiatrist's office, where they may be mistreated for flat and weak foot by means of mechanical appliances which do no good and often cause additional pain. Discreet questioning will reveal the fact that the patient is a sufferer from leucorrhea, and she should be sent to a physician for treatment.

Treatment. Focal infections of all types require treatment at the initial source of infection and therefore are out of the domain of the podiatrist. These cases should be referred to the physician or dentist, as the circumstances warrant. Attempts at local treatment will prove futile, and bring the podiatrist into bad repute. His duty ceases when he has recognized such an infection and sends his patient to the proper person for professional care.

It is a well known fact that the removal of an infected tooth or of a diseased tonsil has often given immediate relief to one suffering from foot pains, due to focal infection. It is equally well known that heel pains, due to gonorrheal causes, have disappeared contemporaneously with the cure of an old venereal lesion. So fully satisfied are the authorities in charge of the Clinics of The First Institute of Podiatry of the utility of such a procedure, that means are now being devised whereby there shall be in nightly attendance, physicians and dentists, to whom are to be referred all cases of foot pains, in which, by exclusion, a diagnosis has been reached that focal infection may be the cause of the same.

MORTON'S TOE AND METATARSALGIA

Morton's toe and metatarsalgia are conditions, so common in the practice of the podiatrist that it is deemed best to discuss them briefly in this volume, although they will be treated most exhaustively in "Podiatry Orthopedics," the next volume of this series.

Morton's Toe or Morton's Neuralgia. When the foot is kept in a narrow shoe, the strain placed upon the fore-foot is so great, that the fifth metatarsal bone is forced upward and the fourth one downward, and the latter bone is made to act as the pillar of the arch In consequence, a severe pain is produced, caused by pressure upon one of the plantar nerves, between the head of the bone and the skin. This condition is called Morton's toe, or Morton's neuralgia, after Morton, of Philadelphia, who was the first to call attention to it.

Treatment. The pain induced by Morton's toe, as stated, is caused by direct pinching of a branch of the external plantar nerve, and it is therefore necessary to relieve the pressure on the head of the bone which causes this condition. This is accomplished by the application of a felt pad about one inch long, three-fourths of an inch wide and three-eighths of an inch thick, properly skived and fastened by some adhesive substance, reinforced with adhesive plaster strips, well behind the head of the affected bone. This will raise the head of the bone so that pressure on the nerve will cease, thus relieving the pain. It is essential to remember that the pad must be placed behind the head of the bone, for if it is put too far forward, increased suffering will result If the case is one in which it becomes necessary to use a pressure of this kind for any length of time, the felt should be discarded, and a plate of metal or some other stable substance should be substituted, with an elevation at the point at which the pressure is desired.

In addition to the device for raising the arch to its normal position, exercises and massage should be prescribed. The exercises should be those which will strengthen the flexor muscles of the toes. Attempting to pick up a pencil or other cylindrical object with the toes, if practised daily for ten or fifteen minutes will ultimately prove effective. Massage, to help develop these muscles and to stretch the shortened extensors, will also be of benefit. The patient should be instructed to wear shoes that are wide enough to allow for the normal spreading of the anterior part of the foot in walking. The waist of the shoe, the portion behind the ball of the foot, should be snug.

Metatarsalgia. The name applied to this lesion is, literally, a pain in the metatarsal region, but is particularly relevant to the condition in which there is a painful depression of the heads of the second, third and fourth metatarsal bones, the bones that make up the anterior arch. This condition is readily recognized by the fact that the heads of the bones are in a straight line instead of forming a concave arc, when the foot is at rest. Upon weight bearing, the normal anterior arch is obliterated.

Treatment. Metatarsalgia is treated much the same as Morton's toe, except that the pad is made large enough to support the three middle metatarsal bones. The pad should be so shaped that it conforms to the contour of the normal arch. Metal or other devices may be worn, if properly fitted, in cases where the pressure is desired for a period of time. Exercises and massage should be used in these cases as well as in Morton's toe, especially the former, for stretching the extensor muscles

A tight bandage around the foot just behind the heads of the metatarsal bones will often give relief in metatarsalgia and Morton's toe; it acts beneficially by preventing the heads of the bones from being forced below their normal level. Adhesive plaster and rubber bands may also be used for this purpose.

The shoe should have a very low heel and a broad toe, so that only a little weight is borne at the metatarsophalangeal joints, thus affording the extensor muscles of the toes a chance to stretch. This type of shoe will cause the patient to experience a feeling of falling backwards, particularly in the case of a woman who has been accustomed to wearing high heels; but this feeling and the strain that is caused on the calf muscles, will soon pass off.

CHAPTER XXV

X-RAYS IN PODIATRY

Roentgenology is the science that deals with the use of the Roentgen, or X-rays, in all their applications. The subject is divided into three parts, each distinct from the other, and with special required study for each part The first branch of roentgenology is known as *roentgenotherapy* or *actinotherapy,* and comprehends the treatment of disease by the use of the X-rays or by other radiant energy.

Roentgenotherapy, to be intelligently applied by the practitioner, requires a thorough knowledge of pathology and is strictly within the province of the licensed doctor of medicine. The second branch variously styled *fluoroscopy, skiascopy, radioscopy* or *roentgenoscopy,* is utilized for examining the various parts of the body by projecting the X-rays through the body and fixating the shadows cast on the fluoroscope. This branch of the science of light is of great assistance in diagnosis and is used extensively in surgery for the location of foreign bodies in the tissues. The third division of roentgenology is called *radiography, skiagraphy* or *roentgenography,* and consists of the making of X-ray photographs by passing the ray through the body in front of a photographic plate. This branch is of great importance to the podiatrist because of the value it possesses in the diagnosis of foot lesions, involving the bony structures; it often clears up a doubt as to the true state of a lesion when other means have failed. The soft tissues through which the ray passes readily appear in light shadow, while the bones, because they are solid, cast a darker shadow on the plate.

Experiments with electricity and with the modifications

of the various currents of electricity, have been responsible for all of the new discoveries and inventions along these lines, and the same may be said of the X-rays.

The two divisions of electric current are the direct and the alternating, named after the direction in which they flow. The direct current moves in one direction and may be likened to the flow of water from a faucet, while the alternating current does not maintain a steady pressure nor does it flow in the same direction continuously. The alternating current, which is commonly used for lighting purposes, reverses its direction of flow and pressure 120 times per second. It is therefore called 60 cycle current, in that it makes 60 complete cycles per second. The alternating current may be likened to the tide, which rises and falls every twelve hours. Instead of passing from ebb to flood and back again each twelve hours, the alternating current, used for illuminating purposes, does so in one-sixtieth of a second.

The alternating current is of most value to the sciences, because its voltage or pressure may be easily changed. Thus it can be raised or lowered by passing it through special apparatus. One particular form of alternating current has a voltage of from 30,000 to 120,000 and can be used for the production of Roentgen rays, if it be transformed into a so-called pulsative or unidirectional high tension current. This transformation is easily brought about by modern Roentgen ray apparatus.

The discovery of the X-rays was preceded by an improvement in the knowledge of alternating currents. Many scientists were experimenting and looking for new rays and currents, and after the invention of the air pump and the production of glass globes, from which the air was removed by means of the pump, Geissler invented the process of sealing platinum into glass and produced the Geissler air pump, which is used to the present day. This made it possible to seal electric conductors into vacuum tubes.

Following this, Faraday and Maxwell developed the

electro-magnetic theory of light and laid the foundation for a theory of the Roentgen ray, which, although later considerably changed, has proven one of the most useful adjuvants to the science of physics. The period between 1840 and the discovery of the X-rays was an active one in electric experimenting Many men were interested in this work, and their observations and discoveries were important in the final discovery of the rays In fact, Roentgen's discovery was fully expected, inasmuch as several investigators, including Sir William Crookes and Roentgen himself, were convinced that rays existed of which they knew nothing The earlier of the two workers, Crookes, had probably produced X-rays, but overlooked them and it fell to Roentgen to become aware of the conditions under which they were produced He called them X-rays or unknown rays, but after a time, they were named after him, and are known in science as Roentgen rays. Roentgen wrote and published three papers on the subject and these have become classics on this topic All of the facts announced by him at that time continue to be accepted, because, notwithstanding all the work done along these lines, they have never been disproven

Experiments have been continuous, and gradually the types of generators and tubes have changed, always improving. Where at first only simple work could be accomplished, the most wonderful things in this art are now being done, with probably many more wonderful things still to come. The dangers to which the earlier workers were subjected have been gradually eliminated, and to-day with proper care, the danger from the X-rays has been reduced to a minor factor. This danger came about from lack of knowledge of what occurred in the tube when the ray was being generated. There are three rays produced, one of which causes destruction of the human tissues, when exposed for a prolonged period of time By preventing the passage of this ray, by the use of lead and lead glass, as protective mediums, the danger has been practically controlled.

X-RAY APPARATUS

The apparatus used in the generation of the X-rays consists of a generator, a vacuum tube and an appliance for holding the tube in a fixed position, called the tube stand.

The Generator. The generators used in X-ray work are of three types, the motor generator, the interrupterless type and the coil generator with a chemical interrupter.

The function of the Roentgen ray apparatus is to produce high potential electric discharges in one and the same direction, or what is known as a unidirectional current. Dependent upon the kind of current used to start with, distinction can be made between the types of apparatus previously mentioned. These types are operated by either direct or alternating current

Direct current apparatus requires an interrupting device for the purpose of producing the necessary change of flux of magnetic lines in the inductive part of the apparatus. Interrupting devices, which are used in connection with such apparatus, are of three kinds *first*, the hammer interrupter; *second*, the mercury interrupter; *third*, the electrolytic interrupter. The function of any one of these interrupters is to break up the continuous flow of direct current into small fragments. Each one of these fragments then produces one impulse of high potentiality, which is then directed through the tube.

The alternating current, as its name implies, is already interrupted, but the impulses are alternately changing direction, passing first in one direction and then in the opposite direction. Hence, if the alternating current is used as a primary source of electric energy, then the secondary or high potential impulses will also be changing their direction alternately. Two methods are used in employing the alternating current as a primary source of energy. The first consists of the suppression of one phase (that which would pass in the negative direction) by means of the so-called rectifier cell. The second consists of producing high poten-

INTERUPTERLESS TYPE GENERATOR

tial impulses which flow in alternate directions, and to then redirect these impulses so that all of those passing through the tube are in the one and the same direction.

Accordingly, X-ray apparatus can be divided into the three classes previously mentioned. The coil, consisting of an induction coil activated by direct current, which is broken into small sections by the interrupter; or the induction coil which is energized by the alterating current of which one phase is suppressed through a liquid rectifier cell, and in which the proper interruptions are again produced by some interrupting device. The most extensively used type of apparatus is known as the "interrupterless machine." This machine operates on either the direct or the alternating current, but, if the direct current is used as a primary source, it is transformed into an alternating current by means of a rotary converter or motor generator set. The alternating current, therefore, either produced or already available, passes into the primary coil of a transformer which changes it into alternating impulses of high potentiality In order to transform them into impulses, all of which shall pass in the same direction, a so-called rectifying system is employed This consists of either a disk or of cross-sticks, which are so arranged that they produce contact with both terminals of the transformer in such a way that current of the same polarity, the unidirectional current, is always delivered to the tube. The name "interrupterless machine" merely implies that the devices used for interrupting the primary current have been eliminated.

There is one other type of apparatus which is built on the principle of an electrically oscillating system Here again a start is made with the alternating current, obtained either from the line or by changing the direct current by means of an interrupter The current is transformed through a so-called step-up transformer into one of high potentiality which is then still alternating. This current oscillates over a spark gap. Parallel to this spark gap a resonator is connected in which impulses are produced that correspond to the discharges over the gap and which, if applied to a specially built, so-called high frequency Roentgen ray tube, will produce X-rays. Since the principle of electric oscillations of a high frequency is used in this type of apparatus, it is generally called the high frequency Roentgen ray apparatus.

Roentgen Ray Tubes. The various types of apparatus

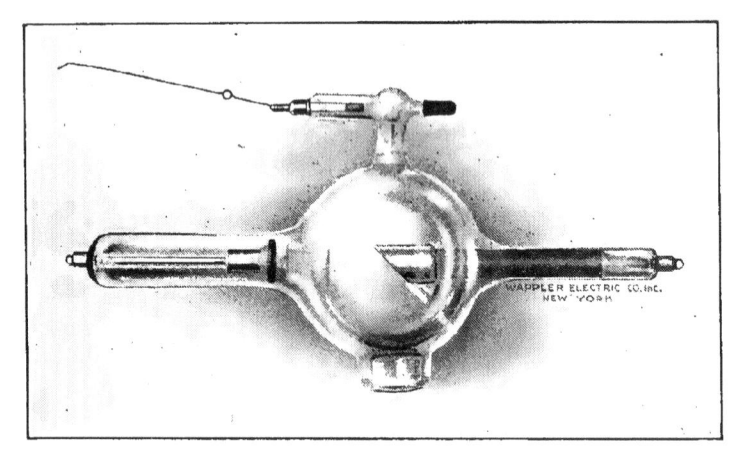

TUNGSTEN TARGET TUBE

previously described require special forms of Roentgen ray tubes. For the coils by virtue of their relatively small capacity, platinum target tubes are generally employed. The capacity of the interrupterless type being considerably higher, the use of a material of greater resistance as a target is necessitated. For this purpose tungsten is generally employed. For the high frequency, or Tesla coils, a tube which embodies a rectifying or valve action device is necessary.

The mechanism of the production of Roentgen rays can be described in the following way: the cathode, or negative terminal of the tube, consists of a hollow spherical surface of aluminum. When this electrode is attached to a negative potential, a stream of negative ions or cathode rays is projected perpendicular to the surface of the electrode. By reason of its curvature, the electrode is therefore focused to produce a converging beam of cathode rays, the area of which is smallest where, in the centre of the tube, the tungsten block or anticathode is placed.

According to whether the area selected for the location of the anticathode is small or large, the possibility to distinguish between fine, medium or broad focused tubes arises. The discharge from the negative electrode takes place, dependent upon conditions which give to the discharge either a high or a low velocity. If the velocity is high, the change from kinetic energy to Roentgen-ray energy will be greater than if the velocity of the cathode ray stream is decreased. In the latter case, the radiations will have less penetrating power. The velocity of the discharge must therefore depend upon the magnitude of the charge on the negative electrode, and also upon the number of gas particles present in the tube at that time. If there is a large quantity of gas present, there will be a reduction in the speed of the ray, due to collision and impact with the gas. The penetration of the Roentgen rays depends therefore directly upon the potential produced by the apparatus and inversely on the gas pressure (or directly on the vacuum) of the tube.

For the purpose of controlling the state of vacuum in the tube, a regulating system has been improvised which, when an electric current is passed through it, liberates a certain amount of gas which passes into the tube proper. This is a convenient device for reducing the vacuum of the tube. Up to the present time, no one has succeeded in inventing an efficient method or device for removing gas from the tube, or a means which would help to increase the vacuum. It is for that reason that operators should guard against reducing the tube unduly. It is a simple matter to reduce the vacuum but difficult to increase it. When a tube becomes low (when the gas content is high), resting the tube

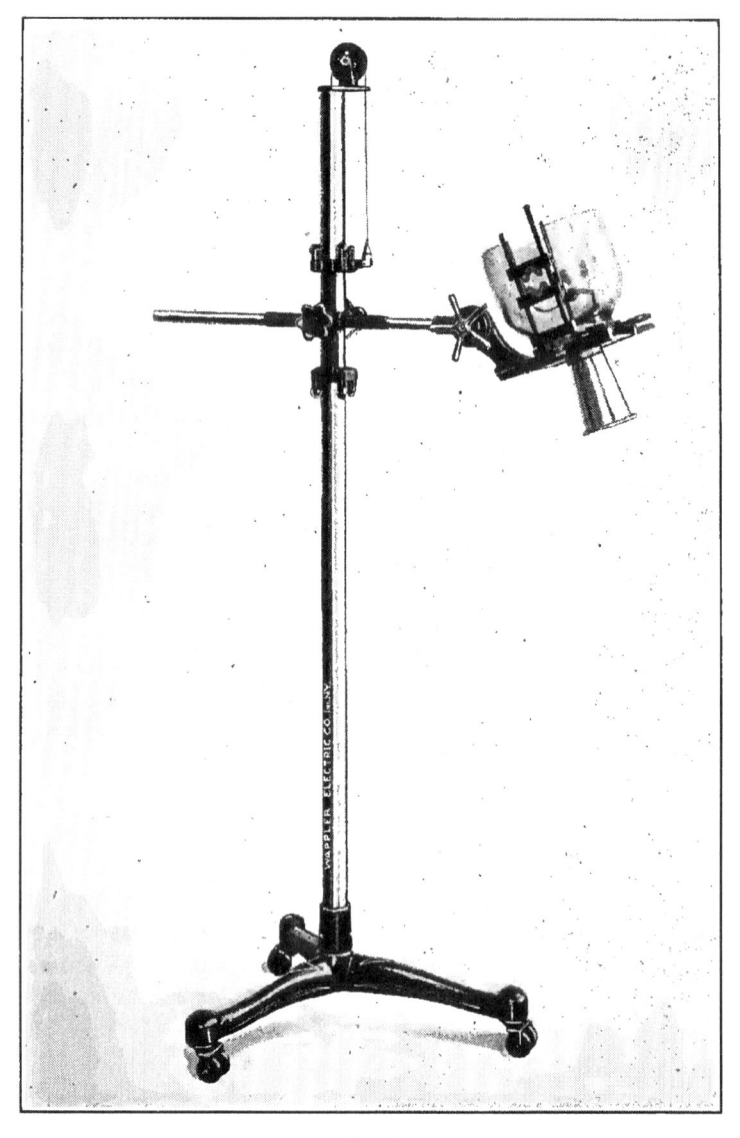

TUBE STAND

by allowing it to remain in its bracket for a period of time, will usually suffice to increase the vacuum.

The proper care of the tube is essential for good radiograms. It should be kept free from dust, and before being used the degree of vacuum should be determined by the testing apparatus on the generator. If the tube is dusty or dirty, the passage of the rays through the glass will be hampered, as these particles tend to deflect the rays from their straight course. If the vacuum of the tube is too high, it will affect the quality of the plate, and if it is too low there will be no penetration and therefore a blank plate

The Tube Stand. The tubes used in Roentgenology are delicate structures and great care must be exercised so as to prevent breakage. To guard against such damage it is necessary to securely hold the tube in a proper device while it is being used. The tube stand should be so arranged that it is possible to raise or lower the tube, with its connections, without being compelled to touch the tube itself, to swing it from side to side, to tilt it forward or backward, or in or out. This is best accomplished by the modern tube stand which is so arranged that after having set the tube in its proper place, it is no longer necessary to touch the apparatus in order to secure all of the above named motions. A careful study of the accompanying photograph will make this clear

The Roentgen or X-rays. The rays generated in the apparatus heretofore described, and named after their discoverer, are of a peculiar character, and although they have proven a boon to mankind, serious trouble and even death has come to those who in their ignorance used the X-rays promiscuously It has been discovered that there are three distinct rays generated when the high potential current is passed through the vacuum tube and they have been named after the first three letters of the Greek alphabet, namely the alpha, the beta and the gamma rays. The *alpha* ray is the ray that is seen in the tube and is of no consequence. The *beta* and *gamma* rays are invisible and it is these rays that penetrate the tissues of the body. To the gamma ray is attributed the harmful effects of Roentgen's discovery. Although the X-ray is used as a therapeutic measure it should only be applied by those who have a thorough knowledge of its properties Prolonged exposure will cause severe burns, and in some cases continued contact with the ray has caused cancer Their action in this respect is due to the actinic quality of the gamma rays. The symptoms of a burn do not manifest themselves until a minimum of a week or ten days after exposure and, when they do appear, they are usually severe. Sloughing of the tissues takes place, and the wounds produced do not heal readily and, in consequence, ugly disfiguring scars remain.

Radiography. This branch of Roentgenology is of most interest to the podiatrist By means of photographic plates, properly exposed and well developed, it is often possible to make diagnoses where other means have failed. It is essential for one who would be correct in diagnosing X-ray plates, to have a thorough knowledge of the structure of the bones of the foot and to understand the meaning of the various shadows cast upon the plate.

When the X-rays penetrate the foot they pass through the tissues, and when they strike a tissue of great density they cannot penetrate it as readily as the rays passing through a tissue of less density. The result is that as the rays pass through the foot they cast a series of shadows on the sensitized photographic plate beneath, the density of which depends upon the tissues through which the rays have passed So, in reality, the plate when finished is not a photograph, as most laymen imagine, but a shadowgraph or, as it is variously termed, a radiogram or skiagram.

For the purposes of producing radiographs that are clear and easily interpreted, it is necessary to have good materials and to follow the technic of developing and fixing the plate in every detail. The photographic plates used in general photography do not, as a rule, give satisfactory results. Plates, with specially prepared emulsions that are adapted for radiography, are preferred. These plates are sensitized with a gelatinous substance containing bromide of silver. When this substance is exposed to the action of the rays it undergoes chemical decomposition, the degree of which varies with the amount of exposure. It is upon this decomposition of the salt that the art of photography depends and so, too, the science of radiography. The plate is then developed.

Developing of a photographic plate consists of making visible the metallic silver which is produced by the decomposition of the silver bromide. This is accomplished by the use of a mixture of chemicals called the developer. The plate is put into a tray about two inches deep and large enough to allow for its easy removal, and the developing solution is poured over the emulsion. Gradually the exposed portions of the negative will appear and developing must continue until every such exposed part has been brought out in its fullest detail. The unexposed portions are then dissolved by placing the plate in a solution of sodium hyposulphite, sometimes called the *fixer* or the fixing bath. As its name implies, this solution permanently fixes the exposed silver, and if the plate were not treated in this manner the entire mass would become blackened upon exposure to light.

The preparation of radiographic plates is carried on in a room that is protected from light with the exception of a dull, red glow from a "ruby lamp" which has no effect upon the plate. The plate is placed into an envelope made of black paper, and this in turn is placed, flap down, into a second envelope of red paper. This insures protection from light rays when the plate is brought out of the dark room. After exposure, the negative must be taken back to the dark room before it is removed from the envelope. After it has been developed and fixed it may be brought into the light with safety.

The length of time required in making exposures varies with the different types of apparatus. When the flow of rays is great, it will require a proportionately shorter exposure. So, too, the length of exposure with a certain type of generator varies with the part being exposed. The bones of the fingers would require less time than those of the leg, while the bones of the head would require more time than either of the above for the production of a clear radiograph. It is essential in all branches of radiography to remember that the part to be skiagraphed be parallel to and in close proximity to the plate. This will prevent elongations and foreshortenings of the shadows cast.

DIAGNOSIS OF RADIOGRAPHS

There are several lesions of the foot commonly arising in the practice of the podiatrist, which are easily recognized by radiographic examination but which otherwise are difficult of diagnosis. Some of these cases are shown in the accompanying pictures, which were selected from a large collection at The First Institute of Podiatry of New York City. They are characteristic of the lesions they depict, and it is needless to emphasize their value as an aid to diagnosis. If a condition involves the bony structure of the foot, clinical symptoms are never so certain that an absolutely positive diagnosis can be made, but the X-ray plate readily reveals such disturbances so that there is no doubt left in the minds of the practitioner as to the exact nature of the trouble. Periostitis, exostosis, fractures, arthritis, bone abcesses, bone ulcers, etc., are thus easily distinguished.

Periostitis. Periostitis is an inflammation of the periosteum, the outer covering of the bone. There are two types, the acute and the chronic, both of which are not really diseases themselves, but are indications of the reaction of the periosteum to some irritant. In acute periostitis the X-ray plate shows a slight destruction of the outer portion of the bone, and a slight thickening of the periosteum, and if suppuration is present, the lesion is a mild osteomyelitis rather than a periostitis.

Chronic periostitis causes an increase in the osteogen-

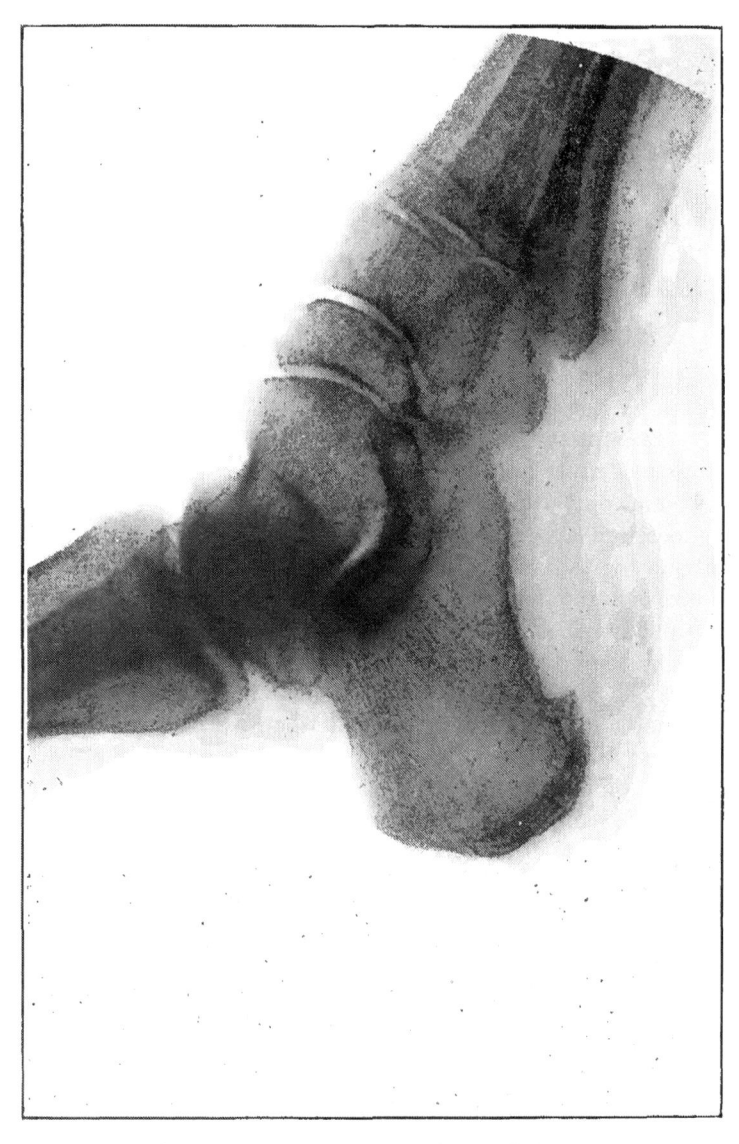

SPUR ON THE UNDER SURFACE OF THE HEEL

etic cells of the periosteum and is common in a great many lesions. Trauma, blows or contusions cause a chronic thickening of the bone-covering with additional bone formation, as do syphilis and superficial abscesses in the soft tissues, in the immediate vicinity of long bones Thus chronic ulcer of the leg over the shaft of the tibia will produce this condition. The picture shows that the even line of the bone surface is lost, and there is a rough, uneven edge, with or without an increase in the bone cells. The entire shaft of the bone is often thicker than normal, especially in the metatarsals, and it is quite common to find one of these bones greatly increased in size. The fourth metatarsal is the one most usually affected.

Exostosis. This lesion is common in the foot, and is a source of great pain and annoyance. It is usually the result of a chronic bursitis which has affected the periosteum over a localized area. Due to the destructive changes brought about by the inflammatory processes, the periosteum is absorbed and the bone cells beneath protrude in the form of a spur which shows on the plate. The most common site of exostosis of the foot is on the inferior surface of the os calcis, under the calcaneo bursa. The part is somewhat swollen and is extremely painful when pressure is brought to bear directly over the growth. The heads of the metatarsal bones on their lateral surfaces are occasionally affected, especially the outer side of the head of the first metatarsal. Lateral pressure gives rise to pain in this type of exostosis. The treatment for all exostoses is purely surgical

Fractures. There are several kinds of fracture, and they are classified variously, but for the purposes of the podiatrist, the following types, with the description of each, will prove sufficient:

Incomplete Fractures, among which are the greenstick and the fissured fractures, are those in which there is not a complete separation of the fragments The greenstick is really a bending rather than a breaking of the bone, and is found mostly in children under fifteen and then only rarely affects the bones of the leg. Fissured fractures are splits or cracks in the bone which do not separate it into two parts and occur occasionally in the fibula or in the metatarsals. They are easily seen in the radiograph by the dark shadow they produce in the region that would ordinarily appear light. This shadow extends over the entire length of the break.

Complete Fractures are the most common type found in the lower extremity and are divided according to the line and the seat of the breach of continuity. Thus we have transverse, longitudinal, oblique and spiral fractures. The radiograph will reveal the nature of the break, and a dark shadow will be cast between the fragments of bone. The most common of these found in the leg are the oblique and the spiral fractures.

Comminuted Fractures are those in which there is extensive splintering of the bone adjoining the fracture or one of the fragments. This class of fracture does not occur in the foot.

Impacted Fractures are those in which the fragments are driven into each other, forming a wedge, thus preventing abnormal motion, so common in other types. This occurs mostly in the neck of the femur.

Crushing or Compression Fractures are those in which the bones are crushed. The spongy portion and the cortical layer are both involved and in some cases the bones may be pulpified. The tarsal bones are subject to this type of fractures as the result of falls from heights, upon the soles of the feet. (See accompanying picture of fracture of the os calcis.)

A simple fracture is one in which a wound of the skin is absent, or if present, there is no connection between it and the broken bone.

If the bone is broken in two or more places or if two or more non-adjacent bones are simultaneously broken, the condition is called a **multiple fracture.**

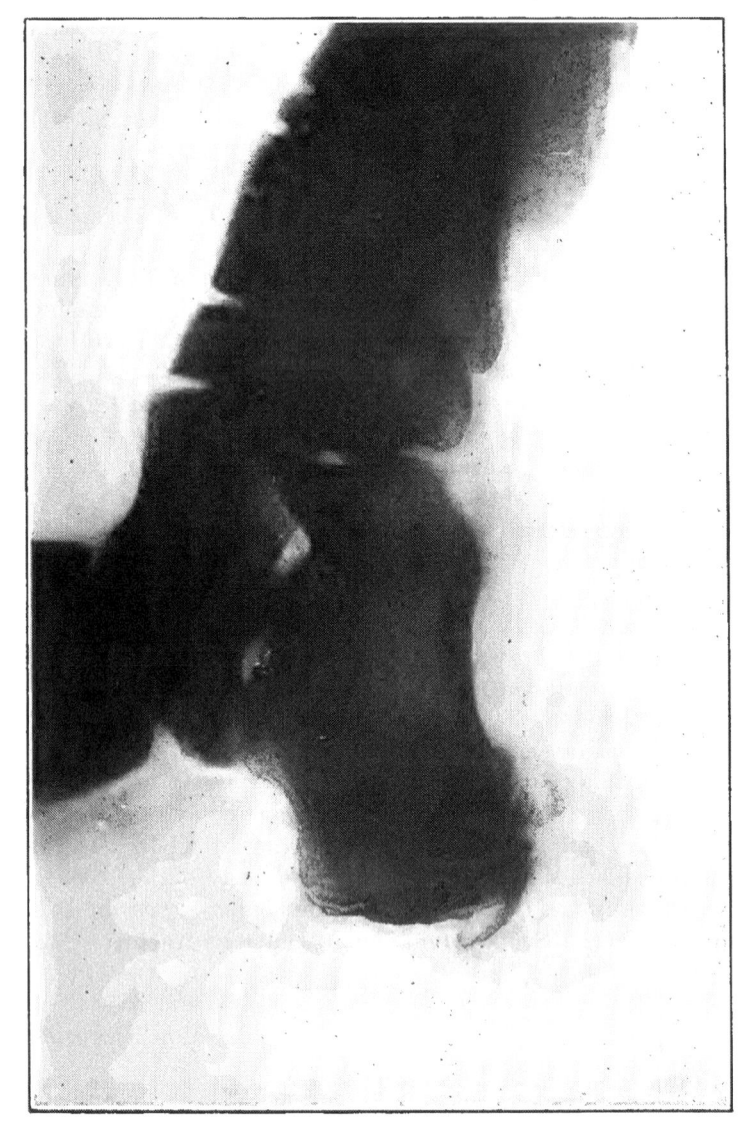

FRACTURE OF THE OS CALCIS

A compound fracture is one in which the fragments of bone pierce the soft tissues and protrude beyond the skin

It is essential in examining a patient who has suffered from a recent fracture, to obtain a history of the case as well as a description of the accident An examination of the part should be made, and the various symptoms such as deformity, abnormal mobility and crepitus should be noted The X-ray picture is then taken and if a fracture is found, the case should be put in the hands of a competent surgeon for immediate and proper treatment.

Sesamoid Bones. The sesamoid bones which are found in the flexor tendons under the head of the first metatarsal bones, are subjected to injury in those who follow vocations in which the ball of the foot is put to great strains Among such may be mentioned dancers and acrobats The normal position of these bones is directly beneath the head of the first metatarsal bone, and when this part is put to a great strain, the bones may become fractured, or they may become displaced The outer sesamoid is usually forced outward and the X-ray picture shows it in the first interosseous space. The inner sesamoid is not affected, but may also be forced outward, and is then found under the outer side of the first metatarsal, in the normal position of the outer sesamoid bone.

Fracture of these bones is not unusual and is a result of a severe injury The line of division is shown by a dark shadow, much the same as in other fractures. One or both of the bones may be involved. It is essential to remember that if the bone is broken, the opposite sides will fit into each other perfectly, whereas, in cases of a freakish nature, in which there are four sesamoid bones, this will not be the case.

Arthritis. Arthritis, or inflammation of the joints, may involve any one or all of the structures which make up joints, viz bone, cartilage, ligaments, synovial membrane and fibro cartilage. The acute forms of inflammation are not detected by the radiogram, but the chronic type leaves

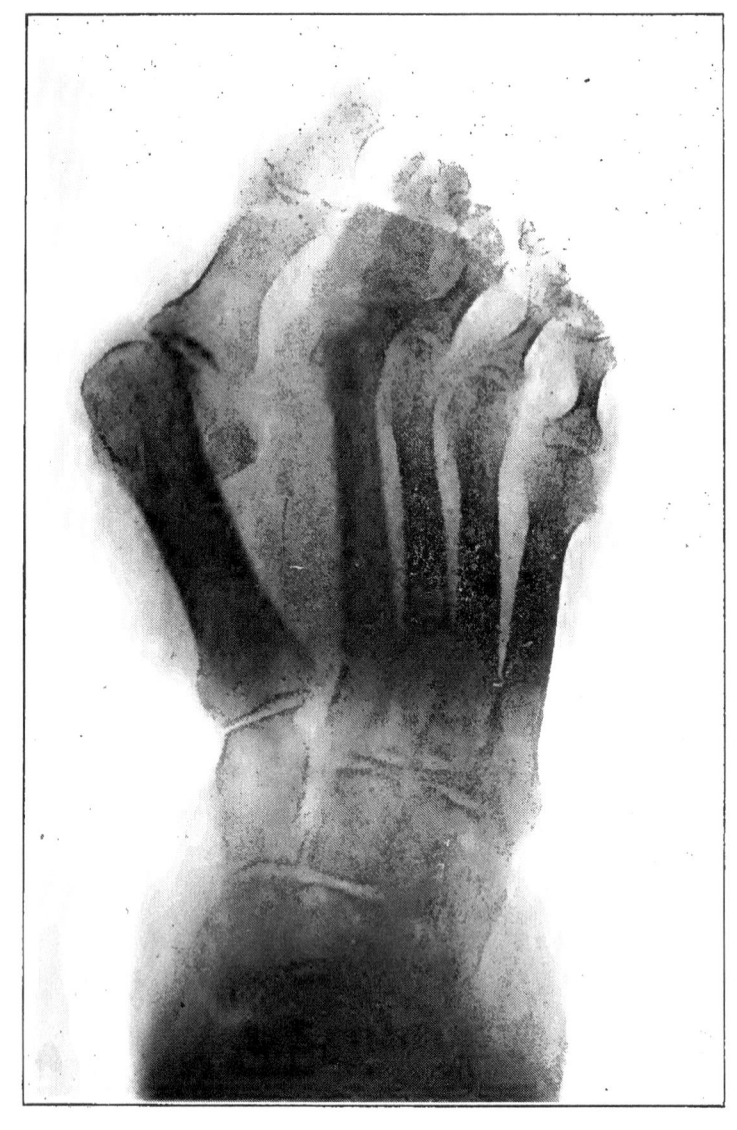

HALLUX VALGUS

its characteristic marks which, when present, are easily seen. The synovial covering of the ends of the bones is destroyed, and shows a rough, uneven surface In cases of long standing, there is complete bony ankylosis, and the shadows of the joint line are completely obliterated. This is particularly true in the tarsal joints, in which the joint lines between the bones can hardly be seen. There is no motion in such joints, and in milder cases, in which no union has occurred, the sensation of crepitus is conveyed to the hand if the joints are moved passively. Tubercular arthritis shows a rarification of the bone with a thickening of the periosteum.

Arteriosclerosis, or hardening of the arteries, is often detected by means of the X-ray picture. Light shadows cast in the normal dark shade produced by the soft tissues, which appear over the course of the arteries, are indications of this condition.

This disease of the arteries causes a change in the vessels whereby there are calcareous salts deposited in the middle coat These salts, containing the metal calcium, are not readily penetrated by the ray, and thus a difference between the artery and other soft tissues is established.

There are many other conditions in which the X-rays are a valuable aid in making diagnosis, but these are of no interest to the podiatrist, being within the exclusive province of the physician and surgeon. The reader is referred to books which deal with the subject of Roentgenology exclusively, for further information upon the subject.

CHAPTER XXVI

THE PODIATRIST'S OFFICE

The equipment of an office of a professional man or woman, whether it be the surgeon, the dentist, the podiatrist or any other of the practitioners of the allied branches of medicine, cannot be set to an absolute standard. There are several factors that govern variations, one from the other, among which are considerations of finance and the amount of available space. Regardless of these differences, however, certain fundamental principles must be observed in equipping such an office, and these depend upon two cardinal requirements. (1) cleanliness, and (2) the comfort of the patient Such an office must be fitted out with the laws of asepsis and antisepsis ever in mind, otherwise it will prove unsafe for the treatment of patients whose feet require surgical attention. Again, the patient must feel at ease while being treated, or revisits will be scarce.

There are other and secondary standards which should be considered among which is the appeal to the eye First impressions often are lasting ones, and an office which makes a favorable impression will help attract patients. One often hears the thoughtless layman express himself, "Go to Dr. Blank for treatment, he has a beautiful office." So it often occurs that a professional person is judged by the equipment in his office, and the effects of such an impression should be considered.

The Waiting Room. The waiting or reception room should be furnished with chairs upholstered in leather or made of solid wood In waiting rooms in which many patients must wait at the same time, and space is valuable, smaller chairs with cane seats are very useful. The table should be of polished wood, covered with a plate glass top. The wood work of the room itself should be white, and the walls should be painted in preference to being papered. Buff is a pleasing color to the eye, and readily matches all kinds of furniture. The floor should be of hard wood, and may be covered by linoleum or rugs. Carpets should not be tolerated, as they are dirty; and even though frequently swept, they become the repositories of dust and of germs.

The Operating Room. The operating room must be scrupulously clean As a white background best shows dirt spots, that should prevail in furniture and in decorations A door, either of glass and wood or entirely of wood, should separate the reception room and the operating room, if hangings must be used, they should be of some washable, white material, that can be readily changed. The floor should be of tile, marble or stone; if these materials are not available, hard wood floors, well polished, are permissible No covering of any kind should be used for the floor of this room. The ceilings and walls should be painted white, and the wood work should be enameled the same color. Tile or marble walls are preferable to plaster or wood No curtains should be used on windows or doors, and if necessary the glass can be frosted to secure privacy. A wash basin, with running hot and cold water, should be in the operating room, and the valves should be controlled by foot levers in preference to hand faucets.

To summarize, everything in the operating room should be of such a character as to make it possible to wash it daily with soap and water. Nooks and corners that tend to collect dust and dirt must be thoroughly cleaned, bearing in mind that disease-producing bacteria will not grow, unless a breeding place be provided for them. Wall pictures and their frames should be selected with a view to having them equally sanitary.

The Equipment. The equipment of a modern office is divided into three classes: (1) the furniture, which, when bought, is permanent, (2) the instruments; and (3) the supplies, which are replenished from time to time as they are exhausted.

Furniture should consist of the following in the order of their importance:

> Sterilizer
> Operating Chair and Stool
> Cabinet
> Glass-Top Table
> Drill
> High Frequency Machine
> Air Compressor
> Galvanic Machine
> Wall Cabinet and Extra Accessories

The authors are not interested in the wares of any manufacturer, and any equipment that is efficient and well made will answer the purposes of the podiatrist. There are many styles of chairs, cabinets, electric machines, etc., on the market and the selection of such furniture and equipment rests with the finances and the taste of the individual.

Chairs should be roomy and have a suitable rest for the patient's back and head. The foot rest should be adjustable and so arranged that the patient's foot is made comfortable, regardless of the position in which it is held. This part of the chair is very important, as upon it often depends the result of the podiatrist's work. If the foot and leg are held so that the patient is uncomfortable or so that muscular cramps are the result, both patient and operator are at a disadvantage which it is difficult to overcome.

There are two types of foot-rests on the market which have proven efficient. One gives support along the entire length of the leg and allows the foot to hang free at the end, and the other gives support at the foot proper and is so arranged that it gives this support no matter in what position the foot be held. The chair itself should be so constructed that no matter how the weight of the patient's body may be distributed, the chair will remain firm, with no danger of spilling its occupant. It is on this account that a chair with a heavy metal base or with heavy spreading legs is best. When the chair is placed in a horizontal position so that the patient is prone, it should be as firm as with the patient in a sitting posture. The stool should match the chair and should be adjustable.

The cabinet is the most important part of the podiatrist's equipment from an aseptic standpoint, for therein are kept the instruments, dressings, drugs, etc. There are many styles and shapes from which to select, but only those that afford proper protection from dust and dirt should be considered. Drawers should be provided for bandages and dressings, and one drawer should be divided into compartments for the various sized shields. This adds to the neatness as well as to the efficiency of the cabinet. Special movable racks which fit into shallow drawers should be provided for the instruments, so that, if necessary, they may be collectively removed, thus avoiding the need for handling each instrument separately. Instrument compartments of this type should be so made that the blades of the various instruments are suspended in the air; moreover such racks and drawers are easily cleaned. Drugs should be kept in special compartments provided with glass doors, or, if the cabinet has no such provision, the bottles should fit in metallic clamps arranged in the rear of the top of the cabinet. Glass tops on the cabinets are best for they are easily cleaned, but white enameled metal tops are quite as good. The towels should be kept in a compartment of the sterilizer, otherwise in a special compartment in the cabinet, one having a glass door being preferred.

Sterilizers may be heated by gas or electricity and when boiling water is not available, even formaldehyde gas is better than nothing for sterilizing purposes. The sterilizer, a necessity and not an ornament, should be cleaned and polished and the water should be changed daily. Unfortunately in the past, practitioners of podiatry did not use the sterilizer with regularity, and one could enter many of these offices and not even find such a contrivance. This state of affairs, however, is becoming a memory because the practitioner, as well as the public, has learned the importance of asepsis and antisepsis. The podiatrist who fails to observe the needs of this dispensation is unworthy of the title he bears.

The sterilizer should be kept on a white enameled table with a detachable metal top, so that boiling water or hot instruments will cause no damage to it, as might occur on a glass-topped table. This table should have a glass shelf below, on which may be kept additional remedial agents for which there is no room in the cabinet.

The surgical drill or rotary file is a valuable asset to the podiatrist in treating the nails, and should be a part of the equipment There are several makes of rotary files, all with the same fundamental structure. The motors and cables are of one type, and are held either by a wall bracket or suspended upon a metal hook, resting on a metal pedestal. When the instrument is kept in only one operating room, the former type is sufficient, but when the drill is moved from one room to another, the latter style is necessary.

Other accessories in the office, such as an air compressor, high frequency coil, galvanic machine, wall cabinet, etc, should be selected with care as to quality, and with judgment as to their harmonizing with the other equipment. If space allows, all of these accessories are desirable because useful, but when quarters are contracted, care must be taken in arranging the paraphernalia that the effect is not such as to give the patient the impression that he is in a podiatry supply shop.

"Cleanliness is next to Godliness," should be the slogan of every practitioner of medicine in any and in all of its collateral branches and the manner in which he conducts his office should be evidence that such is the belief and the practice of every podiatrist.

GLOSSARY

A

a-, an. A prefix conveying a negative meaning—without, not, away from
aa A sign used in prescription writing to indicate equal parts of each ingredient so designated
ab. A prefix signifying from, away from off
abdominal Relating to the abdomen or belly
abduction. Rotation of the foot outward
abnormal Not normal, contrary to the rule or type, irregular
aboriginal. Primitive, existing from the beginning.
abrasion A circumscribed removal of the epidermis of skin or mucous membrane
abscess. A circumscribed cavity in the tissues containing pus
absorption The taking into the tissues, through the medium of the lymphatics or blood vessels, of any material in suitable form
acetanilid An analgesic made from aniline by treating it with acetyl chloride
acetic Relating to vinegar, acid
acid A chemical compound containing replacible hydrogen having a sour taste, and neutralizing a base to form a salt and water
acidum Acid
  a. Aceticum, acetic acid useful as a counterirritant
  a. aceticum glaciale, glacial acetic acid, employed externally as a caustic
  a. boricum, boric acid, dusting powder, antiseptic
  a. carbolicum, carbolic acid, phenol, antiseptic
  a. chromicum, chromic acid, caustic
  a. dichloraceticum, dichloracetic acid; caustic
  a. hydrochloricum, hydrochloric acid, escharotic
  a. iodicum, a white crystalline powder, antiseptic and deodorant
  a. monochloraceticum, a white deliquescent powder, caustic
  a. nitricum, nitric acid, caustic
  a. nitricum fumans fuming nitric acid, caustic
  a. nitrohydrochloricum, a fusing corrosive liquid, caustic
  a. salicylicum, salicylic acid, disintegrant
  a. sulphocarbolicum, sozolic acid, antiseptic and disinfectant
  a sulphuricum, sulphuric acid, oil of vitriol, caustic
  a tannicicum, tannic acid astringent
  a. trichloraceticum, trichloracetic acid caustic
acquired Noting a disease which is not congenital but has taken possession of one at some period after birth.
actinic. Relating to chemically active rays
actinotherapy. The treatment of disease by radiant energy
acute. Of short and sharp duration, not chronic, said of a disease
adduction. Rotation of the foot inward
adhesive. Sticky, causing adhesion
adipose. Fatty, relating to fat
adjacent. Next to, along side of
adjuvants. Agents added to a prescription to assist or increase the action of the main ingredient
adolescents. Youths, those between the ages of puberty and the attainment of full growth
adrenalin. A principle obtained from the suprarenal glands having marked astringent and hemostatic powers
agar. A gelatinous substance prepared from seaweed, and used as a base for culture media
agent. Anything which produces an effect upon the organism
agnail Hangnail, whitlow
albumin A protein contained in the tissues of plants and animals
albuminous. Containing or consisting of albumin
albuminuria. The presence of albumin in the urine as voided
alcohol. One of a series of organic compounds especially one whose formula is C_2H_5OH and called ethyl alcohol
algia. A suffix indicating pain (Exam metatarsalgia—pain in the metatarsals)
alignment Alinement, the act of bringing into line
alkaline Relating to an alkali, having the reaction of an alkali
alkaloid A basic substance found in plants, usually constituting the active principle of the crude drug
alum A double sulphate of aluminum, **burnt a.** alumen exsiccatum
aluminum chloride. A substance used as an astringent in hyperidrosis and bromidrosis
alvpin. A crystalline powder used as a local anesthetic
ammoniated mercury See ungent, hydrarg, amm
ampere. The unit of strength of an electric current
amyotrophic lateral sclerosis A form of progressive muscular atrophy with increased reflexes due to hardening of the lateral columns of the spinal cord
anaerobe A microorganism which thrives best or only when deprived of oxygen
analgesic An agent which causes analgesia or freedom from pain
anastomose To open one into the other directly or by connecting channels, said of blood vessels and nerves
anatomy The science devoted to the study of the structure of organized bodies, more especially the human body

anemia A condition in which the blood is reduced in amount, or is deficient in red blood cells or in hemoglobin
anesthesia Loss of sensation, especially of tactile sensibility
anesthetic. 1 Insensible to touch or to pain or to other stimuli 2 A drug which produces local or general anesthesia
anesthetize To induce anesthesia, to render anesthetic
aneurism. A blood-containing tumor connecting directly with the lumen of an artery
angioma A swelling or tumor due to dilatation of a blood vessel
ankylosis. Stiffening or fixation of a joint
anterior In front of, or, in the front part of
anterior poliomyelitis. Inflammation of the anterior horns of the spine, infantile spinal paralysis
antheloticum or remedium heloticum Remedy for helomata
anti A prefix signifying against opposing (Exam antifebrile — against fever)
anticathode The platinum or other plate in a Crookes tube on which the cathode rays impinge giving origin to the X-rays
antiphlogistic An agent which subdues or allays inflammation
antisepsis The destruction of germs causing disease, fermentation or putrefaction
antiseptic 1 Destructive to the germs of disease fermentation or putrefaction 2 A substance which prevents the action of the germs of fermentation, decomposition, or disease
aperture An opening orifice
apex. The summit or tip
apodal Without feet
apodia Congenital absence of feet
apoplectic Relating to, predisposed to or suffering from apoplexy
apoplexy A sudden loss of consciousness followed by paralysis, due to cerebral hemorrhage or blocking of an artery of the brain.
apothesine A synthetic product used to produce local anesthesia, which came into popular favor at a time when the usually employed local anesthetics were unobtainable because of war conditions
apparatus A collection of instruments adapted for a special purpose
appendage Any part, subordinate in size, attached to a main structure
appendicitis. Inflammation of the vermiform appendix
applicator A slender rod of wood or metal by means of which with cotton, local applications may be made to a part
apus. A monster without feet
aqua Water
aqua cinnamomi. Cinnamon water
aqua fortis Nitric acid, see acidum nitricum
aqueous Watery
arch. In anatomy, any vaulted or archlike structure
argentum The metal, silver
aristol Trade name of thymol iodide, a local antiseptic

armamentarium In podiatry all the means (drugs, instruments, etc) at the disposal of the podiatrist to fit him for the practice of his profession
arsenic A steel-gray metal, one of the elements, arsenic trioxide, white arsenic
arteria Artery, a blood vessel conveying blood away from the heart
arteries of the foot
  a communicans, communicating branch of dorsalis pedis (to plantar surface to join plantar arch)
  a digitales dorsales, digital branches of dorsalis pedis (dorsal surface of the toes)
  a dorsalis pedis, dorsalis pedis artery (dorsum of foot)
  a metatarsae dorsales, metatarsal branch of dorsalis pedis (dorsum of foot to metatarsus)
  a. plantaris lateralis, external plantar artery (plantar surface, joining communicating branch of dorsalis pedis completing the plantar arch)
  a plantaris medialis, internal plantar artery (plantar surface of foot)
  a. tarsae lateralis tarsal branch of dorsalis pedis (dorsum of foot to the tarsus)
arteriosclerosis. Hardening of the arteries
areolar. A tissue made up of loose connective tissue with many interspaces and found under the skin
arsenical Relating to or containing any of the salts of arsenic
arthritis Inflammation of the joints
articulation A joining or connecting together loosely so as to allow of motion between the parts
articular Relating to a joint
ascites An accumulation of serous fluid in the peritoneal cavity
asepsis. A condition in which living bacteria are absent
astasia abasia. Inability through muscular incoordination, to walk or stand, although the muscles functionate normally when the patient is lying down
astragalus. The ankle bone
astringent An agent which causes contraction of the tissues or arrest of the secretions
ataxia A loss of the power of muscular coordination
ataxic. Relating to ataxia
atony Lack of tone or tension
atrophy. A wasting of the tissues of a part or of the entire body
atypical Not typical
auto. A prefix denoting self (Exam autogenesis—self-production)
auto-serotherapic Relating to the treatment of certain conditions by the injection of the patient's own bloodserum
axilla The armpit (pl axillae)
axis A straight line passing through a spherical body between its two poles and about which the body may revolve

B

bacillus A bacterium more especially, a rod-shaped or elongated variety
bacillus aërogenes capsulatis. The specific organism causing gas infection and gas gangrene b of Welch, the same, b perfringens, the same

bacteria Unicellular vegetable microorganisms, usually those which produce disease
bactericidal. Causing the death of bacteria
bacterium fetidum A microorganism producing a stench **b prodigiosus** A microorganism found on food, but not pathogenic
bandage A piece of cloth or other material applied to any part of the body, to make compression, prevent motion and to retain surgical dressings
base. The lower part or bottom In pharmacy, the chief ingredient of a compound In chemistry, a compound which neutralizes an acid to form a salt
belladonna. Deadly nightshade A perennial herb the leaves and roots of which are used in medicine
beneficent. The disposition to do good; of help to
benign Mild in character, said of an illness, not malignant
benzine. A purified distillate of American petroleum
beriberi Endemic neuritis, a specific polyneuritis occurring in eastern and southern Asia It prevails especially in armies, prisons, ships etc, wherever large numbers of men are kept together
bi A prefix denoting two twice or double (Exam bicuspid—having two prongs)
bichloride of mercury A chemical compound, HgCl$_2$, called corrosive sublimate and mercuric chloride It is used as an antiseptic
bifid. Split or cleft bilateral Having two sides, biped Two-footed
bismuth subgallate A yellowish dusting powder, trade name, dermatol
bismuth subnitrate. A white dusting powder with astringent properties
bistoury. A long, narrow-bladed knife straight or curved on the edge, sharp or blunt pointed, employed for opening abcesses, slitting up sinuses, etc
bleb. A circumscribed area of separation of the epidermis due to the presence of a clear non-purulent fluid
blister. A bleb
blood Sanguis cruor; the red fluid circulating in the arteries, capillaries and veins **b plasma,** the fluid portion of the blood as it is contained in the vessels **b serum,** the fluid which is squeezed out by shrinkage of a blood-clot
bones. The hard substances that make up the framework of the body
bones of the foot
  astragalus Ankle bone
  cuboid In front of the os calcis
  internal, middle and external cuneiforms In front of the scaphoid
  metatarsals Five, in front of the tarsal bones
  os calcis Heel bone
  phalanges Fourteen, in front of the metatarsals, two in the great toe and three in each of the four lesser toes
  scaphoid In front of the astragalus
boric acid A powder, soluble in water used as an antiseptic dusting powder
bromidrosis Foul-smelling perspiration

buckskin A leather made from the skin of the buck
buffing. Polishing by means of some soft material, attached to a rapidly revolving motor
bulb Any globular or fusiform structure
bulbar palsy. Paralysis of the tongue and larynx
bulla A bleb
bullous Relating to or of the nature of bullae
bunion An inflammatory swelling of the bursa over the metatarsophalangeal joint of the great toe
bur A small disc or bulb, made to revolve rapidly and used by podiatrists in connection with their employment of the rotary drill, or file
Burow's solution. A solution of alum and lead acetate
bursa (plural, bursae) A closed sac or pouch containing synovial fluid found over joints and where tendons play over bones
bursitis. Inflammation of a bursa.

C

caisson disease. The bends, divers paralysis, tunnel disease, a symptom-complex, occurring in tunnel workers and others working in places under high air pressure when they return too suddenly to the normal atmosphere
calamine Zinc carbonate, a pink powder used as an astringent
calcaneoastragaloid Relating to the os calcis and the astragalus
calcareous Chalky
calcified Hardened by the deposition of lime salts in a part
calcium. A metallic element having a yellow color
calibre. The diameter of a canal or vessel
callositas. Callous, tyloma, a circumscribed thickening of the epidermic layers of the skin
callous Collositas
callus Callosity The bone-like substance thrown out between and around the ends of a fractured bone
calomel Hydrargyrum chloride mite
calor. Heat
camphorated soap liniment. Soap liniment, camphorated tincture of soap
capillary One of the microscopic blood vessels forming the capillary system, intermediate between the arteries and the veins
capsicum The dried fruit of Cayenne, African or red pepper
capsule. A membranous structure enveloping an organ or any other part
carbolic acid. Phenol
carbon An element, occurring in the form of the diamond, graphite and coal
carbon dioxide pencil A mass of solidified carbon dioxide used for the destruction of verruca etc
carborundum. A very hard substance (carbide of silicon) used to sharpen instruments
caries. Molecular decay of a bone
carpal Relating to the wrist
carpus The wrist
cartilage A connective tissue substance

cashmere A woolen fabric made from goat hair
cast An object formed by the solidification of a liquid poured into a mold
castor oil Oleum ricini, a fixed oil from the seeds of Ricinus communis
catalepsy A morbid state in which there is rigidity of the limbs
cataplasma A poultice, a soft magma or mush, prepared by wetting or heating various powders or other absorbent substances
catatonia. Stupor
cathode The negative pole of an electric current
caustic. Corrosive
cautery. An agent used for scarring or burning the skin or tissues by means of heat or of caustic chemicals
c c Abbreviation for cubic centimeter
cell. A minute structure, the living active basis of all plant and animal organization, composed of a mass of protoplasm and containing a nucleus
cellulitis Inflammation of the cellular or connective tissue
centigrade scale A thermometer scale in which there are 100 degrees between the freezing point and the boiling point of water
centimeter The hundreth part of a meter or 3937 (2/5) of an inch
cerate (Lat ceratum) An unctuous solid preparation, containing sufficient wax to prevent it from liquefying when applied to the skin
cerebellar. Relating to the cerebellum or hind-brain
cerebral. Referring to the brain
cerebral cortex The external layer of gray matter covering the hemispheres of the brain
cerebral hemisphere The large mass of brain substance on either side of the great longitudinal fissure
cerebrospinal Relating to the brain and the spinal cord
cerebrospinal meningitis An acute infectious inflammation of the brain and spinal cord caused by the meningococcus
chamois. The skin of the goat family, prepared for purposes of utility
chancre. The initial sore of syphilis
characteristics The traits which mark a substance or condition, and differentiate it from others
Charcot's disease Amyotrophic lateral sclerosis
chauffeur's foot A painful condition of the anterior part of the foot
chilblain. An inflammation of the skin due to exposure to cold and dampness
chimatlon Chilblains an inflammation of the skin due to exposure to cold and dampness
chiropodical Relating to chiropody (podiatry)
chiropodist One who treats the minor lesions of the foot Originally probably, chirurg-podist, a surgeon of the foot
chiropody The study of the minor lesions of the foot Podiatry
chisel The podiatrist's instrument, helotomon
chlorine An element in nature, an irritating, greenish, gaseous element used for disinfectant and bleaching purposes
cholesterin A monatomic alcohol
chorea. A disorder of childhood characterized by spasmodic, involuntary movements of the limbs and facial muscles, St Vitus' dance
chromidrosis A disease of the sweat glands in which the perspiration is colored
chromium A very hard steel-gray element
chronic. Of long duration, noting a disease of slow progress and long continuance
cicatricial Referring to scars or scar tissue
cicatrix. A scar.
circinate. Circular, ring-shaped
circum A prefix denoting a circular movement (Exam circumcision—to cut around)
circumduction. Movement of a part in a circular direction
circumscribed A definitely limited area
claudication. Limping
claw-foot Muscular atrophy with caval contraction of the foot
clavus Heloma, corn
clinic An institution in which medical attention is given to patients who live elsewhere and do not require hospital care
clonic. Marked by alternate contraction and relaxation of muscle
clot Coagulated blood
club-foot Talipes
coagulation Clotting, the process of changing from a liquid state to that of a soft, jelly-like solid
coalesce To grow together, to become one
coaptation The joining together of two surfaces, as in sewing up a wound or setting a fracture
cocaine An alkaloid derived from coca and used for producing local anesthesia
cocoon dressing A dressing made of absorbent cotton covered with collodion
cohesion The power of attraction between the molecules of any substance, keeping the mass from falling apart
collateral Secondary or subordinate
collodial Glue-like A substance which remains permanently suspended in a liquid but does not dissolve
collodion (Collodium) A solution of gun cotton in ether and alcohol
coma A state of profound unconsciousness from which one cannot be roused
comatose A state of coma
comminuted Broken into a number of fragments as in a multiple fractured bone
compound Not simple but made up of two or more parts In chemistry, a substance formed by the chemical union of two or more elements
compress A pad of gauze or other material placed over a part to make compression
concave A surface which is evenly curved inward
concentrated Referring to a solution which has been made strong by evaporation or other means
concentric Having a common centre
concomitant. Accompanying, occurring at the same time
concrete Hardened, solidified into a mass

GLOSSARY

condyle. A rounded articular surface at the extremity of a long bone
configuration External form
congelation Freezing
congenital Existing at birth
congestion The presence of an abnormal amount of blood in the vessels of a part
connective Binding, joining
c tissue The general supporting or uniting tissue of the body
constitutional. Relating to the system as a whole, not local
contact. The touching or apposition of two bodies
contagion Transmission of an infectious disease
contamination Pollution, soiling with infectious matter
continuity. Without a break, absence of interruption
contour. The outline of a part, the surface configuration
contra. A prefix signifying against or opposite (Exam contra-lateral—relating to the other side)
contraindicated Not indicated, as in the purposed use of a remedy or in the consideration of a surgical procedure
contract To shorten
contracture. A permanent muscular contraction, due to tonic spasm or to loss of muscular equilibrium, the antagonists being paralyzed
contused. Bruised
convex A surface which is evenly curved outward
coordination The harmonious working together of several muscles or groups of muscles
core The central mass of necrotic tissue in a boil
corium Cutis vera, true skin, the deeper or connective tissue layers of the skin
corn Heloma, an overgrowth of the epidermic layers of the skin containing a radix, or nucleus
cornification. Conversion into a horny substance
corpuscle A primary atom
corrode. To wear away gradually
corrosive sublimate. Bichloride of mercury
cortex The outer portion of an organ
cosmetic Relating to the care of a person with a view to improving the appearance
cotton The white fluffy fibrous covering of the seeds of the plant, genus gossypium used in surgical dressings
counterextension The resistance or back-pull, made to extension on a limb
counterirritant An agent which causes counterirritation
counterirritation Inflammation or irritation of the skin excited for the purpose of relieving an inflammation of the deeper structures
coup de fouet Rupture of the plantaris muscle, lawn tennis leg
c. p. Abbreviation for chemically pure
cramp. A painful tonic muscular contraction, spasm
creosote A substance obtained from beechwood tar

crepitus The sensation (a crackling) felt when the hands are placed over the seat of a fracture, and the broken ends of the bones are moved against each other
cretinism A disease occurring in the first three years of life and resulting in the arrest of bodily growth and of mental development
crinoline A stiff material with a coarser mesh, and heavier than gauze or cheese-cloth
criss-cross Referring to plaster applied to a part each strip when applied being at an angle to the strip previously applied
Crookes tube. See Chapter "X-rays in Podiatry"
croupous. Marked by a fibrinous exudation
crural Relating to the leg or thigh
crystalline Clear, transparent
cuboid A bone of the tarsus
cuneiform Three bones of the tarsus
curettage Scraping the interior of a cavity for the removal of the abnormal tissues with the curette
cutaneous Relating to the skin
cuticle. Epidermis or outer horny layer of the skin
cutis. The skin
cylinder A geometric figure formed by the revolution of a rectangle around one of its sides
cylindrical Relating to or the shape of a cylinder
cyst An abnormal sac containing gas fluid or a semi-solid material
cytoplasm Protoplasm, the substance of the cell, exclusive of the nucleus It is composed of spongioplasm and hyaloplasm

D

D Abbreviation in prescription writing for da, give detur, let there be given
dactyl A finger or toe
Dakin Solution. A solution compounded by Dr Dakin for the treatment of wounds by means of chlorine gas in solution, applied directly to the parts affected or injured
dancer's foot A painful condition of the great toe joint
decay Slow destruction of an organic substance
debris Fragments, broken rubbish
deformity. A deviation from the normal shape or size, resulting in disfigurement
degeneration. Deterioration, sinking from a higher to a lower level of a type
dehydrating Losing water, being deprived of water
deliquesce To become damp or liquid by absorbing water from the atmosphere
delirium A condition of extreme mental excitement, marked by confused ideas
demarcation. A setting of limits determining a boundary Line of d, a zone of inflammatory reaction separating a gangrenous area from healthy tissue
dementia paralytica General paresis, or paralysis, of the Insane
denuded Deprived of a covering, bared

deodorant. An agent which destroys odors, especially disagreeable odors
depressed. Flattened from above downward, as in fractures of that type
derma The connective tissue layer of the skin, the true skin
dermatalgia. Skin pain
dermatitis Inflammation of the skin
dermatitis calorica Inflammation of the skin resulting from the action of cold or heat
dermatol Trade name of bismuth subgallate
dermatorrhea Excessive skin secretion
dermosynovitis. Perforating ulcer of the foot
desiccant. A skin-drying agent
desication Drying
desquamation The shedding of the cuticle in scales or shreds
developer A solution of chemicals used to develop photographic and X-ray plates
devitalized Deprived of vitality or energy
dexter. Right, in contradistinction to sinister, left
diabetes A disease in which sugar is excreted in the urine, and is also present in the blood. There are two types, incipidus and mellitus. The latter is the diabetes in which sugar is excreted. In the former large quantities of pale urine are excreted
diachylon Lead plaster
diagnosis The determination of the nature of a disease
diapedesis The passage of the blood-cells through the unruptured walls of the blood vessels
diathesis A constitutional state predisposing to any disease or group of diseases
digit A finger or toe
diet Food and drink in general. A prescribed course of eating and drinking
dietetics The therapeutics of food and drink in relation to health and disease
diffuse Spread about, not confined
dioxygen. Trade name for hydrogen peroxide
diphtheria. A specific infectious disease caused by the Klebs-Loeffler bacillus
direct cautery Actual fire or heat applied to a part to destroy it
disbasia angiosclerotica. A disease characterized by intermittent limping
disease Illness, sickness, an interruption of the function of any part of the body
disintegration Separation of the component parts of a substance
dislocation A disturbance of the relation of the bones entering into a joint
dissection The act of cutting apart or separating the tissues of the body in the study of anatomy. In an operation to separate the structures along natural lines. In podiatry, to remove a growth in its entirety and as a whole
disseminatum. Widely scattered referring to heloma d, which is so scattered
distal Farthest from the centre or median line. Opposed to proximal
distension The act of stretching
dorsal Referring to the upper or posterior surface, or the back of any part

douche A current of water or other fluid, directed against the surface or projected in a cavity
drain To draw off the fluid from a cavity
dressings The materials applied to a wound for the purpose of excluding the air stimulating repair, etc
drop-foot. Paralysis of the dorsal flexor muscles of the foot
dropsy. An excessive accumulation of clear watery fluid in any of the tissues or cavities of the body (Latin - hydrops)
duck-shield. A dressing for heloma molle, devised by Alfred Ahrens
duct. A tubular structure giving exit to the secretion of a gland, or conducting any fluid
ductility The quality possessed by some metals to spread and elongate without breaking
dys A prefix meaning bad or difficult (Exam dysphasia—an impairment in the sense of touch)
dyspnea. Shortness of breath, difficult respiration

E

ebullition. Boiling
ecchymosis A purplish patch of the skin caused by extravasation of blood
ectrodactylia A congenital malformation in which one or more fingers or toes are absent
eczema Salt rheum, tetter, an inflammation of the skin characterized by weeping and itching
edema An abnormal amount of clear watery fluid in the lymph spaces of the tissues
edematous Dropsical, marked by edema
effusion Escape of fluid from the blood-vessels or lymphatics into the tissues or a cavity
electrode One of the two poles of an electric battery or of the ends of the conductors connected therewith
electrolysis Decomposition of the tissues by means of electricity
eleidin A deeply staining substance forming the granules of the stratum granulosum of the epidermis
element. A simple substance which has not been subdivided
elephantiasis. Barbados leg. Hypertrophy of the skin and subcutaneous tissues
eliminants. Agents promoting the removal of waste
emaciation. Extreme loss of flesh
embolism Obstruction of a vessel due to a clot or foreign matter, which has been transported to it usually from a thrombus
emollient. Soothing to the skin
emphysema The presence of air in the spaces of the connective tissues of a part
empiric Founded on experience, the treatment of disease based on experience, opposed to rational
encapsulated Inclosed in a sheath or capsule
encysted. Encapsuled, surrounded by a closed membrane
endarteritis. Inflammation of the inner coat of an artery

GLOSSARY

endemic Noting a disease common to a region
endo. A prefix signifying within (Exam endotoscope—a form of ear speculum)
endosmosis. Osmosis in a direction towards the interior of a cavity
endothelium A layer of flat cells lining serous cavities, blood vessels, etc, and cavities not exposed to the air
enervation Failure of nerve force
engorgement. Distension with fluid or other material, congested
enucleate To remove in its entirety
epidemic. Noting a disease which attacks, nearly simultaneously a large number of people in a community
epidermis The epithelial layer of the skin the scarf skin or outer skin
epithelioid Resembling epithelium
epithelioma A cancerous growth originating from squamous epithelium
epithelium The purely cellular, non-vascular layer covering all cavities and surfaces exposed to the air, such as the epidermis, mucous membrane, etc
eponychium. The skin adherent to the nail at its root the nail skin
eradicated Removed
ergot. Spurred rye, rye smut, a drug made from rye
erosion A wearing away
erysipelas An acute spreading inflammation of the skin and subcutaneous tissues
erythema A redness of the skin, rose rash
erythematous Relating to or marked by redness
eschar A slough following a burn or cauterization of the skin
escharotic. Caustic, corrosive, an agent producing an eschar
Esmarch's bandage A rubber bandage wound tightly about a limb in order to exsanguinate the member preparatory to offering a bloodless field for operation
essence of geranium A solution of the volatile oil of geranium
essence of thyme. A solution of the volatile oil of thyme
ether An organic oxide, more especially ethyl ether $(C_2H_5)_2O$
ethics The principles of correct professional conduct as they relate to the public, to the practitioner, and to his fellow-practitioners
ethyl bromide A colorless liquid employed as a local anesthetic
ethyl chloride A colorless liquid employed as a local anesthetic, by spraying
ethylate of soda. A reddish yellow powder, employed in aqueous solution in the treatment of lupus and other skin diseases
etiology. The causes of disease
eucalyptol oil Oleum eucalypti, an oil distilled from the leaves of the Eucalyptus globulus
evaporate To change from liquid to vapor form
evaporation A change from liquid to vapor form
eversion A turning outward
ex A prefix denoting out of, from, away from (Exam excision—to cut out)
excavator. A spoon-shaped instrument used to scrape out pathologic tissue

excision The operative removal of a limb, organ or other part
excrementitious Relating to any cast-out waste material
excrescence Any outgrowth from the surface, especially a pathologic growth
excretion. The process whereby the waste material is thrown out of the body
excretory Relating to excretion
exfoliate. To strip off in layers or sheets noting especially a form of desquamation
exostosis A bony tumor springing from the surface of a bone
expansion Spreading out, an increase in size
exsanguinate. To make bloodless
exsiccant A dusting or drying powder
extension. The act of extending a limb, the position of a limb that is extended
extr cannabis indica A soft solid (Indian hemp) of blackish-green color
extravasated Exuded from, or passed out of a vessel into the tissues
exuberant Copious, plentiful, as exuberant granulations
exudate. To exude, a fluid, or formed elements of the blood, which enters the tissues or any cavity

F

F. Abbreviation for Fahrenheit temperature.
fabella One of two small fibrocartilages or sesamoid bones in the tendons of the gastrocnemius muscle
fabric The structure of anything
fabrics Materials constructed for manufacturing purposes
facet A small smooth area on a bone or other firm structure
Fahrenheit scale. The degree markings on the F thermometer in which the freezing point is 32° and the point of boiling water is 212°
faradic Relating to induced electricity
fasciculi Small bands or bundles of fibres, usually of muscle or nerve tissue
fascia A sheet of fibrous tissue enveloping the body beneath the skin and also enclosing the muscles
fatty degeneration A retrogressive change associated with the appearance of fat in the cells and formed within them f **infiltration.** A deposit of fat in abnormal quantity between and in the cells and not formed within them
felon. Paronychia, inflammation around the nail Whitlow
felt matted wool, unwoven Used for podiatry dressings
femur The thigh bone
fermentation A chemical change induced in an organic compound by the action of a ferment
ferrum The metal iron, the basic ingredient of tincture of the subsulphate of iron
festination The peculiar acceleration of gait noted in paralysis agitans and some other nervous affections
fetid Foul-smelling, having a rank odor
fibre A filamentous element, an elongated cell or cell process
fibrillae Minute fibres

GLOSSARY

fibrin. An elastic filamentous substance derived from the blood after coagulation
fibroblast. A cell produced by the connective tissue in the formation of fibrous tissue
fibula. The external and smaller of the two bones of the leg
filament A fibril, a fine fibre, or thread-like structure
fish skin A preparation used as a covering to wounds, etc, a substitute for oil-silk
fissure A furrow, cleft or slit
fistula A sinus leading from an abscess cavity to the surface
flaccid Relaxed, flabby, without bone
flail-like. Resembling an instrument used for thrashing or beating
flat-foot. Pes planus a foot in which the arch is sunken
flax-seed Linseed Used in making poultices
flexion. Bending, bending of a joint so as to approximate the parts they connect
fluctuation. A wave-like motion felt on palpating a cavity containing fluid
fluffy Feathery
fluoroscope. An apparatus for rendering visible the effects of the X-rays
fluoroscopy. Examination of the inner parts of the body by means of the fluoroscope
flux Flow of electricity or other substance
focal infection. An infectious process which starts at a point remote from the part where the symptoms manifest themselves
follicle A simple tubular gland
fomentation. The application of warmth and moisture in the treatment of disease, poulticing
foot. Pes, the lower, pedal, extremity of the leg
forceps An instrument for seizing anything and for making compression or traction
formaldehyde. An antiseptic gas with a pungent odor The water solution formalin, is used in podiatry
fracture A break, especially of a bone
friction. Rubbing
Friedreich's ataxia Hereditary spinal ataxia
frostbite. Inflammation of the skin and deeper tissues due to exposure to severe cold Chimation severe
fulguration. Lightning stroke Treatment of tumors by means of the sparks of the high frequency current
function The special action or physiologic property of a part
fusiform. Spindle-shaped, tapering at both ends
fusion. Liquefaction by heat, melting

G

G. Abbreviation for gram
gait Specific manner of walking, manner of stepping
gallic acid A yellowish-white substance used as an astringent
gallstone. A concretion, chiefly of cholesterin, formed in the gall-bladder or bile-duct
galvanic. Constant current electricity produced by chemical action
gangrene Death of the soft tissues, en masse,
gas gangrene. Gangrene caused by the bacillus of Welch, gaseous gangrene
gastric Relating to the stomach
gastrocnemius. One of the calf muscles
gastro-intestinal Referring to the stomach and the intestines
gauze A thin loose-meshed cloth employed for dressings bandages, etc
genitalia. The genitals
genu The knee
germ A rudiment A microbe
germicide An agent which destroys germs or microorganisms
ginglymus A hinge joint
glands Secreting organs or excreting organs, such as the sebaceous or sweat glands
gliomatous Relating to a tumor formed of the nerves of the brain and spinal cord
glucose Grape sugar
glutei. Relating to the buttocks
glycerin Glycerinum, a sweet, oily fluid obtained by the saponification of fats and fixed oils
golfer's foot. A painful condition of the dorsum of the foot
gomenol A germicidal, etherial oil obtained from a plant
gonococcus The specific organism causing gonorrhea
gonorrheal heel. A focal infection of the heel caused by an original urethral infection with the gonococcus
Goulard's extract. A solution of lead subacetate
gout. A disease of metabolism characterized by recurrent attacks of arthritis, particularly in the metatarsophalangeal joint of the great toe, though any joint may be attacked, by deposits of sodium biuret in and around the affected joints, and by inflammation of fibrous structures elsewhere (Stedman)
grain A unit of weight, 1/60 dram
gram, gramme A unit of weight equal to 15 4 grains
granulation. The formation of minute, rounded fleshy projections on the surface of a wound in the process of healing
gross. Large, coarse, macroscopic in contradistinction to microscopic
growth. The increase in size of a living being or any of its parts
gt (plural gtt) Abbreviation of drop or drops
gumma. An infectious granuloma, the characteristic lesion of late or tertiary syphilis
gun-cotton. Pyroxylin
gutta percha The dried milky juice of a Malay tree
gypsum. Calcium sulphate **Dried g.** Calcii sulphas exsiccatus, plaster of Paris

H

hair follicle. A cylindrical pit dipping down through the corium and containing the root of the hair
hallux. The great toe, the first digit of the foot
hallux dolorosus Painful toe
hallux flexus. Hammer-toe

hallux rigidus. Stiff toe
hallux valgus. A deformity in which the great toe is bent outwards
hallux varus. Deviation of the great toe to the inner side of the foot away from its neighbor
hammer-toe. A condition of permanent flexion of the mid-phalangeal joint of one or more of the toes, hallux flexus
heloma (plural, helomata). Corn, clavus, an overgrowth of the epidermis, with a central core or nucleus
heloma durum. Hard corn
heloma miliare Seed corn
heloma molle Soft corn
heloma neurofibrosum. Corn containing nerve fibres
heloma vasculare. Vascular corn
helosis The condition of having heloma
helotomeia The surgery of helomata
helotomon. The knife for cutting helomata
hematidrosis. The excretion of sweat stained with blood
hematocele A blood cyst, hematocist
hemi A prefix signifying one-half (Exam hemiplegia—half paralysis)
hemichorea Chorea involving the muscles of one side, only
hemiplegia. Paralysis of one side of the body
hemoglobin The coloring matter of the blood
hemorrhage Bleeding, a flow of blood
hemorrhoids. Piles, a varicose condition of the external hemorrhoidal veins causing painful swellings at the anus
hemostatic. Arresting hemorrhage, styptic
hereditary Transmitted from parent to offspring
hermetically In an air-tight manner noting a vessel closed or sealed in such a way that air can neither enter it nor issue from it
hidrosis. Sweating, especially heavy sweating, hyperidrosis, sudoresis
high frequency. An electric current with a high voltage, and a rapid change in direction from one pole to the other
hirsute. Hairy, pertaining to hair
histology. The branch of anatomy which deals with the cells and the minute structure of the tissues, microscopic anatomy
homogeneous Of uniform structure or composition throughout
homo helotleus. The person having helomata
hone. A flat stone or a piece of leather used to sharpen knives
hookworm. A worm of the genus ankylostoma or uncinaria
hornification. Conversion into horn cornification
Huntington's chorea. Hereditary chorea
hydrocephalus. A condition, usually congenital, marked by an extensive effusion of serum into the cerebral ventricles
hydrochloric acid. See acidum
hydrogen. An odorless, colorless, tasteless gaseous element, the lightest substance known
hydro-therapeutics. The treatment of disease by the use of water, in a scientific way, hydrotherapy
hygiene. The science of health

hyper. A prefix denoting excessive (Exam hyperidrosis—excessive sweating)
hyperemia The presence of an increased amount of blood in a part, congestion
hyperesthesia. Excessive sensibility to touch, to pain or to other sensory stimuli
hyperidrosis Hyperhidrosis excessive sweating
hyperporosis. Excessive formation of callus after fracture of a bone
hypertonicity. A greater degree of tension.
hypertrophy. Overgrowth, general increase in a part, not due to tumor formation
hypodermatic. Hypodermic, under the skin
hysteria. A chronic neurosis or psychoneurosis, characterized by disorders of the will, and partial cessation or exaltation of the individual functions of the brain

I

iasis See osis
ichnogram An imprint of the soles of the feet, showing a series of steps
ichorous. Relating to a thin watery discharge from an ulcer
ichthyol Ichthyolum a brownish oil used in medicine and in podiatry because of the sulphur (from fossil fish) which it contains
ichthyosis. A congenital rough skin due to hypertrophy of the horny layer of the epidermis with diminished sweat and sebaceous secretion fish-skin disease
idiopathic. Noting a primary disease, one originating without apparent extrinsic cause
idiosyncrasy An individual mental or physical characteristic or peculiarity
immersion The placing of a body under water or other liquid
immobility Incapability of moving, the fixed position of a part
immune Free from the possibility of infection.
impacted. Pressed closely together so as to be immovable as in impacted fracture
impermeable. Impervious
impervious. Impassable, impenetrable, to fluids
impingement Used in podiatry to denote the pinching of tissues between two adjacent or opposite bones or muscles
incipient. Just beginning
incision. A cut, a division of the soft parts made with a knife
incompatible Not capable of being mixed without undergoing radical changes
incoordination Lack of harmonious action, as of muscles
indentation. The act of notching or pitting
indolent Inactive, sluggish, painless, or nearly so
induction Production or causation
induction coil An apparatus for the induction of a secondary electric current
induration. Hardening
inert. Slow in action, sluggish

infant A child during the first two years of life, a babe
infection Invasion by living pathogenic bacteria of a part of the body where conditions are favorable to their growth and whence they act injuriously upon the tissues
infiltration The act of passing into or interpenetrating a cell or tissue, said of gases and fluids
inflammation The reaction of the tissues against injury or bacterial invasion, characterized by heat, redness, pain, swelling and impaired function
inflation Distension of a part by a gas or a liquid
inflection. An inward bending
influenza. The grip an acute infectious disease caused by Pfeiffer's bacillus
in-footed. Pigeon-toed, standing or walking with toes turned in
ingrown toe nail Onychocryptosis
inhibition. The diminution or arrest of function in an organ
injection The introduction of a substance in fluid form into the tissues or cavities of the body
innervation Distribution of the nerves in a part
innocuous. Harmless
inoculate To introduce the virus of a disease into the tissues or blood vessels
in situ In position
instep The arch, or highest part of the dorsum of the foot
instrument. A tool or implement
integument The enveloping membrane of the body, the skin
inter A prefix denoting between or among (Exam interdigital—between the fingers or toes)
intercellular Between or among cells
interosseous Between bones
interphalangeal. Between the phalanges
intertrigo Dermatitis occurring between two folds of the skin
intestinal Relating to the intestine or belly
intima The inner coat of a blood vessel
intoe. Hallux valgus
intoxication Acute alcoholism; drunkenness
inunction The administration of a drug in ointment form by rubbing it into the skin
inversion. Bending inward
involuntary Independent of the will, not volitional
involution The return of an enlarged organ to normal size
iodine A non-metallic element occurring in lustrous steel-gray crystals soluble in water and alcohol and used externally as a counterirritant and antiseptic
iodoform. Iodoform, a yellow crystalline powder having a strong, disagreeable odor, employed as an antiseptic dusting powder to wounds and syphilitic sores
ions A group of atoms carrying an electric charge
irritation Extreme reaction of the tissues to an insult or injury, incipient inflammation
ischemia Local anemia due to mechanical obstruction of the blood-supply
ischidrosis. Suppression of the perspiration
ist. An affix denoting an agent (Exam podiatrist)
itis. A suffix grown to mean inflammation of (Exam ostitis—inflammation of bone)

J

jaborandi See pilocarpin
joint-capsule Capsular ligament of a joint
joint-muscle A muscle which causes motion at a joint

K

kakidrosis Bromidrosis
keloids Lesions of a skin disease marked by patches of a whitish color surrounded by a purplish border
keratin. A scleroprotein present in hair, in nails, in horn, etc
keratogenesis The production of horny cells or tissue
keratohyalin Eleidin
keratoma A horny tumor
keratosis. Circumscribed overgrowth of horny tissue
kilogram One thousand grams weight
kinesiatrics The therapeutic employment of movements, movement-cure
kinetic. Relation to motion or muscular movements
Kneipp method. The treatment of disease by water, hydrotherapy
knock-knee Genu valgum
koilonychia Spoon-nail, a malformation of the nails in which the outer surface is concave
Korsakoff's disease Polyneuritic psychosis
kyllosis. Clubfoot

L

labyrinthine. Perplexing, intricate, involved
laceration A tear or torn wound
laity Non-professional persons
lamb's wool. A material used in shielding
lamella In osteology, a thin sheet or scale of bone
lancet A surgical knife with a short, sharp-pointed, two-edged blade
lancinating. Noting a sharp cutting or tearing pain
Landry's disease. Acute ascending paralysis
Langerhans' cells. Star-shaped cells in the deeper part of the stratum germinativum of the epidermis
lanolin. An oily substance extracted from the wool of sheep, adeps lanae
larynx. The organ of voice production
larvae The worm-like forms of insects on issuing from the egg
Lassar's paste An ointment containing salicylic acid, talcum, zinc oxide and vaseline, it is used for eczema
lateral. On the side, as distinguished from medial
lathyrism. Lupinosis, poisoning by flour adulterated with chick-pea
lead. A metallic element
lead and opium wash. A solution of lead acetate and tr opium in water, used to allay pain

GLOSSARY

lead neuritis. Inflammation of the nerves, due to poisoning by lead
lead palsy Paralysis of the extensor muscles of the wrist, due to poisoning by lead, wrist drop
leprosy A chronic disease believed to be due to the presence of the bacillus leprae, or Hansen's bacillus It occurs in two forms, tubercular, affecting the skin, anesthetic, affecting the nerves
lesion A more or less circumscribed pathologic change in the tissues
lethal Fatal, mortal, causing death
leucocyte. A white blood cell
leuconychia. The occurrence of white spots or patches under the nails
leucorrhea A discharge from the vagina of a white, viscid fluid containing mucous and pus cells
leverage. The mechanical power gained by using a lever
lichen planus. A skin disease occurring on the soles of the feet
ligaments. Bands of fibrous tissue connecting two or more bones
ligation. The application of a ligature
ligature. A thread, wire or piece of catgut, tied tightly around a blood vessel a pedicle or a tumor in order to constrict it
limewater. A solution of calcium hydroxide
line of demarcation A zone of inflammatory reaction separating a healthy from a gangrenous area
liniment A solution of a medicament in mucilage starch or other substance, in combination with the white of egg
linseed Flaxseed, used in making poultices
lint. A soft, absorbent material used in surgical dressings
lipoma A tumor of fatty tissue
liquor ferri subsulphate. Monsell's solution
liquor potassae A 5% solution of potassium hydroxide
lisle. A material woven from cotton and silk
liter A measure of capacity equal to a trifle over a quart, 1000 cubic centimeter
lithemia The presence of uric acid, in excess, in the blood
Lobstein's disease. Constitutional fragility of the bones, fractures being produced by slight injuries
locomotion. Movement from one place to another
longitudinal. Running lengthwise, in the direction of the long axis of the body
lordosis Curvature of the spine with the convexity looking anteriorly
lues A plague or pestilence, specifically, syphilis
luetin skin reaction The reaction of the skin in a specific test for syphilis
lumen. The space in the interior of a tubular structure, such as an artery
lunula The opaque whitish semilunar area near the root of the nail
lycopodium. Vegetable sulphur A yellow tasteless powder used as a dusting powder
lymphangitis Inflammation of the lymphatic vessels
lymph. A clear light, straw-colored fluid, which circulates in the lymph spaces or lymphatic vessels of the body.
lymphatics. A series of vessels acting as auxiliaries to the venous system, and containing the lymph
lysis. The gradual subsidence of the symptoms of an acute disease
lysol Trade name of a mixture of soaps and phenols, used as a disinfectant dressing and hand-wash

M

M Abbreviation for (1) mille, a thousand, (2) in prescriptions, for misce, mix, (3) minim, a drop, (4) meter, French measure
macerate To soften by soaking or steeping
maceration Softening by the action of a liquid
mackintosh. A waterproof cloth or tissue used for surgical dressings
macrodactylism. Abnormal size of a finger or of a toe
macroscopic Observable to the naked eye, in contradistinction to microscopic
maculae Small spots or patches on the skin, not elevated above the general surface
Madura foot. Mycetoma, a disease occurring in the East Indies, characterized by large subcutaneous tubercles and nodules which break down and discharge pus
mal A prefix meaning bad (Exam malposition—bad position)
malalignment. Not in normal position
malaria A disease, caused by the presence of a protozoan parasite (plasmodium) of the read blood cells
malignant. Resistant to treatment, occuring in severe form, tending to grow worse, and (in the case of a tumor) to recur after removal Not benign
malingerer. One who feigns disease
malpractice Mistreatment of a patient's ills through carelessness, ignorance or criminal intent
malleolus One of the two rounded prominences on either side of the ankle-joint
manicure. To care for the hands and finger-nails, cosmetically
marasmus Extreme emaciation occurring in children
massage A scientific method of manipulation of the body by rubbing, pinch ing, kneading, tapping, etc
masseur A male who massages
masseuse A female who massages
massotherapy. The therapeutic uses of massage
materia medica The branch of medicine which treats of the origin, preparation, doses and modes of administration of drugs
matrix The formative portion of a nail
maximum The highest limit, the greatest amount possible in contradistinction to minimum, the least limit
M Cp Abbreviation of Master of Chiropody
mechanotherapy Treatment of disease by means of apparatus or mechanical appliances
medicament A medicine, a remedy
medicine The art of preventing or curing disease A drug
medullated Having a soft marrow-like structure, especially in the centre of a part

megalodactylism. Abnormal size of a finger or toe
membrana propria The basement layer of the epidermis, and separating it from the true skin
membrane A thin sheet or layer of tissue serving as a covering or envelope of a part
meningeal. Relating to the meninges or membranous envelope of the brain and spinal cord
menthol A camphor obtained from oil of peppermint
mercuric chloride Corrosive sublimate
mercury An element (quicksilver), compounds of which are used in podiatry
metabolism Tissue change, the sum of the chemical changes whereby the function of nutrition is regulated
metacarpal. Referring to the long bones of the hand between the carpus and the phalanges
metacarpophalangeal. Relating to the metacarpus and the phalanges
metamorphosis A change in form, structure, or function
metastasis. The shifting of a disease from one part of the body to another
metatarsal. Relating to the bones in front of the tarsus, and called the metatarsal bones, they are five in number
metatarsalgia Pain in the metatarsal region
metatarsophalangeal. Between the metatarsal and phalanx
meter A measure of length the equivalent of 39 4 inches
methyl. The radical of wood alcohol
methylene blue A compound of methylene, used as a caustic in treating verruca
microbe. A minute one-celled creation, animal or vegetable, a microorganism
microorganism. A microscopic plant or animal, a bacterium or protozoan
microscopic. Of minute size visible only through a microscope, the reverse of macroscopic
miliaria An eruption of minute vesicles due to retention of fluid at the mouth of the sweat glands
miliary Representing a millet seed in size
milligram One-thousandth of a gram— 1-65 grain
milliliter One-thousandth of a liter— about 15 minims
millimeter One-thousandth of a meter 1-25 inch
milliampere. An electric unit of current-strength, the thousandth of an ampere
milliamperemeter An instrument used for measuring milliamperes of electric current
millet seed A small seed of the millet plant, a grain
minim. One-sixtieth of a fluid drachm, equivalent to about one drop of water
misce. Mix, the character which directs the druggist to mix the ingredients of a prescription
mistura. A pharmacal mixture
mobility. The quality of being movable
molecular. Relating to the smallest possible unit of existence of any substance

moleskin An adhesive substance used in shielding
mollifying Calming, softening
mono. A prefix denoting the participation of a single element or part (Syn uni) (Exam monodactyl—a single finger or toe)
Monsel's solution Liquor ferri subsulphatis
morbid Diseased, pathologic
morphine The chief active principle of opium
morphologic. Relating to the structure of the tissues of the body
morphology The science which treats of the external configuration or the structure of animals and plants
Morton's disease Morton's neuralgia.
Morton's neuralgia A pain in the metatarsophalangeal joint of the fourth toe, also called Morton's toe
motile Having the power of spontaneous movement
mucous Relating to mucous or to the mucous membrane (m membrane), a membrane which secretes mucus, and lines the cavities connected with the outer air
multiple. Occurring in several parts at the same time
mummification. Dry gangrene, shriveling.
muscle. One of the contractile organs of the body, by which the movements of the various organs and parts are effected
muscle-corpuscle. The nucleus of a muscle-fiber
muscle-fiber One of the cylindrical fibers, an inch or more in length and about 1-500 inch in diameter, composing voluntary muscle tissue
muscle-plasma The fluid portion of muscle tissue
musculature The arrangement of the muscles in a part or in the body as a whole
musculus. Muscle Important muscles of the foot
m. Abductor hallucis
m Abductor obliquus hallucis
m. Adductor transversis hallucis
m. Extensor digitorum brevis
m Extensor digitorum longus
m Extensor hallucis longus
m Flexor accessorius
m. Flexor brevis hallucis
m. Flexor brevis minimi digiti
m. Flexor digitorum brevis
m. Flexor digitorum longus
m. Flexor hallucis longus
m Gastrocnemius
m Interosseus dorsalis
m Interosseus plantaris
m. Lumbricalis (4)
m. Peroneus brevis
m Peroneus longus.
m Peroneus tertius
m. Plantaris
m Soleus
m Tibialis anticus
m Tibialis posticus
mustard. The dried, ripe seeds of the white or black mustard plant
mycetoma. Madura foot, a disease of the foot occurring in the East Indies
myelitis Inflammation of the spinal cord, or of the bone marrow (osteomyelitis).

myeloma A tumor due to hyperplasia of the bone marrow
myocellulitis. Inflammation of muscle and cellular tissue
myoclonia Any disorder characterized by muscular twitching
myocyte. A muscle cell
myodynia Muscle pain, myalgia
myology. The branch of science which deals with muscles and their accessory parts
myositis. Muscle inflammation
myotonia Any disorder characterized by tonic spasm or temporary rigidity of a muscle

N

naevus. A congenital mark or discolored patch of the skin, a mole
nafalan A proprietary remedy containing Caucasian naphtha in a soap base
nail Unguis, the horny plate covering the dorsal surface of the distal half of the terminal phalanx of each finger and toe
nail bed. A portion of the distal phalanx covered by the nail
nail fold. A groove in the skin in which lie the margins and the proximal edge of the nail
nail groove. A groove in the distal phalanx in which the nail lies
nail plate. The horny substance which makes up the nail proper
nanomelous. Having very small extremities
narcosis. Stupor or general anesthesia produced by some narcotic drug
narcotic. Relating to or causing narcosis, an agent which produces narcosis
navicular One of the bones of the tarsus of the foot
nebulizer. An atomizer, a vaporizer, an apparatus for throwing a liquid in a fine spray
necrosis. Local death, the death of more or less extensive groups of cells
neo A prefix noting new or recent (Exam neoplasm—new growth)
neoplasm A new growth, tumor
nephritis. Inflammation of the kidney
nerve A collection of fibres in the form of a whitish cord through which stimuli are transmitted from the central nervous system to the periphery, or the reverse
nervousness. A condition of unrest and of irritability to the nervous system
nervus Nerve, a whitish cord made up of nerve fibres
nerves of the foot
   n. musculocutaneus, musculo-cutaneous nerve (dorsal surface and in front of leg)
   n plantaris externus, external plantar nerve (plantar surface)
   n plantaris internus, internal plantar nerve (plantar surface)
   n saphenus externus, external saphenous nerve (dorsal surface and in front of leg)
   n. tibialis anticus, anterior tibial nerve (dorsal surface and in front of leg).
   n. tibialis posticus, posterior tibial nerve (back of leg).

neuralgia Nerve-pain, pain of a severe, throbbing or stabbing character in the course of a nerve
neurasthenics. Those suffering from neurasthenia, or nervous exhaustion
neuritis Inflammation of the nerves
neurofibrous. Containing nerve fibres, said of an heloma
neuroma (plural neuromata). A tumor made up of nerve tissue
N F Abbreviation for National Formulary, a book issued by the American Pharmaceutical Association containing formulas of preparations not official in the Pharmacopeia
nitric acid. HNO$_3$ Employed as a caustic for verrucae
nodule A small node or circumscribed swelling
Noguchi test. A test for tabes dorsalis depending upon an albumin reaction of the spinal fluid, a test for syphilis—a modification of the Wasserman test
non A latin prefix denoting a negation or absence of the quality or fact expressed in the word to which it is prefixed
non-medullated. Without a medulla or medullary substance
non-striated Without stripes or bands
normal. Typical, usual, healthy
nostrum A quack remedy
novocaine A synthetic local anesthetic
noxious. Injurious, harmful.
nucleus The centre of functional activity of a cell, the central portion of an heloma
nutrient. Carrying nourishment

O

obesity An abnormal increase of fat in the subcutaneous connective tissues, corpulence, fatness, general adiposis
obliterated Destroyed by the effects of time, effaced
occlusive Noting a dressing which excludes the air.
official Authoritative, noting a drug or chemical found in the Pharmacopeia
ohm. The unit of electric resistance
oid. A suffix denoting resemblance to the thing indicated by the other part of the word (Exam osteoid—resembling bone)
oil stone. A hone upon which oil is used
oiled silk A waterproof substance used in surgical dressings
ointment. A medicated fatty mixture with the consistency of butter, and employed externally
oligodactylia. A deformity marked by fewer than five fingers or toes on each hand or foot
ology A suffix denoting a special branch of study (Exam podology—the branch of medical science which has to do with the feet in all their relations)
oma A suffix noting a tumor or neoplasm (Exam neuroma—a nerve tumor)
onychatrophia Atrophy of the nails
onychauxis Hypertrophy of the nails
onychia (onychitis) Inflammation of the nail bed or matrix
onychocryptosis. Ingrown toe nail,

onychogryphosis. Hypertrophy of the nails with curvature or deformity
onychoid. Resembling a nail in structure or in form
onycholysis Loosening or shedding of the nails
onychoma. A tumor arising from the nail bed
onychomalacia. Absence of rigidity of the nails, hapalonychia.
onychomycosis. Any parasitic disease of the nails, such as tinea or favus
onychotrophy Nutrition of the nails
onycopathy Any disease of the nails, onychosis
onycophag A victim of the nail-biting habit
onychophosis Calloused nail groove
onycophyma Swelling or hypertrophy of the nails
onychoptosis Falling off of the nails
onychorrexis. Brittle nails
onyx The greek word for finger-nail or toe-nail
oozing Flowing slowly gradually escaping
operation. Any surgical procedure
opisthotonos A tetanic spasm in which the spine and extremities are bent with convexity forward the body resting on the head and heels
organ. Any part of the body exercising a specific function
origin The less movable of the points of attachment of a muscle
orthoform A white crystalline powder used as a local anesthetic and antiseptic.
orthopedics. A branch of surgery which has to do with the treatment of chronic diseases of the joints and spine, and the correction of deformities
orthopedist One who practices orthopedics, orthopaedist
os A bone
os calcis. The calcaneus, the heel bone
oscillate. To vibrate
osis A suffix noting an increase (Exam tuberculosis—an increase in tubercles)
osmidrosis (See bromidrosis)
osmosis The passage of certain fluids through an animal membrane or other porous substance
ossification. The formation of bone
ossiferous. Containing bone
ostealgia. Bone pain
osteanabrosis. Bone atrophy
osteanaphysis. Bone reproduction
ostectomy. Surgical removal of bone
osteitis. Bone inflammation
osteoarthritis Inflammation of the articular extremity of a bone involving the contiguous joint structure
osteochondritis Inflammation of a bone and its cartilage
osteogenesis The formation of bone
osteoma A bone tumor
osteomyelitis Inflammation of the bone marrow
osteopsathyrosis Bone fragility, fragilitas ossium
osteotomy. Bone cutting, usually by means of a saw or a chisel.
ounce (abr oz) A weight containing 48.0 grains, apothecaries' weight
oxidation A combination with oxygen
oxygen. A gaseous element, symbol, O
ozone. A condensed form of oxygen, containing three atoms in a molecule.

P

pachyacria. A bulbous thickening of the extremities of the fingers or toes
pachydactylous Abnormal thickness of fingers or of toes
pachydermia. Elephantiasis.
pachypodous. Having large thick feet
pacinian Named after Filippo Pacini, an Italian anatomist, and noting especially the Pacinian body or corpuscle found in the skin, and which is a touch organ.
palliative. Mitigating, reducing the severity of, noting a method of treatment of a disease or of its symptoms
pallor. Paleness
palpate Examining by feeling and pressing with the palms of the hands and with the fingers
pan A prefix implying all, entire (Exam panhidrosis—perspiration of the entire body)
panaris. Paronychia
papilla A conical elevation found beneath the epidermis, and containing capillary loops and nerve endings
papillary layer The outer connective tissue layer of the true skin, and made up of numbers of papillae
papilloma A circumscribed overgrowth or hypertrophy of the papillae of a cutaneous or mucous surface
papoid. A digestive enzyme from the fruit of the pawpaw, resembling papain
papule. A small circumscribed elevation of the skin containing no fluid, a pimple
papulosquamous. Relating to both papules and scales
para A prefix denoting (1) a departure from normal, (2) an involvement of like parts (Exam (1) parachroma—abnormal coloration of the skin or other parts, (2) paraplegia—paralysis of both lower extremities)
paraffin. A white solid hydrocarbon, having the consistency of wax
paralysis Palsy, loss of power of voluntary movement in a muscle through injury or disease of its nerve supply, loss of any function
paralysis agitans. Parkinson's disease shaking palsy, a disorder marked by muscular weakness, stiffness and tremor
paralysis, pseudobulbar Paralysis of the lips and tongue due to a cerebral lesion
paralyzant Causing paralysis, any agent causing paralysis
paramyoclonus multiplex An affection characterized by sharp, frequently repeated clonic muscular contractions
paraplegia Paralysis of both lower extremities and also of more or less of the trunk
parasite An animal or vegetable organism which lives on or in another from which it draws its nourishment
parasiticide Destructive to parasites
paresis. Cortical paralysis
paresthesia An abnormal sensation, such as burning, pricking, numbness, etc
paretic Relating to, or suffering from paresis

paronychia Inflammation of the tissues around the nail, felon, panaris, whitlow
parresine A paraffine preparation used for burns
passive Not active
pathogenic. Causing disease
pathognomonic Characteristic of a disease, noting certain typical symptoms
pathology The science that deals with the change in function or in structure of an organ or tissue in a diseased state
pedal Relating to the feet
pedarthrocace. Joint disease in children.
pediculis corporis. The body louse
pedicure. One who treats the feet cosmetically
pedunculated. Stalked, having a peduncle, not sessile
pellagra An affection characterized by gastrointestinal disturbances and mental disorders
pelma The sole of the foot
pelmatogram. An imprint of the sole of the foot made by resting the inked foot on a sheet of paper, or by pressing the greased foot on a plaster-of-Paris paste
pelvis Any basin-like or cup-shaped cavity
pemphigus An infection of the skin characterized by the production of bullae
per. A prefix denoting through (Exam perennial—lasting through several years)
perforating Piercing with one or more holes
peri A prefix denoting around or about (Exam periosteum—around the bone)
periarthritis. Inflammation of the parts surrounding a joint
periodic Recurring at regular intervals
peronychia (See paronychia.)
periosteum The thick fibrous membrane covering the entire surface of a bone except its articular cartilage
periphery The outer part or surface, away from the centre
periphlebitis Inflammation of the outer coat of a vein or of the tissues surrounding a vein
pernio Chilblains, chimation mild
perodactylus A monster with defective fingers and toes
peronei Relating to the peroneus muscles
peropus A monster with defective feet
peroxide of hydrogen Oxygenated water, H_2O_2 used as an antiseptic and deodorant
perspiration The excretion of fluid by the sweat glands The fluid excreted by the sweat glands, transpiration
perverted. Turned from what is normal or proper
pes, gen pedis, pl pedes The foot
pes cavus Hollow-foot
pes planus Flat foot
petrogen The proprietary name of refined mineral oil, used as a base for remedial agents **p. iodine.** Iodine mixed with petrogen
petrolatum Vaseline, a yellowish mixture of the softer members of the paraffine or methane series of the hydrocarbons, obtained from petroleum as an intermediate product in its distillation.

phadena A sloughing ulcer
phagocytosis The process of ingestion and digestion by the cells, the substances ingested are other cells, bacteria, bits of necrosed tissue, foreign particles, etc
phalanges Long bones of the fingers or toes, fourteen in number, two on each great toe and three on each of the remaining toes
phenol Carbolic acid
phenomenon A symptom, any unusual fact or occurrence
phlebitis. Inflammation of a vein
phlegmon Acute suppurative inflammation of the subcutaneous connective tissue
phosphoridrosis. Phosphorescent sweating
physical Relating to the body as distinguished from the mind
physics The branch of science which deals with the phenomena of matter
physiology. The science that treats of the functions of the organs and tissues of the human body
picric acid A yellowish, crystalline powder used in burns and eczema
pigment Coloring matter, the coloring matter found in the epidermis
pilocarpin An alkaloid obtained from the leaves of pilocarpus used externally to stimulate the growth of hair
pit. Any natural depression on the surface of the body
pityriasis A dermatosis marked by branny desquamation **p. rubra pilaris**, an eruption of papules surrounding the hair follicles
plantar Relating to the sole of the foot
plantar flexion. A term used to indicate extension of the foot forward at the ankle joint
plaster A solid preparation which can be spread when heated and which becomes adhesive at the temperature of the body
plaster of Paris. Gypsum, calcium sulphate, used in podiatry for dressings and to make casts
plasticity. The capability of being formed or moulded
platinum A silver white metal
pledget. A small mass or tuft of wool, cotton or lint
plexiform. Resembling a plexus or network
plexus. A network or interjoining of structures in the body, especially of veins, nerves or lymphatics
pliability. The capability of being pliable or flexible
plumbism Lead poisoning
podagra Gout especially of the great toe
podalgia Pain in the foot
podarthritis Inflammation of any of the tarsal or metatarsal joints
podiatrist. One who practises podiatry
podiatry The scientific care of the foot in health and in disease
poisoning Administering of poison, state of being poisoned
policeman's heel A painful condition of the inferior surface of the os calcis
poliomyelitis. Inflammation of the grey matter of the spinal cord,

poly A prefix conveying the notion of multiplicity (Exam polyarthritis—simultaneous inflammation of several joints)

polydactylism. More than five digits on either the hand or the foot

polyneuritis. Multiple neuritis

polynuclear. Multinuclear, having more than one nucleus

pompholyx. An inflammatory eruption of the skin of the hands and feet, accompanied by itching and burning

popliteal Relating to the posterior surface of the knee

positive pole. Anode, the chemically active pole of an electric battery, the one connected with the electronegative element

pore One of the minute openings of the sweat glands of the skin

post A prefix denoting after (Exam postmortem—after death)

posterior Behind or after

postoperative. Following a surgical operation

posture. The term applied to the position of the body in space

potassium hydroxide. Caustic potash, a white crystalline mass used in solution form to treat verruca

potassium iodide. A white, crystalline powder used in the internal treatment of syphilis

potassium permanganate. A violet substance used as a deodorant in bromidrosis

potential cautery. A caustic an agent such as potassium hydroxide which forms an eschar without the agency of actual fire

potentiality. A state of tension in an electric source

poultice Cataplasm, a soft mush prepared by wetting absorbent substances with fluids and usually applied hot to the surface

pre. A prefix to words formed from Latin roots, denoting anterior or before (Exam prepatellar—in front of the patella or knee cap)

precursor Forerunner

predisposing. Affecting the body in such a way as to render it vulnerable to the action of the exciting cause

pregnancy. Gestation, the state of a female after conception until the birth of the child

prescription. A written formula for the preparation and administration of any remedy or remedies

process A projection or outgrowth

profuse. Exuberant, liberal to excess

prognosis. The foretelling of the probable course of a disease.

progression. Advance, the act of walking

proliferation Exuberant growth by reproduction of similar cells

prophylaxis. The prevention of disease

propulsion The tendency to fall forward that causes festination in paralysis agitans

protonuclein Trade name of a nuclein preparation derived from lymphoid tissue

protoplasm. Living matter, of which animal and vegetable tissues are formed

prototype The primitive form

proud flesh Exuberant granulations, a fungus growth from a granulating surface which shows no tendency toward cicatrization

proximal. Nearest the trunk or point of origin, opposed to distal

pruritus. Itching

pseudo. A prefix denoting a resemblance, like (Exam pseudomania—pretended insanity)

pseudoarthritis. Hysteric joint inflammation

pseudoankylosis. False ankylosis, fibrous ankylosis

pseudohyperthropic paralysis. Progressive muscular atrophy, a disease of childhood in which fat takes the place of wasted muscle

pseudotabetic (pseudataxic) False wasting, false locomotor ataxia

psoriasis A skin disease characterized by the formation of white scales over rounded, red patches It appears mostly on the extensor surfaces of the elbows and knees

psychosis A disorder of the mind
p polyneuritica, psychosis associated with polyneuritis characterized by failure of memory, hallucinations, and imaginary reminiscences

pterygium. A forward growth of the eponychium with adherence to the surface of the nail

puncture. To make a hole with a small pointed object, such as a needle

purpura. An affection characterized by hemorrhage into the skin

purulent Suppurating, containing or forming pus

pus A fluid product of inflammation, consisting of exuded serum, leucocytes and the debris of dead cells

pustule. A small circumscribed elevation on the skin, containing pus

puttees. Leather leggings worn by soldiers and others who ride horses

putrefaction Decomposition, the cleavage or splitting up of the molecules of a protein resulting in the formation of other substances of less complex constitution, accompanied by the formation of ammoniac and sulphur gases

pyemia. The presence of pus in the blood

pyogenic Pus-forming relating to pus formation

pyrogallic acid. A substance obtained from gallic acid, used in podiatry in the treatment of verruca.

pyrogallol. Pyrogallic acid

pyroxylin Gun cotton, an etherial solution of which makes collodion

Q

quinine and urea hydrochloride A mixture of quinine, as its name indicates, used as a local anesthetic

R

radical As a radical operation, one which removes every trace of possibly diseased tissue, or makes recurrence impossible

radiograph. An X-ray machine

radiogram. An X-ray picture

radiography The science of obtaining X-ray pictures.

radioscopy. Fluoroscopy.
radix. The hard, usually central portion of a corn, root. **r. unguis.** The root of the nail
rancid Characterizing an oil or other fat which is decomposing
rational Reasonable, not delirious or comatose
rays. Lines of light heat or other forms of radioactivity **alpha rays** Rays charged with positive electricity **beta rays** Rays charged with negative electricity **gamma rays.** Waves of motion not charged with electricity
Raynaud's disease Symmetrical gangrene of the extremities
receptacle A storage place
R The abbreviation of the latin word recipe—take, used as the superscription of a prescription
recumbent Lying down
recurrent. Returning, applied to symptoms
redintol A paraffine preparation used for burns
reduce To replace, as a fracture or a dislocation
redundant. Exuberant, more than normal
reenforcement Augmented enforcement, as of a bandage or a dressing
reflex. A reaction, an involuntary movement or exercise of function in a part. **ankle r.,** ankle-jerk, a sudden contraction of the calf muscles, extending the foot when the tendo Achillis is tapped, the subject kneeling on a chair with the foot hanging loosely **Babinski's r**, extension of the toes follows tickling of the sole, usually a sign of organic disease of the pyramidal tracts
patellar r., a sudden contraction of the anterior muscles of the thigh from a tap on the patellar tendon, which brings up the foot, the subject being seated on the edge of a chair with legs loosely crossed, knee-jerk
plantar r, a flexion of the toes following scratching or tickling the sole of the foot
tarsophalangeal, r, flexion of the 2nd and 3rd (sometimes 2nd to 5th) toes when the dorsum of the foot is lightly tapped, indicating an organic lesion of the motor nerve-centres
tendo Achillis r, a contraction of the calf muscles when the tendo calcaneus is sharply struck
toe r., strong passive flexion of the great toe excites contraction of the flexor muscles in the leg, sudden passive extension causes rythmical contraction of the great toe—toe-clonus
regeneration. Reproduction or repair of lost or injured parts
relapse. Return of a disease after it has once spent its force
relax. To loosen, to slacken
remedy. An agent applied to cure a disease or to alleviate its symptoms
renal Relating to the kidneys
repair. Restoration after injury
resect. To cut off, especially to cut off the articular ends of a bone or bones forming a joint
resin The residue after the distillation of turpentine

resolution The arrest of an inflammatory process without suppuration, the absorption or breaking down and removal of the products of inflammation
resonator. An apparatus for producing sounds
resorcin. A phenol derivative used for ulcers
respiration. A function common to all living plants or animals, consisting in man in the taking in of oxygen and the throwing off of the products of oxidation
resorption Removal of an exudate, a blood clot, pus, etc, by absorption
rete Malpighii Stratum germinativum, the lowest layers of cells of the epidermis, the reproducing cells of the epidermis
reticular layer The inner layer of the corium, composed of connective tissue bundles
retrogressive. Degenerative, a reversal of metabolic changes
retropulsion An involuntary backward running or walking occurring in certain nervous affections, a pushing back of any part
reversed. Turned backward or in an opposite direction
rheostat A resistance coil, an instrument used to regulate the degree of resistance in an electric current
rickets Rachitis, a disease occurring in infants and young children, it is characterized by softening of the bones, etc
ridge. A linear bone elevation
rigid. Stiff, inflexible
rigor. Rigidity
rigor m., stiffening of the body from one to seven hours after death
Roentgen rays. X-rays
roentgenography. Radiography
roentgenoscopy Fluoroscopy
roentgenotherapy The treatment of disease by the X-rays
root. In anatomy, the base, foundation or beginning of any part, radix
radix unguis, the root of the nail
rotary file. An instrument used for grinding nails
rubefacient. A mild counter-irritant which reddens the skin
rubor Redness, one of the classical symptoms of inflammation
ruby lamp. A lamp colored red, and used in the dark room for developing purposes It does not affect the sensitized plates
runaround A superficial paronychia
rupture. A tear or solution of continuity

S

S. Abbreviation of Latin, signa-remark the usual introduction to the directions in a prescription
sac. A pouch, a bursa, the capsule of a tumor, the envelop of a cyst
sacro-iliac disease. A disease occurring in the region of the sacrum and ilium
salicylic acid An acid derived from the oil of wintergreen Largely used in podiatry to remove helomata and verrucae
saline solution. A solution of sodium chloride and water in the proportion in which it exists in the blood
salol Phenyl salicylate

saltatory Relating to or marked by dancing or leaping
salvarsan Trade name of Ehrlich's 606, employed in the treatment of syphilis
salve An ointment ceratum, unguentum
sandal. An old form of footgear
sanguineous Relating to the blood
sapo Soap
saponacious Soapy, resembling soap
sapremia Septicemia
sarcoma A malignant connective tissue neoplasm
saturated Impregnated to the greatest possible extent, said of a solution, a liquid holding all of a given solute that it can dissolve
saturnism Lead poisoning
scab A crust formed by the drying of the pus on the surface of an ulcer or excoriation
scalloped Cut in curves
scalpel. A pointed knife with a convex edge
scarfskin Epidermis
scar tissue White fibrous tissue formed in the healing of wounds, cicatrix
scarify. To make a number of superficial incisions in the skin
scarlet red. An organic dye-stuff used in ointment form as an antiseptic and as a stimulant in the treatment of ulcers
sciatic Relating to sciatica
sciatica Sciatic neuritis Neuralgia of the sciatic nerve
sclerodactylia Scleroderma affecting the digits of the hands or feet
scleroderma. A hardening and thickening of the skin with loss of elasticity
scleronychia. Induration and thickening of the nails
sclerosis. Induration or hardening, of chronic inflammatory origin
scoliosis. Lateral curvature of the spine
scorbutus Scurvy
scrofula A constitutional state, occurring in the young and marked by a lack of tissue resisting power
scurvy. A disease marked by inanition, debility anemia, edema of the dependent parts, a spongy condition, sometimes with ulceration of the gums and hemorrhages into the skin and from the mucous membranes
sebaceous. Carrying or producing sebum
sebum The fluid excreted by the sebaceous glands of the skin
seborrhea Overaction of the sebaceous glands
secondary. One of the symptoms of syphilis following the development of the chancre
secretion. The product (solid, liquid or gaseous) of cellular or glandular activity A secretion is stored up in or utilized by the animal or plant in which it is produced, thereby differing from an excretion which is intended to be expelled from the body
secretory. Relating to secretion or to the secretions
sedative. An agent which quiets nervous excitement
semi. A prefix denoting one-half or partly (Exam semi-flexion—midway between flexion and extension)
semis. One-half, noted in prescription writing as ss
senility. Old age
sensitized. Rendered sensitive

sensory Relating to sensation
septic. Unclean, contaminated with bacteria
septicemia. A systemic disease caused by the presence of microorganisms or their toxins in the blood, sepsis
septum. A thin wall dividing two cavities or masses of softer tissue
sequestrum. A piece of necrosed bone which has become separated from the surrounding healthy osseous tissue
serofibrinous Noting an exudate composed of serum and fibrin
seropurulent Containing both serum and pus
serous. Relating to, containing or producing serum
serpiginous Noting an ulcer or other cutaneous lesion which extends gradually over the surface on one side while usually healing on the other
serrated. Notched, toothed
serum A clear, watery fluid that moistens the surface of serous membranes The fluid portion of the blood obtained after coagulation
sesamoid Resembling in size or shape a grain of sesame an oval nodule of bone or fibrocartilage in a tendon playing over a joint surface, most common in the metacarpo and metatarsophalangeal articulations and other joints of the fingers and toes
sessile. Having a broad base of attachment not pedunculated
sheath. Any enveloping structure, such as the membranous covering of a muscle nerve, or blood-vessel
sheep-skin Prepared skin of the sheep, used for shields
shield. An agent used in podiatry to protect a part from friction or pressure
shock A sudden physical or mental disturbance
silver. Argentum, a metal of lustrous white color
s nitrate, largely used in podiatry as a caustic, escharotic and stimulant
s. stick, fused silver nitrate in stick form
sinew Tendon
sinister Of evil import, of bad prognosis, Latin for left in contradistinction to dexter, meaning right
sinistrapodeai. Left footed
sinuous. Tortuous, bending in several directions
sinus A tortuous tract opening on a free surface and leading down to an abscess cavity
sirenomelia. A monstrosity having two lower limbs fused in one
skiagram. A print made from a photographic plate exposed to the action of the X-rays
skiagraphy. Radiography
skiascopy Fluoroscopy
skin The membranous covering of the body, cutis, integumentum
skin-grafting The placing of bits of epidermis or larger strips of the entire skin on a denuded surface in order to supply defects or to stimulate a new skin growth
skiving. The process of thinning shields at their borders
skiving knife An instrument used for skiving
slough Necrosed tissue separated from the living structure

sodium A metallic element The following salts of sodium are used in podiatry
- s bicarbonate, used as a dusting powder in acidity of the skin
- s borate, (borax) used as an antiseptic
- s. chloride, (common salt) used as an antiseptic
- s ethylate, used as a caustic in verruca
- s hydroxide, (caustic soda) used as a caustic
- s. sulphide, used to remove superfluous hair

soggy. Soaked, wet
sole The under part of the foot, the plantar surface
solution. The incorporation of a solid or gas in a fluid
spasm. An involuntary convulsive muscular contraction, cramp
spastic. Spasmodic, convulsive
spatula A flat blade used for spreading plasters and ointments
spatulate. Shaped like a spatula
specific Relating to an individual infectious disease, one caused by a special microorganism, in a special restricted sense, syphilis
sphacelous Necrotic gangrenous, sloughing
spheroidal. Resembling a sphere
spica A form of bandage with overlapping turns
spinal. Relating to the vertebral column
spiral Coiled, winding around a center
spiritus (spirit). An alcoholic solution of a gaseous or volatile substance
Spirochaeta pallida. The protozoan which when present in the blood indicates syphilis
splay-foot. Flat foot, talipes valgus
splint. An apparatus for rendering a part immobile, as in fractures
spontaneous. Occurring without external stimulation
sporadic. Occurring singly, neither endemic nor epidemic
spur A dull spine or projection from a bone
staphylococcus A group of cocci in which the individuals are arranged in irregular masses somewhat resembling a bunch of grapes
stasis. Stagnation of the blood or other fluids
static. In a state of equilibrium or rest, not in action
static ataxia Inability to preserve equilibrium in standing through loss of the deep sensibility
station. Power of standing more or less firmly on one's feet
stereognosis. Ascertaining the form of an object by means of touch
sterile Surgically clean, free from bacteria
sterilization The act of making a person or thing sterile
sterilizer An apparatus for making anything aseptic or germ-free
stimulant An agent that arouses organic activity
stimulation The arousing of the body or any of its parts or organs to increased functional activity
stovaine A local anesthetic, used especially to induce spinal anesthesia

stratum Layer
streptococcus. A group of cocci in which the arrangement resembles chains
streptococcus viridans. A form of streptococcus which grows in green colonies and is not hemolytic; the bacterium responsible for most focal infections in the teeth
striated. Striped
stroma The framework made of connective tissue
strychnine An alkaloid of nux vomica
stump-foot Club-foot
styptic Astringent, hemostatic
sub A prefix denoting beneath, less than normal or typical, inferior, corresponds to hypo (Exam subastragular—under the astragalus)
subacute Not frankly acute, yet not chronic, noting the course of a disease
subcutaneous Beneath the skin
subluxation. An incomplete luxation or dislocation
sudamina Minute vesicles due to retention of fluid at the mouth of a sweat follicle
sudoriferous Carrying or producing sweat
sulphur Brimstone, a chemical element, used in ointment form as a stimulant
super. A prefix signifying in excess, above, superior, same as supra and hyper (Exam supertension—extreme tension)
superficial Near the surface, cursory, not thorough
superfluous. More than sufficient
supernumerary. More than normal in number
supersaturated Said of a solution which holds more than a normal quantity of a solute, and caused by heating the liquid
suppurate To form pus
supra A prefix denoting a position above (Exam supracostal—above the ribs)
surgery. The branch of medicine which has to do with the treatment of disease by means of operative procedures
suture The surgical uniting of two surfaces by means of stitches, with silk thread, catgut, wire etc, the material by which the two surfaces are held in apposition
swab A tuft of cotton or other like material attached to the end of a stick or wire, used for cleansing cavities or applying remedies
sweat-gland. One of the tubular coli-glands in the corium and subcutaneous connective tissue, secreting sweat
swell-foot Swelling and redness of the metatarsus, with pain and disability due to sprain of the ligaments which are frequently detached from the bones
symptomatology. The science of the symptoms of disease
symptoms Any morbid phenomenon or departure from the normal in function, appearance or sensation experienced by the patient and indicative of disease Objective s., one which is evident to the observer Subjective s., one apparent only to the patient
synarthrosis. A fixed articulation
syndactylous Having webbed fingers or toes

synonyms. Words having the same meaning as others
synovia A clear fluid secreted by a synovial membrane and used to lubricate the joints.
synovial membrane. The lining membrane of a joint, secreting the synovia
synthetic. Relating to the formation of chemical compounds by the union of simpler compounds
syphilide. Any skin lesion of syphilitic origin
syphilis. An infectious disease spread by inoculation, usually by sexual intercourse, and due to the spirochaeta pallida
syphiloderma. Syphilis of the skin
syringe. An instrument for injecting fluids
syringomyelia. The presence of cavities in the spinal cord due to the breaking down of gliomatous new formations
systemic. Relating to the entire organism as distinguished from any of its individual parts
systremma A muscular cramp in the calf of the leg

T

tabes dorsalis. Locomotor ataxia, a disease of the spinal ganglia and roots usually found in middle age and often the sequel of syphilis
tactile. Relating to touch or to the sense of touch
talipes. Cyllosis, club-foot in general
 t **calcaneovalgus,** t calcaneus and t valgus combined
 t **calcaneovarus,** t calcaneus and t varus, combined,
 t **calcaneus,** permanent dorsal flexion of the foot, so that the weight of the body rests on the heel, only
 t. **cavus,** hollow foot, an exaggeration of the normal arch of the foot
 t. **equinovalgus,** t equinus and t valgus, combined,
 t **equinovarus,** t equinus and t varus, combined,
 t **equinus,** permanent extension of the foot so that only the ball rests on the ground,
 t **percavus,** an extreme degree of t vagus,
 t. **planovalgus,** t valgus,
 t **planus,** flat-foot, splay-foot—a condition in which the arch of the foot is broken down, the entire sole touching the ground,
 t. **spasmodicus,** a temporary distortion of the foot, usually t equinus, due to muscular spasm,
 t **vagus,** permanent eversion of the foot, the inner side alone of the sole resting on the ground;
 t. **varus;** inversion of the foot, the outer side of the foot only touching the ground
talus Ankle-bone, astragalus
tampon To plug a canal with gauze, cotton-wool or other substance, the substance used for the above purpose is also known by the same name
tangent. A straight line that touches or meets a circle or curve, but does not cut it
tannoform. Trade name of a compound of tannin with ferric aldehyde

tarsal Relating to a tarsus in any sense
tarsalgia Podalgia, policeman's disease pain in the tarsus usually due to incipient flat-feet or to a shortening of the tendo Achillis
tarsometatarsal Relating to the tarsal and metatarsal bones of the foot or region
tarsophalangeal Relating to the tarsus and the phalanges
tarsus The root of the foot, or instep
T B C. (tuberculosis) A specific disease caused by the presence of bacillus tuberculosis, it may affect almost any tissue or organ of the body, the most common seats of the disease being the lungs and joints
teat. Any nipple-like protuberance
technic. The manner of performance of any surgical operation
temper Elasticity or hardness in steel
tenalgia Pain referred to a tendon
tendo Achillis The tendon of insertion of the gastrocnemius and the soleus muscles into the tuberosity of the os calcis
tendon. A fibrous cord or band which connects the muscle to its bony attachment
tenotomy The surgical division of a tendon
tension The act of stretching
tepid Lukewarm, for a bath, 86°F
tertiary The final stages of syphilis
tetanus. An infectious disease marked by painful tonic muscular contractions caused by the toxin of bacillus tetani acting upon the central nervous system
tetany A disorder marked by intermittent tonic muscular contractions
tetradactyl Having only four fingers or toes on a hand or foot
therapeutic. Relating to the treatment of disease, curative
thermal. Relating to warmth or heat
thermocautery. The actual cautery, destruction of tissue by heat
Thiersch's solution. An antiseptic solution containing boric acid and salicylic acid
Thomsen's disease Myotonia congenita An hereditary disease marked by momentary tonic spasms which occur when a voluntary movement is attempted
thrombosis Formation or presence of a thrombus
thrombus A plug more or less completely occluding a blood vessel or one of the cavities of the heart
tibia. Shin-bone, the inner and larger of the two bones of the leg
tinctura An alcoholic solution or extract of a non-volatile vegetable substance, a tincture
 t **arnicae,** used for sprains and bruises,
 t. **benzoini comp;** used for sunburn, chimation, etc,
 t **calendulae** used for sprains and bruises,
 t. **cresolis saponata,** used as an antiseptic,
 t. **ferri chloridi;**
 t **iodi,**
 t **iodi (Churchill),**
 t. **iodi decolorata,**
 t **saponis viridis.**
tinea unguium. Ringworm of the nail
tip-foot Talipes equinus

tissue A collection of cells or of cell derivatives forming a definite structure
titubation. A staggering or stumbling in trying to walk, due to spinal lesion; restlessness
toe. Digitus pedis, one of the digits of the feet
  great t, the toe on the inner, tibial side of the foot corresponding to the thumb
  hammer t, permanent flexion at the mid-phalangeal joint
toe-drop. A drooping of the anterior portion of the foot, due to paralysis
toe separator An instrument used for separating the toes
toe webs The skin at the base of the toes
tonic In a state of continuous, unremitting action, noting especially a muscular contraction Increasing physical or mental tone or strength, invigorating A remedy given or applied to tone up the system
touch corpuscles Special bodies found in the true skin, especially at the ends of the fingers, and used for the sense of touch
tourniquet. An instrument for arresting the flow of blood through a part
toxemia Blood-poisoning, the presence of toxins in the blood
toxic. Poisonous Relating to a toxin
toxin A poisonous substance of undetermined chemical nature, developed during the growth of pathogenic bacteria
transient Not permanent, coming and going
transition Passage from one condition or one part to another
trauma A wound or injury
traumatic Relating to or caused by a wound or injury
tremor Trembling shaking, a disorder of the muscular tonus or loss of equilibrium the normal inappreciable tonic contractions being exaggerated
trench foot. A disease of the present war See full description in the body of the book as per index
tropacocaine. An alkaloid obtained from Java coca leaves, a local anesthetic
trophic. Relating to or dependent upon nutrition
tuberculosis A specific disease caused by the bacillus tuberculosis, it may affect any tissue of the body
tumor Neoplasm, a circumscribed growth, not inflammatory in character
tungsten A metallic element symbol W atomic weight 184, occurring as a gray powder of metallic lustre A form of incandescent electric lamp is made of a tungsten filament
turpentine Terebinthina Prepared in the form of oil and of spirit for external applications
typhoid. Typhus-like, stuporous from fever, same as typhoid fever
tyloma Callosity, tylosis
tyroma. A caseous (cheese-like) tumor

U

ulcer. A circumscribed open sore which shows no tendency to heal ulcus
uncinariasis Hookworm disease
undertoe. Displacement of the great toe beneath the second toe
ungual Relating to the nail

unguentum Ointment, salve
  u. acidi borici, boric acid ointment, used in burns and abrasions
  u acidi salicylici, salicylic acid ointment, used as a disintegrant
  u. acidi carbolici, carbolic acid or phenol ointment, used in burns and in superficial wounds
  u. balsam Peruvianum, balsam of Peru ointment, stimulating
  u camphorae, camphor ointment, stimulating
  u. cantharidis, cantharidal ointment, rubefacient
  u. capsici, capsicum ointment, rubefacient
  u. creasoti, creasote ointment, applied to chilblains, indolent ulcers and various skin affections
  u diachylon, Hebra's lead ointment, employed in hyperidrosis
  u. hamamelidis witch hazel ointment, a soothing application
  u. hydrargyri ammoniati, white precipitate ointment, applied in chronic skin conditions and in tubercular syphilides
  u. hydrargyri oxide rubri red precipitate ointment, used in the treatment of indolent ulcers
  u. ichthyoli, ichthyol ointment, emollient
  u iodi, iodine ointment, used in chilblains and in glandular enlargements
  u picis compositum, compound tar ointment, employed in wounds and in burns
  u plumbi acetatis, lead acetate ointment, astringent application to burns and superficial inflammations
  u resorcini compositum, "soothing ointment", astringent and antiseptic
  u. scarlet red scarlet red ointment, stimulating
  u. sulphuris sulphur ointment, used in scabies
  u zinci oxidi, ointment of zinc oxide, a soothing mild astringent application in skin diseases, burns and abrasions
unguis. Nail, a thin horny transparent plate covering the dorsal surface of the distal end of each terminal phalanx of fingers and toes
Unverricht's progressive myoclonus See Thomsen's disease
uric acidemia See lithemia
uridrosis The excretion of urea or uric acid in the sweat
union The joining together of the opposing parts of a wound
unofficial Not official, said of a remedial agent not described in the pharmacopeia
uremia An autointoxication occurring in certain cases of nephritis or in anuria from any cause
U S P Abbreviation for the United States Pharmacopeia

V

vacuum A space from which the air has been practically extracted
valgus Bending outward, noting a condition of the great toe, in which it is bent outward knock-knees, see talipes valgus

vanadium chloride. A yellowish substance used in bromidrosis
varicose. Relating to or affected with large and tortuous veins
variola. Smallpox
varix An enlarged and tortuous vein, artery or lymphatic vessel
vascular Relating to or containing blood vessels
vasoconstrictors Agents which cause narrowing of the blood vessels, nerves, stimulation of which cause vascular constriction
vasodilators Agents which cause dilatation of the blood vessels, a nerve, stimulation of which results in dilatation of the blood vessels
vasomotor The nerves which have the power of dilating or constricting the blood vessels
vein. A blood vessel conveying blood towards the heart Lat vena
veins of the foot
- v plantaris interna, internal plantar vein (plantar surface, deep)
- v plantaris externa, external plantar vein (plantar surface deep)
- v saphena brevis, external or short saphenous vein (dorsal surface, superficial)
- v. saphena longa, internal or long saphenous vein (dorsal surface, superficial)
- v tibialis anticus, anterior tibial vein (dorsal surface, deep)
- No veins on the superficial plantar surface

verbatim. Word for word
vermiform appendix. A blind sac of the intestine extending from the head of the cecum
verruca. A circumscribed overgrowth of the layers of the skin, including those of the derma (plural verrucae)
vertebral caries Molecular death of the bones of the spinal column
vertigo. Dizziness giddiness
vesicant An agent which when applied to the skin produces a blister
vesicle A small circumscribed elevation on the skin, containing non-purulent fluid, a blister
vesicular Relating to a vesicle, containing vesicles
vibration A shaking, oscillation
vice-versa The terms in the case being reversed
virulent. Extremely poisonous
vocational. Referring to occupation
volatile. Not permanent, evaporating spontaneously
voltage. The electromotive force of a current expressed in volts
vulcanizing Adhering rubber by means of heat

W

wart. A circumscribed hypertrophy of the papillae of the corium (See verruca)
Wasserman test. A diagnostic test for syphilis, based upon the theory of complement fixation
web The skin found at the base of the fingers or toes
wheal An acute, circumscribed elevation of the skin due to edema in the derma
whitlow Felon, paronychia, inflammation of the tissues around the nail
whorl. A set of organs arranged in a circle around an axis
wick. A piece of gauze or other material used for draining cavities
wipe. A piece of gauze or cotton used in wiping instruments
wool-fat Adeps lanae Used as an embrocation in podiatry Lanolin
Woulfe's bottle A bottle with two or three necks, for working with gases (washing, drying, etc)
wound Loss in continuity upon the surfaces of the body
wrist-drop Paralysis of the extensors of the wrist and fingers

X

X-rays. Roentgen rays
xystus Scraped lint, lint made by scraping linen with a sharp instrument

Z

Zander's system Treatment by means of mechanical apparatus giving passive movements
zinc oxide A white powder used as an astringent
zinc stearate. A white powder used as an antiseptic dusting powder
zymotic Relating to fermentation, noting an infectious disease

(We are obligated to Stedman's Practical Medical Dictionary for many of the definitions of medical terms above noted —Editor)

CROSS REFERENCE INDEX

A

Acetanilid 296
Acetic acid 191
Acriflavin 34
Actinotherapy 385
Adenoids 379
Adipose tissue 14
Advent of foot clothing 47
Alcohol 27, 131, 198, 215, 218, 225, 228, 250, 253, 273, 275 301, 331, 334
Aluminum acetate 219, 224, 225, 289, 295
Aluminum chloride 301
Alternate foot bath 53, 299
Alternating current 386
Alypin 144
Ambrene 70
Ammoniated mercury 29, 221, 254
Anidrosis 303
   definition of 303
   derivation of 303
   etiology of 303
   symptoms of 303
   synonyms of 303
   treatment of 303
Anterior arch 184
Antisepsis 19, 20, 21, 24, 33
Antiseptics, general 24
   chlorinated lime 26
   formaldehyde 25
   heat 25
   lime 25
   sublimed sulphur 26
   sunlight 24
Antiseptics, local 26
   alcohol 27
   balsam of Peru 27
   borate of sodium 27
   borax 27
   boric acid 27
   boroglycerine 27
   bichloride of mercury 29
   calomel 29
   Dakin solution 27
   di-chloramin-T 28
   glycerinu'm 28
   hydrogen dioxide 28
   peroxide 28
   iodoform 29
   iodine 28
   liquor alumini acetatis 27
   cresolis compositas 29
   lysol 30
   mercuric chloride 29
   mercurous chloride 29
   peroxide of hydrogen 28
   potassium permanganate 30
   sulphur 30
   phenol 29
   thymol 30
   thymol iodide 30
   unguentum hydrargyri 29
   hydrargyri ammoniatum 29
   sulphuris 30
Apothesine 148
Applicators 91
Areolar tissue 14
Aristol 30, 220, 249, 262, 320, 332, 334

Arsphenamine 378
Arteriosclerosis 404
Arthritis 402
Asepsis 19 32
Aseptic gauze 62
Atrophy of the nails 244

B

Bacillus aerogenes capsulatis 369
Baking 273
Balsam of Peru 27, 180, 193, 198, 199, 221, 247, 262, 277, 295, 320 327 332 335
Bandage scissors 89
Bandages
   description of 75, 76 77
Bandaging 73
Belgian hone 92
Belladonna 298, 299
Benzoated collodion 69
Bichloride of Mercury 29, 199, 218, 273, 274, 289, 318, 328, 334
Bismuth subgallate 220, 249, 262, 313, 332
Bismuth subnitrate 220, 249, 262, 313, 332
Blebs 248, 251, 289, 333
   treatment of 334
Blisters 248, 251
   definition of 251
   etiology of 251
   pathology of 252
   prognosis of 256
   treatment of 253
      ordinary conditions 252
      broken conditions 254
   usual points of location of 252
Bones of the foot 50
   borate of sodium 27, 362
Borated gauze 63
Borax 27, 362
Boric acid 27, 220, 225, 239, 273 275, 302, 303, 318, 320 324
Boroglycerine 27, 312
Brilliant Green 35
Bromidrosis 302
   definition of 302
   derivation of 302
   etiology of 302
   pathology of 302
   symptoms of 302
   synonyms of 302
   treatment of 302
Buckskin 97
Bullae 248, 251, 289
Burns 248, 256
   definition of 256
   pathology of 257
   treatment of 257
Burnt alum 226
Burow's solution 318
Burs 91
Bursitis 263
   definition of 263
   characteristics of 265, 266
   etiology of 264
   location of 264
   pathology of 265

Bursitis—
   removal of pressure for 268
   rest for 268
   strapping of 269
   symptoms of 265
      objective 265
      subjective 265
   treatment of 266
      non-radical 267
      palliative 267
      radical 267

C

California College of Chiropody 5
Callositas 182
   definition of 182
   derivation of 182
   diagnosis of 183
   etiology of 182
   pathology of 183
   prognosis of 183
   symptoms of 182
   synonyms of 182
   treatment of 184
Callosity 182
Callous 182
Callous ulcer 306, 314
   differential diagnosis 316
   etiology of 315
   general causes 315
   local causes 315
   symptoms of 315
   treatment of 317
      cleansing 318
      sterilization 318
Calloused nail groove 205, 237
   definition of 205
   etiology of 206
   symptoms of 206
   treatment of 206
      surgical 207
      medical 208
Callus 182
Calomel 29, 320
Calomin lotion 302
Camphor 361, 362, 363
Camphorated oil 365
Camphorated soap liniment 290
Cannibis indica 277
Capsicum 279
Carbon dioxide pencil 179, 191, 203
Carbon dioxide snow 145
Carrel method 21
Catalepsy 355
Chamois 97
Chauffeur's foot 340
   etiology of 340
   treatment of 341
Chicago School of Chiropody 5
Chilblains 283
Chimation mild 283
   definition of 283
   derivation of 283
   diagnosis of 286
   differential diagnosis of 288

433

434 CROSS REFERENCE INDEX

Chimation mild—
  etiology of 283
  pathology of 285
  predisposition to 284
  prognosis of 288
  symptoms of 284
  synonyms of 283
  treatment of 288
Chimation severe 291
  definition of 291
  derivation of 291
  diagnosis of 293
  etiology of 291
  pathology of 292
  prognosis of 294
  recurrence of 294
  symptoms of 292
  synonyms of 291
  treatment of 294
Chiropodists of America 2
Chisel 81
Chlorazene 37, 168
Chlorinated lime 26
Chromic acid 301, 303
Chromidrosis 304
  definition of 304
Clippers 86
Cocaine 143
Cocoon dressing 65, 184, 335
Cold applications 271
Colloidal silver 363
  gold 364
Collodion 68
  benzoated 69
  ichthyolated 69
  iodized 69
  medicated 68
  salicylated 70
Colorado Pedic Society 9
Connecticut Pedic Society 9
Copper sulphate 320
Corium 13
Corns 149
Corrosive sublimate gauze 62
Cotton 64
Counter irritation 270 278
Creoline 318
Cutaneous manifestations of super-acidity 329
  characteristics of 329
  definition of 329
  etiology of 330
Cuticle scissors 89

D

Dancer's foot 341
  treatment of 341
Dakin solution 21, 27, 35 168, 318
Deodorant 26
Derma 13
  blood supply of 14
Dermatitis calorica 291
Dermatitis congelationes 283
Dermatol 220, 320, 334
Diachylon 300
Diagnosis of radiographs 397
Di-chloramin-T 28, 37
Direct cautery 191 202 222, 224
Direct current 386
Disinfectant 26
Dressings 60, 218 258
  moist 60
  evaporating moist 60
  non-evaporating moist 60

Dressings—
  occlusive 61
  dry 61
  ointment 61
Drill 90
Dry dressings 61, 220, 312
Duck shield 174

E

Electric experiments 385
Electricity 270 280, 296
Electrolysis 178, 191, 200
Ephidrosis 297
Epidermis 12
Epithelioma 189
Ergot 298
Erythema pernio 283
Ethyl bromide 145
Ethyl chloride 145
Ethylate or soda 196
Evaporating moist dressings 60
Excavator 84
Excessive sweating 297
Excision 191, 198, 222
Exostosis 399

F

Fabrics for dressings 62
Faradic Current 281, 290 296, 304
Felon 239
Felt 98
Felt adhesive 99
Ferri subsulphate 227, 232
Ferric chloride 232
Fish skin 73
Fissured toe webs 171
Fissures 248, 330
  definition of 248
  etiology of 248
  treatment of 248, 331
  technic 249
Flat foot 340
  symptoms of 340
  treatment of 340
Flavin 34
Fluoroscopy 385
Focal infection 379
  modes of 380
  relationship between the foot and, 380
  treatment of 381
Foot care of adolescents 55
Foot care of adults 56
Foot care of infants 53
Foot care of soldiers 57
Foot gear, modern 47
Forceps 85, 88
Formaldehyde 25, 44, 299, 301
Formalin 319
Fractures 399
  comminuted 400
  complete 400
  compound 402
  compression 400
  crushing 400
  impacted 400
  incomplete 399
  multiple 400
  simple 400
Freezing method of anesthesia 146
Frost bite 291
Fulguration 177, 191, 199

G

Gall bladder 379
Gallic acid 298, 332
Galvanic current 304
Gangrene 293 294
Gas gangrene 365, 368, 369
Gas infection 369
  antitoxin for 372
  bacteriologic diagnosis 372
  destruction of bacillus 371
  etiology of 369
  removal of necrotic tissue 371
  symptoms of 370
  treatment of 370
Gauze 62
  borated 63
  corrosive sublimate 62
  iodoform 62
  plain aseptic 62
  squares 63 64 219 314
  uses of 63
Geissler air pump 386
Glands 14
Glossary 411
Glycerinum 28
Golfer's foot 341
Gonorrheal heel 380
Ground itch 368
  treatment of 369
Guaiacol 290
Gutta percha tissue 72

H

Hard corn 150
Heat 25
Heloma 149
  definition of 150
  derivation of 149
  synonyms of 150
Heloma disseminatum 179
  definition of 179
  diagnosis of 180
  etiology of 179
  pathology of 180
  prognosis of 180
  symptoms of 179
  treatment of 179
Heloma durum 150
  diagnosis of 154
  etiology of 151
  pathology of 152, 153
  prognosis of 155
  symptoms of 150
  treatment of 156
    dissection 160
    non-radical 159
    palliative 157
    preventive 156
    operative 158
    radical 158
    shaving 159
Heloma miliare, 179
Heloma molle 169
  definition of 169
  diagnosis of 170
  etiology of 170
  pathology of 170
  prognosis of 171
  symptoms of 169
  treatment of 172
Heloma vasculare 174, 190
  diagnosis of 175
  etiology of 174
  pathology of 174
  prognosis of 175
  symptoms of 174
  treatment of 175

CROSS REFERENCE INDEX 435

Helotomon 81
Hematidrosis 304
  definition of 304
Hemorrhage 31
Hidrosis 297
High frequency current 177, 199, 281 290, 296
High heels 48
Honing 92
Hookworm 368
Hot applications 270, 304
Hydradenitis 305
  definition of 305
Hydrogen dioxide 28
Hydrogen peroxide 28, 218 228, 289
Hydrocystoma 304
  definition of 304
Hydrotherapy 270
Hygiene of the foot 51-291
Hyperidrosis 297
  definition of 297
  derivation of 297
  etiology of 297
  pathology of 297
  prognosis of 298
  symptoms of 298
  synonyms of 297
  treatment of 298
Hypodermic method of anesthesia 145
Hypodermic syringe 90, 146
  uses of 147

I

Ichthyol 180, 193, 198, 199, 251, 254, 262, 276, 290, 295, 296, 320, 332
Ichthyolated collodion 69
Idrosis 297
Illinois College of Chiropody 5
Illinois Pedic Association 8
Impervious coverings 72
Incorporated Society of Chiropodists (England) 6
Indolent ulcer 306, 314
  etiology of 315
  symptoms of 315
Infection 213
  treatment of 227
Infected heloma 167
Inflammation
  symptoms of 177
Ingrown nail clippers 86
Ingrown nail forceps 85
Ingrown toe nail 205, 210, 237
Instruments 78
  applicators 91
  burs 91
  care of 92
  chisel 81
  excavator 84
  helotomon 81
  history of 79
  honing of 92
    Belgian hone 92
    oil stone 93
    Swatty hone 93
    technic 93
  hypodermic syringe 90
  ingrown nail clippers 86
    forceps 85
  iris tooth forceps 88
  nail chisel 82
    clippers 86
    file 91
    groove gouge 83

Instruments—
  scraper 84
  polishing 94
  rotary file 90
  scalpel 80
  scissors 88
    bandage 89
    cuticle 89
  selection and care of 78
  skiving knife 92
  soft corn spoon 83
  spatula 84
  special, for ingrown nail 85
  standardization of 80
  thumb forceps 86
  toe separators 91
  wiping of 95
Iodoform 29, 320
Iodoform gauze 62
Iodine 28, 215, 295
Iodized collodion 69
Iris tooth forceps 88

J

Jaborandi 304

L

Lamb's wool 99
Lanolin 276
Lassar's paste 320
Laws governing chiropody
  New York 8
  California 8
Lead and opium wash 273, 275, 318
Lewi, Maurice J 4
Lime 25
Lint 66
  shielding 67
Liquor alumini acetatis 27, 273, 274
Liquor cresolis compositus 29
Lister, Joseph 22
Local anesthesia 143, 158, 198
  reaction of 148
  technic of 145
Locomotion as an aid in diagnosis 343
  classification of gaits 347
  Ataxic gait 352
    static ataxic 352
    static spinal ataxic 353
    cerebellar 353
      titubating 353
      reeling or staggering 354
  Choreic 354
    festination 354
    hysteria 355
    myotonia 355
    saltatory 355
    stumbling 354
  Paretic gait 347
    mild 347
      Charlie Chaplin 349
      hobbling 347
      intermittant limping 348
      pompous 347
      shuffling 348
      tottering 348
      waddling 348
      wobbly 348
    moderate or flaccid 349
      prancing 350

Locomotion—
  steppage 349
  spastic or severe 350
    cross legged 351
    dragging 352
    dromedary 352
    ill-defined spastic 352
    mowing or hemiplegic 351
    small step 351
  elements of 343
    gait 344
    posture 343
    station 344
  methods of diagnosis 345
    ichnogram 345
    observation 345
Lymphatics 15
Lysol 30 318

M

Massage 250, 270, 279, 280, 259, 296, 304
Mazamorro 368
Medicated collodion 69
Menthol 276
Mercuric chloride 29, 273, 274
Mercurous chloride 29
Mercury 378
Metatarsalgia 139, 141, 382
  treatment of 383
Methylene blue 196
Miliaria 304
  definition of 304
Miscellaneous foot lesions 357
Moist dressings 60, 270, 273
Moleskin 195
Moleskin adhesive 97
Monochloracetic acid 191
Monsell's solution 227, 232
Morton's neuralgia 382
Morton's toe 139, 140, 382
  treatment of 382
Muscles 15
Mustard 279

N

Nail chisel 82, 215
Nail clippers 86
Nail file 91
Nail groove gouge 83
Nail matrix 16
Nails 16, 50
Nail scraper 84
Naked foot 46
National Association of Chiropodists 3, 9, 10
Necrosis 293
Nerves 15
  medullated nerve fibres 15
  non-medullated nerve fibres 15
Nitric acid 176, 191, 194, 225
Non-evaporating moist dressings 60
Novocaine 144 198, 216

O

Occlusive dressings 61
Office 405
  accessories 409
  cabinet 408
  chair 407
  cleanliness of 405
  comfort of patient 405

CROSS REFERENCE INDEX

Office—
  equipment 406
  operating room 406
  rotary file 409
  sterilizer 408
  waiting room 405
Office equipment 405, 406
Ohio College of Chiropody 5
Oil stone 93
Oiled silk 72
Ointment dressings 61, 220, 270, 275, 313
Onychatrophia 244
  derivation of 244
  diagnosis of 246
  etiology of 244
  pathology of 245
  treatment of 246
Onychauxis 241
  derivation of 241
  diagnosis of 242
  etiology of 241
  pathology of 242
  treatment of 243
    palliative 243
    radical 244
Onychia 238
  derivation of 238
  diagnosis of 238
  etiology of 238
  pathology of 238
  treatment of 238
Onychitis 238
Onychocryptosis 210, 237
  definition of 210
  derivation of 237
  etiology of 210
  complications 212
  prognosis of 229
  treatment of 214
    allowing nail to grow long 234
    complicated cases 221
    excision 222
    method of procedure 223
    no lateral cutting 235
    palliative method 216
    proper boots and hosiery 235
    packing 233
    prophylaxis 230
    radical method 216
    uncomplicated cases 215
Onychophosis 237
Onychoptosis 247
Onychorrhexis 247
Onychygrophosis 241
Orthoform 320
Osmidiosis 302
Oxygen 300, 366

P

Painful feet in women 381
Panaris 239
Panghao 368
Papillary layer 13
Papilloma 185
Paraffin No 7 70
Paraffin No 7-11 70
Paraffin preparations 70, 258
  application of 71
  conclusions 261
  precautions in using 258
  removing dressings of 259
Parresine 71
Paronychia 239
  derivation of 239

Paronychia—
  diagnosis of 240
  etiology of 239
  pathology of 240
  synonyms of 239
  treatment of 240
Paronychitis 239
Pasteur 22
Pasteur serum 365
Pedic items 2
Pedic Society, State of California 7
Pedic Society, New York State 1
  officers 1
Perforating ulcer 324
  characteristics of 325
  etiology of 324
  prognosis of 327
  symptoms of 326
  treatment of 326
Periostitis 397
Pernio 291
Peroxide of hydrogen 28
Petrogen camphor 280
  iodine 280
Phenol 29, 198, 289, 302
Pilocarpin 304
Plaster 105, 106, 107, 117, 120
Plaster of Paris bandage 74
Podiatrist 2
Podiatrists office 405
Policeman's heel 341
  treatment of 341
Polydrosis 297
Potassium hydroxide 176, 184, 191, 195, 196, 209, 225
Potassium iodide 378
Potassium permanganate 30, 301, 303
Potential cautery 191, 192
Poultice 272
Pressure method of anesthesia 146
Proflavin 34
Protonuclein 320
Proud flesh 213 216 221 251
Pruritus 333
Pyrogallic acid 191, 196

Q

Quinine and urea hydrochloride 144

R

Radiography 385-395
Radioscopy 385
Redintol 71
Reticular layer 14
Rhode Island Chiropody Society 9
Roentgenography 385
Roentgenology 385
Roentgenoscopy 385
Roentgenotherapy 385
Rotary file 90, 149

S

Salicylated collodion 70
Salicylic acid 173, 176, 181, 184, 191, 197, 208, 233, 277, 378

Salvarsan 379
Sandal 47
San Francisco Chiropody Association 6
Scalpel 80
Scarlet red 221, 277, 314, 320, 327, 332
School of Chiropody of New York 4
Scissors 88
Sebaceous glands 14, 15, 17
Seborrhea 305
  definition of 305
Seed corn 179
Sesamoid bones 402
Sheep skin 98
Shields and shielding 96, 173 269
  adhesive substances 104
  aperture for 101
  definition 96
  location of parts to be shielded 100
  manufacture of 99
  materials 96
    adhesive felt 99
    adhesive moleskin 97
    buckskin 97
    chamois 97
    felt 98
    lamb's wool 99
    sheep skin 98
  method of skiving 103
  preparation of 99
  skiving of 101
  strapping of 105, 107
  thickness of 100
Shielding, specific 107
  dorsal surfaces 138
  fifth toe 120
    built up half-moon 127
    dorsal surface 120
    strapping for 121, 126
    lateral surfaces 128
    strapping for 128
    interdigital surfaces 128
    strapping for 128
  great toe 107 113
  interdigital surfaces 118 119
    strapping for 120
  intermediate toes 113
    dorsal surfaces 113 115
    ends of 116
    strapping for 117
    lateral borders 137
    lateral plantar half-moon 136
    metatarsalgia 139, 141
    Morton's toe 139 140
    metatarsophalangeal articulation 130
      oval 130
      half-moon 131
      modified half-moon 132
    os calcis region 137
    plantar surfaces 132, 133
    strapping for 134, 135
Silver nitrate 191, 195, 226, 231 248, 249, 250, 256, 290 319, 320, 332
Simple ulcers 306, 311
  treatment of 311
Sklagraphy 385
Sklascopy 385
Skin 11
  anatomy of 12
  layers of 12
  physiology of 17
Skiving 101, 103

CROSS REFERENCE INDEX 437

Skiving knife 92, 104
Spatula 84
Sodium bicarbonate 332
Sodium hydroxide 191
Soft corn 169
Soft corn spoon 83
Soft soap 362
Sterilization 39
  dressings 40
  field of operation 30, 40
  hands of operator 41
  instruments 39
Sterilizing apparatus 42
Sterilizers 42, 408
Strapping 105, 106, 107 117, 120, 121, 128, 134, 269
Stratum corneum 12
Stratum granulosum 12
Stratum lucidum 12
Stratum mucosum 13
Subcutaneous areolar tissue 14
Sublimed sulphur 26
Sudamen 304
  definition of 304
Sudorrhea 297
Sudatoria 297
Sudoriferous glands 15, 17, 49
Sulphur 30, 33, 299, 335
Sunlight 24
Sutures 198
Swatty hone 93
Syphilitic ulcer 327
  symptoms of 327
  treatment of 328
Syphilis 189 241 373
  blood tests for 377
    Wasserman 377
    Noguchi 377
    luetin 378
  color of 374
  course and duration of 378
  definition of 373
  derivation of 373
  diagnosis of 374
  differential diagnosis of 377
  distribution of 374
  etiology of 373
  form of 374
  pathology of 373
  plantar syphilide 375
  synonyms of 373
  treatment of 378

T

Tannic acid 248, 332
Tannoform 249, 332
Teeth 379
Temple University 5
Tetanus 365
The First Institute of Podiatry 5
Thiersch's solution 318
Thumb forceps 86
Thymol 30

Thymol iodide 30, 220, 249, 262 312, 332, 334
Tr Benzoin Comp 249 251, 289, 331
Tr Iodine 184, 278
Toe separators 91
Tonsils 379
Trench fever 358
Trench foot 357
  complications in 365
  crust formation in 363
  etiology of 358
  extensive invasion in 364
  general treatment of 365
  prevention of 361
  prognosis of 360
  reparation stage of 365
  simple edematous 362
  stages of 357
  symptoms of 359
  treatment of 360
  vesicular 363
Trichloracetic acid 191, 194
Turpentine 279
Tyloma 182
Tylosis 182

U

Ulcers 306
  callous 306
  definition of 306
  etiology of 306
  exciting causes of 308
  granulation of 310
  indolent 306
  pathology of 308
  perforating 306
  predisposing causes of 307
  simple 306
  syphilitic 306
  varicose 306
Uncinarial dermatitis 368
Ung Acidi borici 313
Ung Acidi tannici 313
Ung Balsam of Peru 314
Ung Eucalypti 314
Ung hydrargyri 29
Unguentum hydrargyri ammoniati 29, 221 313, 332
Unguentum sulphuris 30, 221, 262, 276
Ung zinci oxidi 314
University of Massachusetts 5
Urethra 379
Uric acid diathesis 212
Uric acid and the nails 335
  changes in size and shape 336
  treatment of 337
  discoloration 335
  treatment of 335
  prognosis 337
  texture changes 336
  treatment of 336
Uridrosis 304
  definition of 304
Uterus 379

V

Vanadium chloride 300
Varicose ulcer 321
  bandaging for 324
  etiology of 321
  symptoms of 322
  treatment of 322
Vascular corn 174
Venereal warts 190
Verruca 185
  definition of 185
  derivation of 185
  diagnosis of 189
  etiology of 185
  pathology of 187
  prognosis of 190
  synonyms of 185
  treatment of 191
  varieties of 188
  where found 187
Verruca arida 185 188
Verruca humida 185, 189
Verruca vulgaris 188
Vibration 281
Vocational foot disorders 339

W

Walking 57
Water 52
  properties of 52
Water itch 368
Water pox 368
Water sores 368
Weak foot 339
  appearance of 339
  symptoms of 339
  treatment of 339
Welch bacillus 360
Wet dressings 60, 218, 239, 270, 273, 311
White precipitate 29, 221, 254, 378
Whitlow 239

X

X-ray apparatus 388
  generator 388
    coil 390
    interrupterless 390
  tubes 391
    vacuum regulators 392
  tube stand 394
X ray plates 394
  developing of 396
  fixing of 396
X-rays 300, 385, 394
  dangers of the 387
  discovery of 386
  experiments leading up to 387

Z

Zinc oxide 261, 313 320
Zinc stearate 313
Zinc sulphate 320